Plots & Schemes That Brought Down Soeharto

by Richard Mann

GATEWAY BOOKS

CONTENTS

Preface

To know, or even to be able to guess what might happen next in Indonesia, it is essential to understand the events leading up to the resignation of former President Soeharto and his replacement by President Habibie.

Focusing on the events which led to the fall of Soeharto is no mere academic exercise. Business people, too, want to know why he was brought down and by whom.

Those favouring political reform in Indonesia will surprise some readers of this book, particularly the evolving attitudes and policies of the United States towards Soeharto and particularly the evolving policies of the Indonesian military.

People interested in Indonesia who want to know who holds power there and who influences the powerholders will want to read this book.

It has been produced in record time and is a detailed, event by event, account of all that led to the fall of Soeharto.

The book was written in Malaysia, Singapore and Indonesia but, fortunately, the author was in Indonesia during the month of May and at other critical times.

In the writing of the book I have drawn on 20 years association and knowledge of Indonesia as well as over 30 earlier publications about investment, business and tourism.

**Jakarta,
Indonesia**

Richard Mann is a British political scientist and economist, author and publisher, specialising in Asian affairs, especially Indonesia. His wife Jenny is Indonesian and the couple have two children, Ian and Sarina, at universities in the United Kingdom.

5

6

CHAPTER ONE

Sow What
Ye Shall Reap

The seeds of the massive opposition to President Soeharto which erupted in May 1998 had been sown nearly two years earlier, during the run-up to the 1997 General Election. Many would say that they had been sown earlier still, at least a decade before. What happened after July 1996 were just the final straws that broke the camel's back.

Over the years a strong sense of injustice had developed among Indonesia's people, from many classes and walks of life. As the Soeharto years accumulated, morality and legality not only did not show any signs of improvement but in the eyes of many people, actually declined. Small benefits could be snatched as easily from the hands of the poor as big benefits could be stripped capriciously from the rich, or perhaps taken from one set and given to another. Objectivity was everywhere replaced by subjectivity, connections and favouritism. Corruption, collusion and nepotism flourished as never before, from the largest deals involving the most powerful people right down to the smallest unit of government and social responsibility in the villages. A sense that nobody was watching what went on in business or, if they were, that nobody really cared, led to the most blatant and dangerous manipulation of the business system as a whole, including banking. After Soeharto's fall, villagers were as fast in ridding themselves of corrupt officials as were their sophisticated urban counterparts. In Jakarta, the capital, Soeharto had created

7

a ruling elite and while they might decry the excesses of his family, there were as many who feared his departure as those who prayed for it. Soeharto's network of patronage stretched through the bureaucracy, the military and into every corner of the casino of business. There were many with their own hefty stakes in the house that Pak Harto built. Intellectuals generally had no such stakes and could speak out.

From the Government's point of view, no price had apparently been too high to pay for political and social stability, including the use of overt and clandestine brute force - against political opponents, against workers asking for at least a living wage or even against peasant farmers trying to protect their land from developers. Members of any of these categories often ended up branded as "subversive."

The New Order Government was generally believed to be capable of just about anything in the names of 'Development,' 'Stability' and 'Unity.' The requirements of 'development,' often seen as only making a handful of Government-backed rich richer, usually overrode all other considerations; the quest for stability at all costs usually meant the capping of all debate hostile to Government and the determination to maintain a unitary republic led to war conditions in three provinces. What was known at the "security approach" to politics ensured that everybody, everywhere towed the New Order line or paid a high price for disobedience.

In the wake of the 1965 bloodbath which hastened the end of Indonesia's first president, Sukarno, law and order was understandably welcomed. So, too, was the following decade of economic growth after two decades of economic anarchy which had ended with Indonesia's economy in a complete shambles. But, after more than 30 years, for the Government to seek to justify its "security approach" by regular invocations of a lingering communist menace or of other dark and threatening forces stretched the imagination. Most people felt that the days of the "security approach" were long over - or should have been long over.

Throughout the 1990s, as the economy boomed, the gap between rich and poor widened. Some, perhaps too many, felt left out of the growth process more or less altogether. Ranking at the top of President Soeharto's blunders list was failure to take into account the sufferings and frustrations of Indonesia's 'little people', the millions of low income informal and factory workers faced with earnings and wages which never seemed to let them get significantly ahead of prices. Even farmers had been outraged when their land was taken over at derisory prices so that the fertile hectares could be turned into golf courses for the wealthy. Such projects were usually undertaken by major developers, if not conglomerates - either members of the charmed circle around Soeharto or simply too rich, powerful and well connected to be stopped by officialdom or anyone else.

There had been warning signs of impending trouble. In Surabaya, in June, 1996, have-nots had angrily attacked and destroyed 10 Christian churches, not because they were Christian necessarily but almost certainly because their congregations were largely ethnic Chinese, a minority strongly believed by the 'common people' to be favoured by the regime and to have grown rich at the expense of so-called indigenous people - meaning non-Chinese. Two years later the frustrations of the 'little people' were to explode with terrible violence.

The Armed Forces, as the Government's ostensible enforcer, were widely feared. In Jakarta in 1998, doubts still lingered about the Armed Forces' (Angkatan Bersenjata Republik Indonesia or ABRI) shooting into a crowd of 2,000 Muslim worshippers at Tanjung Priok 14 years earlier, in 1984, and there was a perennial demand that "missing" people be located. It was alleged that 600 people died or "disappeared after Tanjung Priok." Even 14 years later, after the fall of Soeharto, it was still possible to mobilize a crowd of 15,000 to commemorate the incident and demand justice. In 1991, in Santa Cruz Cemetery, Dili, East Timor, ABRI fired on 3,500 mourners, killing as many as 115 and wounding many others. After the fall of Soeharto a stream of stories began to emerge of alleged military excesses in the "operational zones" of East Timor, Irian Jaya and Aceh, North Sumatra. These and other operations were seen as yet another manifestation of the Government's iron-fist, "security approach."

Indonesia is made up of many disparate peoples, some so different ethnically and culturally that if they were independent countries it could be readily understood. Those furthest away from feeling 'Indonesian' such as in East Timor, Irian Jaya and even Aceh, needed plenty of space around them within which to exercise a level of self determination consistent with membership of the Indonesian commonwealth. They also needed to feel that they were not being bled of funds and resources badly needed for provincial development. But the unitary approach, like the security approach, kept the provinces strapped in a straightjacket. If they tried to move an arm or a leg the central government would deploy its enforcer to crack down. According to media reports, the crack downs were often characterized by intimidation, rapes, kidnappings and terror.

After the fall of Soeharto, residents of these areas and domestic

9

and international human rights organizations began to speak of "rampant abuse" of human rights. The Indonesian language 'Merdeka' newspaper said on August 8, 1998, that the people of these provinces felt that they had been stripped and plundered by Javanese colonialists. Few of ABRI's alleged abuses and excesses have been forgotten by the people, especially those who now have only fading pictures of their loved ones, missing, killed or presumed dead.

The New Order's "security approach" was also equipped with a frightening, unbridled and unaccountable, covert intelligence system, applied not against foreign enemies but against ordinary Indonesians. Key units of this apparatus reported directly to the President. All too frequently activities of these units, including covert operations overseas, for example, in Papua New Guinea aimed at weakening the Irianese independence movement, were unknown and unapproved by people outside the circles of those directly responsible.

Loekman Soetrisno, a social science lecturer at Gadjah Mada University, Yogyakarta, spoke of a "psychology of fear' keeping informed members of the nation silent. Feudalism and ignorance guaranteed the silence of many others.

But ABRI as a whole was by no means the Government's unquestioning accomplice. For more than two decades official ABRI philosophy had embraced a more neutral and a more equitable position for the security forces. Indeed, the 1945 Constitution required it. ABRI was by no means committed to the idea of President Soeharto being repeatedly re-elected beyond two terms. And ABRI generally favoured increasing openness and democracy. The military's aspirations were always torpedoed by President Soeharto's demand for total obedience to the Executive. Not only did ABRI resent its lack of independence and its lack of influence where it counted most - over the President - but for more than a decade resentment had grown at the unbelievable greed of the President's children, greed which sometimes touched interests of their own, including state enterprises in which they had a stake.

In the late '80s ABRI tried again to distance itself from President Soeharto to the extent of changing the object of the soldier's oath from the president to the state. President Soeharto fought back and laid waste such notions, including some of the key enunciators, such as then Armed Forces Commander, General L. B. "Benny" Murdani. While President Soeharto himself came from ABRI, whenever the military tried to push forward President Soeharto pushed them back, not merely to where they had been before but to a position of much less power and influence. Less power and influence equated to less access to appointments and business opportunities. There was to be no doubt who was the real commander of the Armed Forces and the undisputed power in the land. ABRI resentment simmered.

President Soeharto sought to counter military pressures by civilianizing his Government, most notably by entering into a new relationship with certain Muslim elements grouped around the Indonesian Association of Muslim Intellectuals (ICMI) which had been formed in 1990. Throughout the 90s, President Soeharto played to the Muslim gallery, encouraging and patronizing the Muslim civilian community as a counterweight to ABRI, ironically, also Muslim dominated but by a completely different group. It was a complex web and within it President Soeharto sought to identify but not associate politically with conservative, traditionalist Islam while keeping modernizing or reformist Islam close but not closer than arms length.

Throughout the '90s there was a constant tension between the President and the Armed Forces. So long as Soeharto retained power, at the end of the day, constitutionally he was the boss, the supreme commander of the armed forces. Unless ABRI was prepared to risk acting unconstitutionally they were stuck. Unless, of course, some crisis came along which brought the old man down! But, then, within ABRI there were those who favoured succession and those who favoured the status quo. In the general elections of 1988, ABRI had flirted with being seen to support the Indonesian Democratic Party, (PDI). By 1996, President Soeharto destroyed this alternative by ousting the real strength of the party, President Sukarno's eldest daughter, Megawati Sukarnoputri. He also helped tip the balance of ABRI's loyalty toward the status quo by promoting family members and former adjutants to key positions, for example, General Wiranto and Let. Gen. Prabowo, the President's courageous but allegedly sometimes hot tempered son-in-law.

By 1998, if the people's resentment was ready to explode there were many even within ABRI who felt that they had just about reached the end of their tether. The people's anger had been fuelled critically by the onset of the worst economic crisis any Indonesian could remember. And the angry people blamed the Government, especially its chief architect, President Soeharto. ABRI's doctrine preached that it stood with the people. If the people opposed their President where would this leave ABRI? Events would soon show.

ABRI was even given encouragement from overseas. Discussing Indonesia's bleak economic future, the prospect of the imposition of a currency board and the possibility of growing popular unrest Britain's 'Economist' magazine said in a leader on February 21, 1998: " The hope must be that Mr. Soeharto's army backers will prove less loyal than they now seem if violence spreads and if such financial discipline (as the CBS) is imposed. The Army has a special place in Indonesian life; there are even seats reserved for officers in the country's Parliament. Though the Army can be brutal and corrupt, it is probably the most reliable institution remaining in the country and is thus best-placed to begin the process of change - even towards democracy."

Ten years before anything would finally be done to end the New Order's "security approach", in 1989, at Magelang Military Academy, General Edi Sudrajat called for an end to what he called the "foot stomping, father knows best style of leadership." The military, he said, did not wish to be mere "fire extinguishers" for those in power. In March, 1996, a year before President Soeharto's re-election for a seventh term, Chief of ABRI's Sociopolitical Affairs, Let. Gen. Syarwan Hamid would use identical words. He told University of Indonesia students that ABRI was "no longer willing to clean up the mess left by other people's incompetence." The 'Jakarta Post' of March 25, 1996 quoted him as saying that ABRI would "no longer be a repressive force" and, incredibly, to the public at large, that ABRI was "willing to be controlled." One of the messes they got into in July, 1996 was the forced occupation of the headquarters of the PDI. Can we infer from these 1996 statements that what happened at Jalan Diponegoro was to ABRI's distaste? Did it become for ABRI one of the key factors in bringing down Soeharto?

In September, 1998, ABRI Chief of Sociopolitical Affairs. Let. Gen. Soesilo Bambang Yudhoyono was quoted be the Jakarta media as saying that ABRI had been given too many tasks and roles to fulfill and had become too powerful as a result. Syarwan Hamid had previously held this same post. Was this what he was referring to when he spoke of the need for "control." And if ABRI really was "too powerful" was it all of ABRI or just certain special units, units commanded by Soeharto loyalists, perhaps? Was it these special forces units that even mainstream ABRI felt were out of control? Let. Gen. Soesilo pointedly regretted that ABRI "had been blamed for past unrest, mass killings and human rights violations" - hardly achievements of which professional soldiers could be proud! A few days earlier, in ABRI's defence, Armed Forces Commander Wiranto had stressed that whatever had been done had been done at the orders of the Government and that ABRI could not be blamed exclusively. But both men left the indelible impression that

ABRI had not liked carrying out some of these orders and a new emphasis placed on defence rather than internal security pointed to a yearning for a diminished role in domestic politics and a more orthodox role for the military. Later in the month Hermawan Sulistyo of the Indonesian Institute of Social Sciences would be quoted in the 'Indonesian Observer' as saying that KOPASSUS troops should cease to be used for political purposes. Even now, there were many in ABRI who doubtless agreed. KOPASSUS units had been increased once Let. Gen. Prabowo became commander in 1994 and promptly and successfully argued for an increase in the number of KOPASSUS from three to five. Who dared refuse the President's son-in-law?

All the signs of ABRI resentment at the role of the special forces, especially KOPASSUS, and resentment at some of the domestic political policies they were asked to carry out were there, but was President Soeharto listening? Or, if he was listening, was he so confident that he had made ABRI his creature by hand-picking its commanders that he chose to ignore such evidence?

In March, 1996, nine months before the 1997 general elections, there had been quiet fury in significant sections of ABRI when then Army Chief General Hartono had said that ABRI members were also cadres of GOLKAR, an approach which conflicted diametrically with the military's ideal to be above politics. It also infuriated political groups outside GOLKAR who wondered loudly who there was to protect them. Edi Sudrajat, now Minister of Defence and Security, emphasized that ABRI "comes from the people, was raised by the people and will serve the people." The Coordinating Minister for Political Affairs and Security, the late General (ret) Soesilo Soedarman said that in the upcoming elections ABRI would be neutral, directly contradicting Hartono, soon to lose his military post and be appointed Information Minister in the last Soeharto cabinet. ABRI Chief of Social and Political Affairs, Let. Gen. Syarwan Hamid, said that Hartono had made the statement in a 'personal capacity." ABRI's resentment at being shackled to GOLKAR was coming over loudly and clearly. Were there special reasons why this resentment should be at fever pitch now? Were there aspects of what the Government was asking ABRI to do for it of which the military commanders heartily disapproved?

When, in the wake of Soeharto's fall from power, General Wiranto said that ABRI should from then on be "above political parties" and defenders of all, he placed himself at the end of a line of thought which had begun way back in the 70's and had been nursed amid mounting frustration for over two decades. It may even have begun in 1945 or before. When Indonesia's new president, B. J. Habibie, announced that in future a president would only serve two terms, ABRI might have written his speech. At last, after 32 years, ABRI was feeling its way towards a more democratic role and, hopefully, one more respectful of basic human rights. Really, their very survival now depended upon it.

Addressing an ABRI leadership meeting at the State Palace, Jakarta in March, 1996, President Soeharto was at his 'best'. The 'Jakarta Post' of March 30, 1996, quoted him as calling for "stern measures" against any who attempted to break the rules during the forthcoming elections. Additionally, he was quoted as saying that "ABRI had the obligation to prevent the emergence of any elements which may disturb national unity." In other words, the political status quo would be defended by force and any not in favour were by definition against. Those against would soon be the objects of search and, in some cases, destroy missions by the military's special forces. Apparently seeing no contradiction, President Soeharto went on to say that "On the other hand, as a socio-political force, ABRI must help open the chances for the people to express their idea and channel their creativity." What critics made of this was summed up by M. Mahfud, Director of the Postgraduate Programme of the Islamic University at Yogyakarta when he said that all talk of political changes was meaningless without the consent of the president. While the President may have appeared to have given consent, in reality, what he meant by "opening the chances for people to express their ideas" was only that more people should feel free to contribute to the goals of the New Order through the channels laid down by the regime.

Indonesians generally saw less of the military's good side than its bad. In practice ABRI **was** Soeharto's "fire extinguisher." Many felt themselves to be living in a terror state where anything was possible except life without fear within a structure of impartially and equitably administered laws. Even elements within ABRI wanted reform - those who took seriously their mission as partners in good government. But all the levers of power in this terror state were controlled by one man, Soeharto. The President's power could be deployed with devastating force against civilians and military alike. Against his power a uniform was no defence. Suspicion began to deepen dangerously that Soeharto's use of the levers had as much to do with his own survival and family interests as with the Government he led. After 32 years was he ruling in anyone's interest except his own? If he was, why didn't he give some of the people some of the reforms they craved? Why didn't he give some of the regions the air they needed to breath?

Despite obvious tensions, ABRI seemed to remain firmly under presidential command. Nothing had dramatized the point more than pictures of Soeharto in October, 1997 in his new 5-star general's uniform inspecting his troops on parade. Yet even on this ostensibly happy day the tensions persisted. Again, we find the President using the phrase that "ABRI is obliged" to do this or that - as if he knew that not all of his commanders agreed. In this case, the General was saying that ABRI "was obliged" to ensure that the March, 1998 meeting of the People's Consultative Assembly went smoothly. Did this reminder mean that there were officers who would like to see the winds of genuine democracy blow through the Assembly, winds which might perhaps blow away their commander-in-chief?

The stability for which the New Order Government had become famous had been badly fractured by a spate of riots throughout 1996 and 1997, some of them communal. As usual there were suspicions that some of the riots were being deliberately orchestrated to undermine, if not to bring down, the regime. At the October 5, 1997, ceremony at Halim Perdanakusuma Air Base, the President warned that Indonesia might face more violence in the future. He warned or counselled that ABRI would need to use more persuasive rather than directly repressive measures to deal with the upsurge. He was quoted as saying: "We still cannot identify precisely the root of the intergroup conflicts. At the same time we must ensure that such social upheavals will not happen again in the future. ABRI needs to evaluate the forms of this new threat....it needs to develop all necessary policies, strategies, systems and procedures to prevent and counter the threat." This sounded more like advice for the intelligence services or the special forces than for ABRI as a whole. Indeed, such statements and others not published may have been interpreted by certain officers as calling for a stepping up of covert "persuasion" before incidents and riots called for the use of outright force. Did ABRI agree with this approach or were they being lectured and cajoled? Were there some who agreed and some who didn't. Aside from those who agreed were there some senior officers who would rather see the burning issues dealt with than the building of any new apparatus of "persuasion."

If ABRI resented some of the orders it was given, some of those susceptible to them resented the orders even more. Among ordinary people, there was a general feeling that people in uniform could do pretty much what they liked to lesser mortals, if they so chose. Sometimes, at the behest of their government masters, they did choose and the people resented being pushed around with no redress. What was the point complaining to the bureaucracy or to the courts when these were also under the presidential heel? In Nipah, Madura, it took three years from 1993 until 1996 for villagers whose land had been earmarked as the site of a dam, to obtain justice after troops opened fire on protesting villagers. In the farms and in the factories there was a strong sense of the arrogance of power, a strong and growing sense that the Government had no ear for the needs and wants of Indonesia's "little people." Even the forest fires which raged more or less unchecked throughout 1997 led to many people concluding; "The Government doesn't care about us." The omnipotent Government could do whatever it wanted and no machinery existed which could be used to fight back, much less to obtain a fair hearing and justice. Big developers or logging companies with connections could apparently get away with anything, provided only that someone powerful in the Government agreed. Connections, corruption and collusion reached unimagined heights (or depths) during Soeharto's last years. Connected businesses could flout environmental laws, flout codes of employment and working conditions, float wage and benefits regulations, flout trading rules - flout anything they wished so long as they had powerful backers. Corporate Indonesia, including the state banks, became the plaything of the ruling family and its supporters. If they needed money, which bank manager dared to refuse? If they wanted a project who dared defy them?

The big and connected businesses most visible were often ethnic Chinese owned, sewing in the minds of many deep resentment against the privileges and wealth these ethnic Chinese enjoyed - privileges and wealth all too soon ascribed to all ethnic Chinese, irrespective of their true economic position. The disregard for rules and laws meant the disregard of people and while non-ethnic Chinese bosses may have been no better than their ethnic Chinese brethren, in practice popular hatred was reserved near exclusively for ethnic Chinese business operators and employers. If the ethnic Chinese despised the indigenous people the arrogant and unsympathetic words and deeds of some of Indonesia's Chinese made the feeling entirely mutual.

Resentment had been bubbling and boiling for years about the avarice of Soeharto's family, often damaging to peasant and company president alike, often damaging to the interests of ABRI. If the President's family wanted land for some project it had to be made available. If the

16

President's family wanted a particular contract they had to get it. If the President's family wanted a specific project it had to be theirs. Whatever the President's business friends wanted they had to be given. Often these demands raised costs and consumer prices. Often they threatened the very viability of rival enterprises, including state owned enterprises. In the wake of the First Family's business demands and suspected mountainizing fortune was a growing tailback of angry and frustrated people. The Soeharto's had managed to upset just about everybody, rich and poor alike, most critically, even from among the class created and succoured by the New Order. President and government alike seemed studiously devoted to economic growth and social welfare but by 1998 it had become too clear to be hidden in any conceivable way that the road to development had also been the path to personal enrichment of the Soeharto family. The President maintained he had no money and challenged doubters to prove the opposite. But with suspected family ownership in 3,200 companies few could doubt that the children had money - and lots of it.

In 1996, like President Soeharto himself, the New Order had looked old and tired. In the President's case the external evidence was deceptive. Those who knew him say that he was strong, alert and knowledgeable to the end. After the death of his wife, Ibu Tien Soeharto in the Spring of 1996, Soeharto seemed to dig in, to bunker down, to be more stern and less approachable then ever. His system seemed more ossified than ever. Though from time to time he might hint at more openness or at more regional autonomy, in practice, he was unswervingly committed to the ideology of Pancasila and to the unitary state, a state which had to be run his way and no other. As resentments against him swelled, his power looked unassailable. But was it? Signs outside many of the offices of the New Order were rusty and crumbling, relics of events and policies which took place or were inaugurated 32 years ago. Was Soeharto's power a similar illusion? Was Soeharto truly an omnipotent leader invincible behind the shield of ABRI and a labyrinth of patronage? Or had he become a single elderly man whom more and more people resented and who could actually just be walked forcefully out of office? At this stage the answers were unknown, even frightening.

If the President was anything to go by, the regime's face was set firmly and sternly against change. It seemed set to cling to the rusting signboards and the old ways until the bitter end. "Stern and tough measures" seemed to be the only things the Government had to offer those able to muster sufficient temerity to say: " Please may we have a little change, a little openness, a little fairness." The young, particularly, craved to see an end of the old man and of his ways. They had never known any other leader. They wanted change. Soeharto was old. They wanted youth. Change, youth, a new generation, new ideas - all were blowing in the wind.

A young professional interviewed by 'Time' magazine in August 1996 was quoted as saying: " We want this country to be on a par with our neighbours in terms of rights. We are achievers and we would like to compete freely within our system. We would like to be promoted based on merit, not connections. At the moment, there is not enough space within the Indonesian political system for us to express ourselves. We are suffocating here and we can't stand the military."

Professionals were suffocating, workers felt cheated of the fruits of development, peasant farmers wanted to be allowed to go on tilling land that had been theirs for generations until the Government said it had to be given up for development. Upon this situation the economic crisis and drought imposed mass unemployment, want and even starvation.

In this new situation, were events as fully under the President's control as he or anyone else might have thought? As the economy collapsed around him, first the students and then the intelligentsia had begun to speak out more and more loudly against President Soeharto and his regime. President Soeharto knew that his very survival hinged on restoring growth and prosperity to the economy. The people had allowed him to govern in his way while he delivered these things. Now he could not. How patient would the people be? Bad governance was already being blamed for the decrepit economy. After the March elections, shaken by the economic collapse and the scale and intensity of the criticisms against him, Soeharto was driven to promise limited reforms. The President could see that not to do so at this time might lead to his ousting. But he placed the inauguration of the reforms safely far away, after 2003, when his current term of office expired. At this realization there was a public outcry and waves of student protests which grew in intensity each day. Total reform was needed now yet the President was putting it off. In whose interest. people asked themselves? And they thought: What if Soeharto was still fit at aged 82? Could there be another five years of him after that? Another five years of political suffocation! Another five years of regional imprisonment! The nation squirmed. The prospect was unendurable! The markets and the rupiah dived!

Soeharto had been appointed acting president in 1967, after

seizing the initiative to restore order in the wake of the alleged murder of six Army generals by members of the Indonesian Communist Party as the prelude to a coup. The circumstances of his gaining presidential power have always been the subject of debate, never more so than after his fall from power. By 1998, there were allegations that Soeharto had known about the plot to murder the generals but had taken no action, thus paving the way for him to take command of the armed forces and subsequently to gain presidential power. Doubts were expressed about whether the generals were murdered by communists at all. There were hints that it may have been a left-leaning faction from within the security forces themselves. There had always been doubts about the legality of Soeharto's power insofar as it was alleged to have been based on a letter of authority from President Sukarno which had subsequently been 'lost.' There was talk of pro-Soeharto involvement by the CIA, Britain's MI6, the Government of Australia and even the anti-PRC, KGB. However, it came about, by 1967, Soeharto had replaced Sukarno as president.

Less an intellectual than his predecessor, Sukarno, the charismatic man who led Indonesia to independence from the Dutch in 1945, order was almost a religion to Soeharto. Sukarno, too, had been troubled by the indiscipline of his country, introducing what he called "Guided Democracy" in 1957. Since independence, a new government had been sworn in roughly every 18 months and disagreement was rife. The dozens of political parties in existence would not agree to "Guided Democracy" any more than later, under Soeharto, it would be easy to win agreement for Pancasila (not until 1988). As a result of the parties failure to agree, in 1957, all were banned by the then Chairman of the Supreme War Authority, Abdul Haris Nasution. At independence the President had enjoyed little power. By 1957 he had it all. Essentially President Soeharto repeated the pattern and for the same reasons. The last thing anybody wanted was a return to the political bickering of the 1950s. Not only to the political bickering but to the corruption, inefficiency and ultimately the complete breakdown of the economy. The number one priority for Soeharto's New Order was the maintenance of political stability as the essential shield behind which economic growth could take place and prosperity achieved for increasing numbers of people. Political bickering was to be eliminated forever by implementation of the state ideology Pancasila, a philosophy of discussion and consensus derived from Indonesian village life, almost from family life. Indonesians were to be one big, seamless, family. Deviants would be dealt with by ABRI.

By the mid-'90s this political straitjacket screamed to be thrown off by those suffering at the bottom of the social pile and by the inhabitants of brutalized provinces. Professionals and private business people, now more numerous and more educated, also wanted more say in their governance, not to mention accountability and an end to corrupt practices which had turned Indonesia into a "high cost" economy. Generally speaking, about 30 percent of a company's revenue might have to be earmarked for illegal bribes and levies. More than ever, ABRI resented being the "enforcer" and "fire extinguisher" of a man now widely reviled. Soeharto faced no mass opposition because, under the "floating mass" policy the mass had been more or less kept out of politics for years. Other than the PDI, he faced no serious organized political opposition thanks to the role of GOLKAR and the weakness it guaranteed other political parties - there were only two others. With over 30 million members, the Nahdlatul Ulama (NU) led by Abdurrahman Wahid could have been a potent political force but the organization had opted to stay out of politics. So, too, had Amien Rais, leader of the 20 million strong Muslim Muhammadiya. Many Muslim's were deeply morally outraged by the excesses of the Soeharto Government but there was no political vehicle through which this outrage could be expressed. Stacked with his own hand-picked commanders, Soeharto believed he faced no threat from ABRI.

Indonesia's middle class, including ethnic Chinese business people, were increasingly unhappy with the ethos of corruption in which they were obliged to operate. They were apoplectic over the business excesses of Soeharto's family. Intellectuals found common ground with critics of the regime across the whole range of issues. They also had complaints of their own. The time had come to speak out yet the Government seemed more determined than ever to stamp out all opposition - ranging from the opposition of individuals such as Megawati Sukarnoputri to the growing demands not only for improvements to Pancasila democracy but for wholesale systemic change. "Reformasi Total" was becoming very much the order of the day! While the criticisms of business were narrow and relatively muted, intellectuals and students felt driven to criticize and protest across the board.

The intelligentsia could be defined as students, college faculty and professionals, and combined, represented a substantial force for change. The mere fact that there was now demand for systemic change showed the new mood of the intellectuals and sections of the middle class. Commenting on this new mood, former minister, Emil Salim, was quoted as saying that Indonesia needed to reappraise the building blocks of its political foundations. He said that there had been many social changes and advances in 30 years and: "A denial of these changes may jeopardize political stability and disrupt economic stability and the development process." How right he was to be proved to be. Dissident members of the middle class wanted a bigger slice of the political cake and the lower classes needed a larger slice of the economic cake. In the short-term, the PDI drew support from both these groups. In 1996, there was really no where else to go. It was this support that Soeharto felt he had to neutralize before it turned Megawati into a potent political force.

Meanwhile, there was mounting frustration at overwhelming presidential and executive power. How much longer could the old man go on? How much longer could the people afford to let him go on? Indonesians were patient people, they valued harmony, they knew how to respect their leaders. But enough was becoming enough! The President was steering government stubbornly in directions in which more and more people objected to going. Not only had he no solution to the economic crisis beggaring many Indonesians but his policies were thought to have contributed very significantly to the process. The issue of presidential leadership and succession now became critical.

M. Mahfud slammed both houses of Indonesia's Parliament as "mere rubber stamps to legitimize the President's rulings. It's quite a bitter pill to swallow but this is the reality of Indonesian politics." All parliamentarians had to be approved by the Government and none other than the three approved parties could contest elections - Golongkan Karya (GOLKAR) representing the bureaucracy and the Armed Forces, the Christian-Nationalist Democratic Party of Indonesia (PDI) and the Islamic United Development Party (PPP). Ministers were only appointed to "assist the president."

More and more individuals and groups were frustrated at the way in which the Government outlawed "free expression." Asked one observer: "What political institutions can the younger generation turn towards as a channel for their demands and aspirations?" In June, 1996, even the Speaker of the House of Representatives, Wahono, spoke about the Government's "excessive fear" of political openness. This was significant because Wahono was a former GOLKAR leader as well as a retired Army Let. Gen. He warned that if established channels failed to accommodate the public's desires "social disturbances would escalate." A few days after Wahono spoke, President Soeharto ruled out any change to the political system he had created. He was quoted as saying: "We will not change a system which has proven effective, let alone if it is only to serve the wishes of a few people." Politically bound and gagged, the people struggled in their bonds.

There was anger over corruption at all levels of the government and bureaucracy - especially when the corrupt were protected - like Eddy Tansil, who allegedly escaped from jail in May, 1996 after being found guilty of defrauding state owned Bank Pembangunan Indonesia of US$620 million - or the public was asked to pay higher prices for services where the cost was already inflated because of the need to pay bribes or because of the obligation to channel business through family owned companies. There was anger over the lack of independence of the judiciary and growing mistrust of court judgments.

The Government was a constant target for allegations of human rights abuse. Members of the security forces seemed to have to be frequently apologizing for breaches of discipline. In May, 1996, three students had been killed by the security forces in Ujung Pandang during the forcible dispersal of a demonstration. A year earlier members of the Cavalry 6 assault battalion "went wild" in Medan launching a "series of violent attacks against residents" after a private was killed by a hoodlum. Two years later Medan would be the scene of an orgy of violence by the have-nots against the haves (largely ethnic Chinese).

The wealth gap was widening. The poor's resentment of the rich was rising fast, a resentment deepened among the teeming urban and rural kampongs by television dramas which depicted the lifestyles of Indonesia's middle and upper classes as decadently lavish - compared to conditions at the bottom of the social ladder. Food supplies had to be supplemented by imports, including rice. Prices were increasing. Workers everywhere, on land or in factories, were getting tired of working for the low wages of which their Government liked to boast to foreign investors. For many, low wages meant inability to cover the cost of necessities. Social unrest was boiling up among the urban labouring classes. The number of land disputes was on the increase as developers sought to take over land used by poor farmers for subsistence. Persistent drought put a premium on land retention and cultivation and in some areas where the drought bit hardest starvation became a very real spectre.

As the pot of unrest boiled, the Soeharto regime tightened the lid until it was ready to explode.

Even 1995 had seen the beginnings of discontent, especially among Indonesia's millions of have-nots. Despite the dramatic reduction in the numbers of those living below the poverty line to below 22 million, many Indonesians remained poor. Not only poor but most of them still lacked such basic facilities as piped water, sanitation and garbage disposal. Many resented the wealth of ethnic Chinese Indonesians they saw around them, controlling trade and apparently enjoying government favours and support. The support most resented was the turning of a blind eye to the flouting of regulations. Whatever the ostensible cause of a riot the underlying cause was always really frustration at want and injustice. Any riot could quickly turn against perceived symbols of the sufferings of the poor - the ethnic Chinese and the Government.

If there was widespread jealousy of the ethnic Chinese there was equally widespread resentment of the Government. Officials were perceived to act high-handedly and without regard to the feelings and interests of the poor. There was thought to be widespread collusion between corrupt officials and developers. The Government seemed only to have the interests of the rich at heart. Communal and religious conflicts flared, aggravated by the Government policy of transmigration under which people from overpopulated areas were sent to live in islands with space to spare, frequently bringing together people of different religions and ethnicity who kept themselves very much to themselves except when transgressing on each other's rights or being victims of misunderstandings. Many of the transmigrants were Javanese or Balinese, the presence of the former fueling long-standing outer island fears of "Javanese colonization.'

There had been riots in Flores over an allegedly biased judicial decision against a Christian; Catholics and Muslims had fought in East Timor where the extent of indigenous longing for independence would only become fully clear after the earth-shaking events of May, 1998. In February, 1996, one man died, 350 people were forced to flee and 80 houses were burned when East Timorese rampaged in the town of Ambeno.

In October, 1996, in the East Java towns of Situbondo, Panarukan and Asembagus, 10,000 Muslim youths attacked, damaged or destroyed more than 20 Christian churches, schools and orphanages in addition to destroying cars and motor cycles. Five people died. Shops and a court building were also damaged. Muslim leaders apologized and appealed for calm. Ostensibly the incident was over a sentence imposed on an alleged Muslim blasphemer which the mob considered too light. The alleged blasphemer was thought to have sought shelter from the mob in a Christian church. Anger against the court soon turned to "frenzy" against any and all thought to enjoy unfair advantages, especially the local ethnic Chinese who are mostly Christian. The area also had a history of disputes with government owned companies and with the armed forces over land appropriation.

Anti-Government sentiments burst out again in December, 1996, when thousands of people rampaged in the West Java town of Tasik-Malaya over alleged mistreatment by the police of three local Muslim teachers whom the police accused of mistreating one of their sons. Shops and even factories were burnt and over 400 troops from the Siliwangi military command had to be deployed to restore order.

In January, 1997, hundreds of roadside vendors and public order officials fought in the Jakarta suburb of Tanah Abang. Government vehicles and offices were damaged or destroyed.

Troops had to be deployed in West Kalimantan after local Dayaks fought Madurese newcomers transported there via government transmigration programmes, destroying hundreds of houses, killing four and resulting in 21 people missing. An incredible 14,000 people were made homeless by the unrest. In February, there was more fighting in West Kalimantan.

Also in February, anti-ethnic Chinese and religious riots broke out in and around Bandung partly over a company's alleged failure to pay Idul Fitri (Islamic New Year) bonuses and partly over the disturbance of Muslim prayers by an ethnic Chinese woman. At Rengasdengklok, near Bandung, more than 70 houses and 70 shops were destroyed in the riots as well as nearly 30 vehicles burnt or damaged. More than 40 Christian churches and Buddhist monasteries were damaged or destroyed.

In many parts of Indonesia, the pot of discontent was boiling and bubbling. Desperation and violence filled the air. 'Review Indonesia' quoted retired General Soemitro as saying: " They (the Government) have to understand the signs that are present. There are signs of many things happening now. Clearly it is the time to make some changes so that it doesn't get more chaotic." Soemitro meant constructive changes but, as usual, the Government opted for more of the security approach.

The frequency and scale of riots around Indonesia was so serious that in January, 1997, the Government announced that riot alert centres would be established throughout the country. Many felt that the establishment of the centres had as much to do with security for the June, 1997, general elections as with the ongoing problems.

In March there were riots in Praya, Lombok, when a government office, shops and homes were attacked. President Soeharto said that he was very concerned to establish the cause of all the riots and to identify remedies. There were the usual allegations of "third parties" masterminding the riots from behind the scenes. To observers the causes seemed plain enough and they did not include phantom "masterminds." Soeharto slammed the observers and analysts for reaching "hasty" conclusions. Recent violence continued to be blamed by the Government on "dissident and subversive groups from left and right extremes seeking to discredit and undermine the Government." Incredibly, President Soeharto blamed "small groups of Maoist activists" for many of the riots, citing as an example, the Maoist tactic of fomenting revolution in the countryside and then using rural areas as bases from which to capture power in the cities. Saner voices at home and abroad urged him to focus on poverty and injustice as the causes. Pinning the blame on Maoists, now discredited even in China, was hardly conducive to furthering good relations with the ethnic Chinese.

Behind many of these riots could be plainly seen the policies of the New Order - the unitary state concept, transmigration, favouritism - approaches which had created issues, issues now magnified and multiplied by the onset of the economic crisis. With all authority monopolized by the Government from the pinnacle of power in Jakarta down to the smallest village, dissidents were left with nowhere to turn and with no recourse other than violence.

Riots and the corresponding state violence deployed to control them and even to anticipate them as well as efforts by the intelligence services to locate the "ringleaders" spawned a climate of violence and terror. Unscrupulous employers sometimes made use of this climate of terror to employ off duty ABRI lower ranks to maintain "security" at their workplaces. As in the case of the young female trade union activist Marsinah, enforcing "security" could mean death - Marsinah's bore all the trademarks of the involvement of elements of the military. She was beaten, raped and subjected to gross torture before being killed.

Some of the riots reflected negative consequences of stubbornly enforcing the unitary state, including provincial protests against central government authority and the melting pot strategy of throwing all Indonesians together as if their ethnic antecedents didn't exist. The unitary state also bred resentment of Java and Javanese, especially if they moved to live in non-Javanese areas. Other riots reflected simmering ethnic Chinese-pribumi tensions, frequently taking the form of Muslim-

Christian outbursts but rooted in economic jealousy the perceived injustice of ethnic Chinese seeming to be Government favourites. The fact that the New Order Government treated the ethnic Chinese as a separate and almost alien group in its midst did nothing to foster understanding and assimilation.

For whatever reasons, tempers were now on an extremely short leash and were exploding with increasing frequency. Outspoken Minister of Transmigration, Siswono Yudohusodo said that the riots reflected a "sickness" of the Indonesian people the major symptom of which was short tempers, lowered rationality and heightened emotions. It is doubtful if Siswono really believed that the Indonesian people were "sick." More likely it was the safest way to make the point that the people were getting very angry and fed up. Muslim scholar, Nurcholish Madjid, said that the situation was so tense that even a petty argument could spark riots. Both men cited unethical practices of some government officials as being among the reasons for the people's frustration, coupled to corruption, collusion and manipulation. Meanwhile, they said, many people faced injustices, poverty and unemployment. Psychiatrist, Professor Dadang Hawari, said that the riots gave people an opportunity to vent their emotions. Astrid Susanto, a Professor of Mass Communication and Director for Social, Political and Cultural Affairs at the National Agency for Development Assessment said that in a riot people did things they would never dream of doing as individuals. Later, when terrible riots erupted in Jakarta, 'Time' magazine of May 25, quoted one looter as saying: " I have never done anything like this before but we can't afford to buy anything any more." Other analysts warned of a danger that the people were losing trust in all Government agencies, including the Armed Forces, and that care should be taken in branding all rioters as neo-communists. In May, 1998, these comments would take on new meaning.

President Soeharto may really have believed or chosen to have believed that some of the rioters were communists. But, on paper, three decades of steady economic development had raised millions up out of poverty. Based on the statistics, who could believe that there were still so many in want that their anger could erupt uncontrollably and be directed at the very agency which was supposed to have been lightening their burdens - the New Order Government.

Despite the accumulating mayhem, foreign observers seemed largely not to notice. Politics had long been off limits as a discussion topic. Some may have harboured suspicions about the true nature of the governance practiced by the New Order but politics were usually dismissed as an internal affair. No foreign businessman wanted to offend the Government of Indonesia or President Soeharto. Many foreign governments with trade interests at stake took the same view. "Delinkage" of politics and business was the order of the day. The general feeling was that Adam Schwartz was right and that Indonesia was a "nation in waiting" - waiting for President Soeharto to step down. Until then nothing much could or was likely to happen.

Prior to May, 1998, Indonesia's economic growth roared from one success to another, in 1996 reaching a dizzying 8 percent, much of it assisted by liberally lent foreign capital. Foreign direct investment was running at a record US$30 billion a year. There was even talk of an investment blow-out. Domestic bank loans were at a record high. The economy was tipped to become the world's fifth largest by the year 2020. Jakarta was touted as an incipient regional and financial centre. The capitalization of the Jakarta Stock Exchange was expected to reach US$ 244 billion as early as the year 2000. Inflation was projected to remain well below 7 percent per annum and the government managed rupiah-dollar exchange rate looked stable for the foreseeable future. This glittering record of apparent success masked problems that would soon explode into the open with devastating force.

To be sure, there had been doubts. Enjoying record breaking growth and, despite Government assurances to the contrary, analysts and foreign observers felt that Indonesia's deregulation and market liberalization drives were slowing down. Many foreigners had long suspected that successive packages were strictly tailored to perceived needs, opportunities and pressures of the moment and not as a result of a genuine comprehensive ideological commitment. Few seemed to think or, if they thought, seemed to be overly worried that perhaps the deregulation had gone too fast - especially in the banking sector. Imports were rising; the current account deficit seemed to be widening dangerously to almost US$8 billion in the 1995-96 fiscal year, although still only 3.5 percent of GDP, a level generally regarded by international experts as still safe. At US$63 billion public debt was beginning to seem excessive and some of the foreign loans were costing too much. There were warnings from the IMF and the World Bank to take care. There was a spate of early repayment of high interest public loans by Finance Minister Mar'ie Muhammad, critics thought, incurred imprudently by the previous government. State bank bad debt had risen to US$3.5 billion. Attempts were made to better control and pace major government projects requiring large offshore capital inputs and imports. Foreign and domestic economists talked of a need to cool down the economy, to reduce soaring imports and to strongly increase declining exports. There was a hope and expectation that bank loans would fall and that increases in the money supply could be held at 18 percent.

More social disquiet was sewn in April, 1996, when bus, taxi and air fares had been hiked from between 9.2 to 66.7 percent. Meanwhile the Government Finance Comptroller unearthed 15,732 cases of irregularities in the management of state finances. There was a growing chorus of complaint about Indonesia's 'high-cost economy', meaning bribes and unofficial levies. With the central government holding 93 percent of taxation capacity it was argued that local administrations had little choice but to exact their own levies. Partly to try to head off growing labour unrest, in April, the Government also introduced new higher minimum wage levels but many companies complained of difficulty making the new payments, especially when bribery and corruption kept their costs artificially high.

Sofyan Wanandi, Chairman of the Gemala Group, spoke about the arrogance of power and its apparent injustices. He was quoted as saying that the lack of effective means for people to express opinions different from those of the Government was leading to the creation of new unofficial alliances and groups, especially among those who felt that economic and other benefits accrued only to those close to the power-holders. Sofyan was an outspoken champion of fair play and while, as an ethnic Chinese, he may have thought himself a member of the highest circles of power, his sharp comments had not gone unnoticed. Later, his name would be found mysteriously on a list said to have been in the possession of anti-regime activists suspected of making bombing devices. Because he was in Australia at a time when he was needed for questioning in connection with the incident he was branded as not being a "good Indonesian." It seemed that his years of hard work to ingratiate himself had apparently stood for nothing. After the questioning this vociferous man was seldom heard from. On February 6, 1998, 'Asiaweek' noted: " Some critics accuse the Government of setting up the whole incident to cow the public and of using Wanandi...as an example." Had there been a Government ploy to silence Wanandi it had worked.

Agricultural expert, H.S. Dillon, also spoke about the arrogance of power and its affects on the farm sector where there was, he said, - " for the first time ever, a deficit in the trade of food and live animals." Nevertheless the booming economy ensured that most criticisms, fears and doubts would be marginalised. For many foreigners, the boom, hid what might otherwise have been worrying social and political developments.

The intelligentsia and students were disenchanted and frustrated; the business class was fed up; workers and farmers were angry over being badly and unfairly treated. Almost imperceptibly, the grievances of all classes were beginning to coalesce into a single set of demands - for a new president, a new government and for justice. Political and social dissatisfaction was dangerously close to the surface and rumbling with ever increasing volume. Yet, observers, especially those who knew President Soeharto well, were forecasting no major political changes in Indonesia, not only in 1997 and 1998 but not even before the year 2005. In his state of the nation speech on August 17, 1996, - Independence Day - President Soeharto, as always, had said that reforms were certainly possible - but, only within the paradigm established by the New Order. Critics labelled this paradigm "rigid" and "static." Some might even have added "dead." Academics warned of an "ever increasing gap between the power holder's and the public's aspirations," a situation they described as "dangerous."

President Soeharto was not deterred. Just over a month later he described growing demands for a multi-party political system as "unrealistic" and claimed such a system would " unravel all the hard work that has gone into building the present system." "It would be impossible to add another political party," President Soeharto was quoted as saying. "Those who insist on a multi-party system similar to what they have abroad, or to the one we had a long time ago, are automatically asking that we repeal the five political laws that we enacted by consensus. This will be a setback. This is clearly unrealistic if we look at the history of this country in the last 20 years and at the way we have upheld the law and implemented the Pancasila ideology and the 1945 Constitution."

At the end of May, 1996, with a new general election only a year away, outspoken government critic, Sri Bintang Pamungkas, removed from the House of Representatives a year earlier, had defied New Order convention and established a coalition of Government critics by founding a new pro-reform party, the Indonesian Democratic Union Party (PUDI). The formation of new political parties was severely frowned on by the Government but Bintang cited the 1945 Constitution as the basis for his action. He said the Constitution "guarantees the people's right to assemble and associate." Bintang had recently been found guilty of slandering President Soeharto and, pending appeals, had been sentenced to 34 months in jail.

Writing in the 'Jakarta Post' on June 12, political scientist, Mochtar Pabottingi said: " Only a handful of Indonesians could emulate the courage, energy and vision of Sri Bintang Pamungkas in contemporary Indonesian politics. Since five or six years ago, he has not only expressed his ideas with rare frankness and clarity, but followed them up with concrete actions. Undeterred by personal harassment, dismissal from the House of Representatives and recent trial and conviction for defaming President Soeharto, over a week ago he established PUDI." Kahar Badjhuri of Diponegoro University was quoted as saying: "He (Bintang) deserves to be called a hero of the political movement." What was the aim of PUDI? - total reform of Indonesia's political system. The 'Jakarta Post' commented in a leader on May 31: " After three decades of national development, we have emerged as a stronger nation. Nobody in this country wants instability and chaos but a greater measure of democracy will not hurt us and will even make us a stronger nation."

The Government said "No" to political reform and openness. Bintang and his supporters said "Yes." Eventually Bintang went to jail, only to be released two years later after Soeharto had been brought down. Soeharto should have listened to Wahono. The handling of Bintang's case was a major blunder.

Apart from growing generalized opposition to the lack of openness in Indonesian politics, there were many other pinpricks goading unrest. There had been widespread resentment at the way in which, in February, 1996, "Tommy" Soeharto had been exempted from import duty and luxury sales tax, ostensibly to build an Indonesian national car. In fact the 'Timor' car was made in and imported from Korea and then sold in Indonesia at prices which undercut all competitors. The imports added to the widening current account deficit. Even if the car was a good idea, it was universally thought wrong in the extreme to give it to a man who had neither experience, capital nor even an assembly plant. It was the most blatant example to date of the way in which the Soeharto family gained unfair advantage. Most importantly, the car and other examples of favouritism set Indonesia on a collision course with the World Trade Organization and sent out the signal that Indonesia was not serious about levelling its business playing fields.

An article in Singapore's 'The Sunday Times' on August 18, 1996 said: " The car project decision, accompanied at around the same time by an announcement giving effective protection to a domestic firm producing propylene, went against the grain of commitments by a government that vowed to be outward looking and which intended to plug-in to a free and open international trade and investment regime. Both decisions also revived notions about politically well connected groups gaining from the system because the beneficiaries in both instances were firms associated with Mr. Soeharto's sons. The cumulative affect of all these events has been to bring the issues of political reform, leadership succession and a more level economic playing field into sharper focus."

Eighteen months later there had been a public outcry when it was revealed that a private shoe company owned by Soeharto's grandson, Ari Sigit, was claiming to have won a monopoly from the Government to sell shoes to millions of students across the country. The shoes were said to be expensive, bringing huge profits to the owners of the shoe company - "trillions of rupiah," according to Amien Rais. The climate of public opinion had become so hostile that President Soeharto felt obliged to make a statement saying that he "completely disagreed" with any plan to force students to buy expensive shoes. The shoe scandal was almost the straw that broke the camel's back. The Soeharto family were famous for their rapacity. Now, it seemed, they were even prepared to augment their suspected fortunes by exploiting poor school children, struggling to pay their fees.

As 1996 had opened, in Irian Jaya, Irianese separatists had sought to dramatize their demands by kidnapping 13 people, including foreigners. President Soeharto's son in law, the US trained Brig. Gen. Prabowo was in charge of the military's rescue force. Meanwhile an Indonesian platoon commander was on trial at the Irianese capital of Jayapura, accused of issuing unclear orders to his men which resulted in the deaths of Irianese villagers. In March, in Timika, Irian Jaya, thousands of local tribesmen ran amok after hearing rumours that one of their people had been killed after being hit by a vehicle owned by PT Freeport Indonesia, a company in which the Soeharto's are shareholders. According to Reuters, the situation was so serious that Soeharto's son in law and troopers from the Army's special forces were rushed to the scene. Three months later, at Nabire, thousands of Irianese attacked and damaged government offices and the local GOLKAR office after failing to secure jobs in the civil service. East Timor, it seemed, was not Indonesia's only "forgotten war."

In Jakarta, Indonesia's capital and power centre, it was not regional unrest that was agitating the country's intellectuals and interest group leaders so much as Government moves aimed at neutralizing opposition in the run up to the 1997 general elections. These moves outraged and offended not only for their intrinsic evil but because of the rot they seemed to expose in Indonesia's political system as a whole.

On July 19, 1996, in the 'Jakarta Post,' University of Indonesia lecturer, Kastorius Sinaga, drew attention to a statement signed by Abdurrahman Wahid, leader of the Muslim Nahdlatul Ulama, Lt. Gen. Bambang Triantoro, a former chief of staff of the Armed Forces Social and Political Affairs and former cabinet minister, Frans Seda. The well known public figures had signed a "Statement of Concerns" about developments in Indonesia's political climate. The signatories promised to distribute an incredible five million forms to the general public, inviting them to express their concerns about recent political developments. In a country where politics was traditionally taboo this was an amazing development.

Abdurrahman Wahid, better known as Gus Dur, knew what he was talking about. In January, 1996 State Minister for Research and Technology, B.J. Habibie had sent a message to the NU leader saying that it would be better for his organization if Gus Dur resigned. Gus Dur was a long-standing critic of the Indonesian Association of Indonesian Muslim Intellectuals (ICMI), launched in 1990 to rally Muslim elements around the New Order regime. He was also leader of the Forum Demokrasi, a group including some of the Government's staunchest critics. As a sample of the NU leader's comments, he was quoted as saying at Yogyakarta on April 7, 1996: " The National Constitution is good enough and there is no difficulty implementing it. But every day we see the Constitution violated." In a probable sideswipe at ICMI he added: " Moslem scholars have even joined the group who have resigned and adjusted themselves to the situation, helping to preserve the status quo." Gus Dur had come to power in 1994, defeating rival contender Abu Hasan. For the past year Abu Hasan had been encouraged to set up a rival executive board within the NU in a bid to topple Gus Dur. Implicitly Habibie's message was aimed at backing Abu. By mid-year, however, Gus Dur was firmly in control. Someone's tactic of promoting a rival board had not worked. Among the NU leader's most far sighted comments was his view that looming financial and social crisis would trigger dissent among the political elite and, most importantly, provide an opportunity for pro-democratic elements. May 1998 would prove him correct with a vengeance.

Kastorius Sinaga wrote: "Today, real politics have seemingly been reduced to the art and science of power management. Not surprisingly the elite power brokers see politics as a skill by which they mobilize forces to achieve their own political objectives and maintain the status quo. In this perspective, moral considerations are a far cry from the prevalent Machiavellian conduct: the end justifies the means. Political moves are now targeted at the short-term aim of safeguarding a group of people's interests. No wonder intervention, intimidation and violence have become the rule of the day. In such a climate law is compelled to serve political interests, and the executive power is increasingly beyond the control of other democratic institutions like the House of Representatives and the mass media. Such unprincipled behaviour is now affecting Indonesian politics. A series of issues reflect this, including the constriction of the mass media, the imprisonment of pro-democracy activists, the recall of outspoken House members, the threatened dismissal of a judge who wanted to cleanse the Supreme Court of collusion, the interference with the Batak Protestant Church to rid its leadership of those critical of the Government and the overthrow of the Indonesian Democratic Party's leadership", he might have added, for the same reason.

In his last point, Kastorius was referring to a special congress of the PDI, backed by the Government, and held in Medan, North Sumatra on June 22, 1996. The Congress, backed and partly financed by the Government with security provided by the Armed Forces ('Jakarta Post,' June 22, 1996) had been convened allegedly because PDI branches across the country had allegedly requested it - the declared objective: to discuss the record of the Party's leadership; the hidden objective: to remove democratically elected Megawati Sukarnoputri as the Party's head.

Megawati Sukarnoputri must have been giving President Soeharto sleepless nights. First and foremost, as head of the PDI she would, of course, be eligible to run for president in March 1998. Were there reasons why President Soeharto would not want former President Sukarno's daughter to become President of the Republic and Commander-in-Chief of the Armed Forces? Publicly, at least, the reasons were two: Mega had called for presidential terms to be limited to two and, more importantly, for the dismantling of the Soeharto's "vast business empires." (Time magazine, August 12, 1996.)

Despite all the warning signs of stirring opposition, on June 22, 1996, at a special Government backed Congress in Medan, Megawati was duly ousted from the leadership of the PDI. In the run up to the Congress and while it was taking place there were large-scale street demonstrations in Jakarta during which 100 people were injured when the security forces sought to impose 'order.' Jakarta PDI chapter chairmen tried in vain to meet the Home Affairs Minister, Yogie S.M. and the Coordinating Minister for Political Affairs and Security, the late Soesilo Soedarman. At the end of the proceedings on June 22, the new leader was once again Soerjadi, ironically, the man who had recruited Megawati to help the party improve its polls standing in the first place, back in 1987. In insisting that he retake charge, the Government was forcing Soerjadi to eat a large portion of humble pie. If Soerjadi had calculated that Megawati's Sukarno family connections could be used to boost the number of seats held by the PDI in Parliament how wrong he was to be made to be. It may have pleased President Soeharto hat a man who had once called for a limit to presidential leadership terms was now likely to go down with the PDI into hoped for political oblivion.

By the end of the first week of July, when the Government had issued forms to political parties to be used to draw up a list of candidates for the 1997 general elections, it was very clear that Megawati's faction was to be ruthlessly sidelined. Megawati herself was barred from taking part in the 1997 election as leader of the PDI. Megawati resorted to legal action, filing a storm of lawsuits against government officials and the 1,000 participants in the Medan Congress. The lawsuits were launched in the heat of the moment. Two months later, on advice from Megawati's close friend Gus Dur, the PDI leader agreed to withdraw them. It is likely that Gus Dur felt that Megawati would only be subjected to all kinds of unpleasantness without any result. Gus Dur said that he believed Megawati was a person "facing cruelty." He was quoted as saying: "I totally support Megawati in her struggle for democracy."

In the wake of the Medan Congress, anti-Government groups gravitated toward Mega as never before. In its July 11, 1996 edition, the 'Far Eastern Economic Review' described how a "network of non-government organizations (NGOs) were proffering support for Megawati, hoping she will emerge as a powerful symbol of resistance." Bambang Widjojanto, President of the board of directors of the Indonesian Legal Aid Foundation was quoted as saying: "We can use this event (the Medan Congress) to start to organize ourselves to develop 'people power' to challenge the Government."

The 'Review' said that the Foundation had become an "anchor for a new pro-Megawati coalition of 30 NGOs, called the Indonesian People's Council. "The Council claimed to represent students, workers, women, human rights victims and journalists. The NGOs shared the broad aim of improving economic welfare at the grassroots level and

34

abolishing five fundamental laws deemed to be politically oppressive. Under these laws only the PDI, the PPP and GOLKAR were approved political parties and the Republic's president was elected by his own appointees. The laws also governed the formation and operation of the People's Consultative Assembly (DPR) and the House of Representatives (MPR), mass organizations, regional administrations and elections.

Muchtar Pakpahan was out of prison and again working among Indonesia's labourers as head of the Workers' Welfare Union - unrecognized by the Government. Students had been organizing since three were killed during a demonstration against hikes in transport fares in April, 1996. Attempts were now made to establish links across the country. Based on the 1997 election results majority of the PDI rank and file supported Megawati and based on the number of seats lost by the PDI and gained by other parties thousands of PDI supporters heeded Megawati's call to - of becoming golput (a non-voter). from voting during the election. But they were always there, aggrieved and waiting for an opportunity for justice.

Critics dismissed the Indonesian Peoples Council as marginal but did Pak Harto? Megawati had been ousted from the leadership of the PDI and was automatically out of the running for president in '98. But would she now emerge as the leader of a Philippine-style people's power movement and, if so, with what consequences for the Government? Who might her supporters turn out to be? What issues concerned them? How angry were they becoming? Even if they were not sought at once, answers to these questions were deemed vital and unusual methods would in future be used to obtain them, methods which contributed massively to Soeharto's fall.

Meanwhile, Muslim activist Ridwan Saidi, Secretary General of the Masyumi Baru was quoted as saying that "Muslim clerics will fill mosques with praise of Megawati and preach that democracy was an integral part of Islam." At a press conference on July 1 the 'Review' quoted him as saying: " We are sympathetic towards Megawati and we want to help as a supporting element in the struggle for democracy in Indonesia." Megawati's rights, he said had been "unfairly robbed." Another coalition member was the Toba Batak Church whose ruling board had become badly fragmented as a result of alleged Government meddling to gain its own ends. Muchtar Pakpahan's Workers' Welfare Union backed the pro-Mega coalition as did the Student Solidarity for Democracy, spurred by the death of three students in Ujung Pandang in April, 1996. Although the Nahdlatul Ulama was not part of the group, the 'Review' noted that its leader, Abdurrahman Wahid, also known as Gus Dur, had "publicly declared his sympathies for Megawati." Members of the NU's youth wing, the 40,000 strong Indonesian Islamic Students Association had already taken to the streets to show their support for Mega. NGO spokespeople said that "morally" they felt obliged to support Mega as part of their battle to strengthen civil society and one executive from Megawati's board was quoted as saying: " The PDI problem is no longer an internal problem but the problem of the entire nation." The 'Review' said: " In all this, activists sense a new momentum for change fuelled by long standing grievances over economic disparities, underemployment, rural displacement, censorship and corruption." An NGO veteran was quoted as saying: "This is an opportunity we cannot afford to miss." The People's Council was said to be bent on expanding its base and to be framing programmes aimed at abolishing politically repressive laws and enhancing economic welfare.

The Government sought to sideline Mega while encouraging the media to promote her Government-backed rival, Soerjadi. For a while, at least, time was needed to see whether Soerjadi's leadership would take root and what forces it would attract. Time was also needed to see if the bluster surrounding Megawati's ousting would really turn into a people's power movement or would just fizzle out. How had the "dispute" in the PDI come about and why?

At elections in 1993 the PDI had fared well, increasing its seats in the House of Representatives to 56. In 1987 the party won 40 seats and in 1982 only 24. Government suspected that a major cause of its success was the involvement in the party of Megawati, daughter of Indonesia's first president, Sukarno, increasingly idolized by many, especially the poor. Her election to the PDI leadership was feared to give the party an even more substantial boost at the polls. By June 1996, Megawati herself was forecasting that, in free elections, the Party would "get 80-85 percent of the vote" Such predictions must have sent shivers down government spines. After the 1993 election, the ruling GOLKAR's majority had slumped. The Government determined then and there that all the stops should be pulled out in 1997 to ensure that its majority was restored and increased.

Megawati had been elected at an extraordinary Party Congress in Surabaya in December, 1993. She had replaced Soerjadi who had served as chairman since 1986. The leadership wrangle had been protracted, requiring three congresses before it was finally resolved in Megawati's favour. By early 1996 it seemed to Soeharto, if not to his

Government, that Megawati posed a serious threat and had to be neutralized. Within the PDI, party members loyal to Soerjadi, currently Deputy Speaker of the hand-picked House of Representatives, were encouraged to demand a special "leadership congress". Megawati was quick to point out that the demand was inconsistent with Party statutes because it was not made by chapter and branch leaders but by rank and file. Consistent or not Government "listened" to the rebels and unilaterally sanctioned their request for a leadership congress to be held in Medan, Sumatra. The rebel group whipping up the 'rebellion' was led by Megawati's deputy, Fatimah Achmad, an ally of former leader Soerjadi, who moved quickly to establish an organizing committee for the illegal Congress. Medan was a Soerjadi stronghold. There were flat denials that a leadership review meant unseating Megawati as chairperson of the party's central board. Even while the Government backed the Congress to the hilt, its spokesmen continued to agree that Megawati was the lawful leader of the PDI - which of course she was until proved otherwise.

Soerjadi supported Fatimah's rebellion but denied he had ambitions to become leader again. According to the 'Jakarta Post' Soerjadi had been "booted out" from the chairmanship because of "impending criminal prosecution" relating to his alleged role in the beating of several party members. The Government ostensibly stood on the sidelines while a leadership 'dispute' between Soerjadi's and Megawati's factions ran its course, entering the play only to support Megawati's rebels - much as it had supported pro-Government elements in an earlier "dispute" which had wracked the Toba Batak Protestant Church.

Soeharto's downfall can be traced directly to his handling of this alleged "dispute." Tampering with a church in Sumatra might have seemed a small issue. Tampering with the PDI national leadership in the politically charged atmosphere of mid-1996 was asking for disaster. As Indonesian political scientist, Soedjati Djiwandono was to write later: "What seems to have been unanticipated (by the Government) is the strength of that reaction (from Megawati's supporters) and the support that Megawati's faction continues to enjoy." Undoubtedly the ousting of Megawati was Soeharto's first major political blunder. Djiwandono went on: " Megawati has become a symbol of and a rallying point for the increasing demand for change, reform, greater freedom and democracy." Underestimating these demands was a second major Soeharto blunder, especially once they were deepened by heavy handed excesses by elements of the security forces. Djiwandono concluded: " The regime should not fail to read the writing on the wall." If not the regime, Soeharto, at least, failed to read the writing.

On June 6, 1997 the 'Jakarta Post' had said in an editorial: "Over the last few months, there have been rumours that a 'final solution' to remove two prominent figures from Indonesia's political scene has been drawn up. The targets are Megawati Sukarnoputri, chairwoman of the Indonesian Democratic Party (PDI), and Abdurrahman Wahid, chairman of the populist Moslem organization Nahdlatul Ulama (NU). The two are reportedly considered potential threats in the upcoming People's Consultative Assembly (MPR) session scheduled to convene in March 1998. One of the items on the agenda is electing a new president." The attack on Gus Dur failed; the attack on Mega succeeded.

After Megawati's fall, the 'Jakarta Post' wrote: " What has happened to the PDI is deplorable. The use of such a contemptuous method to topple a constitutionally elected party leader is not merely a political setback for Indonesia but also a tragedy for our embryonic democracy. It is conceivable that the whole sorry scheme might backfire. But we fear that unpleasant things could happen if the situation gets worse. This could disrupt our national stability." The 'Post' was right on all counts.

In fact, the Government had not only been concerned about March 1998 but also about the even nearer general elections in June 1997. The Government had been determined to slash the electoral showing of the PDI and also to make sure that Megawati posed no challenge to Soeharto's unanimous re-election for a seventh term. It was never likely that Gus Dur would pose such a challenge, but, despite its denials, the NU had been suspected of somehow being behind some of the riots which had often pitched Muslim against Christian. Plus, Abdurrachman Wahid was a persistent Government critic. Even shadows terrified the Government these days.

Megawati later claimed that letters from branch leaders supporting the special Medan Congress had been forged. Her claim was given credence when some of the branches retracted their backing for Soerjadi. Sixteen members of the Party's national board had been involved in the plot but all had been sacked on the eve of the special Congress, making it impossible for them to continue to represent the Party. Megawati accused the 16 of abrogating party statues which allowed a congress only once in five years. The 16 responded that their dismissal was illegal because it required 15 votes and the decision had been taken by only 11. No such congress could be held without government permission and the most important aspect of the affair in Megawati's eyes was that the go-ahead for the Medan Congress had been willingly given by the Home Affairs Minister. Not only did he willingly grant permission but he was even at the Congress to declare the proceedings officially open. The Armed Forces ensured that there were no incidents. Organizing committee member, Untung Sutomo revealed that the Government had even put up some of the money to help defray the expense of organizing the special congress. "It wouldn't be ethical of me to say how much the Government has given," he was quoted as saying. When President Soeharto formally met Soerjadi on July 25, thereby recognizing him as the sole and legitimate leader of the PDI, he warned of anti-Government forces at work within the PDI, using methods reminiscent of the Indonesian Communist party. By inference, Soerjadi was the person to combat such forces, not Megawati.

For a while Megawati and her supporters tried to ignore the result of the Medan Congress, insisting that she remained the duly elected leader. Her faction continued to occupy PDI headquarters at Jalan Dipenogoro, Jakarta. Later, until it was closed for allegedly violating planning permission, Megawati's PDI occupied a new headquarters in Condet, south Jakarta. While still vowing defiance at Jalan Diponegoro, thousands of her supporters rallied at the headquarters daily in what were termed Free Speech Forums. 'Time' magazine of August 12, 1996 said: " The free speech forums " became the most outspoken forum(s) in Indonesia for decades. Poets, Islamic scholars, feminists, environmentalists and critics of all descriptions took turns in venting their pent-up frustration and rage before ever larger crowds that spilled off the sidewalks and blocked traffic every day for more than a month. Others took to the streets to protest the Government's backing for Soerjadi. Foreigners suddenly found themselves sharing the streets with riot police and armoured cars. Certain streets were regarded as off limits, especially close to the PDI headquarters. With 259 of the Party's 306 branches said to support Megawati it was easy to understand her confidence. Supporters called for a referendum of party members to settle the leadership issue once and for all.

Following the Medan Congress many of the activities of Megawati's faction were deemed illegal, including party meetings and, of course, the Free Speech Forums. The Forums drew huge crowds and the Government accused Megawati of allowing them to be used as a platform for anti-Government propaganda. On July 22, Armed Forces Commander, Gen. Feisal Tanjung, had vowed to clamp down on the free speech forums which he said had "disrupted public order" and were "unconstitutional." Megawati's camp feared that the PDI headquarters would be taken over by her rivals and she ordered her supporters to "defend" it.

The General's threat had drawn immediate fire from the media. In a leader the 'Jakarta Post' on July 24 said: "The warning issued by Armed Forces Chief General Feisal Tanjung on Monday to ban the free speech forum at the Indonesian Democratic Party headquarters on Jalan Diponegoro, Jakarta, for being "unconstitutional" and inciting people "to overthrow the Government" is rather disturbing. It is appalling, because one would think that such a serious charge as treason - which carries the penalty of life in prison or the death penalty if proven in court - should be backed up by solid evidence. So far, one has yet to see it. Without sufficient proof, one might think that the plan is a mere excuse by the authorities to take over the headquarters from the Megawati camp and to stop Megawati Sukarnoputri from continuing her fight to maintain her position."

Despite the protests, on July 23 the commander ordered a halt to the Forums. There was no sign of compliance from Megawati. Indeed, she publicly vowed to continue. Officials of branches loyal to her were now hauled in by the police for "questioning," especially any involved in organizing the Free Speech Forums.

On July 27, 200 of her supporters were brutally ejected from the Party's headquarters by a force which included 800 "PDI supporters" (note, not members) trained by the security forces. In fact, as early as July 4, media reports claimed that Soerjadi had asked the Indonesian Armed Forces directly to assist him take over the PDI headquarters. In the event, it seems that they did so. According to Malaysia's 'Sun' newspaper of May 25, 1997: "Investigations by several human rights organizations on both the storming of the PDI headquarters and the riots contradict the official version. An extensive report by the Indonesia-based Alliance of Independent Journalists, the Institute for Studies on Free Flow of Information and the Bangkok-based, Asian Forum for Human Rights and Development found that security officers took an active role in the attack on the PDI headquarters while riot police blockaded the building, making no attempt to stop the attack while preventing Megawati supporters from coming to the aid of their colleagues. An Amnesty International investigation, which included interviews with people at the scene, concluded that the security forces played a major role in the storming of the PDI building." Initially eyewitnesses said that riot police stood back and watched before giving their backing to the invaders. The chief of the

Central Jakarta Police Office, Lt. Col. Abubakar Nataprawira said that Soerjadi had requested police help to "protect" the headquarters. In an October report into the takeover, the National Commission on Human Rights said: " The Government security apparatus involved itself in an excessive and partisan fashion, and acted beyond its function as an agent of political development and as security apparatus." The Government and the Armed Forces denied that they had played any role other than preserving order.

At first Soerjadi denied that his supporters had taken part in the raid on PDI headquarters, even though the attackers wore T-shirts emblazoned with the message " Supporters of PDI 4th Congress in Medan." On August 1, the 'Jakarta Post' quoted him as admitting that he had, in fact, "mobilized 2,000 of his supporters to take over the headquarters." According to the National Commission on Human Rights, only one day before the take-over, the rival camps had agreed to meet and settle their differences peacefully. "Soerjadi's camp broke its word," Commission Chairman, Marzuki Darusman was quoted as saying. Almost a year later, Malaysia's 'New Straits Times" on May 28, 1997 revealed that 51 men came forward to say that they had been tricked into assisting Soerjadi. The 51 were all members of a rehabilitation centre for troubled youths. They sued Soerjadi for failing to pay them Rps 200 million promised to them for taking part in the raid. All said that they were Megawati supporters and hadn't realized what they were being asked to do. In the immediate aftermath, Soerjadi's Secretary General, Buttu R. Hutapea denied that violence had been initiated or even used by his faction's supporters. Later, on August 30, he admitted that he had actually led the raid. He and his supporters attacked by hurling stones and Molotov Cocktails into the building. Many of Megawati's supporters were injured as a result. Two years later, on July 28, 2998, Soerjadi himself was quoted by the 'Jakarta Post' as saying that "the Government must be held responsible for the incident." He claimed that the Government had meddled in the internal affairs of the PDI to bring about the Medan Congress of 1996 which unseated Megawati and that the Government had also been involved in the attack on the building used by Megawati as her headquarters. In both cases, he said, ABRI involvement was also prominent to the extent of paying and escorting delegates to Medan and backing the takeover of the Jakarta headquarters.

A group of 36 US congressmen filed a petition with Minister of Foreign Affairs, Ali Alatas asking the Indonesian Government to ban the Pemuda Pancasila youth organization, one of GOLKAR's youth wings, which they claimed was responsible for the attack on the PDI headquarters. The petition also called on the Government to make known the names and whereabouts of all those arrested.

There were now, in effect, two PDIs - Soerjadi's and Megawati's. Historian Onghokham said in the 'Jakarta Post:' " The formation of PDI Soerjadi was done in such a cynical and rude way, and its dependence on the Government is so obvious, that it can no longer be said to be functioning as a party." The 1997 general election results would show that his was absolutely true. Soerjadi's PDI secured only 3% of the votes.

The eviction led to widespread riots in Jakarta. Later on the morning of the takeover, hundreds of youths began to gather on Jalan Diponegoro. As the day wore on they were joined by thousands of others chanting "Long Live Megawati" and insulting the security forces. They pelted the police with stones. Troops charged the demonstrators with tear gas, rattan sticks and canes. The mob retaliated by rampaging through nearby streets stoning and burning vehicles and buildings as they went. The mob had to be charged again before it dispersed.

Police had taken away about 170 people from the PDI headquarters and a further 246 were arrested during the street riots. It would be October before any of them were put on trial. They were defended by 11 lawyers, all members of the 3,000 strong Public Defenders of Indonesian Democracy, an organization founded by R.O.Tambunan to help handle the legal battles faced by Megawati and her supporters. Their occupations were given as (petty) traders, taxi and bajaj drivers, bus conductors, construction workers, car mechanics, car washers and bicycle repairmen. As usual in events of this kind in Indonesia, a number of people went "missing" - the Indonesian Legal Aid Foundation said it was 76. Subsequently, the Government expressed strong surprise at the number of people alleged to be "missing" and, indeed, some were rediscovered. According to the 'Jakarta Post' of August 16, 1996, volunteers investigating cases of missing people had found their task difficult to impossible because witnesses were afraid to speak out. In a statement the Jakarta Social Institute (ISJ)said: " Potential witnesses...are obviously frightened and refuse to have anything to do with this case. The 'Post' added: " Houses of victims, or the families of victims, are reportedly being "tightly guarded" by plainclothes officers and terrorized by phone calls from unknown parties. The National Commission on Human Rights and the Jakarta Legal Aid Insatiate were each undertaking investigations into the fate of riot victims, alive or dead. Both reported that it was as difficult to obtain information from hospitals as from witnesses, victims or relatives. The ISJ spoke about post-riot fear turning into a long lasting "trauma."

During the riots, three people were killed and 22 buildings were destroyed and burned, including an expensive block owned by the hapless Soerjadi. Stock prices fell on news of the unprecedented rioting, the rupiah "slumped" to Rps 3,100 to the US dollar and there were fears that foreign investors might now be deterred from proceeding with their plans in Indonesia.

In the wake of the riots, Jakarta military commander, Maj. Gen. Sutiyoso said he was ready to issue an order that future rioters were to be shot "on sight." "We have our limit of tolerance," he was quoted as saying. Armed Forces Chief of Sociopolitical Affairs, Let. Gen. Syarwan Hamid, said that the Army had a standing order not to open fire on the rioters but he hinted this might be cancelled if more riots erupted. "Don't try us again," he was quoted as warning."

The riots - as opposed to the takeover of the PDI headquarters - were blamed by the Government on a small organization known as the Democratic People's Party (PRD). The Party had been around for a couple of years, emerging in 1994 as the People's Democratic Union and had the avowed intention of building a pro-democracy movement across Indonesia. The PRD was apparently an umbrella group for students, workers and farmers. Knowing the fate of political parties in Indonesia, other than those approved by the Government, it had maintained a shadowy existence. Its presence had often been alluded to by government officials when they spoke of "third parties" and "invisible groups" etc. The language used in the group's statements may have seemed inflammatory back in 1994. By 1998 it seemed as if the entire opposition was using similar words - words which the Government always maintained equated to those used by the banned communists.

Five days before the storming of the PDI headquarters the People's Democratic Party declared itself, presumably in the belief that the hour of revolution had come. According to Malaysia's 'Sun' newspaper, in its manifesto the Party said: "There is no democracy in Indonesia. The authorities of the New Order regime dominate the political arena through brutal, cruel and unconstitutional methods." The Party said that the fruits of Indonesia's economic growth had been monopolized by a "small elite," workers had been "economically oppressed, terrorized and even killed," peasants found it "increasingly difficult to defend their rights as they are confronted by the military when they resist capitalist encroachment." Elite-only politics, an intrusive military, a politically controlled judiciary, corruption and nepotism, they said, had created a "bankrupt system." The Party called for the wholesale dismantling of the New Order regime, including political and electoral laws.

On July 8, 1996, the Party had been able to mobilize 20,000 workers in Surabaya. ringing loud alarm bells in the corridors of power. The Surabaya rally called on supporters to back Megawati. The 'Sun' said: " The PRD declaration in support of Megawati indicated the unprecedented galvanizing of a constitutional and a mass based party, forming a potential political force.' The Government said that the Party's structure, aims and propensity for mass action mimicked the banned Communist Party. The riots which followed the take over of the PDI headquarters were said to be the latest example of the Party's attempts to overthrow the legitimate government of Indonesia.

Let. Gen. Syarwan said that the PRD had piggybacked an "uprising" on the back of the conflict between rival factions of the PDI. Within a little more than two weeks the Party's leader, Budiman Sudjatmiko and 170 other activists had been arrested. Many would later be sentenced to between 7 and 13 years in jail. Branches in Surabaya and Yogyakarta were raided and closed down. While the arrests went on, bomb hoaxes at the city's glittering business towers maintained an atmosphere of tension and anxiety. The Government implied that it was the work of subversives. Opposition members thought that it might be the work of the Government. Catholic Priest, Father Ignatius Sandyawan was interrogated in Jakarta for sheltering alleged PRD activists.

The security forces seized the opportunity to haul a number of activists in for questioning, irrespective of whether they were members of the PRD. Muchtar Pakpahan was among them. Soothsayer, Permadi Satrio Wiwoho, a loyal Sukarnoist, was also questioned about the riots. It began to look as if anyone and everyone who had ever openly criticized the Government was now liable to be hauled in for "questioning." PDI legislators were swept up in the net. Ridwan Saidi, a former legislator who then chaired the Indonesian People's Assembly, a loose coalition of NGOs was also brought to book. Former 'Tempo' Editor, Goenawan Mohamad was brought in as a witness along with human rights campaigners H.J.C. Princen and Mulyana W. Kusumah. Former Jakarta governor, Ali Sadikin was also interrogated as a witness against Pakpahan who, he told the press, was only trying to improve the lot of workers, an activity he described a "good." Gus Dur was mentioned as a possible witness. The Attorney General, Singgih, said ominously that there was always a possibility that witnesses could become suspects.

There was almost certainly a hope that the hunt for "reds" and the calling in of witnesses would by themselves intimidate actual and potential opponents. Of course, in the long term it didn't. The campaign just made everyone even more fed up and frustrated.

The riots and destruction of property had infuriated Soeharto. That buildings should be burned and smashed by lawless, stone throwing mobs clearly brought him close to apoplexy - especially when he suspected that those behind it were the allegedly anti-Pancasila, communist-like members of the PRD. He ordered all rioters brought to court for punishment. And he ordered the "questioning" to identify troublemakers to continue at full strength. Soeharto accused that the PDI had become infiltrated by the PRD. He said that the PRD's political manifesto issued on July 22, 1996, showed that its thought and actions resembled the outlawed Indonesian Communist Party. He accused the group of attempting to replace the state ideology, Pancasila, with "something alien to us." "They are exploiting poverty and social disparity problems to start a revolution," he was quoted as saying. Even Megawati was accused of having links to the PRD, an allegation she promptly denied. In a satirical twist, referring to Soerjadi's takeover of PDI headquarters, Megawati was quoted as saying: " Soerjadi has justified all means in order to reach his goals, something which resembled the ways of the outlawed Communist Party."

Activists in organizations with links with the PRD such as the Indonesian Students Solidarity for Democracy were arrested. Twenty-eight alleged PRD activists were also detained in Bali. The Indonesian Legal Aid Foundation quickly revealed that Budiman Sudjatmiko's father had never been a communist but had been a member of the Islamic Hisbullah group. The father of student activist, Garda Sembiring, was a retired army officer - certainly not a communist. The Foundation condemned the arrests.

The Government pressed its case that the views and activities of the PRD resembled those of the defunct Communist Party. Chief Spokesman for the Armed Forces, Brig. Gen. Amir Syarifudin said that the alleged PRD actions on July 27 amounted to an "embryonic coup d'etat" and he added that the objective of the PRD was definitely to turn Indonesia into a communist state. With communism dead everywhere, such allegations looked increasingly wild and wide of the mark. In January, 1997, Soedjati Djiwandono, a member of the board of directors of the Center for Strategic and International Studies would write: " One would think that accusing anyone of being communist-inspired or communist influenced simply on the basis of similar tactics sounds like an effort to find a scapegoat." Commenting on the social and political unrest that had characterized 1996 he added: " We should accept the possibility that ......those acts of violence may represent genuine grievances against injustice." As with so many other developments in a world so different in 1996 from what it had been in 1966, President Soeharto failed utterly to correctly divine social grievances and aspirations and massively underestimated the yearning for change and for justice.

Meanwhile, President Soeharto was quoted as saying that the PDI, PRD and other groups were using democracy and human rights issues as a mask behind which to carry out activities aimed at toppling the Government. In the recent past the Government had warned of "formless organizations" engaged in subversive activities. The elements around the PDI and PRD were now identified as these organizations. A manhunt was launched to round up activists. Gen. Feisal Tanjung described the PRD as a "front line" threat and said that the Armed Forces were determined to track down the "masterminds" behind it. These, he was quoted as saying, would be "crushed" before they bred "new troublemakers." The media generally took the view that the events of July 27 were being used by the Government as an excuse to hunt down all those suspected of opposition to the New Order. Amnesty International agreed. Members of dozens of organizations loyal to the Government were called out to rally in support of the military's actions against the PRD and other organizations and to re-swear the oath of allegiance to the regime. More than a few of the rallyers looked as if they would rather be somewhere else. Ministers and organizations loyal to the Government dutifully condemned the July 27 riots.

Police summoned Megawati and three PDI legislators in connection with the riots, a summons which, in the case of a Member of the House of Representatives or a Member of the People's Consultative Assembly the PDI claimed needed authorization from President Soeharto. No written authorization could be found and the Attorney General ruled that it was unnecessary. The summons related not only to the events of July 27 but also to "crimes committed between June 17 and July 28, 1996" - the time when Free Speech Forums were being held daily.

In the wake of the July 27 seizure of the PDI headquarters and the termination of the Free Speech Forums, 20 foreign ambassadors expressed concern to the Government and demanded an explanation. A delegation of 11 members of Indonesia's National Commission on Human Rights told visiting US Secretary of State, Warren Christopher, that, this time, "the Government and ABRI had gone too far." This was the first time such a phrase had been used - but by no means the last.

As the battle with Megawati had dragged out and President Soeharto had visited Germany for a medical check up, Indonesia's currency and stock markets registered their concern. There was fear of social and political instability in the wake of the PDI affair and there was fear that President Soeharto might be seriously ill and that if he died suddenly chaos would ensue. The rupiah slumped and share prices fell in companies with links to the Soeharto family.

To millions of Indonesians, Megawati and the PDI seemed to stand for Indonesia's 'little people', in stark contrast to GOLKAR and the Government which seemed to represent and care about only the rich. The 'little people' were increasingly fed up with being at the bottom of the income pile and wanted change. They were fed up with only having ever known one president - Soeharto. And, in common with even sections of the middle class, they were fed up with the commercial favouritism enjoyed by Soeharto's children and by his supporters from among Indonesia's ethnic Chinese. Arguably Soeharto's most major miscalculation was the extent to which the greedy commercial activities of his children were despised and hated. Power and its misuse, nepotism, wealth and corruption seemed to characterize the later years of the New Order Government while, in retrospect, the years of Sukarno's presidency seemed to stand for national pride, social care and, above all, morality. Few people alive could remember that the Sukarno years were also ones in which cabinets rose and fell annually and the economy ended in the same kind of shambles it would reach in 1998 under Soeharto.

To the Government, Sukarno's daughter, Megawati, seemed to pose a dangerous threat of actually bringing about the change wanted by many at the grass roots - change it was hoped by them would result in openness, fairness, honesty, transparency and greater income equality. At the very least her leadership could drag down GOLKAR's majority at a time when the Government was determined to show that it was more popular than ever. At its worst it could severely disrupt the presidential elections to be held in 1998. The election of president was usually unanimous. What if Megawati's PDI refused to nominate GOLKAR's choice - which everyone assumed would be Soeharto.

And there was another factor. In the case of the ousting of Megawati, we cannot assume that the Armed Forces as a whole were unwilling co-conspirators. PDI legislator, Aberson Marle Sihaloho had continually criticized the dual function of the army for being both a military and legislative force. The legislator's attacks could not have been welcome to conservative, pro-status quo, elements in the military who had recently seen their stake in the House of Representatives reduced from 100 seats to 75. Subsequently, Aberson was charged with defaming President Soeharto. They might not have been welcome even to reformists who, while wanting change, nevertheless believed and had a vested interest in the military's dual function.

Political observer, Riswandha Imawan commented that the Government-assisted strategy of ousting Megawati from the PDI chairmanship had turned Megawati from a " small wave" to a "tidal wave" in Indonesian politics. "She has now become a leader and a symbol for whoever still believes in moral principles and political ethics." He went on: " The common assumption that the recent Indonesian Democratic Party congress in Medan was nothing less than the beginning of a bigger disaster seems to hold some credence. The Congress has helped launch a new political force in Indonesia. No longer does Megawati belong solely to the party. She has captured the hearts of those outside the party as well. People who are not satisfied with today's monolithic political mechanism, including individuals ostracized by those within the circle of power as a result of increasingly 'personalized' politics." 'Time' magazine commented: " In a matter of five weeks, Megawati has become a full blown opposition figure, the very first in the Soeharto era. Whether she likes it or not - and no one is certain how she feels or what she intends - Megawati has become a rallying symbol for discontented citizens...."

What was the monolithic political mechanism, the circle of power, personalized politics? Indeed, when the term 'government' was used what was meant? The generally accepted belief was that for 'government' one should read Soeharto. But extreme care had to be taken in mentioning the President by name because if he felt "insulted" the insult giver could serve a long jail term and suffer other significant banishments, deprivations and losses. But in reality the Government was Soeharto. Even the 1945 Constitution stipulated that ministers were merely presidential assistants. At the launch of a project of "Tommy" Soeharto's one minister began a speech in "Tommy's presence with the words: "This is embarrassing. I am only the Minister."

The Megawati crisis not only sparked anger among the 'little people.' It also kindled and fanned flames of unrest among students, the intelligentsia, professionals and broad sections of the indigenous middle class not connected with the Government. The independent Election Monitoring Committee (KIPP) called for the 1997 elections to be cancelled in the wake of the PDI scandal.

The emergence of KIPP was an interesting phenomenon. It was formed before the destabilization of the PDI at a time when Government critics had higher if not high hopes that the 1997 general elections might bring about some change in Indonesia's political life. Its leader had been chief editor of the outspoken 'Tempo' magazine, closed in 1994 with two others, 'Detik' and 'Editor.' After protracted legal proceedings the ban on 'Tempo' had been declared lawful by the Supreme Court in June, 1996. A veritable shadow government of non-government organizations had grown up sharing common criticism of the straightjacket within which they felt they political lives had to be lived. Many of these now fell into line behind KIPP including: the Indonesian Prosperous Labour Union, the Indonesian Students Solidarity for Democracy, the Democratic People's Association, the New Masyumi and the Legal Aid Institute. In Aceh, West Kalimantan, Yogyakarta and Bali branches were quickly established.

Kastoius Sinaga commented: " For the first time pro-democracy, non-governmental groups have closed ranks in forming a coalition through the poll watchdog....As a coalition of middle class and progressive intellectuals, the committee comes close to being the fulfillment of a dream long cherished by NGOs in Indonesia. The founding of the new poll watchdog is closely related to the people's increasing participation in politics. For decades political participation has been reduced to serving the interests of the Government's development programmes through the implementation of the 'floating mass' policy and the 'security approach'. In recent years there has been an increasing demand for political reform. People have begun to challenge the Government's authority in the nation's political life."

As evidence of the challenge, Kastorius listed some of the shadow organizations which had sprung up: The Indonesian Farmers Committee - in opposition to the Government sponsored Indonesian Farmers Association; the Association of Independent Journalists as a counter to the official Indonesian Journalists Association and the Indonesian Prosperous Labour Union- in opposition to the Government sponsored All Indonesian Workers Union Federation. Said Kastorius: " The rival non-Governmental institutions wish to accommodate the aspirations and interests of the common people and to exert some influence on state policies."

General Feisal Tanjung immediately branded KIPP as unconstitutional because he said: "The 1945 Constitution makes no mention of independent electoral monitoring committees. It (KIPP) is obviously unconstitutional." The Government's National Election Supervision Committee, presumably also not mentioned in the 1945 Constitution, and headed by Army General Singgih said that his organization accepted the existence of KIPP so long as it did not interfere with the forthcoming election. "If it does, we will smash it," he was quoted as saying by the 'Jakarta Post.'

For years, foreigners doing business in Indonesia had chosen to all but ignore political developments. Suddenly, the ousting of Megawati brought not only howls of protest but determined opposition from Indonesia's hitherto silent and apparently docile people. There had been complaints from foreign governments in the past about human and worker rights abuses in Indonesia but the brushing aside of Megawati as the democratically elected leader of the PDI brought an avalanche of demands for explanations and information - information which would now go into political memory banks around the world for future reference and user.

The Chairman of the Institute for Strategic Studies of Indonesia, Rudini, was quoted as calling on the Government to handle the PDI "dispute" with care. "Please consider the adverse impacts of the dispute. Careless handling of the dispute may plunge the nation into disintegration." Accusing the Government of taking a succession of wrong decisions in relation to the PDI, Rudini went on: " All of the necessary decisions should have been made with the interests of the nation in mind, not those of a certain group." To their cost, the "certain group" chose not to listen. The leader of the Central Java Chapter of the Muslim Nahdlatul Ulama, Muslim Rifai Imampuro, said prophetically that the PDI rift would only end when President Soeharto recognized Megawati as the true leader of the PDI. Even Sudomo, Chairman of the Supreme Advisory Council, was quoted in the media on July 29 as saying: " The Government should not have meddled." Here was a rare insight into even a loyal supporter doubting 'government' policy and tactics.

To the Government, its handling of the PDI may have seemed like just one more step along the tried and tested road to self-preservation. To society at large it was evidence of what was increasingly seen as a deep sickness in Indonesian public life.

Unfortunately for the regime, its maneuverings were no longer observed only in Jakarta or Medan. Washington, the champion of world democracy, was also watching. Five days before her faction was evicted from the PDI's Jakarta headquarters, Megawati met with US civil rights activist Jesse Jackson. The American sympathized with Megawati's hope for a free and fair election in 1998 and with her view that if it wasn't fulfilled, this time, the world would be watching.

On July 23, US Secretary of State, Warren Christopher, flew into Jakarta. One of his interests were the events concerning the PDI. Christopher said that after his visit he would "report to President Clinton." Christopher predicted that there would be an increase in demands for greater liberty and free expression in Indonesia. " How Indonesia responds to those demands will have important implications for the future of this great country and the entire region." He also mentioned that the US planned to raise human and labour rights issues at the forthcoming World Trade Organization ministerial conference in Singapore - a development fiercely resisted by Indonesia and specifically by President Soeharto. Meanwhile, at a seminar in Jakarta, human rights activists characterized progress in human and labour rights in Indonesia as "very inadequate."

In retrospect, the ousting of Megawati as leader of the PDI can be seen as the beginning of the end for Soeharto. At stake was not the future of one woman but of democracy in Indonesia. Onghokham, writing in the 'Jakarta Post' on August 3, 1996 said: " Megawati's popularity has grown fast among the people, beyond the confines of the PDI. She is seen as a victim of Government interference. In short a succession has taken place within the ranks of the opposition. Megawati has at present become the main opposition leader with deep roots in society and outside the political parties. All the discontented people, people eager for change, reformists and others are now behind her. No other recent Government policy has obsessed society more than the PDI policy."

Ominously, for the Government, students had commenced hunger strikes against the Government's alleged "meddling" in the affairs of the PDI by backing the Medan Congress. The students also focused on Government efforts in July to fire Deputy Chief Justice for General Crimes, Adi Andojo Soetjipto, after he had drawn attention to widespread collusion in the supreme court. In the aftermath of his disclosures, in June, Chief Justice Soerjono had set up an investigating team. The Team's unusually rapid conclusion was that there was no evidence to support Adi's claims. Commented Adi: " How could it (the Team) have concluded that there has been no collusion in the face of so much evidence to the contrary?" Ominously, in view of its 1997 election performance and subsequent events, the United Development Party (PPP) warned that the "Supreme Court's credibility " had slumped to an "alarmingly low level. People are marching in the streets and students are going on strike in protest at the Chief Justice's plan to sack Adi Andjojo," a spokesman was quoted as saying. The banners of student demonstrators demanded an end to collusion - and the introduction of democracy. The protests and marches were only a tiny precursor of what was to come in May, 1998. Interestingly, in view of what would subsequently happen to him, Muladi, a law professor and Rector at the state run University of Diponegoro in Semarang was quoted as saying that the conclusions of Chief Justice Soerjono's investigators were "far from satisfactory." Muladi subsequently became minister of justice, appointed by Soeharto and retained by President Habibie.

Justice Adi's revelations about the rottenness of the Supreme Court fanned the flames of public unrest. And there were other explosive issues. In Surabaya, students had been jailed in July for allegedly inciting street protests in which 10,000 workers demanded increased wages. Military officials reportedly tried to liken the activities of organizations to which they belonged, including the PDI, to those of the banned Indonesian Communist Party. Information Minister, Harmoko, warned that communists could try to infiltrate the media - ominous indeed to those familiar with Government crackdowns. President Soeharto accused "interest groups" of "exploiting discontented labourers, peasants and impoverished urban communities to serve their own interests." Detainee, Pontoh, an alumnus of the Sam Ratulangi University in Menado, was quoted in the press as responding: " They know that's not true. They only say it in order to grind us down. There's no way our movement can be equated with communism."

At around the same time the little known Chairman of the State Planning Agency (BAPPENAS), Ginandjar Kartasasmita warned that the wealth gap posed serious challenges to the Government. He said that poverty and equality could stoke social anger and affect the political situation. He also warned that while many people valued stability they disliked the Government's firm actions in maintaining it. He was quoted as saying that in modern Indonesia: " People are more critical, increasingly assertive in their rights and refuse to be treated badly."

Writing in the 'Jakarta Post,' Juwono Sudarsono, Vice Governor of the National Resilience Institute, Jakarta, said: " ..the single most important lesson of the July 27 riots may be the one addressed to the Government and its supporters by the urban middle class. That lesson lies in the urgent need to provide swifter, wider and deeper social and economic outreach to the increasing urban underclass, particularly those who have neither access to employment, the requisite skills needed to ascend the social ladder, nor to the credit structure which tends to favour the well connected. For the vast majority of (urban dwellers) living in an urban environment increasingly impregnated by market advertising and consumer lifestyles, there exists a cumulative sense of severe deprivation, which is easily exploitable, motivating them to acts of desperation and destruction." These would turn out to be prophetic words indeed. he went on: " It remains to be seen whether today's government leaders and the affluent middle class will heed the lessons to be learned from the steps not taken in the last 22 years." Indeed, it did!

Former minister, Emil Salim, said that Indonesia would not survive the challenges of the 21st century without a strong civil society. He was quoted as saying that the first step to such a society was empowerment - "women, children and youths, indigenous people, non-governmental organizations, employees and labourers, farmers and scientists, all need to be empowred. Freedom of expression, as guaranteed by the 1945 Constitution should therefore be implemented in the spirit of the time. He also called for greater regional and local autonomy.

The Government had reason to be extra nervous about the 1997 general elections. Throughout the country there had been ample and violent evidence that the people were restless. Scholars and political activists widely felt that the elections would be a sham to legitimize the status quo and were demanding empowerment, democracy, transparency and fairness. There was widespread cynicism over nepotism, corruption and collusion.

While GOLKAR was planning a landslide victory there were more and more who resented the very thought of it. Feelings in some areas had become so sensitive in relation to GOLKAR that when at the start of the year the Surakarta (Solo) mayoralty painted all its street furniture yellow, the party colour of GOLKAR, rival party activists were enraged and clandestinely painted all the objects white.

In March, John Pieres, a staff lecturer at the University of Indonesia Law School, expressed the hope that the new people's representatives would have the quality and the courage to supervise and correct the Executive. He was quoted as saying: " The public is now demanding leaders with high moral, spiritual, professional, managerial and intellectual standards." The Government was under fire, the political system was under fire, the legal system was under fire. In a hearing at the House of Representatives at the beginning of the year, Edi Sudradjat had high-lighted issues detected by the military as likely to provoke social unrest - the general demand for more democracy, resentment of unfair treat-ment, dissatisfaction with wages and salaries, arbitrary dismissals, un-employment, increased prices and racial and religious intolerance.

The first quarter of any year was generally relatively quiet. In fact, 1997 had opened with more than a fair share of disturbances around the country and snowballing criticism of the status quo. The first quarter was the time of Christmas, Chinese New Year and the month-long Ramadan holidays. By March, the holiday mood was over and everyone's attention was becoming focused on the upcoming elections. In addition to the elections, the issue of presidential succession gained momentum to the point where calls began to surface for the President to resign. President Soeharto took the trouble to respond, saying that he was per-fectly willing to step down provided it was done by constitutional means. Both the President and his Armed Forces Chief, Gen. Feisal Tanjung, both threatened to "clobber" anyone who tried to bring down Soeharto using unconstitutional means. At the beginning of March, Gen. Feisal revealed that 60, 000 troops were being prepared to ensure smooth general elections.

As 1997 opened, the Government was determined that its show-ing in the general elections scheduled to begin on May 29 should be improved. Hardly a day seemed to pass without Information Minister, Harmoko, being televised or photographed somewhere in Indonesia rallying the people to GOLKAR. When elected to the post of party chair-man in 1994 he had vowed to enhance GOLKAR's majority. Based on his experiences in the field, in the run-up to the presidential elections of March 1998, Harmoko would duly report to Soeharto that the nation wanted him as president for a seventh term. Whether truthfully or not, when President Soeharto finally stepped down in May, 1998, he was said to have commented: "Why was I assured that the nation wanted me?" Perhaps what happened at Soeharto's 77th birthday celebration provided the clue. Nobody turned up. Out of power, the nation's true feelings about its president could be displayed. In power, there may have been felt a deep need to dissemble. Parri passu with the effort to boost GOLKAR's standing had been the perceived need to weaken sig-nificant opposition, especially the PDI.

As the run up to the election commenced, the Government could congratulate itself on having gone as far as possible to slash the elec-toral chances of its chief rival, the PDI. By March, 1997, the Party was said to be on the verge of bankruptcy. The PPP was not considered a formidable threat, having mustered only 17 percent at the last election and thought to be lacking either charismatic leaders or convincing and attractive policies. In case there was any doubt, in February, members of constituent organizations of the ruling GOLKAR, such as the country's six million civil servants, were reminded that they "must" vote for GOLKAR. In some quarters, there was doubt. At the end of February the Indonesian Institute of Sciences, based on a survey result, recommended that civil servants should be free to vote for the party of their choice. The survey found that the theoretical obligation of civil servants to treat all citizens equally was severely undermined by their forced loyalty to GOLKAR. The PDI and PPP had long complained but to no avail. Again in theory, according to the 1985 law on political organizations, civil servants can vote for any party. In practice they could be disciplined by superiors if they failed to vote for the Government. The Armed Forces announced that it would support GOLKAR. If there were officers who craved change, clearly their perception was that this was not the time.

Having taken steps to increase its own vote and minimize competition from the opposition the Government began to ensure that the election ran "smoothly." As usual, all 2,000 candidates contesting the 425 seats in the House of Representatives were screened for suitability. Seventy five seats were reserved for ABRI. The 500 seats of the People's Consultative Assembly, which met only once in five years, were all government appointees. Electors would not vote for candidates but for party symbols and after the election legislators would be appointed depending on their party's electoral performance and on their place on the list. The higher up the list the greater the priority for appointment. A major structural weakness of the system was that voters and their representatives had only a very nominal and tenuous relationship. Among those deemed suitable for appointment were the wives and children of high ranking government and military officials. The list included President Soeharto's daughter, Siti Hardiyanti Rukmana and his son, Bambang Trihatmodjo.

The nepotism involved was so blatant that it provoked Minister of Defence and Security, Edi Sudradjat to speak out. He was quoted as saying: " Recruitment of legislative candidates should not be based on their proximity to or relations with government and military officials. Even GOLKAR legislator, Syafrinus, was quoted as saying: " I find it hard to believe that some officials say there is nothing wrong with nepotism in recruiting members of the House of Representatives. Outspoken government critic, Amien Rais, slammed the nepotistic selection saying: "I'm afraid we'll then get a House of Representatives which deviates from its function, namely giving voice to the people's aspirations, and becomes a mouthpiece for the Government. Neither Amien nor Gus Dur were included in the list. From January 1997 onwards, when the candidates for the new Parliament were announced, nepotism would become an increasingly major issue in Indonesian politics - especially in March, 1998, when President Soeharto unveiled the Seventh Development Cabinet, including his daughter and his archest of cronies, "Bob" Hasan.

As usual, campaigning among the 125 million voters was permitted only during the two weeks before the election, from April 27 to May 23 with a five day "cooling-off" period preceding polling day. Unusually, the competing parties were encouraged to stage only indoor rallies to avoid feared disturbances of the peace. Local administrations were warned not to sanction large gatherings of people in the run up to the elections. All campaign broadcast speeches were to be screened by the Government's General Elections Institute, a limitation which triggered waves of criticism from political activists and scholars. The PPP even threatened to boycott the entire election and, at the least, flouted campaign restrictions by staging massive street rallies in several cities. PUDI also threatened to boycott the polls, something Sri Bintang Pamungkas had promised practically since his party's founding.

The contestants in the election and Indonesia's political society as a whole was firmly focused on three major issues: democratization, implying empowerment and transparency as well as end to corruption and collusion, the need to radically change the political "status quo" and the issue of President Soeharto's successor. To some observers changing the status quo and choosing a new president were euphemisms for wholesale political change and for the entry into politics of a new generation. At this stage there was still hope that the 1997 general elections would bring about some of the changes people were demanding. There was still hope that 74-year-old, President Soeharto, would not stand for re-election in March, 1998. Up to this point he had not said that he would. Indeed, he hadn't even been asked.

Political scientist, Riswandha Imawan, from Gadjah Mada University was quoted as saying: "Up until now (discussion of) the succession issue has been postponed. It looks as if this time (1998) round it has to happen. Once the democratization issue has started rolling, it will continue to do so and there won't be a single force able to stop it." The Government seemed to understand this. Spokesmen stressed that they were ready to promote empowerment and responsible freedom within Pancasila democracy. Cynics and critics doubted the commitment. In theory Pancasila democracy promised a cooperative democracy within which participants could disagree while avoiding exclusivism. In practice, it was difficult to impossible for the voices of dissenters to make themselves heard. With President Soeharto seeming to equate almost any alternative to his interpretation of Pancasila democracy with "anarchy" and "chaos" what chance could they possibly have? 'Review Indonesia' warned: "Public response to campaign speeches shows that the country cannot afford to take for granted the growing aspirations of society at large. These include the younger generation, who are more educated and more exposed to globalization than ever before. Their enthusiastic and at times violent response to the campaigns shows that there exists a burning desire for some kind of change for the better."

True to pessimistic forecasts, the 1997 general elections turned out to be the most violent in Indonesia's history, involving a fair amount of actual "burning." In 1992 only eight people had died, in 1987, only 12. In 1997 the death toll reached nearly 300 as frustration and anger exploded. Despite the advice not to stage outdoor rallies there were mass mobilizations and pitched battles were fought between rival groups. In Jakarta alone over 80 died; in Banjarmasin, South Kalimantan there were 136 fatalities and hundreds of buildings destroyed by fire. The violence in Banjarmasin was described as the "worst of the New Order era." Much of the spleen was vented against the ruling GOLKAR by thousands of green clad supporters of the PPP which, despite expectations, increased its share of the vote to almost 23 percent. The carefully hatched rules were flouted by all parties but there was deep resentment at the way the ruling GOLKAR apparently favoured itself and discriminated against rivals. The election spotlight remained firmly on the PPP throughout the campaign, its giant rallies bringing it supporters into frequent conflict with GOLKAR supporters and with the security forces. Tear gas and warning shots were fired to disperse crowds. Frustrated campaigners occasionally rioted, stoning security personnel and damaging or destroying property. The National Commission on Human Rights said that the campaigns of the PPP and the PDI had "spread terror throughout communities". "Campaigners have banged on motorist's cars, honked their horns, revved their motorcycle engines and shouted at pedestrians."

After not only a violent campaign but what many perceived as a one sided campaign, heavily favouring the Government, GOLKAR won the election with a record 74.30 percent of the votes - compared with 68.1 percent five years ago. GOLKAR Chairman, Harmoko, was quoted as saying: " This is proof that the people of Indonesia agree with the existing political and electoral systems besides being a big legitimization for (President Soeharto's) New Order Government." How wrong subsequent events were to prove him!

The PPP notched up 22.64 percent of the vote and Soerjadi's PDI a sad 3.05 percent. In practice, despite the outcome, if the election had shown anything, it had been the growing hatred of GOLKAR. In an editorial a year earlier, the 'Jakarta Post' gave clues as to why GOLKAR was still able to win handsomely. It said: " ...one can easily get the impression that a certain political party is still living in the mindset of the 1970s, with its officials practicing the old strategy of coercion and putting pressure on voters to vote for their party. In this information age, little can be concealed from the public and such wrongdoing will merely fuel resentment and animosity." The 'Post' did not say which party it had in mind. Dissatisfaction with GOLKAR's win in Madura was so deep that 3,000 troops had to be deployed to restore order after riots broke out over alleged irregularities in vote counting. A recount was scheduled.

The election had been billed by the Government as a "Festival of Democracy." Many critics felt that it had been a festival of repression. A post-election survey conducted by the Center for Strategic and International Studies, concluded that the election had shown no improvement over those in previous years and may even have been a "setback." Presenting the survey, T.A. Legowo was quoted as saying: " There have been many indications of violations to the principle of a direct, general, secret, fair and just election." he was quoted as adding that the right to hold a general election had been arrogated exclusively to the Government, with the role of poll contestants being reduced to a mere formality. He was quoted as adding: " Domination of government officials and Armed Forces officers in the election committee line-up has restricted the participation of political parties and the public. This confirms the possibility of vote-rigging and other violations." Vote-rigging had been the subject of the public fury in Madura. Public complaints were higher than ever not only about vote-rigging but also about intimidation, about violence and about the increased public control of the entire election process. The Center warned prophetically that if the Government continued to use general elections only as a means of maintaining the status quo instead of reflecting the aspirations of the people "this nation will slide even deeper into political decay." Surprisingly he did not say, "violence and anarchy."

CHAPTER TWO

In the eye of the currency storm

Despite more than two years of massive and escalating evidence of unrest around the country and the most violent general election in Indonesia's history the Government felt pleased. It had achieved what it set out to do. It had not only won the election but, as hoped, had increased its share of the vote. But, just as everything seemed to be turning out right for the Government things began to go badly wrong for the country.

In early June, 1997, with the elections over and another massive 74 percent win under its belt, the Government felt confident. It basked in an atmosphere of political security, a rupiah stable at about Rps 2.4 to the US dollar, high and rising forex reserves of US$28 billion plus, low inflation and a trade surplus. Bad things were happening to the Thai bhat but, at this stage, whatever they were, seemed specifically Thai and Thailand was a long way away from Indonesia. Nevertheless the currency contagion rolled south and in other directions besides, infecting Malaysia, the Philippines, South Korea and, all too soon, Indonesia.

As the rupiah dipped against the US dollar few of Indonesia's leaders were seriously worried. How many times had they been told by the world's experts that Indonesia's fundamentals were strong and that its macroeconomic management was virtually faultless!

There had been some mild warnings, not only to Indonesia but also to other members of the Association of Southeast Asian Nations (ASEAN). Toward the close of 1996, IMF chief, Michel Camdessus had warned of rising current account deficits. Most countries in the region thought them manageable, especially Indonesia, whose deficit was within the accepted range of approximately 3.5 percent of Gross Domestic Product (GDP). In the month after Indonesia's general elections the IMF warned of weaknesses in Indonesia's banking sector. There were references to mounting unrecoverable loans and even to bank insolvency.

In its 1997 country report the World Bank had praised Indonesia's fiscal policies and congratulated it on its prudent foreign borrowings and even debt management. However, in line with new thinking within the Bank, the report had talked about bad business practices, poor business structures and slow Government action to bring about improvements. After a year of record economic growth the warnings seemed to command little attention. The World Bank's criticisms seemed little more than a description of the culture of normal business in Indonesia - a culture which had so far provided more opportunities than it had posed problems. Even in early September, Standard & Poor was still able to say: "Basically, we don't see Indonesian banking as another Thailand."

From the Indonesian Government's point of view, if there were weaknesses of the kind cited, it was thought that most of them would be found in the private sector, which since 1988, had been given its head to drive and lead Indonesia's economic growth. Problems created by the private sector were the private sector's to solve.

One of the problems being faced by the private sector and about which the Government and Bank Indonesia was entirely in the dark was the volume of private short-term offshore debt. As June led into July and on into August dollar demand from Indonesia's corporates rose noticeably, driving the rupiah down. The demand for US dollars was by no means limited to Indonesia but had its counterpart in Thailand, Malaysia and South Korea. In Indonesia, the money-men scratched their heads, started digging, added up the numbers and slumped back in their chairs in shock. The level of private debt, repayable in 18 months or less and subsequently estimated by one banker as requiring 8 years to repay, seemed enormous. Looking at turnover, profits, and even assets, there was no way that the bills would be paid! Forex dealers and hedge fund managers began to beat a retreat. As July wore into August, global investment funds had also become alarmed. Bad debt meant bad investments for their clients. By early August the world's mutual funds were thought to have dumped up to US$15 billion in southeast Asian currencies - about the same amount as local Governments had spent defending the ringgit, baht, peso, rupiah and, finally, even the Singapore dollar. Again the rupiah dived.

An atmosphere of unease had settled over the region in August, as currencies headed downwards in line with the perceived mismatch between currency values and economic fundamentals. Nervous markets watched more and more economic damage being inflicted by falling currencies throughout the region, damage which brought beleaguered currencies under new rounds of pressure from selling. The pressure on the rupiah became remorseless but was still described as a crisis of 'sentiment'. The reasons why overseas forex speculators and fund managers didn't like what they saw in Indonesia seemed incomprehensible and inexplicable to most Indonesians, told so often and by such reputable people that their fundamentals were strong. Each time the rupiah dived, market confidence dived with it. The more bearish and negative the dealers became, the higher Bank Indonesia felt obliged to hike interest rates until, at the end of August, private banks were charging borrowers 40 percent and more.

Earlier in the month, the still bemused Government was prompted to protect its reserves by first widening its support band for the rupiah to 12 percent and then, in mid-August, with the rupiah at Rps 2.755 to the US dollar, to abandon the band completely and, for the first time in Indonesia's history (since 1945), simply float the rupiah. Demand for US dollars was too remorseless to counteract. To a free marketeer like Bank Indonesia's Governor, Soedradjad, in any case deeply engrossed in the implications of the globalisation of financial markets and free trade within the Association of Southeast Asian Nations (ASEAN) early next century, freeing the currency must have possessed a hard-to-resist logic. It was also in line with advice now being taken routinely from the IMF. Later the start of the collapse of Indonesia's economy would be dated from this fateful decision.

In any case, a modest and bearable de-facto devaluation of the rupiah from Rps 2,400 to one US dollar to Rps 3,500 to one US dollar, promised to assist Indonesia's flagging non-oil and gas (non-MIGAS) exports against worsening international competition. It should also help to depress imports and lower the current account deficit - both highly desirable objectives. At this stage, Bank Indonesia Governor Soedradjad did not have accurate figures describing the amount and term of private sector offshore borrowings and could not guess at how low the rupiah might sink if dollar demand turned from the steady to the torrential in a very short space of time.

The Government had watched Thailand, Malaysia and the Philippines throw away billions of US dollars of their reserves in a vain attempt to halt the slide of their respective currencies and, after already seeing US billions disappear down the drain, had no intention of repeating the same 'mistake.' The float took the pressure off the Government's reserves but it left the currency fully exposed to the frosty, negative, sentiments still blasting it. As dollar buying pressure mounted and the rupiah sank steadily, to protect the currency, the Central Bank resorted to the tried and trusted instrument of again raising interest rates. In the circumstances, it is hard to see what else could have been done. The Government had to at least try to protect the value of the rupiah by raising interest rates and, if that failed, it would score no points by throwing good money down the drain in a useless rear-guard action aimed at creating adequate rupiah scarcity.

For the first time in Indonesia's history, a floating rupiah gave the world an opportunity to register what it truly thought of the country by its attitude to the currency. And what it thought was evidently mostly bad. A factor not well understood in Indonesia was the massive negative view of the country in the influential Western press - a view which definitely influenced 'sentiment'.

This view was that President Soeharto and his family were draining the country of funds for their private use and had no desire to eradicate from the bureaucracy and business corruption on a scale said to be ruining the economy. Whenever there seemed to be a chance to make big money, the Soehartos were alleged to favour themselves and their friends. It was said that it was this access to the national cookie jar that compelled President Soeharto to cling to power into his late 70s with the prospect of his continuing in power until he reached the age of 81 - making him one of the world's longest ruling leaders.

In addition, despite all the talk of the constitutionality surrounding his succession, foreigners feared that, without the grooming of a successor, chaos could break out and instability ensue. Indonesia's apparent inability to put out some of the world's worst forest fires also created a very bad impression of the country's management - especially since, later, Environment Minister Juwono Sudarsono confirmed what had long been suspected, namely that 65 percent of them were caused by commercial companies, many of them in the category of those favoured by the Government. To these current issues could be added the lingering perceived problems of East Timor, Aceh and Irian Jaya and alleged rights abuses by a Government consistently characterized as little more than an authoritarian dictatorship.

While foreigners certainly couldn't be said to know all there was to know about Indonesia, its economy looked weighed down by debt and the regulatory and legal environment in which the debt would, or would not, be repaid seemed far short of standard international practice. Indonesia had now earned the reputation of being one of the most corrupt countries in Asia, placing a large and heavy question mark over its reliability, the environment was becoming seriously ravaged, threatening domestic health and even the global climate. If spasmodic riots were anything to go by, the people were becoming potentially dangerously restless. Even sections of the upper class were talking about the normally unmentionable - a looming political crisis accruing to the Government's apparent inability to solve Indonesia's worst crisis in three decades.

Against this background, following the float, the rupiah fell to another record low but Governor Soedradjad, assured that this was to be expected and "temporary." In fact, among those who thought they knew that Indonesia wasn't as bad as critics painted it, there was a widespread feeling, even among some foreign observers, that the currency had basically 'overshot.' Within a week, there was indeed some small cause for congratulation because the tumbling rupiah appeared to recover somewhat, rising by over 11 percent. There was even dollar selling and short-term rupiah buying on the basis of jacked-up interest rates. The 'Jakarta Post' quoted one local dealer as saying: "I salute the Government's success in stabilizing the rupiah. It proves that our economic fundamentals are really good." The long-beleaguered stock market gained ground.

However, by the end of August, constantly rising interest rates and a constantly devaluing currency were inflicting greater damage on the economy and revealing critical weaknesses in the way most business was done in Indonesia. To the suspected inability of Indonesia's private sector to repay its offshore loans, swingeing interest rates now threatened a tide of domestic bad debt, bank insolvency and even large scale bankruptcies.

As the currency crisis had developed, the Government of Indonesia had been in constant contact with the IMF and other international agencies. At the end of August, the IMF now turned a microscope on Indonesia, searching out the underlying problems. Like the Indonesian Government itself, the IMF focused its attention on the ramifications of the nose-diving rupiah. There was still an assumption that Indonesia's 'fundamentals' were firm. Its recommendations can be summarized as: keep expenditures and prices low and seek to maximize state revenues.

The Fund's Executives chose to take the view that negative market sentiment stemmed principally from such economic distortions as monopolies and subsidies - characteristics of Indonesia's economy that domestic critics of the Indonesian Government and laissez-faire America had long cherished overturning. The Government was urged to promote economic efficiency by further and consistent deregulation and particularly by scrapping monopolies, which, it was claimed, had the effect of keeping prices artificially high. Such measures would enhance the country's weakening competitiveness. The Government of Indonesia was also urged to proceed with eliminating business restrictions which led to rent seeking and abuse and to do more to apply transparent regulations evenly, especially those relating to the collection of tax - a source of revenue more important than ever as the currency devaluation diminished the contents of the Government's coffers. In this way costs would be kept down and revenues and efficiency boosted. Implicitly, reform of the banking system was urgent.

The so-called bailout strategy devised by the IMF had contained another component which, while it did not sew the seed, certainly fanned the flames of doubts even some Indonesians now had about their entire political system. War on corruption, which was blamed for a host of economic, social and moral problems in Asia, had been adopted as the IMF and World Bank's theme in 1996 so it was perhaps not surprising that these concerns should have been at the top of their list in Indonesia. The IMF had placed great emphasis on transparent, fair and good governance being crucial to Indonesia's ability to recover from the severe lack of confidence among investors.

From the Indonesian Government's standpoint, none of the kind of general jabs the IMF had made at Indonesia's culture of Government and business amounted to much more than ideological huff and puff and its response could be expected to be equally woolly.

Meanwhile, in the real world of economic activity, some corporations snapped up dollars for offshore debt repayment, while others held onto theirs rather than change them into rupiah, dollars became scarce with their value rising at a rate commensurate with the fall of the rupiah. While before it had been only the crisis of 'sentiment' pushing down the rupiah, now large-scale dollar buying had to be added into the mix of reasons for its precipitous decline. At the same time, domestic prices began to creep up, especially of imported goods, threatening to push up inflation dramatically.

Far from seeing a country with firm fundamentals, what the market now felt it saw was an economy with a dangerously widening current account deficit - equal to almost one third of national reserves, a currency so fiercely under attack that the rest of Indonesia's reserves risked being quickly drawn down, a growing inability to service or settle offshore loans, a rising tide of domestic bad debt and the spectre of corporate and bank failures - plus all the other factors foreigners identified as promoting lack of confidence. Suddenly, rock solid Indonesia began to look like a country increasingly unable to pay its way.

And its Government either didn't seem to know what to do or acted only in a half-hearted manner. It was feared that one reason for its being half-hearted might be that corporations with the largest offshore debts might be politically well connected, disposing the Government to indulge them rather than confront the problems. Little did many know that the real reason was that, at this stage, the Government still had very little idea of who owed what!

Throughout September, the Government instigated a number of measures aimed at enhancing opportunities for foreign investors, at reducing imports, at holding down public foreign debt and at slashing public expenditure to better fit the new value of the rupiah. The steps were generally welcomed as equivalent to a voluntary IMF austerity package.

The IMF issued a statement saying that it was "very impressed with the steps announced by the Government of Indonesia." First Deputy Managing Director of the IMF, Stanley Fischer, was quoted as saying: " The IMF has been very impressed by the fact that Indonesia has moved decisively in the foreign exchange market, on the budget and on structural measures in the economy." He added that the measures were the reason why "Indonesia is seen so positively in international capital markets."

By the third week of September, despite the IMF's optimism about Indonesia, other experts were beginning to give voice to the hitherto unmentionable. Perhaps the 'currency' crisis was an economic crisis after all. Or perhaps the currency crisis had triggered an economic crisis. Indonesian economist, Mari Pangestu, of the Centre for Strategic and International Studies, warned of falling GDP growth on the back of continuing high interest rates and declining corporate and consumer spending, accompanied by rising inflation caused by the impact of the long dry spell and by rising fuel prices. The possibility of rising exports was the only bright spot on the horizon, she said.

As October opened, the rupiah plunged down toward Rps 4,000 to one US dollar and analysts described traders as in a "panic selling mode." The issue for the market now was very squarely that of Indonesia's solvency. Could corporations pay what they owed, at home and abroad? Could domestic banks meet their obligations? Could and would the Government find some way of bailing out the debtors? Was there still hope for the economy? The market doubted it and the rupiah continued to fall.

With no sign of any halt to the rupiah's slide and talk of "panic" in the air, the general feeling in Indonesia was that perhaps the Government had little alternative but to turn to the IMF for heavy-duty help - although few seemed very clear what help was being sought. Few understood why they needed any help! If only the rupiah would stabilize it would be business as usual! In any case, the IMF had already been consulted. Measures had been taken which the Fund had praised. Why hadn't the market responded positively? What else could be wrong? What else could be done?

On October 8, the Government decided to emulate Thailand and South Korea and turn to the IMF for "technical assistance." At the same time, it sounded out multilateral agencies, including the IMF, about the prospect of support funds for Indonesia's reserves. President Soeharto stressed that, at this stage, proud Indonesia was not asking the IMF for money, only technical assistance. He was quoted as saying: "We've already set up our own reform programmes and we've asked the IMF to look at them because of their experience."

In the days that followed the announcement of the turn to the IMF, markets seemed to be optimistic and, by October 10, the rupiah rose to around Rps 3.400 to one US dollar and stocks gained. Even though it slipped slightly the following week, there was nevertheless said to be hope and optimism in the market. To those whose dominant fear was insolvency, the word 'bailout' associated with the IMF truly had the ring of magic. In a leader on October 7, the 'Jakarta Post' said: "To be fair, the Government has done almost everything in its power in dealing with the crisis. Many of its responses this past one-and-a-half months have won praise from international lending agencies: from the decision to float the rupiah, and the shelving of huge and costly Government projects, to the new economic deregulation package announced in early September."

The reprieve to the rupiah, following the Government's request for IMF assistance, was short lived. What the market most wanted to see - a solution to Indonesia's private, offshore debt problem - wasn't forthcoming. Indeed, the Government had expressly said that it wasn't asking the IMF for money and ruled out any role for itself in settling the private sector's overseas bills. The market maintained its stubborn downward course. It seemed that the only thing that would satisfy it was money! And money handled by a solvent banking system with all its leaky holes firmly plugged! Despite all that had been said and done the market took the view that more had been said than done. The market was only interested in real fundamentals, not what seemed to be a lot of hot air about 'reforms.' To outsiders, the Government of Indonesia still seemed to be hoping that the crisis would solve itself and that all that was required was a few ameliorative measures to help weather the storm.

Although Indonesia had only asked the IMF for technical assistance, Western diplomats in Jakarta lobbied the Government to accept whatever cash aid was needed for a 'bailout' and to be prepared to accept whatever reform 'medicine' the IMF might prescribe.

Discussions between the Government of Indonesia, the IMF, the World Bank, the Asian Development Bank and bilateral sovereign lenders took place throughout October and on October 31 the IMF announced a US$23 billion aid package for Indonesia to be accompanied by a package of reforms aimed at restoring international confidence. The cash was to be provided by the IMF (US$10 billion), the World Bank (US$4.5 billion), the Asian Development Bank (US$3.5 billion) with US$ 5 billion from "Indonesia's own foreign assets." There would be an additional US$20 billion funding from bilateral donors including: Japan (US$ 5 billion), Malaysia (US$ 1 billion), Brunei (US$ 1.2 billion), Singapore (US$ 10 billion) and the United States, (US$ 3 billion).

The multilateral and bilateral aid package was to be used largely for very specific purposes, such as trade finance or banking reform. Psychologically, it was thought likely to overcome any fears the market may have had about possible national insolvency - although there was never any suggestion that the funds would be used to augment reserves which might be fed into the market to improve dollar liquidity. The notion that the package was any kind of bailout was a misnomer from the beginning.

The vice-president of Hong Kong-based, Morgan Stanley Asia Ltd., Timothy Condon, was quoted as saying in Jakarta on November 4, that the IMF funds promised that Indonesia would be the first to escape the monetary hurricane sweeping the region. "What is needed in Indonesia is confidence that the rupiah will not go into free fall as the short-term debt overhang is unwound. The IMF is precisely what will deliver this confidence." A month earlier, Dennis de Tray had said much the same thing: "What we need to do is to put together a package that is so good that we can say to the world, financing will not be a problem."

Unlike the September package, some of the October 31 reforms looked as if they might have teeth, although by no means all seemed relevant to the country's ongoing and deepening problem of debt. Since the October package was basically a continuation of what had been begun in September, once again, Government promised to trim its spending but now it also promised to dismantle certain trade and price distorting monopolies, to do away with the local content programme for automobiles, to push ahead with trade deregulation generally, to abide by any decision of the World Trade Organization regarding the Timor car and to introduce measures to boost exports and to restore health to Indonesia's entire financial sector, including the capital market, insurance and pension funds, financial institutions and banks.

Many of these measures looked like the result of the West's crusade to bring about global free trade on level, Western-marked-out, playing fields. The more charitable said that the reforms would allow Indonesia to operate more efficiently and reliably in accordance with international standards and norms. Whether their funding really weighed in creditors' minds or not, the opportunity had also been taken to target the underwriting by the Government of allegedly unviable projects, such as the manufacture of aircraft and cars. To strengthen and help clean up the banking system the IMF had specifically allocated US$8 billion. Experts from the US Federal Reserve Bank and the Federal Deposit Insurance Corporation were to assist Indonesia with the needed reforms. Whatever the reforms achieved, the one thing that they didn't do was to pay any debts and this was virtually the sole hub of Indonesia's economic problems.

There had been heated debate over the direction of Government spending, with the New Order Government happy to balance its books and avoid a deficit and the IMF pressing for a surplus equal to one percent of GDP. The difference between the two positions was broadly that the Government's position seemed to guarantee some growth while that of the IMF seemed to risk recession, a condition the Government naturally wanted to avoid and, in any case, thought unnecessary. The market was cautious about all this. A recession would obviously make the debt problem close to insoluble.

Certainly, if long-term devaluation reduced Government revenues, projects would have to be postponed or cancelled, otherwise the Government really would end up with a huge which it was already clear, foreign funding sources had no wish to pay. But the IMF's harping on the need to cut Government expenditures at this time seemed more to reflect its experience in other parts of the world than Indonesia's. The crisis aside, it wasn't Government spending and debt which had triggered the confidence crisis in Indonesia but that of the private sector - an issue untouched either by the Government's reform package or by the IMF.

Indonesia's private sector was already screaming from the hurt inflicted by persistently high interest rates and while the Government wanted to be seen to be aware of this and to be promising to reduce rates, at the same time, the IMF and its supporters were adamant that it must commit to keeping interest rates high and at a level likely to maintain the stability of the rupiah. By trying to keep interest rates down, the Government wanted to head-off a recession it feared might develop while the IMF insisted that only its 'medicine' of high interest rates would save the economy.

From the market point of view, the October reforms, enacted on international advice, amounted to little more than an effort to achieve good housekeeping under circumstances of increasingly free trade. Banking reforms, though included, would inevitably be very long-term. On the day the package was announced the stock market again fell and the rupiah was described as "dithering' at Rps 3.625 to the US dollar. Economist, Nyoman Moena, summed up the mood in the marketplace. He was quoted as saying acidly and succinctly: "the Government needs to move beyond that (the October reforms) to satisfy the market." The package's failure to address the offshore private debt issue, the insistence on a budget surplus and high interest rates made the package a lot less than attractive to Indonesia's government and business sectors.

To restore banking sector solvency and to impress markets and investors, the IMF argued that what was needed was for bankrupt banks to be closed down. Rumour had it that the IMF wanted 50 banks shut down. Reliable Jakarta foreign banking sources put the number at 42. It was hard to see how this would reassure lenders or even the markets. To send this strong, allegedly positive signal to the market, immediately after the October 31 deal with the IMF, 16 of those banks which were deemed to be the most flagrant violators of best banking practice were closed down and 9,000 employees laid off with three months severance pay, commencing December. Finance Minister, Mar'ie Muhammad, confirmed that bad debts meant that all the banks had more liabilities than assets. Because of continuing losses they resorted to the inter-bank market for emergency funding, always short-term and high inter-est - occasionally as high as 75 percent or more.

Depositors with less than Rps 20 million in any of the banks could be reimbursed from one of three state banks, Bank Rakyat Indo-nesia, Bank Dagang Negara and Bank Negara Indonesia. Sums of this scale accounted for 93.7 percent of all deposits at the banks, or some 600,000 accounts. Reimbursements were slated to begin on November 13, to prevent anxiety among depositors. Other depositors could hope to recover some or all of their money from what remained from the sale of bank assets after tax. Owners and shareholders would also be held responsible for any losses to clients.

First reactions, even from Government critics, were generally positive. But as time passed, instead of sending the strong, positive signal to the market presumably anticipated by the IMF, the closure of the 16 banks, at least two of which argued that they were not insolvent or badly run, led to growing panic about the stability of the entire bank-ing system. Large private banks were suddenly cautious about having foreign currency transactions with smaller ones; some joint venture banks severed their ties with such banks, the public began moving money en masse from private to Government banks, which it hoped would be more stable. To try to retain clients, private banks were obliged to push up their interest rates far above those of the state banks to as high as 70 percent. Despite this, some people began withdrawing their money from the banking system altogether. To head-off panic and possible bank runs, the Government said that no other banks would be closed. Such a prom-ise flew directly in the face of the IMF but the Government had decided that, if possible, no 'medicine' was better than bad 'medicine'. Although the Government had guaranteed that all small depositors at the closed banks would get their money back there was still an element of public clamour until everything became clear. In the event, it was not until Feb-ruary 20, 1998, that all depositors finally received a Government guar-antee of reimbursement in the interest of "justice".

State banks and not private banks were traditionally accused of having the largest amount of bad debt. The long-term plan for the state banks remained privatization, as much as anything else to raise fresh funds. The state banks now suddenly benefited from a windfall. In the wake of the bank closures there was a veritable stampede of clients away from what now seemed to be highly risky private banks and into the state banking system, perceived as likely to be propped up by the Government at all costs and therefore essentially no risk.

There can be no doubt that the Government agonized long and hard over the decision to close insolvent banks. If they did nothing about the banking system, market sentiment would remain negative. If they did too much or the wrong things, panic might spread, threatening the entire system. Worse still, whether banks were closed or not seemed not to be the issue. The nub of the crisis was the repayment of debt. How would bank closures facilitate this?

The Government had clearly felt that its new measures would be enough to satisfy the market and not only were the public reassured that there would be no further bank closures but there were also no overt signs of the more drastic reforms demanded by the IMF - an attack on monopolies across the board - including, but not merely, the state logistics agency, BULOG, the removal of subsidies and the withdrawal of funds and favours from unviable enterprises such as Industri Pesawat Terbang Nusantara (IPTN), the state aircraft manufacturer and PT Timor, the putative manufacturer of the putative national car.. Funds for PT Timor were a special drain on the banking system with little hope of any rapid repayment to lending banks.

To take these further steps seemed to many to be tantamount to bringing about a sea change in the culture and way of life, not only of the New Order Government, but of virtually the whole society which had grown up with it and around it. There was widespread skepticism about whether such things would ever happen. Vested interests in the status quo were legion and extended throughout the business community.

In Indonesian Government circles, with continuing uncertainty about what was causing the monetary crisis and IMF-fanned optimism that it would be short lived, the public thought it detected wavering as to whether all the doomed banks would really have to close. During his November visit to Jakarta the IMF's, Michel Camdessus, had said breezily: "I believe the stabilization of the rupiah and financial stabilization itself shouldn't take a long time." The feeling that the crisis was one of 'sentiment' affecting 'currency' was persistent and widespread; belief in Indonesia's 'strong fundamentals' was enduring. Against this background, it was hard for many of the players in Government and in business to be able to understand either the gravity or the longevity of what was happening around them.

71

On November 7, the Government announced that some of the capital projects postponed back in September would be allowed to proceed after all, several of them linked to the President's family. The presidential decree giving the projects the go-ahead was actually signed on November 1, the same day as the announcement of the IMF package - so certain was the Government that the problems Indonesia faced were no too deep going and that the IMF's 'magic' would work rapidly.

While the Government of Indonesia stopped and started, IMF Managing Director, Michel Camdessus bolstered the Government's confidence that the IMF package would be enough to soon solve the immediate problems and restore confidence. He said in Paris: " I am very satisfied with by market reaction to a multi-billion dollar aid package for Indonesia. The rupiah has consolidated and confidence has begun to return."

US Assistant Secretary for International Affairs, Timothy Geithner, commented: "The markets have reacted quite favourably to the programme so far, which is a testament to the clarity and force with which the authorities have acted and the credibility of the authorities' commitment to a strong programme." World Bank President, James Wolfensohn, was quoted in the Jakarta Post' as saying: "I think the Indonesians are very, very committed to try to get this (programme) done and, under Mar'ie Muhammad, the Finance Minister, my guess is that you will see a lot being done." Later on, it was easy to say that the Government of Indonesia had been over confident but with this sort of backing who could blame them for thinking that they were on the right track and everything was turning out all right after all. In Kuala Lumpur, on November 5, for the G-15 Summit, President Soeharto seemed to shrug off the crisis with the thought: "The Indonesian crisis is actually now a crisis of confidence in the rupiah and this is what we are trying to revive."

For a while, some things actually did look better - the rupiah-US dollar exchange rate for example. But the stock market kept its nose pointing downwards amid regional gloom and uncertainty.

On November 11, with little sign of any improvement to the value of the rupiah, IMF boss, Camdessus flew in to Jakarta in what was described by the press as a "show of confidence." Hopefully, a visit like this would make the longed-for IMF 'magic' effective at last. At Soekarno-Hatta International Airport, Camdessus rose to the occasion and, smiling and confident, told the assembled media just that - he was confident. Next day, after a meeting with President Soeharto, he repeated his message, adding that he had found the President's personal commitment to the reform programme extremely encouraging. At the airport he had gone out of his way to stress that the reforms to be implemented were not the IMF's but Indonesia's - supported by the IMF. "With this programme I trust that Indonesia will be in better shape and better equipped for long-lasting growth after the time of difficulty. I'm certain that the crisis will be a blessing in disguise and that Indonesia will leave it stronger than it was before."

What the "time of difficulty" was likely to be like was described by economist Kwik Kian Gie - "We may witness the bankruptcy of many companies, the laying off of workers, the abandoning of building activities, the decline of sales and low occupancy rates at hotels,. Many traders will leave their outlets at shopping malls because they cannot afford to pay their dollar denominated rents, unemployment will increase and economic growth will slow down." - enough difficulties to be going on with....

Continuing to see the offshore debt-triggered, economic crisis firmly before them and witnessing the Government's apparent shilly-shallying, market observers asked themselves whether the Government of Indonesia had really understood the seriousness and magnitude of the crisis and of the problems it faced in restoring confidence? Would it really go ahead with the proposed budget cuts, needed more than ever as rupiah devaluation slashed state revenue? And did the closure of the 16 banks point to determination to clean up the whole system or was it just token. By now, behind the scenes, the Government was working closely with US advisers on necessary reforms but from the market point of view nothing much seemed to have changed. The debt overhang was still in place, confidence about its repayment was still declining and deeper financial problems were building up fast in many important sectors of the economy.

By the third week of November, the steps taken apparently somewhat half-heartedly to date were now said by most commentators to have signalled that Indonesia was not serious about doing what the market was said felt had to be done - cleaning up the whole banking system, indicating a solution to the ever more pressing problem of ballooning short-term, private, overseas debt and attacking monopolies and subsidies. Naturally, the persistent devaluation made the dark clouds over the banking sector look even blacker.

Markets, of course, are in reality inanimate, so we have only subjective opinions and analysis to guide us as to what really needed to be done. Assuming that markets are most interested in buying and selling, paying and being paid, we can reasonable expect that it was the debt problem and its ramifications that was really the root cause of the entire crisis. The debt problem led to other problems which the markets felt had to be corrected. Who can do business with insolvent banks or corporates? On top of the root problem of the debt and the ancillary problems this triggered the IMF weighed in with a programme of institutional and procedural reforms which it said were essential to enable Indonesia to survive its current crisis and ameliorate any which may occur in the future.

On November 18, Finance Minister, Mar'ie Muhammad, suddenly stressed the importance of curbing private sector borrowings. At last, the private offshore debt was identified squarely as the villain of the piece! Mar'ie blamed the precipitous fall of the rupiah on panic among private sector companies, all scrambling in the market at the same time to buy dollars to pay off their debts. Obviously some of them were even trying to make payments ahead of time in case the rupiah slumped even further. He revealed that Indonesia's total offshore debt stood at US$117 billion in September, 1997 with a fall in the public portion to US$52.3 billion but a rise in private borrowings to US$65 billion. The debt service ratio was expected to rise to 34.5 percent or about 3 percent above Government estimates. Approximately 43.3 percent of the foreign loans were denominated in US dollars, 39.5 percent in Japanese yen and 17.2 percent in other currencies. According to the Bank of International Settlements, 59 percent of Indonesia's private offshore debt was short-term. The Finance Minister was quoted as saying: "To reduce the burden on our balance of payments, we need to curb private sector borrowing." What Mar'ie did not say, but the Bank of International Settlements did, was that, of the private sector's US$65 billion debt, US$34.2 billion was short-term, meaning repayable in 18 months from the date of securement. The Bank estimated that US$20 billion would fall due between November, 1997 and May, 1998. The fact that later other assessments of this debt would crop up and that foreign news media were able to spook the markets even more by quoting unsubstantiated and perhaps inaccurate figures points up graphically the problem created by the absence of any effective monitoring and recording system by Bank Indonesia. This debt mountain was the time bomb ticking away beneath Indonesia's economy. This was largely the reason for the huge dollar demand and the continuing fall of the rupiah.

While they may not have possessed fine detail about how much was owed and when it was repayable, the Government certainly now realized that debt repayment was a large part of the reason for Indonesia's currency problems. Indeed, as dollar demand increased, the topping up of state reserves suddenly looked more important than had perhaps first been thought. The fact that the sums promised to Indonesia by international financial institutions and bilateral donors exceeded the country's short- term debt was calming to observers but seemed to have little impact on players in the marketplace. Presumably, those who knew the IMF also knew that its funds would not be used to directly pay down debt. As always, it was a case of seeing being believing. Until the debts were paid the market refused to relax.

The news for the market on November 20 was not good. Newspaper headlines in Jakarta screamed "No bailout for private debtors." The only good element was that the Government promised to help debtors negotiate roll-overs with foreign creditors. Next day, the Jakarta Stock Exchange dived to a four-year low and the rupiah sank to Rps 3.625 to one US dollar. Whether, by strict definition, it was or wasn't a crash, Paribas Asia Equity chief, Robert Allison, was quoted as saying: "It's a crash." In the absence of accurate data and of positive statements from the debtors, it is not clear whether this pessimism was justified or not. However, the market was in no mood to take chances.

Bank Indonesia Governor Soedradjad revealed that at least US$9.6 billion of Indonesia's private sector debt was due to be repaid before the end of the current financial year, providing little hint or chance of a respite for the battered rupiah. The Governor said that the information had been obtained from a recent survey of custodian banks, reports from commercial banks, from corporate borrowers and, incredibly, from publications! In the markets and the media, there was speculation about how much money might have been borrowed by companies in the largely unregulated short-term debt market, especially promissory notes.

Whereas, at the beginning of the month, the appeal to the IMF had been described as being for technical help, Soedradjad now said that the approach to the IMF was, in fact, to try to convince the world that Indonesia had the money to pay its bills. Practically to a man, foreign experts and observers had thought this all along. It was confirmed. Much had been said and done, tried and failed and despite his official optimism, at the close of the stormy month of November, with the rupiah having tipped the 3.700 mark to one US dollar, President Soeharto went to Mecca to pray.

There is no doubt that, as December opened, the President was feeling frustrated. He was besieged by an enemy he could not see and against whom he could launch no 'strike.' Around him, even the experts were saying that no "quick fix" was in sight. Echoing similar but more acid comments by Mahathir Mohamad, President Soeharto lamented: "The hard work and sacrifices over several decades that have been exerted for social and economic development are being wiped out overnight." Like Prime Minister Mahathir there can be little doubt that the President and others in the Government were not merely frustrated but perhaps even bitter because the crisis seemed no fault of theirs. Hadn't they been told ad nauseam that their economic management was first class!

While the Government sought solutions to the crisis President Soeharto appealed to the nation to unite and for all sections of society to help each other weather the storm. At the same time, human rights campaigner, Marzuki Darusman, was quoted as saying that even those Indonesian people suffering most were unlikely to join social unrest so long as they were confident that the Government was doing its best, that all sections of society were treated fairly and that the supply and price of basic food items was maintained. Of course, if it should happen, jobless, penniless or starving people would not be likely to stay quiet for long.

The so-called IMF bailout might have provided a solution had the money been delivered immediately and had it been fed into the market to maintain the dollar supply. This did not happen and, even if it had, it would have greatly increased Indonesia's public debt, something the Government naturally wanted to avoid. Foreign crisis-related aid was very much regarded as stand-by, unless project specific and as many other ways as possible were sought and tried to influence the market, short of injecting borrowed dollars, and without burning up dwindling reserves. The issue wasn't even whether the private sector could pay or not. There was simply too much debt to be repaid in too short a time. The answer had to be a debt roll-over and the Government wanted this as eagerly as some of the companies now having trouble servicing or repaying what they owed.

At the end of November, Finance Minister, Mar'ie Muhammad, had visited Japan to urge a roll-over of some of Indonesia's private sector debt. Given the scale of Japan's own banking sector problems, this initiative had seemed doomed from the outset, if not to outright failure, at least to limited success. Japanese banks were said to have lent Indonesian companies about US$20 billion, with South Korean banks accounting for a further US$12 billion. No visits were made to South Korea, itself, now one of the major targets of the regional crisis. Now, in December, the Finance Minister decided to go to the US, this time taking with him representatives from leading private companies, a suggestion emanating from the Indonesian Chamber of Commerce and Industry (KADIN). At an estimated US$4.5 billion in bank loans, US exposure to Indonesia was relatively slight, four times less than the amount owed to European banks. The mission to the US had two objectives: 1) to try to get some of the private debt rolled over and 2) to boost confidence in Indonesia's commitment to reform. The business leaders included: Mochtar and James Riady from Lippo, Ciputra, Sofyan Wanandi, Sukmawati Widjaja of the Sinar Mas Group and Aburizal Bakrie, representing KADIN. In all probability the Americans were in no mood to agree to roll-overs. What most wanted was to get their money back and get out. In the ensuing months this would understandably come to be seen as the attitude of most if not all foreign lending banks. Later, nervousness among international bankers about Indonesia's dwindling ability to pay its debts would result in even Indonesia's export trade being severely impeded after foreign banks refused to recognize Indonesian letters of credit.

Before Christmas, the US's Standard & Poor downgraded Indonesia's sovereign debt and Moody's Investors Service downgraded Indonesia's foreign currency ceiling for bonds. Moody's also put on review the financial strength ratings of five state and one private bank. Moody's was quoted as saying that the downgrade reflected: " the deterioration in the country's financial position as a result of a more than 50 percent drop in the valuation of the rupiah and a drop in investor confidence."

While the market was acutely concerned about the stability of Indonesia's banking system and the solvency of its corporations there was also that underlying chronic fear that the country lacked political stability until President Soeharto appointed a capable and convincing successor. The President was aged 76 (life expectancy in Indonesia is around 64) and had recently undergone a round of tiring transcontinental travel to South Africa, Namibia, Saudi Arabia and Canada. Instead of resting during the long flights it was President Soeharto's custom to spend the time working. While the President's doctors were adamant that he was healthy, nevertheless, upon his return to Jakarta on November 28, a trip to the Summit of the Organization of Islamic Conference (OIC) in Tehran scheduled for December 9 - 11, was cancelled. Earlier, it had been announced that President Soeharto would attend an informal summit of ASEAN in Kuala Lumpur on December 14 to discuss the regional crisis and possible further neighbourly responses. The day before the summit was due to open, the trip was called off. Even a family outing to pay homage at the tomb of Madame Tien was cancelled.

Already jittery markets began to fear the worst. When the trip to the ASEAN summit in Kuala Lumpur was called off, people feared that the President might actually die. Rumours spread like wildfire that he was in hospital or already dead - not only in Indonesia but in Singapore, Hong Kong and Japan. Defence Minister, Edi Sudradjat, even found it necessary to deny that the military were planning to maintain stability by mounting a "coup." The rupiah slumped to Rps 4,600 against the US dollar - the largest single-day drop in recent history. To assuage fears, it was necessary for friends and family to speak out and for the President to be seen in the media as being still very much alive. Unfortunately, one photograph showed him in the garden of his home, dressed informally in a sarong, watching and listening to a pet parrot - hardly the right image for a man the markets hoped was in firm command of one of the world's larger economies with a population of 202 million.

Doubts about the President's health grew faster than the speed of light, not only to rumours about what might happen if he died, but to a new dimension for Indonesia's economic crisis. A problem that had begun on the basis of "negative sentiment," that had snowballed into a "currency crisis," that had developed into a crisis of "confidence" in the economy as a whole, that had ballooned into a full-scale "economic turndown" was now said to have become a "political crisis." Hashim Djojohadikusumo, Chairman of the Tirtamas Group and a shareholder in one of the 16 banks closed on IMF advice, was quoted as saying: "The rupiah's depreciation is really crazy. This has become a political problem and we need a political solution to the problem."

Just as offshore private debt had slowly come to be perceived as the basis of Indonesia's economic difficulties now bad governance was being firmly identified as the reason why this situation had a) been allowed to develop and b) Indonesia's bureaucratic, legal and commercial institutions were in such poor shape to weather the storm.

At the University of Indonesia in December, a seminar on good governance was held, with respected Muslim intellectual Nurcholish Madjid telling delegates that Indonesia's economy could only recover if there was transparency in the implementation of all policies as well as accountability to the people. Echoing the IMF, he said that the nation and its leadership must be willing to engage in a radical programme of economic and political reform. In a leader on December 18, the 'Jakarta Post' said: "It is certainly no coincidence that the growing public calls for political reform should be gaining in strength during these times of monetary turmoil. As the current crisis proceeds with no hope or sign of abating any time soon, it is becoming more and more clear to many Indonesians that economic and monetary decisions are not taken in a political void. For the average Indonesian, who stands to lose the most, it is becoming increasingly frustrating to observe that, being outside of the decision-making process, there is nothing whatsoever that he and she can do to influence the course of developments. If anything good has come out of the current crisis, it may be the growing comprehension that the need for accountability and transparency in Government is no longer a choice, but a reality - that is, if we are aspiring to become a modern nation capable of standing on par with other members of the global community."

From the outset, the IMF had placed heavy emphasis on good and transparent Government as being as much a likely solution to Indonesia's currency and economic crisis as the macro and micro-economic measures it proposed. And although there were many Indonesians who might have agreed, until mid-December, there were few who were prepared to speak out boldly in its favour. This public clamour to link the demonstrable failure to find a solution to the economic crisis with a failure of political leadership would rise to a crescendo in the New Year.

As the rupiah dived below Rps 5,000 to one US dollar, and the stock market plunged to a four-year low, a public chorus broke out claiming that the October 31 IMF package had failed and that Indonesia's economy was sicker than ever. Kwik Kian Gie was quoted as saying: " .... people do not believe in the rupiah's stability. They believe that the rupiah will continue falling and they are hastily buying dollars." Speculators were busy in most markets, especially Singapore and London, exchanging rupiahs for dollars. This was a new development, at least in semantics. Until now the rupiah had been said to be being forced down by the demand for dollars to meet debt payments. Now it was said that people generally had lost confidence in the national currency.

A few days before the Christmas holiday, the rupiah slumped to Rps 6,000 to one US dollar. Inflation had increased to the highest monthly levels in 10 years, prices of even basic goods were rocketing upwards to socially dangerous levels, bankruptcies were rising, whole industry

sectors were paralyzed, the number of newly unemployed was beginning to run into millions, even the supply of a very popular food was
threatened by the fact that 80 percent of poultry farmers couldn't afford
imported feed for their chickens.

The President could see that the IMF medicine was not working, the people felt that the Government was doing too little too slowly
and, but for the upcoming Christmas, Chinese New Year and Muslim
holidays, a potentially explosive social situation was building up. Those
who dared to raise prices or were foolish enough to hoard were increasingly subject to summary mob retribution. While foreigners were feared
to have lost confidence in the economy, among the people of Indonesia,
a new and potentially far more serious crisis of confidence was brewing
- in the Government itself. On the eve of Christmas 1997, it was not only
clear that the market wanted to see Indonesia's debts repaid but that
the nation was beginning to ask for an account of how the country's
finances had been allowed to fall into such a state.

Indonesian Sociologist, Loekman Soetrisno, blasted Government
officials for their response to the economic crisis. He was quoted as
saying: "We had been claiming that the fundamentals of our economy
were strong when in fact they were not. This habit of denial is demonstrated not just by officials but by us as a nation." Abdurrahman Wahid,
leader of Indonesia's largest Muslim organization, the 40 million strong,
Nahdlatul Ulama (NU), added that even though people were dying in
famine stricken areas Government officials denied there were food shortages. He was quoted as saying: "When facing a crisis we behave like an
ostrich...we pretend there's no problem...we bury our heads in the sand."
Amien Rais, Chairman of the 28 million strong Islamic Muhammadiyah,
spoke about a decline in the Government's "legitimacy". He was quoted
as telling a seminar at Gadja Mada University, Yogyakarta, that social
unrest, brawls among the unemployed and protests against certain Government policies were indications that the Government was "losing its
political and moral legitimacy."

As the year closed, the rupiah had lost almost 75 percent of its
value, the Jakarta Stock Exchange had lost about 80 percent of its value
(down from US$100 billion to US$23 billion), projects were being cancelled thick and fast, corporate and bank debt was rising, businesses
were scaling back and winding down, millions were being thrown out of
work and the severe drought was sparking fears of food and water shortages, in some worst-hit areas, fears that became reality.

Franz Magnis-Suseno wrote in the 'Jakarta Post' on December

31: "While the year 1997 is coming to an end our economy is tumbling into an abyss. The rupiah's fall through the Rps 6,000 to the US dollar barrier is not only a psychological shock, it is simply economically unsustainable. It must be reversed, otherwise what we have built up during he last 30 years would be cut by a third and we would find ourselves where we were about 16 years ago. Millions of people would in the end lose their source of livelihood and the danger of large-scale riots would become increasingly likely.

"Up till now our Government has taken the right steps and pointed in the right directions. But the fact is that all this is just not enough. And time is running out if we want to avoid total economic collapse with all its terrible consequences. The compulsive buying of dollars.......is a sign of a complete loss of trust in the rupiah. And this means nothing less than the loss of public trust in the Government's ability to safeguard people's livelihoods. People have lost faith in our Government. The question is not whether this lost of trust is justified or not - it is a fact. And this fact becomes more obvious as officials continue to act as if the situation was not so bad and that the public should not be alarmed. This is, in fact, the Indonesian way. Nothing other than decisive, inspiring leadership can save us now. Only decisive leadership by the Government can restore public confidence - without which there is no way out of the crisis.

"What would decisive leadership mean? First, a clear, unequivocal acknowledgement of the graveness of our situation. Second, there needs to be a clear, credible sign that the Government, in taking steps necessary in the national interest, would override all personal interests - even for groups up to now deemed untouchable. This action should at the same time clearly show a commitment to national solidarity, meaning that while asking Indonesians to make sacrifices, the Government would show that it demanded real sacrifices from those in power."

As 1998 approached, with its March election of a new president and vice- president and the appointment of a new cabinet, there were ever increasing calls for "new blood" in the country 's leadership. The 'Jakarta Post' said in an editorial that "....problems and differences are tackled in the same old way as they were 20 to 30 years ago: by persuading people to conform, if possible, and clamping down on dissenters, if necessary. New blood is needed to revitalize our national energy." Ominously, at the beginning of December representatives of the Association of Indonesian Law Students Council had called on the People's Consultative Assembly not to renominate President Soeharto for a seventh term. They were soon followed by representatives of the Communication Forum of Jakarta Youth and Students, bearing an identical message. The 'Jakarta Post' quoted Irfan Gani, representative of Islamic students from Bandung as saying: "It's a sin if we let (Soeharto) lead the country (again).. we'd better place him in a respected place for a person whose time has come to enjoy his retirment." These were mild beginnings of what would all too soon become a national movement of protest against Soeharto, a movement which he ignored at his peril.

Virtually from the close of the 1992-3, parliamentary and presidential elections there had been voices raised against corruption, collusion and nepotism in Indonesia. And there had been a rising tide of voices in favour of openness, a concept the President had cautiously endorsed provided, as always, it did not threaten political, social and economic stability. The heavy-handed closure of three magazines in 1994 seemed to bring this flirtation to an abrupt end. Had there been no cataclysmic economic crisis, these voices may have amounted to little more than an 'acceptable' background 'noise.' But once the crisis bit in all its terrible, unforgiving and unrelenting savagery, corruption, malpractice, collusion and ineptitude were trumpeted as the causes. While it was realized that President Soeharto had not caused the problem, his style of Government and even his continued presence as President of the Republic, now appeared to some as a barrier to the changes the market was demanding and without which Indonesia seemed to risk sinking to its knees - or lower.

Political scientist, Soedjati Djiwandono, wrote: " We are waiting for a change in the political scene. The same political system has been in power for over three decades, a record surpassed only by Cuba's President, Fidel Castro. The political system is not functioning fully and properly. There is a growing tendency toward a growing concentration of power in the hands of the Government's Executive branch and, by contrast, a continuous weakening of the representative bodies power - one of whose main functions is to exercise control over the Executive branch. Indeed, one would wonder, especially in the light of what has always appeared to be the Executive branch's dominant role in the People's Consultative Assembly steering committee, whether the President is really mandated by the MPR (House of Representatives) or the other way around. There are increasing demands for greater public participation, greater freedoms of expression and association, an effective mechanism of control, judicial review, an antitrust or anti monopoly law, and a presidential term limitation - in other words for greater democracy and justice."

First, the call had been for transparency in business. Now, the call was for transparency in government. From a crisis of sentiment, to a currency crisis to an economic crisis, by the end of 1997, Indonesia appeared to have arrived at a political crisis - the first since 1965. Said the 'Jakarta Post: "Behind an economy that has made tremendous progress until recently, there has lurked the dark shadow of monopoly, favouritism, nepotism, public distrust of the rupiah, institutionalized inequality and a weakness of supervision. Politically, Indonesia lacks transparency, an uncertain succession scenario, increasingly weak legislative and judicial bodies, rampant corruption and a freedom of expression which has been turned into an art of whispers."

On the first day of trading after the New Year Holiday, Asian currencies were said to have "taken a pounding" with the Thai baht, Malaysian ringgit, Philippine peso and Indonesian rupiah all being sold down to new record lows. By January 6, the rupiah had slumped precariously close to Rps 7,000 to one US dollar and political as well as economic concerns in the market were now cited as the reason. The 'Jakarta Post' quoted "dealers" as saying that political concerns ahead of the convening of the People's Consultative Assembly in March to elect a president and vice president accelerated the fallout of the rupiah against the US dollar. "The political atmosphere approaching the General Assembly poses another important factor in the rupiah's decline," a dealer was quoted as saying.

The General Assembly was important for a reason other than the election of the new president and vice-president. It would also be the time when the state budget for the next fiscal year would be finally approved as well as the state guidelines leading up to a new five-year-plan - Repelita VII. The debate about the budget had continued with December opinion veering firmly towards an austerity budget based on the losses the Government must sustain as a result of the devaluation of the rupiah and the decrease in tax revenues.

Before the Assembly met normal practice was to release a draft of the forthcoming budget. But the nearer the budget approached the more voices were heard - or at least read - saying that, above all else, the budget must promote growth. There began to emerge widespread concerns about the IMF's insistence on a contractionary one percent budget surplus of a kind which had also emerged in Thailand. More or less at the same time that the draft budget was being framed in Indonesia, in Thailand, the Government of Prime Minister, Chuan Leekpai, was saying that it might have to renegotiate aspects of its IMF package, especially the requirement for a one percent budget surplus. As in Indonesia, the Thai currency continued to plunge, despite the advice of the IMF.

As if to highlight the differences in approach, the January 4 edition of the 'Jakarta Post' carried a front page headline which read "Govt Must Make Hard Choices In New Budget" while on the very next page the heading was "Budget Must promote Growth: Business people". Aburizal Bakrie, the Chairman of KADIN, was quoted as saying: " We are relieved to hear that President Soeharto said that the next state budget would increase in size." Pontjo Sutowo, Chairman of the Hotel and Restaurant Association was quoted as saying: "The budget has to ensure that the development process continues." However, on balance, opinion was on the side of a 'care and maintenance' budget which would allow whatever development seemed possible. With revenues falling unthinkably, what other realistic approach could there be?

The draft budget was made at a difficult time, when no one dare predict what the rupiah's exchange rate against the US dollar would eventually be. But decisions had be made by the drafters and, convinced as they were, that Indonesia's fundamentals were really strong, that the currency had "overshot," and that the market, in effect, would soon come to its senses, the figure of Rps 4,000 to one US dollar was chosen. Given that, even as President Soeharto delivered his budget address to the House of Representatives, on January 6, the rupiah shot down almost to Rps 8,000 to the dollar, the choice of Rps 4,000 to the dollar seemed high optimism. Immediately and unfortunately that was exactly how the market perceived it.

For those who favoured an austerity budget, including the markets and the IMF, there was also a public relations downside to the budget. Thanks to the devaluation of the rupiah, it showed an increase of 32 percent in Government expenditures, chiefly for the purpose of servicing public debt and also to continue to subsidize fuel - a subsidy anathema to the IMF but essential to all the millions of poor throughout Indonesia whose incomes wouldn't tolerate even a small increase. Any rise in the price of fuel - priced in US dollars - affected everything from lighting and cooking to transportation and livelihoods, and was extremely sensitive. Back in November, all four factions in the House of Representatives had urged the Government not to do anything to raise fuel prices - a sure confirmation of the importance and sensitivity of this matter. Although the Government wanted to be seen to obey the IMF's advice to remove subsidies, to do so at such a time would have been to invite massive social unrest. It would also have fuelled inflation. Head of Indonesia's Central Bureau of Statistics, Sugito Suwito, was quoted as saying: " If there is a drastic cut in subsidies, then inflation will of course, shoot up quickly."

The Government was caught. It wanted to please the IMF but had also to look after its people and guard against inflation. The sum of money set aside to subsidize fuel prices was actually increased. Later, the Government revealed that to 'meet the IMF halfway, so to speak,' from April 1, while the poor would continue to be subsidized, there would be price increases for aviation turbine fuel, aviation gas, premium and industrial diesel and kerosene and automotive diesel for industrial and commercial use. The price of automotive diesel for public transport would also be kept low. Vital fertilizer subsidies were retained. Development spending was increased by a modest 5.6 percent, principally for poverty alleviation and equitable development programmes.

With state revenues falling, extra money had to be found from somewhere both to tread water and to meet the cost of even marginal growth. Increases in foreign aid and in revenues from oil and gas sales were identified as the principal means to achieve this. The price of oil was assumed to be US$17 per barrel. Public capital inflows would be used to cover a current account deficit expected to have fallen to US$5.39 billion from US$ 6.35 billion the preceding year. The budget made no mention of the one percent budget surplus being insisted upon by the IMF but the Finance Minister was quoted as saying that the Government still aimed to try to achieve it.

President Soeharto now stressed that a number of development projects, including those specially targeted by international loan agencies because of his family's involvement, had been and would remain postponed and that there could be no increase in already low civil service salaries. His main point was that the New Order Government was committed to deepening the reforms suggested by international advisers and, by promoting economic efficiency, would do its best to smooth out the impact on less privileged groups.

Critics branded the budget as "too optimistic", particularly the assumptions about the rupiah/US dollar exchange rate and the price of oil, which, at US$16.13 per barrel on January 6, had slumped to a two-year low and was already below the budget forecast. The prospect of increased pumping from Iraq threatened to push down the price still further. When the Assembly met in March to ratify the budget, oil had slumped to US$13.00 per barrel. Most wondered how the 1 percent surplus required by the IMF would be achieved.

On the eve of the budget, the IMF had taken to the war path to pressurize Indonesia into doing more to implement agreed reforms. The 'Washington Post' quoted an unnamed IMF official as saying: "We would like to see the senior leadership in Indonesia stand up and be counted on the reforms." The official was quoted as saying that if Indonesia did not implement the reforms in full, although it had received US$3 billion from the Fund in November, the country could very well not be given the next tranche of US$3 billion. This would be serious. All those who had pledged financial help to Indonesia, including for trade financing, had done so as part of the IMF package. If the package was stopped, their help would be stopped.

The public record for Indonesia did not look good. A merger of state banks, over which the Government had direct control, had been announced but progress seemed very slow. Private mergers were also moving slowly, on the basis of a policy of "persuasion" by Bank Indonesia Governor Soedradjad. The closure of insolvent banks had been far below IMF expectations. The dismantling of monopolies had either not happened or appeared to outsiders to have been fudged. Subsidies were still in place for the very good reason that to remove them at this time might be to risk a country-wide conflagration as ordinary people with low incomes vented their anger on the easiest available targets - shops and Government offices.

On the other hand, liquidity was so tight that 80 percent of Indonesia's corporates listed on the stock exchange were said to be on the brink of bankruptcy. From the point of view of Indonesia's corporates, the IMF-backed policy of high interest rates to defend the rupiah was beggaring the country. What the corporates and the banking sector needed most was more liquidity, not less. While the IMF and the Central Bank governor favoured the use of high interest rates the corporate sector was screaming that it was dying. President Soeharto agreed, but the Government was caught firmly in the middle. If interest rates were lowered and liquidity improved the IMF would say that its reforms were not being carried out. Carrying them out could mean the death of Indonesia's corporate sector. The Government tried to adopt a balancing position between the conflicting forces, promising that interest rates would be reduced as soon as circumstances permitted while maintaining them at high enough levels to satisfy the IMF.

In January, the persistent, region-wide, demand for US dollars was gathering new momentum. Across Asia there was talk of a "dollar drought." In a significant report on January 7, Reuters quoted dealers as saying: "It's a drying up of US dollars that is causing all the regional currencies to plummet to record lows." In January a 'Jakarta Post' report revealed that, since June, the US dollar had appreciated by a staggering 300 percent against the rupiah. Around the region the value of the US dollar was topping half-decade highs.

Here was another story completely. Indonesia had first been told that corruption and mismanagement had resulted in an historic loss of investor confidence. Then it had been told that, because its private sector looked unable to pay its bills, there was a mismatch between currency values and fundamentals. Then it was told that people had lost faith in the rupiah. Now it was being told that what was really causing the currency crisis was a shortage of American dollars. It goes without saying that loss of confidence in regional currencies led to an unusually high demand for US dollars, not only from local people but from US fund managers selling out. But when one realizes that this demand was taking place at a time when the greenback was at a six-and-a-half-year high, one can readily forecast the consequences and the problems. Interestingly, according to the Bank of International Settlements, the percentage of Asia's private debt, due to mature in 1998, was actually LESS than in 1997.

While US commentators were blaming Asia for bringing its woes upon itself, the fact of the matter was that the Clinton Administration was promising to deliver to the US the first budget surplus in 30 years - roughly the same amount of time that the New Order Government had been in power. According to APP the deficit for the 1997-98 fiscal year would be only US$22 billion, down from the almost US$ 360 billion forecast when the Democrats took office.

As the rupiah collapsed, the political dimension of the crisis intensified. Fitch IBCA were quoted as saying the political as well as economic stresses were rising in Indonesia since President Soeharto's Government had drawn much of its legitimacy from economic success. The 'Jakarta Post' quoted Mohamad Sadli as saying bluntly: "the Government must be replaced."

In its leader of January 8, the 'Jakarta Post' was as forthright as it is possible to be. The leader concluded: "The way it stands now reforms could happen in one or two ways: by orderly and peaceful means through the MPR, or outside the MPR, which could possibly be chaotic and, God forbid, violent. Those who call the shots must now decide what it is to be."

The Government was in a corner. The IMF's 'medicine' did not work and, domestically and internationally, many, if not most people, thought that the Government of Indonesia was itself to blame. The Government and President Soeharto faced a barrage of criticism and condemnation at home and abroad.

On January 7, University of Gadjah Mada sociologist, Loekman Soetrisno feared the worst if the economic crisis continued - aggravated by prolonged and widespread drought. He warned: " When we're talking about the need to fill stomachs, people will do anything, including steal." Little did he know! Asked why the Government couldn't solve the problems he said: "They can't resolve it because at home and abroad people no longer trust the Government. The Government should adopt a new strategy to regain that trust. It should change its strategy in facing the people. The Government should be willing to release Sri Bintang Pamungkas (leader of his own recently proclaimed political party). Why is he charged when he didn't do anything?: We cannot let the Government continuously violate human rights. Let (labour leader) Muchtar Pakpahan go. Let the PRD activists free. Why is the Government doing this if it is wasting time, money and impairing the image of our nation? Acknowledge Megawati Sukarnoputri as the chairperson of the PDI. Don't keep on hounding her. If the Government does all these things, then they can regain trust at home and abroad. The Government should stop inferring that some groups have a bad intent toward the nation. The Government should stop looking for a scapegoat. It is the Government themselves who are at fault for improperly managing this country." One by one incidents and issues had occurred throughout 1996 and 1997. Each had been dealt with in the same way and from the same Government perspective. Each had remained lodged and had accumulated in the public mind. They would haunt President Soeharto throughout the remainder of his presidency . In the end they would bring him down.

On January 11, an IMF team arrived in Jakarta to 'help' Indonesia out of the economic quagmire into which it found itself sinking rapidly beneath and around it. The IMF team had arrived in town determined to discuss their entire package, from ideology, through the state budget to the promised disbursements of money. The Government of Indonesia was under heavy pressure from the money markets and prominent leaders of free market economies. President Soeharto and his ministers promised the IMF that they would work harder to achieve the reforms already agreed and would review the controversial state budget.

For a few days in January 1998, there was a mood of optimism abroad as world leaders and financial experts converged on Jakarta to work with Indonesia's Government to craft the definitive rescue package. Britain's 'Daily Telegraph' said in a report that: "The world rallied yesterday around President Soeharto of Indonesia..." - January 14, 1998. The money markets seemed to be impressed and for a few days the rupiah hovered with some stability at Rps 10,000 to the US dollar. The 'Jakarta Post' quoted a dealer as saying: "Talks between the world leaders and President Soeharto have set most currencies in the region to strengthen against the American greenback." A sour note was the downgrading of Indonesia's sovereign risk by Thomson Bankwatch. The agency said that recent calls for President Soeharto to resign had greatly increased political uncertainty in Indonesia at a time of mounting economic crisis and even social unrest.

The media reported that the IMF was focusing on three 'targets:' - structural reforms, revising the controversial budget and stabilizing the currency. In fact, it is more likely that the Fund discussed all its recommendations to date with the problems created by the draft budget simply being added in. Reforms to the now critically damaged banking sector and an end to 'crony capitalism' were presumably at the top of the list. As to stabilizing the currency this was an issue the Fund had never addressed, except with its proposals for long-term reforms.

Crony capitalism and the problems of the banking system led straight to the President and his family. US Deputy Treasury Secretary, Larry Summers, met President Soeharto in Jakarta. The US was deeply concerned lest its contribution to IMF aid simply went into Soeharto family pockets via the banking system. Summers said that he thought that President Soeharto "recognizes the need for strong steps to reform the economy." According to Britain's 'Daily Telegraph:' " Chief among these reforms is the need to break up the vast business empires built up by his children, Run with cheap credit from manipulable state-owned banks, the profligacy of these family firms lies at the heart of Indonesia's malaise." President Soeharto was once again in a difficult position. Just how difficult was made clear by a headline in 'Newsweek' of January 26: "The Indonesian ruler's kids own a vast chunk of the nation. Can the IMF force them to let go?" The US and the IMF were blaming the Soeharto family for much of the financial mayhem; identifying the Soehartos as the centrepiece of the ongoing problems. Would the President give in to their demands that he rein in his family? Could it be done? If not, was his own position threatened?

With President Soeharto's apparent agreement with the reforms the IMF said must be made, a new agreement was signed in good faith on January 15. The announcement of the 50 point Letter of Intent between the Government of Indonesia and the IMF was welcomed by a near deafening chorus. The Indonesian public generally wanted to believe that the IMF deal meant a new lease of life for the rupiah. There were measures to raise government revenue, boost exports, remove trade restrictions, abolish monopolies and levies, to speed up privatization of state enterprises and to halt funding of state aircraft manufacture and of the so-called national car, the Timor.

The most unpalatable aspect of the new deal struck with the International Monetary Fund (IMF) IMF was bowing to the Fund's insistence that there should be zero economic growth. Such a scenario posed very great risks and dangers in a country with an already huge underemployed and unemployed population, with over two million new jobseekers entering the market each year. Insistence on a budget surplus threatened to increase the risks. The removal of subsidies, especially fuel, was also danger-packed. The IMF's insistence that the inflation rate should be fixed at 20 percent was also frightening to Indonesians - although, actually, probably still too low, given the depth of the rupiah's devaluation. Some foreign experts were already predicting inflation of 60 to 90 percent. Price rises in Indonesia could easily trigger violent riots. The Fund's insistence, for budget purposes, on fixing the rupiah exchange rate at Rps 5,000 to the US dollar was about as low as it was thought safe to go if overseas debts were to have any chance of being repaid and corporate and bank solvency maintained.

Market reaction remained pessimistic and, despite minor ups, stayed doggedly down in quiet trading. Standard & Poor again downgraded Indonesian banks. 'The Times' of London, quoted a Western banker as saying: "I am still pessimistic, especially about Indonesia's short-term prospects. I am not convinced that President Soeharto will implement everything he promised today, and even if he does it will be very painful for this country. If we don't see progress by the end of next week, I think the rupiah could well plunge to below 10,000 (to the US dollar) again. He will have to move extremely quickly this time. A stock-broker economist was quoted as saying: " Mr. Soeharto does not have a good track record of reform so I don't think that market confidence will return until we see some concrete steps, particularly in the finance sector."

Some Indonesians, too, were pessimistic. From a practical point of view, former Indonesian Mines and Energy Minister, Subroto, wrote on January 19: "The reform package is OK but market players did not respond enthusiastically because they do not see that any of the massive reform measures will address the core problem that caused the monetary crisis - the private sector's huge debts."

On January 20, Government critic and IMF 'believer', Kwik Kian Gie, wrote in his front page column in the 'Jakarta Post': "I must admit that economist, Rizal Ramli, is right when he said that I was starting to doubt the merits of the IMF's intervention." In Jakarta, small groups of students began demonstrating against the IMF. One banner read: "Don't sell out the honour of the nation to the IMF." Kwik said that the markets lack of confidence in the IMF's recommendation had kept the rupiah down at Rps 9,000 to one US dollar, holding out the near-certain prospect of debt default, bankruptcies, bank failures and large scale unemployment. He said: "There has been no mention of how the rupiah might be shored up in the short-term."

The aid package assembled by the IMF now totalled US$43 billion but Kwik said there was no indication of what this money was actually for or whether it would be used to support the rupiah. He went on: "In some people's eyes the Letter of Intent signed, created an impression that the IMF merely wants to take over Indonesia's sovereignty while overcoming the economic crisis without distributing any money. This has been reinforced by the assigning of an IMF Executive to the Economic and Monetary Resilience Council.....if there is no clear explanation about the planned utilization of the aid, we suspect that the IMF might not have any plans to disburse the US$43 billion but merely wants Indonesia to achieve a current account surplus in 1999 at the cost of the extraordinary suffering of its people - which may also include social unrest. if such suspicions are true, the IMF's involvement will cause deep concern because it will be seen as being dictated to be a foreign party. Moreover, the ownership of good domestic companies may have to be transferred to foreign investors. Many people have told me that they were sad to see Camdessus standing with his arms folded as he witnessed the President sign the (January) Agreement imposing hardships on Indonesians but offering no significant assistance from the IMF. That gave a distinct impression that the President had 'lost a battle.'"

Speaking for those who felt that the dreadful economic crisis had been triggered by government corruption and ineptitude, Y. B. Mangunwijaya, described as a noted social worker, architect and novelist wrote: "Everybody knows that the best way to accomplish the common and desired goal would be the willingness of the responsible decision makers, or maker, of the past, to step down to make possible the abolition of corruption, collusion and nepotism and transform the whole economic, social and political structure into a better one."

Suddenly it was open season for reform. It no longer mattered whether the reforms were long or short-term, economic or political. From the commencement of its advice the IMF had unearthed layer after layer of economic ineptitude which screamed for reform. They had associated this ineptitude with a chronic need for good governance. Now, a feeling was abroad in Indonesia that the whole political and economic infrastructure was rotten and that the rottenness of the political system had somehow led to the rottenness of the economy. The British 'Economist' was allowed into Indonesia with the front cover showing President Soeharto in a 5-Star army general's uniform and with the headline "Soeharto Step Down." Voicing his thoughts about the upcoming presidential in March 1998, Amien Rais stressed that the single most important goal was transparent, clean and just government. Though the numbers of the apostles of change willing to speak out publicly was still small, they were growing, as the crisis made people increasingly desperate and forced them to look for some new scapegoat for their woes.

On January 15, 20 prominent Government critics, including Amien Rais, Megawati Sukarnoputri, Supeni and Ali Sadikin called on the Government to abandon its violation of the principles of the 1945 Constitution and of Pancasila. It was clear that what the group wanted was wholesale political change, especially empowerment of institutions and the election of a new president to replace Soeharto. Amien Rais said pointedly: "I hope that the 1,000 MPR members will also listen to the people's aspirations and side with their political interests." There were calls for Amien and Mega to stand as presidential candidates. In their hearts both knew that this was impossible and that the likelihood of the Soeharto-chosen People's Consultative Assembly refusing to nominate Soeharto for a seventh term was remote to non-existent. In Bogor, students rallied to demand that the Government take immediate steps to "cope with the current economic turmoil."

On the money market, as if to give the lie to the IMF's claim that its 'medicine' would cure Indonesia, continuing high demand for dollars dragged down the rupiah still further, on January 20, reaching Rps 10,500 to one US dollar. And, neither in the Agreement nor anywhere else had the IMF done anything to tackle the central problem of the private, offshore debt. The Head of ING Barings Regional Economic and Debt Research Unit, Chris Tinker, was quoted as saying at a Bank conference in Jakarta: "Restoring confidence (in the rupiah) requires clarification of what is going to be done with the private debts. Without this clarification the bear rally will continue." Writing from London on January 26, William Keegan wrote: "One of the problems the Asian situation has highlighted is that the IMF does not know how to handle crisis in the private sector."

The markets agreed with Keegan. Next day the rupiah shot down to close to Rps 17,000 to the US dollar. Share prices fell by almost 5 percent. As usual, the problem was massive dollar buying. And the dollars were now in even shorter supply as offshore banks operating out of the financial centres of Singapore and Hong Kong choked off the supply for fear of a banking collapse in Indonesia. The 'Jakarta Post' reported dealers as urging, once again, that some solution be found to the problem of the offshore private debt.

Even before the rupiah shot down to Rps 17,000 to a-dollar, international dealers were firmly of the opinion that urgent steps absolutely must be taken to halt and reverse the fall of the rupiah. In London, 'The Sunday Times' published an analysis by Michael Sheridan and David Smith which quoted SocGen Crosby's Nilesh Jasani as saying: "We are at a point of dramatic action." A paper co-authored by Jasani and Manu Bhaskaran suggested Indonesia and other countries in the region might have to abandon floating currencies for pegs or capital controls. The paper went on to say: " At current levels the economic damage that could be caused by the market has reached proportions that cannot be tackled by simple liberalization of foreign ownership rules or monetary/fiscal tightening. Governments, most particularly in Indonesia, and to an extent in Thailand and Malaysia, need to not only stem the fall but pull the currencies back up by at least 20 percent for economic survival."

Later in the month, it was easy to get the impression from the media that President Soeharto was the only man thinking about implementing a Currency Board, flying in the face of all 'expert' advice, but this was far from being the case. Many of those involved in the markets could see plainly that, unless the collapse of the rupiah could be stemmed, and stemmed quickly, Indonesia could collapse. President Soeharto and his Government were painfully aware of this. The IMF and its backers were apparently not.

ABN-AMRO Indonesia Bank Country Manager, Cees de Koning wrote on January 23 that after careful reading, he had concluded that the Agreement between Indonesia and the IMF was only half a programme. He said: "The IMF programme can be seen as half a programme since it does not directly address the fundamental question of how to keep Indonesian companies in positive foreign currency cash flow positions. The IMF programme for Indonesia addresses many structural reforms, including for the banking sector. But since it is designed to enhance the country's economic efficiency over time, how many companies will be left to take advantage of it? The IMF makes foreign currency loans available to the Government, but these funds are not meant to go to the private sector. The funds are meant to support the Government to raise confidence in the rupiah. Maybe it is not within the IMF's duties to maintain the financial health of the Indonesian private sector, but, in order to get the country back on its feet, the private sector's crisis should get at least equal priority , if not higher, than the structural reforms. A programme for both is needed. Over time, getting companies back on their feet leads to a much faster return to healthy economic growth rates, low inflation and a much stronger rupiah."

Indonesia's economic crisis showed no let-up. At the end of January a Western diplomat was quoted by the 'Far Eastern Economic Review' as saying that the crisis had gone beyond reforms. "...more reforms are not the answer. It's too late in the day." Cees de Koning had earlier been quoted as saying that, economically speaking, in Indonesia it was "one minute to midnight." Singapore Prime Minister, Goh Chok Tong, now described the crisis affecting ASEAN as " the biggest test since the Second World War." - 'Financial Times,' UK, January 12, 1998.

Evidence of how poor most Indonesians were was now showing up increasingly in the form of sporadic riots. In Java, Nusa Tenggara and Sulawesi mobs went on the rampage to protest rising prices. The monthly inflation rate hit a 25-year high of nearly 7.00 percent. There was speculation that there could be no increase in minimum wage rates in 1998, already admitted by the Government to cover only 96 percent of basic needs. The minimum wage for Jakarta is Rps 172,500 or at Rps 10,000 to one US dollar, just US$17.25 per month. Even at Rps 5,000 to the dollar it would only rise to US$34,50. Per capita income had slumped nearly 80 percent since the crisis began. Reuters reported that market analysts now expected Indonesia's GDP growth to be not zero but minus 4 percent! The World Bank promised to disburse US$1 billion to Indonesia in February to assist drought-hit needy farmers and to procure medical supplies for public hospitals and rural health centres.

On February 8, there was a hint of 'official' confirmation of what many market participants and analysts had suspected since before

Christmas - Indonesia might be forced by the collapsed rupiah to try to peg it through the use of a Currency Board. Confirmation that such a possibility was being discussed came, not from the Indonesian Government, but from IMF chief, Camdessus. The 'Jakarta Post' quoted him as saying in New York: " It's an option available but it's not the only one." He added: " If the (IMF) programme fails to restore the rupiah because of the lack of cooperation from the Government, then a Currency Board would not be the solution."

Here were the seeds of a conflict which was to drag on through the remainder of February and last until after the meeting of the Parliament between March 1 and 11. Indonesia was desperate to peg its currency because it believed that the IMF's 'medicine' had not worked. The IMF said that Indonesia could never afford and could never properly manage a Currency Board until reforms were carried out, and this, the Fund said, were being frustrated by the Government. Critics felt that the Government was thinking of introducing the Board merely to mask its unwillingness to carry out reform. Nothing was further from the truth.

On February 9, President Soeharto was quoted as saying in Jakarta, using characteristically strong military language, that he hoped to "kill" speculators attacking Indonesia's currency. For weeks, he had been discussing the Currency Board system with Baltimore University's Professor Steve Hanke, the US pro-peg expert he had last met in Istanbul eight months earlier while attending the D-8 Summit. Jesuit in his promotion of Currency Boards, Hanke was a man with a mission, whose sales-pitch fell on unusually receptive ears.

Immediately a Currency Board began to seem like a serious possibility, analysts divided into two camps: those for and those against. The market simply took whatever steps were necessary to protect its investments, especially off-loading dollars. On Tuesday, February 10, the rupiah rose 30 percent since Monday, touching the Rps 7,000 to the US dollar mark. Whether a Currency Board would work in Indonesia and would be good for the country in all economic aspects was another matter. An editorial in the 'Jakarta Post' on February 11 said: "Such a system would be an easy target for currency speculators and huge foreign exchange reserves are needed to defend the chosen rate of exchange. Furthermore, many of the other factors required to successfully run a Currency Board system, such as a sound banking system, low inflation and good governance, are not yet present. Political independence for the CBS must also be guaranteed."

Supporters of the peg in Government and business simply

wanted to see a halt to the decline in the rupiah and a return to more normal business conditions, indeed to enter a situation in which Indonesia's stalled businesses could resume. Critics said the peg would require massive reserves because every rupiah in circulation would have to be matched by a dollar and that the peg could lead to a surge of demand for dollars resulting in swingeing interest rates to continue defending the rupiah at its new pegged level - notionally Rps 5,000 to one US dollar. Moreover, neither the Central Bank nor anyone else would control interest rates which, instead, would be left to automatic adjustment by the market.

With the rupiah strengthening to up to Rps 6,000 to the US dollar in anticipation of a Board, on February 11, Finance Minister, Mar'ie Muhammad, confirmed that Indonesia would introduce a Currency Board. The 'Jakarta Post' quoted the Minister as saying: "The primary objective of the system is to restore public confidence in the rupiah and the banking system. The Government will strictly control the growth of the money supply to curb inflation and to restore an orderly and stable economic condition." Steve Hanke confirmed, from his office in Baltimore, that he was finalizing plans to implement a Currency Board in Indonesia. By now, Hanke had been appointed an adviser to the Economic and Monetary Resilience Council. The IMF directorate felt snubbed and spurned. Even as early as the very next day, February 12, market doubts about a Currency Board had outweighed its perceived benefits and the rupiah had slipped down again to Rps 9,000 to one US dollar.

There were widespread price riots in Java with reports of rioters attacking security forces with machetes and of the first fatalities, in Java and in Lombok, east of Bali. Security forces stepped up tracking down alleged hoarders of essential supplies including baby formula, cooking oil, instant noodles and flour, immediately releasing the items to the market to contain price rises. In some places troops sold kerosene at special low prices. Students at some Islamic boarding schools undertook to carry food into even the remotest villages of East Java. In several places throughout Indonesia 'tycoons' distributed free food to the poor.

At the University of Indonesia campus at Depok, around 2,000 students demonstrated in favour of guaranteed supplies of food, jobs, lower prices and political reform. 'The Jakarta Post' carried a report that the students were demanding the resignation of the New Order Government for failing to keep the people's mandate. More people-based riots (as opposed to students) were reported as taking place in Sulawesi and Sumatra.

Significantly, expatriates now began to pour out of Indonesia, not because they wanted to leave particularly, but either because Indonesian companies could no longer afford their dollar salaries or because rupiah salaries made it impossible for them to service personal or family commitments abroad. A year ago there had been 100,000. By December, according to the Ministry of Manpower, there were only 48,000. More than 17,000 left for good during the Christmas and New Year holidays alone. For some of those remaining, the US, French and Australian embassies warned their nationals to be extra alert in case public security deteriorated. In the capital there was indeed a steady increase in media reports of robberies but the overall security situation remained normal.

The escalating unrest prompted ABRI to make an in-depth view of developments. And they didn't make it alone. Armed Forces chief, General Wiranto and ABRI's head of Sociopolitical Affairs, Maj. Gen. Bambang Yudhoyono took the initiative to call together not only other ABRI members but also retired officers, ex ministers and even experts from outside ABRI, especially academics. While the major drama was playing on the economic stage, failure to cure Indonesia's economic ills was having ever increasing political repercussions. If social unrest developed how should ABRI respond? If political unrest developed, how should ABRI respond? What if the crisis forced President Soeharto to step down without completing his term? Who would step up? Who could ABRI support? To ABRI, 1998 seemed packed with dangers and possibilities. One of the matters agreed was that never again should there be, in effect, a lifetime president. Two terms was enough. More importantly, the brainstormers foresaw a reduced role for ABRI in the political arena and even a reduction of its representation in Parliament. The military were fed up with being the mere tool of the Executive.

Pictured with Professor Steve Hanke on February 13, President Soeharto was smiling broadly with the smile of someone who sensed that he had at last found a secret weapon which could be used to 'kill" the speculators ruining Indonesia. But the more enthusiastic the President became, the more skeptical became the markets .

For the first time, the IMF was reported as condemning the introduction of a Currency Board to Indonesia. "We have concluded that a lot of options need to be in place before a Currency Board would make sense," the 'Jakarta Post' quoted Stanley Fischer as saying on February 13. On the 15th, Michel Camdessus wrote formally to President

Soeharto cautioning him about the drawbacks of pegging the rupiah against the dollar and threatening to terminate the IMF's so-called bailout. This letter must have infuriated the entire Government. For the first time, there was talk now in the media of a "standoff" between the Government of Indonesia and the IMF. US Treasury Secretary, Robert Rubin, added his voice to the chorus of dissenters. ASEAN economists, meeting in Manila, also condemned the idea as likely to "aggravate the regions financial crisis." The 'Post' quoted Asian development Bank Institute Dean, Jesus Estanislao, as saying: "The contagion effect of the financial crisis in southeast Asia stemmed from having stubbornly pegged interest rates at unrealistic exchange rate levels. Why would anyone want to repeat the problem?" Australia urged Indonesia to take the IMF 'medicine' and abandon the Currency Board. German Finance Minister, Theo Waigel, repeated the thought. President Clinton rang President Soeharto to voice his concerns and to urge Indonesia to obey the IMF "in full."

Meanwhile, after canvassing all factions in the House of Representatives, House Speaker, Harmoko, was quoted by the 'Jakarta Post' as saying: " I have talked to all the four factions of the House and all came out in support of the CBS (Currency Board system) as they are confident the system will stabilize the rupiah rate and restore certainty for economic and business activities.

Despite being a holiday month, February had been busy in Indonesia as the Government twisted this way and that, tried this and that, rushed from one problem to another to try to achieve what alone could solve the crisis - the stabilization of the rupiah. The country's leaders were shocked and panicked. What had gone wrong? What should they do? The advice of the foreign business community resident in Indonesia had been sought; there were long meetings with the representatives of foreign chambers of commerce and heads of foreign banks. The foreigners were invited to speak frankly. Given Indonesia's allegedly strong fundamentals, such was the official and unofficial bewilderment at economic events that even whispers of plots to destabilize the currency and topple the President began to emerge. Society became more restless and more desperate.

The IMF's relationship with Indonesia had soured progressively until, at the end of February, ABN-AMRO's, Eugene Galbraith, could be quoted by the 'Jakarta Post' as placing " a large share of the blame for Indonesia's woes on the IMF, which he said had handled the situation badly. "While the IMF's prescriptions to steady the staggering Indonesian economy were 'uncontroversial', its (the IMF's) way of dealing with the country's leaders undermined their authority and failed to recognize political realities." Galbraith described the IMF as 'petulant' in its early dealings with the country over the Asian crisis. "On the topic of the Currency Board, the way the IMF dealt with Indonesia was disgraceful. Giving an ultimatum to a sovereign nation does not create a fertile environment for good political dialogue."

It could now be seen that the IMF's relationship with Indonesia broke down into several parts. At the level of behaviour, as Galbraith said, the record of the Fund's officials had not been good. They did not understand Indonesia or Indonesians. Its structural reforms, while capable of imposing hitherto unimaginable 'soundness' on Indonesia's economy, seemed to the Indonesians to be irrelevant in the short-term and, in some cases, in any term. Knowing themselves, they feared some of the legal and regulatory reforms would take years to introduce - the reason why there are so many presidential and ministerial decrees in Indonesia. Finally, there were the Fund's specific measures relating to money supply, interest rates, the state budget, measures to decrease costs, including the thorny question of subsidies and steps to increase revenue. Some seemed harmful, others unlikely to solve the immediate crisis.

It has to be borne in mind that, by February, the Government of Indonesia believed that it was facing complete economic collapse with all its terrible social and political consequences. It felt that if solutions could be identified embodying the idea of 'salvage' they should be tried first. The Government meant well. Culturally and traditionally, Indonesians must help other Indonesians. Crisp, Yankee-style reforms inflicted licketysplit on a suffering nation were simply not in its book of options.

IMF anger about alleged Indonesian Government foot-dragging over subsidies and legal and regulatory reform brought down a storm of condemnation on Indonesia's head. But there were reasons - the prospect of social unrest, the imminence of a new Government, the uncomfortable speed with which everything seemed to have to be done. While the Government of Indonesia had been perpetually accused by the IMF and many others of being slow in its implementation of the IMF Agreement, in fact, against the background of the traditional pace of change in Indonesia, changes had been introduced practically at the speed of light. Such was the seriousness of the situation. Such was the urgency of the Government's approach.

Anything relating to subsidies, to measures which could raise consumer prices or to the creation of shortages of items considered to be essential, such as palm oil had not been actioned or had been actioned partially. With no system of social security, no social safety nets, millions of poor people and a real fear of the consequences of shortages of items deemed essential the Government of Indonesia simply could not act. It would have been irresponsible to act. It would have courted certain unrest. Later, when it had developed some understanding of the specific realities in Indonesia, the Fund would relent somewhat on issues which threatened to raise prices or create shortages.

Throughout February there had been widespread unrest in drought hit East Java. College students had spearheaded food riots in South Sulawesi. In scenes reminiscent of what would happen later in Jakarta, students were joined by their high school colleagues and by labourers and shops and offices pelted with stones. In Surabaya wealthy Chinese business people distributed free food to the needy. Shopping malls and prominent buildings in the business district were under military guard. The threat of unrest was real enough!

In Indonesia, the press and sections of the 'intelligentsia' were in full cry against the Government for its alleged failure to implement the reforms agreed with the IMF. Asked the 'Jakarta Post' in a leader on February 26: "Has the Government executed the reforms to which it is now committed in a firm and consistent manner? The answer, after scrutinizing the 50 points of reform contained in the IMF agreement, is a resounding no." Actually, the answer was a resounding: 'partially.'

As the opening approached on March 1 of the General Session of the People's Consultative Assembly, the reforms agreed with the IMF and the possibility of a Currency Board remained in process - as did the 'stand-off with the IMF.

CHAPTER THREE

The ides of March
- good reason to beware!

The President was undoubtedly looking forward to the March election. He had been the target of an unprecedented barrage of demands to resign or retire and his Government subjected to the most fundamental criticisms. What he needed now was a reaffirmation that he was still Indonesia's favourite son, that the mandate of power was still his. His nomination was already assured and the Armed Forces had specifically said that their informal sounding-out of opinion at grass-roots level across Indonesia indicated that this was the choice most people wanted. Not only could the President be assured of re-election but his nominee for vice president, B. J. Habibie, had been accepted by all factions. The foreign media were saying that President Soeharto had worn out his welcome and that as vice president, Minister Habibie would be a disaster. If the President now secured a unanimous, resounding mandate for a new five-year term, some of the ground would be cut from under his critics' feet, at home and abroad.

The President's dream was his critic's nightmare. Writing in the 'Jakarta Post' on February 19, political scientist, J. Soedjati Djiwandono described Indonesia's political institutions as: "Dysfunctional, paralyzed and ossified" - hardly a basis for confidence in what was about to happen at the People's Consultative Assembly. He went on: " GOLKAR, after three decades in power, and the two (other) political parties, do not act to channel the changing aspirations of society, particularly our younger generations. The increasing number of riots and demonstrations in the face of the deepening economic crisis are indicative of the disaffection felt by many people. To dismiss any expression of discontent or disagreement with the official line as "unconstitutional" is an indication of just how nervous those in power are. In any case, differentiating the constitutional from the unconstitutional is a power supposedly only vested in the judiciary, not the Executive branch... Barely two years ago, those in power even went so far as to arrogate to themselves the right to interpret the statutes of the PDI to determine the legal status of its leadership.. Furthermore, to attribute the cause of recent riots to "engineering" by "certain quarters" in society in order to "cultivate and spread hatred of the Government" is to fail to read and grasp the political mood of the people and is in keeping with the Government's habit of finding scapegoats for the ills of society."

It is all too likely that President Soeharto read the political mood only too well. But he was stubbornly determined to tough out not only his current term but a new one as well. Whether he had read the mood in ABRI equally well was a moot point. ABRI commanders were making tough statements about ensuring a peaceful meeting of the People's Consultative Assembly, about barring dissension from the proceedings and about reformists sticking to the 1945 Constitution and the institutions established by the New Order within its framework. But some of them, at least, were thinking other thoughts. They had already been brainstorming the elements of Indonesia's crisis and possible solutions.

A clue to which way new winds might be blowing in ABRI was given on Friday, February 28, 1998, when Defence Minister Edi Sudradjat was quoted by Singapore's 'The Straits Times' as saying that the mass rallies taking place across Indonesia against soaring food prices and in favour of political and economic reform were "natural in a democracy." He was quoted as saying: " To have different opinions from other people is part of democratic life." He was quoted as adding that the opinions expressed at such rallies were " constructive" and might be beneficial to the forthcoming session of the full Parliament. The report was also carried in the 'Jakarta Post' which said that the minister was mainly referring to rallies held at Jakarta's University of Indonesia and at Gadjah Mada University, Yogyakarta. Sudradjat was now retired from the military and was asked by the media about the participation in one of the demonstrations of retired General Hariadi Darmawan. Sudrajat clarified that the General had taken part in his capacity as Chairman of the University of Indonesia Alumni Association.

It was not by any means unusual in Indonesia for retired military personnel to make comments critical of the New Order Government. Indeed, it was virtually a permanent feature of Indonesian politics. But Minister Sudrajat's statement seemed different because of its timing and because, after all, he was still a serving minister. President Soeharto had been warning about elements bent on undermining and destroying the Government. MPR ABRI faction leader, Let. Gen. Hari Sabarno had warned that no attempts should be made to disrupt the proceedings of the forthcoming meeting of Parliament - proceedings which all knew did not include discussions of the causes and solutions to the economic and political crisis ravaging Indonesia. Military commanders had backed the President's calls for stern measures against those found guilty of fomenting sedition or disturbances. Indonesia's students were making the loudest disturbances of all yet here was a minister describing them as "natural."

Was ABRI now increasingly susceptible to the same divisions and dissensions as in society as a whole? Were there those who remained obedient to the President and to the status quo while others saw the necessity of some of the changes advocated by the students? Did these include ABRI's new commander, appointed in February, 1997, General Wiranto? Of course, there had often been distention within ABRI and in his role as commander-in-chief of the Armed Forces the President had always been able to deal with it. He must have felt that he still could. He must have felt that, by and large, if it came to a showdown with critics who could be shown to be destructive and irresponsible elements, even subversive elements, ABRI would, as usual do his bidding. Still, Minister Sudradjat's statement might have rung alarm bells - especially since the students he was condoning carried banners saying: "Soeharto is the root of our problems." Students everywhere held the Government responsible for the country's economic problems and everywhere were demanding political change, especially a change in leadership. Was the Defence Minister endorsing such views?

The 11-day People's Consultative Assembly opened at the national Parliament on March 1, 1998 amid massive security and even more massive cynicism. All parties and factions had already endorsed Soeharto for a seventh term and also his nominee, B. J. Habibie as vice president. There would be discussion in response to the President's first day accountability speech and he would make a speech of acceptance. Of the worst economic crisis pummelling Indonesia since World War II there was to be no debate. Critics slammed the meeting as a stage managed farce.

Respected former minister, Emil Salim had declared his readiness to stand for the vice presidency. Amien Rais had said he was ready to stand for the presidency. Despite the prior agreement of the factions, until the last moment the media reflected Government fears that backers of rival candidates, at least for the vice presidency, would seek to disrupt the proceedings. There were official fears that such disruptions would be linked to supporters outside the Parliament - hence the unprecedented security. Twenty five thousand troops and police stood ready to maintain order, significantly, twice the number on stand-by or deployed in 1993. The intelligence services doubtless already knew what Indonesian Prosperous Labour Union leader Muchtar Pakpahan admitted to investigating police officers on March 12, namely that he had distributed leaflets calling for nationwide protests during the Assembly. The protests were aimed at pressing the Government to reduce prices, raise basic wages, prevent layoffs and abolish KKN (corruption, collusion and nepotism) and monopolies. To try to nip in the bud such protests or other disturbances, unknown hands had been kidnapping political activists for several months prior to the Assembly. Later, the unknown hands would be traced to ABRI's special services unit, KOPASSUS and its then leader, President Soeharto's son-in-law Let. Gen. Prabowo.

The activists were detained and questioned and some were released. Some are still "missing" at the time of publication in October, 1998. Later it would emerge that the activists were kidnapped to discover what they were doing, what their organizations were doing, what other organizations were doing etc - a clumsy way of obtaining intelligence and one which seemed to show that the penetration of key social organizations by relevant units of ABRI was less than omnipresent. Based on a comment by Jakarta military commander, Maj. Gen. Sjafrie Sjamsoeddin, such activists were suspected of forming part of "Indonesia's opposition movement network." By "opposition" the Government seemed to understand "enemy" and used the security forces against them accordingly. Amien Rais later blasted the Government for accusing the student movement of having been infiltrated or masterminded by certain "adverse" parties. He was quoted as saying: "Please, stop making those haphazard statements. It does not make any sense at all." Over recent years there had been many similar accusations of "communists," "Maoists," " formless organizations" and now the "opposition movement network." Government critics had consistently poured scorn on such fancies or fabrications, pointing out that they did nothing to solve the nation's economic and political problems.

Of course, as we saw earlier, from July 27, 1996 onwards, if not before, critics of President Soeharto had certainly been increasingly speaking out and even linking themselves together in groups and loose associations amounting to considerably broad-based coalitions aimed at bringing aboput reform. While the Government could be said to have brought the problems on itself, nevertheless, it can be readily understood that mounting evidence of growing opposition from a variety of sources had triggered alarm - not only an alarm but an urgent desire to find out more about who intended to do what.

As the March meeting of the People's Consultative Assembly got under way, President Soeharto doggedly followed his congress programme to each constitutional letter. Although there were to be no emergency sessions on the parlous state of the economy, President Soeharto emphasized the economic achievements of his Government - achievements on which its 32-year record rested narrowly. He spoke of improved per capita income, now seriously eroded, the growth in employment opportunities, now savagely cut back, the reduction in poverty, now sharply increased. He acknowledged that prosperity had not been spread evenly - an understatement in view of the events of May. The contrast between past performance and present reality was so extreme and striking that it was difficult for the President to be taken seriously.

For the benefit of critics at home and the IMF abroad, the President had gone out of his way to underline his seriousness about (economic) reform and, by implication, the seriousness of his soon to be appointed new cabinet and government. To ram home the point, and also reflecting Indonesia's sincerely held belief, referring to Indonesia's Agreement with the IMF, President Soeharto added: "In accordance with the set schedule, we have carried out parts of the programme while the other parts will follow later. We are firmly committed to implement this programme in its entirety." A few sentences later, the President repeated again: "I have started and will continue to implement the economic and financial reforms which have the support of the IMF." His repetition of this key point shows the depth of his concerns that people weren't listening, important people, such as officials of the IMF and leaders of powerful and influential foreign Governments. The foreign media especially seemed not to want to hear or to believe.

105

Pointing up his differences with the IMF, President Soeharto said: " Despite the fact that we already have, and have started to carry out clear and fundamental reforms and restructuring programmes, there are no signs yet that the situation has improved. On the contrary the people's life is becoming more difficult." Corporations, he said, were forced to reduce their activities, unemployment was growing, prices "skyrocketing." What was a consequence of this - not perhaps entirely visible or understood by foreign experts who only stayed briefly in the capital city at 5-star hotels before returning to what was, in effect, another world, among the developed countries? "The public becomes restless. Even the slightest misunderstanding sparks greater unrest. The situation becomes even worse when there are individuals who fish in the muddy water."

Anyone who knows Indonesia also knows how dangerously volatile and explosive the population can be. One of the Government's nightmares was undoubtedly of an orgy of destruction by rampaging mobs after which there would still be no solution to Indonesia's economic problems and even less chance of a return of international business confidence.

A short time later, the President repeated for a second time the thought: " ...there are no signs of improvement yet." Did the foreign experts and government leaders really understand Indonesia's position? They were doing as much as they could as fast as they could under crisis conditions but still the economy was going down and the sufferings of the people were going up. Did no one understand how potentially explosive this was? It was an equation which without the shadow of a doubt could see Indonesia explode in flames.

The President now hit firmly on the head the nail of contention with the IMF and the root problem bedevilling the economy: "The key problem is the stabilization of the exchange rate of our rupiah at a reasonable level. Unless this is achieved, I do not see any possibility of improvement within a short period of time. This is why I have asked the IMF and other heads of Governments to assist us to find a more appropriate alternative. I refer to the more appropriate concept as IMF-Plus." The President revealed that "I, myself" am "carefully and cautiously" contemplating the introduction of a Currency Board. If anyone else had any other solution for halting the slide of the rupiah they had certainly been very quiet about it. It was all very well for foreigners to talk about reforms which would make Indonesia "stronger" in "two to three years" but President Soeharto and the Government had to find a solution as quickly as humanly possible or face the risk of chaos, a risk which grew every day the crisis continued, with every new price increase, with every new redundancy, with every new imported goods shortage. Factory and office workers, housewives, children, the sick, students - all were affected and some were increasingly vociferous.

The President referred to measures being taken by the Government to try to safeguard Indonesia's millions of poor people through job creation programmes, to try to help skilled people who had lost their jobs with entrepreneurial training and to try to increase the supply of food through more efficient farming and the bringing into cultivation of industrial and marginal lands. Touching on another thorny discussion point with the IMF, the President said pointedly: " To facilitate (...) distribution, to provide certainty, and to maintain a stable and reasonable price, the Government provides subsidies for imported food and medicine. These subsidies are covered by the state budget."

In reality, Indonesia's millions felt that the Government was doing precious little to help them. The General Assembly seemed little more than a monument to the power of the New Order. The millions now facing the worst hardships of their lives wanted no displays of power, no platitudes, no excuses. They wanted solutions. And this was precisely what they didn't get.

Mindful of the public mood, in the wake of the speech, the leaders of the United Development Party (PPP) and of the Indonesian Democratic Party (PDI), both criticized the President for concentrating only on the Sixth Development Cabinet's economic record and failing to mention any need for political change. Even PDI chief, Soerjadi joined in and was quoted as saying: " corruption, collusion and business monopolies" were at the root of the present crisis. The Petisi (Petition) 50 Group of Government critics, mostly retired ABRI officers, and formed as long ago as May, 1980, also condemned the speech.

In fact, President Soeharto had mentioned political unrest when he touched on the "anarchic" events of July 27, 1996 surrounding the takeover of the Jakarta headquarters of the PDI from supporters of Megawati Sukarnoputri. He said that "any government" has the responsibility to protect society from such acts. He added that if there were people who wanted political changes, the changes should involve and be limited to improving the existing system and not seeking to replace it - the very real fear motivating the political kidnappings and interrogations.

In Jakarta alone 172 people had been arrested since mid-February for participating in street rallies and protests. Some were charged with politically related activities, others with spreading hatred of the Government. Thirty four were charged with taking part in unlawful street rallies. Amien Rais had been informed that he would be questioned for organizing a meeting at which speakers had called for a million protesters to flood Jakarta's streets on March 1, for making remarks which "tarnished" the Government and for "slandering " President Soeharto - allegations which, if proved, could result in lengthy prison sentences.

After the President's accountability speech to the General Assembly nothing had changed; the markets and the masses continued to face the full force of the deepening economic crisis and continued to demand political solutions. Students at campuses across Indonesia refused to let the issue of government corruption and ineptitude die. Wherever there were demonstrations there were banners calling for an end to corruption, collusion and nepotism - a demand which many thought had heightened relevance once the new cabinet was announced. The demonstrators were still tolerated and even encouraged by the security forces so long as they did not stray off campus. Many faculty members stood behind their students. Some demonstrators requested a dialogue with the representatives now meeting in general assembly.

The appointment of a new cabinet by President Soeharto was now only days away. The composition of the cabinet would be crucial in determining how Indonesia would face the very serious problems it confronted and how Indonesia's people would fare in the months ahead. The students now included in their demands that " the Government form a cabinet with members who have good moral reputations" - the Salemba Declaration of March 2, 1998 in Jakarta. In Parliament, the call was taken up by the United Development Party (PPP). The Party demanded that state officials should declare their wealth before taking office. Although they made little apparant progress with the demand for clean government, later, President Soeharto would respond to the call to audit top officials by asking them to privately declare their wealth and assets. Since the declaration was to be private, the public perceived the measure as but another New Order cosmetic.

In Bandung, Surakarta, Salatiga, Purwokerto, Surubaya, Bali and Ujung Pandang the students were also on the march, demanding economic and political reform and a change of leadership. At Surabaya, a handful tried to stage hunger strikes in support of political reforms. As the days ticked past more and more students joined the campus rallies until thousands were involved - possibly as many as 10,000 nationwide.

Seeing that there was now no chance of the General Assembly discussing the very serious issues facing the country, student leaders condemned the whole affair as "stage managed" and demanded a "new president." As usual, the security forces restricted the students to their respective campuses but there appeared to be no witch-hunt of leaders or follow-up arrests. Significantly, the students were strongly supported by their deans and lecturers. At some campuses the students sold rice, sugar and cooking oil below market prices to the needy and called on the Government to lower the prices of basic essentials.

Meanwhile, the General Assembly granted President Soeharto the special powers he had suggested he needed as early as August, 1997, while addressing 500 legislative candidates in Bogor. The powers enabled the President to take emergency action, including dissolving Parliament and banning political parties, whenever he considered the security and development of the nation in jeopardy. The University of Indonesia's Arbi Sanit was quoted as saying that the powers amounted to allowing the President to take over the running of the state. Such action could be taken without consulting the House of Representatives and need be reported only ex post factos. Observers wondered aloud if the special powers would involve the re-establishment of the Operational Command for the Restoration of Security and Order. Indicative of the mood of some in the Government, on March 6, troops in full battle gear were parachuted onto empty land near the University of Indonesia's Jalan Salemba Raya campus in central Jakarta. Earlier, a similar exercise had been conducted in Glodok, presumably to reassure the ethnic Chinese. Meanwhile, Information Minister Hartono announced that the Government would sue 'Detektif dan Romantika' magazine for portraying President Soeharto as a king.

The General Session took place against an economic crisis amounting to a national tragedy. Yet the Assembly was not allowed to discuss or even to reflect this tragedy. Representatives were outraged when ministers who were supposed to be interested in their views actually left the chamber while they gave them. There were accusations that such ministers showed blatant disrespect to the Parliament. Even President Soeharto was absent when his accountability speech was being critiqued.

Exactly one year earlier, even before the economic crisis broke across Indonesia, a seminar in Yogyakarta had been discussing the urgent need for political empowerment. The speakers were by no means students or well-known government critics. Sayidiman Suryohadiprojo was a retired army general, Roekmini Astuti Koesoemo was a retired police general and Ginandjar Kartasasmita was serving Minister of National Development Planning. Some of the speakers proposed changes to Indonesia's political system, others said that the system was fine but needed to be operated more equitably. Ginandjar Kartasasmita noted that among government officials "empowerment" was a concept which had "not caught on." Roekmini had joined the National Commission on Human Rights and was a former legislator. She was quoted by the 'Jakarta Post' of March 9, 1996 as saying: that ..."the current political system has failed to accommodate the wishes of the people because those in power refuse to yield to the demands for democracy." Roekmini was quoted as saying: "They (the powerholders) want to preserve the status quo. What they don't know is that by preserving the status quo they're sowing political discontent."

Even without an economic crisis such discussants had been talking about the growing and pressing need to reassess the role of the office of president, the frequency with which parliament met, the selection process and even the calibre of representatives and the electoral process. "All representatives must be elected by the people and not appointed," Sayidiman was quoted as saying. This was one whole year before the Assembly of March, 1998, By March, 1998, such views dominated the reform movement and were being backed be individuals and groups from many segments of society, including within the Armed Forces.

An article in the 'Jakarta Post' of March 4, by Budiono Kusumohamidjojo seemed to sum up what many Indonesians felt as the Assembly slipped irrelevantly passed. " After 30 hard working years put into developing the economy and improving living standards, we have ended up on the brink of national bankruptcy (again). This is a tragedy because the drive for development was, and still is, heavily burdened by corruption, collusion, nepotism, manipulation, hypocrisy and lies. Authoritarianism and the use of force have become more and more intense over the years, as those involved took ever greater measures to defend their political irresponsibilities.

"Nationwide riots over the past two years should have been seen as a sobering and unequivocal signal that an end must be put to all such scandalous aspects of Indonesian political life. A failure to return to fair and sensible principles will undoubtedly block the road to a just and prosperous society, as set out in the 1945 Constitution as our country's ultimate political goal. The fear now is that after the Republic's golden anniversary the majority of the Indonesian people will not tolerate the current situation any more.

"The nation must rethink how it wants the face of modern Indonesia to look. We call for the establishment of a clean government, and good governance, respect for genuine democracy, compliance with the law, equality for all in the eyes of the law, respect for justice and observance of human rights. The people of this country are entitled to these basic rights of civilized society."

As public clamour mounted outside the sterile rubber-stamp Parliament, inside the General Assembly the dominant GOLKAR and ABRI factions were driven to promise political reform. GOLKAR's Nazaruddin Syamsudin was quoted by the 'Jakarta Post' as saying: " GOLKAR is ready to (introduce) reform now that the people are ready..(but not) revolutionary reform (which) changes the political structures." - precisely the element people wanted to see changed. GOLKAR colleague, Rully Chairul Azwar, was quoted in the same report as saying that the changes could take place during "the next five years." Student leaders said they hoped that any changes would be "real" and not "artificial."

On March 5 a significant event had occurred. A delegation of University of Indonesia students arrived at the Parliament building intent on delivering a petition. No faction would meet them - except ABRI. The students demanded that president Soeharto's accountability speech be rejected, that the political leadership be changed, that the legal system be reformed and that those holding public offices returned to the path of serving the people. The National Commission on Human Rights praised ABRI for meeting the students and called for positive follow up. Two days later, the media were talking about " a more receptive attitude from the Government and military towards their (the students') concerns. On March 9, in a leader, the 'Jakarta Post' said: " The military authorities seem to be exercising a virtue of tolerance toward the thousands of students now staging anti-Government demonstrations at various Indonesian universities." The leader went on to note that in 1965, during a similar time of economic collapse, the students had played the role of an opposition to then President Sukarno. ..."today's students also believe that the only way to save the country from the current economic catastrophe is a succession of the national leadership." The Post hoped that Indonesia's legislators were listening but feared that they were not.

Market fears that a second tranche of IMF money from the IMF would not be released now came to reality. With the General Assembly

111

still going on in Jakarta and Indonesia effectively without a Government, on March 6, the IMF announced from Washington that there would be no further discussion of more cash for Indonesia until April, when a new Government would have taken office and there had been time for its officials to discuss latest developments with the new team. The world press seemed to interpret the delay as some kind of punishment for Indonesia. In fact it reflected the reality that there was temporarily no government in Jakarta. Other than delay what else could be done? The money could not realistically be given because there were still many uncertainties and still much information lacking about a highly volatile and rapidly changing economic situation. The fact that all normal government business seemed to have come to a stop during the General Assembly did not help matters.

Outgoing Foreign Minister, Ali Alatas, while confirming that Indonesia wanted to implement its agreement with the IMF in full, explained: " We need time before we can start implementing them (the reforms) because the nation is currently concentrating on the constitutional process of the General Session." He was quoted as adding that the reforms would resume after a new cabinet was formed. The IMF accepted the reality of this and its team went quietly on with its investigatory work in Jakarta. The world saw only more procrastination in Jakarta.

To the world outside, the IMF Agreement had not been implemented in full. In early March, the Fund, backed by leaders of the developed countries and by most international media, insisted that Indonesia stop its foot dragging and gulp down the IMF's 'medicine' in full. Indonesia simply couldn't do it. It was too dangerous and could only lead to frightening levels of chaos. Anyway, it believed it had already swallowed hefty doses in record time. Indonesia seemed incapable of explaining; the IMF seemed incapable of understanding. The world media portrayed this comprehension gap as a stand-off, as stubborn Indonesia refusing to carry out the well intentioned advice of the IMF - mostly because the Government was in some way trying to protect its or its supporters vested interests.

The Government's room to maneuver with the IMF was increasingly limited. Reflecting rising prices, inflation in February reached nearly 13 percent in the month and fears were expressed about the effect on fuel, power and transport prices of going ahead with the IMF Agreement to remove subsidies. Other fears were expressed about the possible rescindment of the ban on palm oil exports, a move which it was said would send essential cooking oil prices skywards. Meanwhile, the foreign media called for the ban to be lifted, mistaking its intention and even mistaking the industry's structure, describing the ban as a new "monopoly."

When former US Vice-President, Walter Mondale, had walked through President Soeharto's door on March 3, sent as a special envoy by President Clinton to persuade him to fully implement the IMF reform package, the President looked decidedly strained. With all the pressures upon him to go beyond the package and, after the many times he had stressed that the package had not worked, here was Mondale to press the same ineffective course upon him once again. By all accounts Mondale's case was weak. He was reported to have told the President that Thailand and South Korea were on the road to recovery because they had followed IMF advice! While they may have been on the road to someone's definition of 'recovery,' in fact, Indonesians could see that Thailand and South Korea were also suffering from the administering of too much of the wrong 'medicine.' In any case, the President was under the impression that, as far as possible in the time available, Indonesia **had** followed the IMF programme. This meeting represented a serious disjunction. Mondale was said to have complained later, at a press briefing in Dallas, Texas, that he could not illicit a firm decision from the President about proceeding with the IMF reforms or about the prospect of a Currency Board. How could he? The President could not at this stage afford to spurn an apparently viable option. It was an impossible request. Mondale's report fanned international negative opinion against President Soeharto. After meeting President Soeharto in Jakarta, Mondale was quoted as saying: "It's our view that the way to deal with the severe currency problems here is to deal with the underlying forces that are driving the rupiah towards its weakness. There are no quick fixes that provide an alternative."

Meanwhile, as seemingly the whole world criticized the prospect of the introduction of a Currency Board in Indonesia, stock market prices rose in response to President Soeharto's plan to benefit from IMF assistance AND a Currency Board - now dubbed "IMF-Plus." The 'Jakarta Post' quoted David Chang, Head of Research at Trimegah Securities, as saying that, "rising inflation and the unstable rupiah rate against the American dollar were the country's most urgent issues in the short-term, before proceeding to the implementation of long-term reforms agreed to with the IMF." The market saw what the President saw. The IMF's suggestions were long-term. Indonesia's needs were short-term. The 'Jakarta Post ' went on: " Most stock analysts in Jakarta shared a common view that pairing the IMF reforms with some other elements, such as pegging the rupiah to a foreign currency at a fixed exchange rate, would improve the country's ailing economy."

Tjandra Kartika, Head of Research at Mashill Jaya Securities, was quoted as saying that the market was speculating "that the IMF-Plus plan would include a fixed exchange rate for the rupiah and a new programme for rescheduling and reducing Indonesia's mounting foreign debt. This is really positive for the market because the Government addressed both the (country's) short-term and long-term problems at one time. The market welcomes the Government's strong commitment to introduce new bold measures to complement the IMF reform package."

On March 11, 1998, the 77-year-old President Soeharto was duly re-elected with B. J. Habibie as Vice President and despite a deep feeling that the election meant that nothing had changed, there were high expectations of the incoming cabinet. The new ministers would be crucial in rebuilding confidence in Indonesia. Vice President Habibie spoke of preparing Indonesia for the era of globalization - actually, under current conditions, just about the last thing Indonesia should have been preparing for. Still, it all sounded good, new, optimistic!

What the general public thought of this election was as instructive as the ongoing demands of students. The 'Jakarta Post' quoted Ratmokaryo, a taxi driver as saying: " I'm not surprised President Soeharto has been elected. I do have many hopes in my mind, but I'm afraid no-one will listen to me because I'm just a cab driver. The monetary crisis has created many difficulties I almost cannot bear. My earnings have dropped sharply while prices are skyrocketing. I don't really care who the president and vice president are. The most important thing for me is that the crisis is over as soon as possible." Then there was housewife Yulianti: "My wish is simple: the Government should not make our husbands unemployed." Or cashier, Yanie, who said: " I'm concerned because Pak Harto has again been reelected. He has been there for too long. He was the president when I was born and he still is. I want to see change. How is it possible that I have only known one president so far?" Finally Diah Pratiwi: " A clean and more democratic government is obviously a must." Most of the issues were there in these simple comments - President Soeharto too long in power, too little democracy and no sign of a solution to the economic woes. Worse still, with the General Assembly as evidence, was anyone with power and influence really listening?

Whether or not President Soeharto really had been waiting to draw renewed strength from his confirmation for a seventh term of office, on the very day of the announcement of his acceptance of renomination, a new, tough, line seemed to be taken with the IMF. The President was quoted as saying that some of the IMF's recommendations were against Indonesia's 1945 Constitution, which he was sworn to implement "to the letter." President Soeharto was said to be chiefly concerned about Article 33 which stipulates that: "The economy shall be organized as a common endeavour based upon the principle of the family system. Branches of production which are important for the state and which affect the life of most people shall be controlled by the state. Land and water and the natural riches contained therein shall be controlled by the state and shall be made use of by the people." The President was quoted as saying that the IMF's package for Indonesia was based on 'Liberal' principles and therefore not consistent with the family approach taken in Indonesia - 'Liberal' meaning free market. To the world press, President Soeharto's citing of the Constitution seemed a mere flimsy excuse for continued alleged foot dragging.

Undoubtedly, President Soeharto was sincere in wanting to cooperate with the IMF, if he could. When he couldn't, he would feel it his duty to explore other options - and there appeared to be several. A Currency Board was one, another was pegging the rupiah to a basket of currencies. To obtain the additional foreign exchange reserves required in any pegging scenario, there was still hope that, if the IMF turned its back on Indonesia, friendly countries might advance the funds. Also, there is always a strong undercurrent of feeling in Indonesia that the country is too big and too strategically important to be allowed to collapse. In Washington and other influential world capitals there was the same underlying feeling. Could the US and the world really afford to let Indonesia collapse? The problem was that foreigners had blind-sided themselves with their obsession with President Soeharto and his leadership. A quite unreal battle line had been drawn between President Soeharto on one side and the IMF, the US and others on the other side. As 'The Far Eastern Economic Review' commented on March 19: "They (the US) can cut off Indonesia, possibly tipping the world's largest Muslim state into an ocean of civil unrest. Or they can succumb and bail out Soeharto on his terms...." There was no bail out!

The President was by no means alone in his doubts about the efficacy of the IMF's programmes. Long-time Government critic, Kwik Kian Gie wrote in March: "President Soeharto...was right when he said that strengthening the rupiah value was an undebatable must. We must have a serious discussion with the IMF, asking for its support to stabilize the rupiah's value as soon as possible. If the IMF does not agree to support us in this way we could abandon our agreement with it. The most important unsolved factor is how to obtain an adequate level of foreign exchange reserves to support our rupiah strengthening measures. Looking for an adequate amount of foreign loans would be very difficult, but not impossible if the newly established cabinet is regarded as credible by the international community."

With nothing having been achieved at the 11-day General Assembly except the re-election of President Soeharto and his deputy, at 30 campuses throughout Indonesia, up to 20,000 students kept up their demands for political change. They were warned not to stray from the campuses. The gist of the students demands was that before they would be willing to return to their books, " The Government must show concrete steps" to eliminate the corruption, collusion and nepotism identified by the students as being at the root of Indonesia's economic crisis. The National Commission on Human Rights demanded to know what had happened to missing activists. One was Desmond J. Mahesa, a director of the Nusantara Legal Aid Foundation. The other was Pius Lustrilanang, of whom the world would hear much more later. Pius was a member of SIAGA, a loose association which supported Megawati Sukarnoputri. The Commission had already sent letters to the relevant military and police commands and said they would send more. None had been answered.

In Indonesia and overseas, all eyes were now on President Soeharto. Who would be in the new cabinet? Would they be capable men and women? Would they be the exceptionally capable men and women the crisis seemed to call for? Would their appointment herald new hope? Would it instill new confidence at home and abroad? The 'Jakarta Post' quoted the Chairman of the Indonesian Footwear Association, Anton Supit, as saying: "The new cabinet must have a clear vision and be professional. The bottom line is integrity and capability. After that, everything will follow and we won't have to worry about corruption and collusion any more." Sri Mulyani Indrawati, a senior economist at the University of Indonesia, was quoted as saying: "What we have now is not merely a currency crisis but a crisis of public (and international) confidence in the Government."

Around the world, Indonesia and foreigners interested in Indonesia waited with baited breath for the news to break.

When it came, the international media was appalled. The line-up included one of the President's daughters, Siti Hardiyanti Rukmana and his long time friend, "Bob" Hasan, a man most associated with the foreign media's favourite targets of monopolies and cronyism. According to the 'Jakarta Post' the new state minister of Food, Drugs and Horticulture, Haryanto Dhanutirto, had been found guilty in 1996, while transport minister, of using state funds for his own personal use. Subsequently, he had returned the money. The 'Post' added that Minister of Tourism, Art and Culture, Abdul Latief, had been under fire the previous year, accused of using funds from the state insurance company, Jamsostek, to finance discussions relating to a controversial new manpower bill. Latief later acknowledged that he had taken US$2.8 million "under instructions of President Soeharto."

Yet, behind the media hysteria, the President had recruited men and women, often with relative youth on their side, frequently foreign educated, occasionally because some faction or interest had to be represented, but in majority of cases because the candidates had a track record of achievement as well as commitment to stability, development and self reliance. Naturally, as their leader, the President wanted people around him that he could work with and who broadly agreed with his general thinking, though they may disagree on details. His and the new cabinet's objectives were no secret: stability, development, self-reliance and resilience. With an eye to the campuses and other sources of demands for 'clean' Government, the President asked his new cabinet members and their spouses to declare all fixed or liquid assets. The reports would not be made public except if ministers faced corruption charges. The President also asked his ministers to donate their first year's salaries to the poor, relying instead on ministerial allowances and benefits. Provincial governors were also obliged to declare their wealth.

The new cabinet reflected precisely what the President felt Indonesia needed, as well as his own need to be surrounded with friends and even family who he thought could best help him lead Indonesia through the current crisis and into the next millennium. While condemned in some quarters, his choice of businessmen "Bob" Hasan and Tanri Abeng were hailed in others as bringing to the cabinet an element of hard-headed business expertise as well as channels to private sector support and even funds. The new Finance Minister, Fuad Bawazier and Central Bank Governor Sjahril Sabirin were well qualified, with proven track records, but were perhaps more inclined to back Indonesia's perceived interests than to follow foreign doctrine and ideology. Of course, they were also loyal Soehartoists.

While a pragmatic businessman, the new Minister of Industry

and Trade, Mohammad "Bob" Hasan, could be counted on to take a tough, even abrasive line, with those thought to be trying to push Indonesia in directions its Government preferred not to go. The new Coordinating Minister for the Economy, Finance and Industry, Ginandjar Kartasasmita, was a pragmatist as well as a nationalist, capable of building bridges to the world beyond Indonesia's borders as competently as demolishing them. Among his initial statements he was quoted as saying: " ..I regret that the heated debates on the CBS (Currency Board) have caused some misunderstandings with the IMF which are now trying to be mended." He was quoted as saying also: " However, we will go ahead with our reform programme with or without IMF assistance." One of the President's sons, Bambang Trihatmadjo, was quoted by 'The International Herald Tribune' on March 11, as saying that: "Indonesia would go it alone rather than submit to foreign dictate. If necessary, we can rebuild this country starting from ground zero."

Opinion about the new cabinet overseas was near uniformly negative. It was said to be made up of friends and cronies of the President - dashing all foreign hopes of an end to so-called cronyism. It was also said to be a slap in the face for the IMF.

In action, the new cabinet line-up looked good, their statements more promising than usual, their actions along the right lines. President Soeharto seemed to be taking a less conspicuous position, in the background, leaving more of the daily work to his newly appointed ministers, including to his vice-president who some thought might be the long awaited successor. Even before his re-election the comment had been made that because of his age President Soeharto might now have to leave more to others and even to cut back on foreign travel. Of course, no one was under any illusion that President Soeharto could not step forward every bit as quickly as he appeared to be stepping back. There was no suggestion and, given the President's role in the 1945 Constitution, there could be no suggestion, that President Soeharto was anything less than in complete control of his government.

With a new government in place, the IMF now sent a senior director to Jakarta. On March 17, Asia-Pacific Director, Hubert Neiss, arrived, briefed to review progress and prospects. Despite having staff in Jakarta since well before Christmas, somewhat incredibly, special teams now had to be set up - at this eleventh hour - to undertake the review: for monetary policy, banking, the 1998-99 budget, structural reforms and debt restructuring. Had reviews and reports not been made to IMF headquarters by its staff on the spot? Had they not been called for by the IMF directorate? And, to the lay observer, none of the subjects to be reviewed had a single hint of any practical role for what the IMF was most valued - its money. If it wasn't going to give any money (assuming Indonesia actually needed this kind of help) why was it involved in Indonesia at all? One day after Neiss's arrival, Ginandjar Kartasasmita was quoted as saying: "On the Currency Board system, we will not adopt that for the time being because for that there are some requirements that we haven't been able to fulfill, especially sufficient foreign exchange reserves to support it." The IMF had won this round.

With a senior IMF official in Jakarta, in the preferred face-to-face environment, Indonesia now officially asked the IMF to be more flexible in its approach to the country's problems. Surprisingly, the IMF agreed. BULOG Chairman, Beddu Amang was quoted as saying: " The IMF understands that the subsidies of certain strategic commodities, such as food, feed meal and medicines, are still needed. Fuad Bawazier was quoted as saying that private companies had not come forward with available warehouse space to enable BULOG to end its activities as planned on February 1 and that, therefore, the Agency would continue its work - with IMF blessing. He confirmed that, subsidies and BULOG aside, basically, the Government was still prepared to implement its agreement with the IMF in full. Australian Indonesia specialist, David Ray, from Melbourne's Centre for Strategic Economic Studies slammed the IMF for insisting on the withdrawal of subsidies and the dismantling of BULOG. He wrote in the 'Jakarta Post' on March 21: " For many Indonesian producers and consumers, the dismantling of the very institution charged with the responsibility of providing food security and price stability could not have come at a worse time. While the operations of BULOG have long been exploited as a tool for rent seeking activities by politically well-connected business groups, it has nevertheless served to hold down or stabilize prices for ordinary Indonesians. He warned that, since December, 1997, average prices for rice, flour and cooking oil in Jakarta had risen by 23 percent, 28 percent and 62 percent respectively - a recipe for a mounting social explosion. Unemployment hovered close to 9 million; underemployment at over 18 million. Poverty and want was rising - fast.

Students were maintaining their sporadic demonstrations. Leaders said that whereas their protests could be characterized as a moral movement, since they had failed to influence events at the recent People's Consultative Assembly, some of them felt that "moral force alone was no longer adequate. We need something more permanent, some organizations which include other elements in society." Political observer, Emha Ainun Nadjib was quoted by the 'Jakarta Post' as saying: "There should be a synergy between the students and other elements in society...to establish a people's power movement."

In their harping on corruption, collusion and nepotism, the students were reflecting widely held disenchantment with the morality of the New Order Government. Unleashed beyond the campuses, their campaign might enjoy widespread public support, especially from Muslim communities emboldened by a new sense of rightness and even power. Amien Rais articulated these beliefs and frustrations and after the conclusion of the People's Consultative Assembly he was quoted as saying that he would give the new government six months to "prove itself." Student leaders had latched onto his comment and were saying the same thing. Another clock appeared to be ticking, a new time-bomb smoldering. Many believed that the students would not back down until their demands were met. Perhaps ABRI thought so, too.

On March 19, Armed Forces Commander, General Wiranto, offered the students a dialogue and the first meeting took place in Bandung on March 25. Some student leaders demanded a dialogue with President Soeharto. At first, Government spokesmen ruled out the idea on grounds either of "protocol" or "impracticality." General Wiranto said that it depended on the President. Eventually, the President was quoted as saying that he had no objection to meeting student leaders, just as he frequently met with other groups, as diverse as farmers, fishermen and athletes. He looked forward to any "concrete proposals on how to boost development." Development was not a subject that interested the students and the presidential response indicated that the old, familiar, New Order political straightjacket was still firmly in place. The students wanted to talk about poor leadership, bad governance and immediate, practical solutions to the economic crisis, especially the problem of high prices. In Jakarta the cry was raised for a special session of the just concluded People's Consultative Assembly. The numbers involved in demonstrations continued to rise and one newspaper was interested to comment that "security was noticeably more lax than for previous days."

Dialog between ABRI and demonstrators was a novel experience for both sides. The Rector of Gadjah Mada University, Ichlasul Amal, was quoted as saying that neither the students nor the military were ready to dialogue. "The students were often not ready to defend and describe what it was that they meant by political reform. The military officers were not ready (to respond to the students) either." A further dialogue between the military and the Gadjah Mada students was refused by the demonstrators on the grounds that the agenda had been prearranged and therefore precluded free and open discussion. It seemed that the students needed to go away and define their positions and that ABRI would have to make up its mind whose side it was on, a demand now beginning to be raised by Government critics.

On the day of the dialogue, Army Chief of Staff, General Subagyo Hadisiswono was quoted as praising Amien Rais, a man the state police had said they wanted to question. The General was quoted as describing Amien's criticisms of the Government as "mature" and "wise." He was quoted as adding: " ABRI also respects student opinions because they are the future of the nation." With him was Let. Gen. Prabowo, the President's son-in-law. Did he really endorse such sentiments? Prabowo had apparently not been included in the closed door dialogue with the students. Retired General Soemitro expressed support for the students but warned against violence which, he said, could lead to an "emergency." He further warned that such an emergency could result in " a physically strong leader but without strong intelligence (presumably meaning bad judgment) appearing and taking control of the situation." A few days earlier, responding to questions, Let. Gen. Prabowo had ruled out the possibility of a military coup - a rumour increasingly rife in the capital. Talk of a coup was perhaps understandable, given the severity of the crisis, the apparent weakness of the Government and mounting protests but the reference to an "emergency" by a retired senior officer was more interesting. Restoring order in the wake of an "emergency" need not be as part of a coup; it could simply involve a reshuffle of commanders, replacing the 'soft' with the 'hard.' Was Soemitro warning of the undesirability of social unrest reaching the level of an emergency or was he hinting that someone was ready to take advantage of such a situation? If so, who was it?

On March 27, Amien Rais reported that he had met Armed Forces Chief of Sociopolitical Affairs, Let. Gen. Susilo Bambang Yudhoyono and other officers at Yogyakarta's Sheraton Mustika Hotel. The other ABRI leaders were Chief of the Armed Forces Intelligence Agency, Maj. Gen. Zaky Anwar Makarim, Chief of the Diponegoro Regional Military Command, Maj. Gen. Mardiyanto and Chief of the Pamungkas Military District, Col. Djoko Santoso. According to Amien the officers had told him to keep up his criticism of the Government for the good of the nation. For obvious reasons the meeting was significant. It was also significant for the less obvious reason that, like Amien Rais, the officers were Muslim. General Wiranto is also Muslim. Amien told the media that the meeting was a reunion and intended to strengthen Silaturahim - an Islamic word usually used to describe the bond between Muslim brethren. Not only were Indonesia's Muslim intellectuals, loosely represented by Amien Rais, fed up with the immorality of the New Order regime under President Soeharto. It appeared that Muslim elements in ABRI's officer corps felt the same way. Doubtless all decent and right thinking people of whatever religion felt this way but after years of feeling sidelined there can be no doubt that some of Indonesia's Muslims were now ready to take a stand correcting some of the abuses of the Soeharto years.

On March 29, General Subagyo was quoted as going even further in support of Amien. The 'Jakarta Post' quoted him as saying: " ABRI has never considered Amien Rais as an enemy. We've never made any Government critics our enemies. ABRI will always take the side of the people in its every decision regarding state affairs and politics." What must President Soeharto have made of this? The 'Jakarta Post' in a leader described the military's comments as " a welcome whiff of fresh air which it said had come as "somewhat of a (welcome) surprise."

Between times, Amien Rais and Nurcholish Madjid spoke at a discussion at Jakarta's Al Azhar Grand Mosque. They sharply criticized leaders who used Islam to gain national legitimacy. There criticism was so pointed as to be almost funny. Nurcholish was quoted as saying: " If a leader fails to live up to good leadership as taught by Islam, the legitimacy of the Muslim majority would be eroded. Don't be deceived by formal piety, don't be blinded by leaders who are able to enter the Kaaba, don't take the haj and the umrah (minor haj) as evidence of good and pious leadership. " Who could he have had in mind? He went on: " We need to go back to the essence of what constitutes good leadership. There are leaders who say their prayers just for political legitimacy, leaders who can't even be honest to their children" (and tell them that what they're doing is wrong). The Muslim scholar said that no matter how great, a nation would be destroyed if its administration was unjust and punished the common people for small errors while letting so-called leaders escape with great mistakes. "People who have been unjust, despite saying their prayers and entering the Kaaba will be destroyed. The essence of leadership is justice and trustworthiness." Amien said that a good leader should be concerned for his people and not with self aggrandizement and that he should be trustworthy and accountable. "Corruption, collusion and nepotism practices are all the result of poor accountability."

On March 29 the Indonesian Legal Aid and Human Rights Association urged the Government to do more to locate missing political activists. In addition to Pius Lustrilanang and Desmond J. Mahesa, missing since early February, since March 9, Haryanto Taslam, Deputy Secretary of Megawati's PDI had also gone missing. Haryanto had organised an anniversary meeting at Megawati's house in 1997, deemed illegal. Megawati's Secretary General, Alexander Litaay said that he had reported the case to the security authorities but had received no reply. The Association also reported that several students had gone missing after demonstrations at Lampung University two weeks earlier. Even a cursory browsing of the daily media engendered nagging thoughts. Every few days, or so it seemed, someone was going "missing." All very strange - and ominous!

The military brass had apparently told Amien that he could look forward to even bigger dialogues between ABRI and students. At least some ABRI commanders apparently felt that it wasn't necessary to kidnap people and violate civic and human rights to obtain information. Why not just talk to them? Almost simultaneously it was announced that General Wiranto would meet student representatives from 17 universities in Jakarta on April 4. Military leaders said that they would talk to the students as "equal partners" in Indonesia's development process. Minister of Defence and Security, Armed Forces Commander, General Wiranto, was quoted as saying: "The dialogue is of national importance for mutual understanding." In the event the students refused to take part. Instead, General Wiranto promptly opened a dialogue between ABRI and leaders of 32 youth organizations. The meeting took place on April 11 and covered much the same issues as were being raised by the students.

In Yogyakarta, demonstrations turned ugly when students tried to march off campus and take their protests to the streets. On April 2, 88 people were injured in scuffles with security forces. There were smaller demonstrations at other campuses. On April 7, the Government called on university rectors to control their students. Minister of Education and Culture, Wiranto Arismunandar, was quoted as reaffirming that students were prohibited from engaging in "practical politics." Nahdlatul Ulama leader, Abdurrachman Wahid was quoted as saying that the student demonstrations were showing signs of "destructive anarchy." Meanwhile, university lecturers were quoted as saying that attempting to ban students from engaging in political activities had "no legal basis." The students certainly agreed because they were unfazed. Writing in the 'Jakarta Post,' political scientist, J. Soedjati Djiwandono said: " The General Session of the People's Consultative Assembly, the supreme governing body of the nation's political system, ended last month, having indicated not the slightest interest in the issue of reform. Whatever the case may be the students deserve to be listened to. So far, they have only been heard, loud and clear." Soedjati continued into interesting territory: " The present student protests.....have yet to enlist and enjoy the support of the military. Hence, the possible significance of a dialogue offered by the military leadership."

On April 13, the Executive Board of the Indonesian Muslim Student Movement was quoted as saying that: "The best way to achieve political change in Indonesia is through a people power movement." This was the second time the phrase "peoples' power" had been used. Rebellion, if not revolution now seemed firmly in the air.

On Thursday, April 16, in a significant written address to the Army's special force, (KOPASSUS), President Soeharto warned that ABRI could use "repressive measures" if peaceful persuasion failed to calm boisterous students. The message was significant because it was addressed to KOPASSUS, a force which would later be blamed for all kinds of clandestine and even illegal activities. The student demonstrations had been gathering momentum since the collapse of the rupiah in January which had forced up prices across a wide front and made it more difficult for students to pay their fees. Their pleas that Indonesia's worst economic crisis since independence be discussed by the House of Representatives in March had gone unheard. Student anger over rising prices had switched to fury with the Government as a whole, especially President Soeharto. Was the President now planning a formal crackdown? Was this his message to the assembled red berets?

As significant as Soeharto's message was another from Army Chief of Staff, General Subagyo Hadisiswoyo. He reminded the special forces not to become an "exclusive" corps, distanced from the people. Why did he feel it necessary to do this? Was KOPASSUS in danger of becoming an exclusive corps? Of even greater significance for later events, had this exclusiveness been deliberately fostered by President Soeharto's son-in-law, Prabowo, when he was commander? Did the suggestion of "exclusiveness" hint at a division in ABRI between Prabowo and Soeharto loyalists and the main body of ABRI? According to the 'Jakarta Post' of April 17, General Subagyo added: " The People are not the enemy of the Armed Forces (ABRI) because ABRI are the people's soldiers." Why was it necessary to issue this reminder? Did ABRI's top brass suspect KOPASSUS of having been engaged in anti-people activities? What were these activities? Kidnappings, perhaps?

Clearly, from the record, these were confusing times for ABRI's officer corps. The President and the Government were telling the military to keep control but segments of the military agreed with the demonstrators. In practice there was an oscillation between clamping down and supporting. Clandestine forces were kidnapping and abusing people to abstract politically related information. Mainstream ABRI was treating the people as "partners. Were there now two very definite camps within ABRI? Those around Let. Gen. Prabowo, now commander of KOSTRAD, the military's strategic reserve, and those around General Wiranto!

According to the Foundation of the Indonesian Legal Aid Institute the number of activists still missing had now risen to 11 - out of a one time total of 21. Reports said that 10 had returned. Those still "lost" included: Faisal Rezha, Rahardjo Waluyo Djati, Andi Arief and Nezar Patria from Gadjah Mada University, students Aan Rusdianto and Mugianto, Herman Hendrawan from Surabaya's Airlangga University. Munir, the Foundations Deputy Chairman for Operational Affairs was quoted as saying that: " If the activists were guilty of committing a crime, they should have been brought to trial, not kidnapped. All of those missing were outspoken critics of the Government.

On the last day of March ABRI spokesman Brig. Gen. A. Wahab Mokodongan was quoted as saying: How can people say that ABRI is behind the disappearances when our personnel have painstakingly searched high and low for the missing individuals?" Which part of ABRI was he speaking for - Prabowo's or Wiranto's? He went on to say that the National Police had been ordered to investigate - a difficult task if the culprits really were from units of ABRI, rogue or otherwise! And Jakarta Regional Military Commander, Maj. Gen. Sjafrie Sjamsoeddin was quoted as saying: " I wonder if people have evidence to back up their allegations." ABRI has become famous for making denial its first response to an unpleasant allegation and its second a demand for evidence. Rogue elements would be safe in the knowledge either that no evidence would be found or that victims/witnesses would be too afraid to come forward.

ABRI refused to give up on its idea to dialogue with the students. On Saturday, April 18, no fewer than 15 ministers attended a meeting with students arranged by the Armed Forces. Unfortunately, according to the 'Jakarta Post', "only about 50 students" turned up with no one at all from the University of Indonesia, the Bandung Institute of

Technology and Gadjah Mada University, Yogyakarta. Generally speaking the students felt that neither ABRI nor the Government were committed to a programme of total reform. Some said that they found ABRI "defensive." Former Minister Siswono Yudohusono was quoted as saying that it was significant that GOLKAR ministers attended the meeting at all and he urged GOLKAR to play a leading role in introducing reforms. He was quoted as saying: " The recent dialogue between the Armed Forces, intellectuals and students indicates that the Government understands the demands for sweeping reforms. I think that the demands for reforms aim to create better conditions and that's why I hope the Government will respond positively." The Government had understood the demands but did it understand the inescapability of implementing them? The students thought not.

The day before, 10,000 students had rallied at Surabaya, allegedly marching three kilometres through kampongs, where they were joined by members of the public sharing their concern to lower prices. The students demanded a new national leadership and an end to corruption, collusion and nepotism. More than 16,000 students were reported as rallying in Ujung Pandang, the capital of South Sulawesi. Groups numbering from a few thousand to a few hundred rallied elsewhere. A pattern became established of daily student rallies at various campuses across the country, typically involving around 30,000 students and typically with the indulgence of at least some members of administration and faculty.

The Government was increasingly concerned about the ongoing protests. ABRI was not only concerned but interested. The President was talking about the possibility of "repressive measures." The Government and the President were one and the same. But was ABRI? Theoretically, yes but did the high command now agree with the Government that repressive measures might have to be used to silence the students or were some of the ABRI commanders beginning to believe that the students had a point. Did General Subagyo's comment about ABRI not being the enemy of the people send a message as loud as Soeharto's? Was ABRI planning to back the students against the President?

April 1 was the first day of a new financial year and there was widespread anticipation that Indonesia must reach a new agreement with the IMF around that time. Hopes were raised further by the arrival of the IMF's Stanley Fischer who was quoted as saying: "It is understood by everybody that it is a crucial moment for Indonesia's economy and the carrying out of the (IMF) programme is essential for its success."

Interviewed by state television on the eve of the announcement of a yet another new agreement between the IMF and Indonesia, Fischer stressed that the new deal was the key to a recovery of confidence in Indonesia. And he underlined that it was not the signing of a new agreement that mattered so much as its implementation. The Fund had compromised on its demand for a budget surplus, compromised on its demand that subsidies be scrapped immediately, compromised on its demand that BULOG be terminated but otherwise its position remained unchanged, particularly that no funds would be disbursed until the agreed reform programme was carried out. Fischer spoke in an opinionated, school masterly and even condescending manner, as if the Fund was really doing Indonesia a very big favour. But was it?

So far, only US$3 billion had been disbursed under circumstances in which the public at large were not even convinced that Indonesia needed money. In his interview, Fischer made it clear that the Fund would not be paying any of the offshore debts. If there were to be bankruptcies, the Agency had recommended a new bankruptcy law. If banks became insolvent, the Fund supported their closure. If the closure of insolvent companies instilled confidence, high interest rates would generate even more and these also the Fund supported. On the ideological side, far removed from an actual solution to the current crisis, Fischer insisted that monopolies must not be reinstated and that there should be a new anti-monopoly law to prevent it. Indonesia he said, faced the prospect of recovery with the IMF or inflation and disorder. On April 8, when the new agreement was announced by the Coordinating Minister for Economy, Finance and Industry, Ginandjar Kartasasmita, the impression persisted that, for the time being the Fund was playing a strictly advisory role, with the promise of funding but with no actual disbursements.

The new, third Agreement, was announced between Indonesia and the IMF on April 10. The budget had been revised again, forecasting a growth contraction of 4 percent, inflation at 17 percent and the barrel-price of oil at a more realistic US$14.50 instead of US$17.00. There would be a budget deficit of 3.2 percent which would be partly made good by foreign loans and partly from revenues from the sale of state companies. Subsidies were allowed on rice, soybeans and fuel while those on foodstuffs, drug raw materials, animal feed and energy were to be removed by October, 1998 - six months after the new Government took office. Ginandjar confirmed that to help companies pay offshore loans Indonesia would implement a Mexico-style solution with the Government guaranteeing debtors access to foreign currencies to repay their debts at a "reasonable" rate. He stressed: "There's not going to be a government bailout or a government subsidy." He was quoted as saying that the Government was looking at a three to four year time-frame within which the debts would be settled rather than the eight years applied in Mexico. A new bankruptcy law would be available to those who could not settle. The policy of high interest rates was confirmed but small and medium sized companies and cooperatives would be offered credits at subsidized rates. A number of taxes with revenues going to local Government were increased by as much as 5 percent but all local levies, official and unofficial, were abolished. There was no mention of a Currency Board.

Few things illustrate how complete a surrender to the IMF was this third agreement than the decision to maintain high interest rates. The question of whether rates should be high or low was not just a matter of the balance the Government felt it needed to maintain be-tween the interest of the rupiah and the interests of the corporates, it was not just a matter of disagreement between the Government of Indo-nesia and the IMF. Interest rates were a genuinely contentious issue.

On March 27, 'Asiaweek' had quoted World Bank chief econo-mist, Joseph Stiglitz, as saying: "...our econometric studies tend to sup-port the view that high interest rates have more deleterious effects on financial systems than do devaluations." He went on: " Many believe that you need to increase interest rates to sustain exchange rates. Still, the evidence of that in the current situation is much more ambiguous. In Latin America, raising interest rates showed that Governments were doing something about macroeconomic imbalance. Here (in Asia) the econo-mies were in macro-balance. In that context, excessively tight monetary policy could lead to high levels of unemployment and bankruptcy, un-dermining the overall strength of the economy."

Indeed, it could. Indonesia had become the living proof!

A few days earlier, Harvard economist, Jeffrey Sachs had been quoted in 'The Straits Times' of Singapore as saying: "High interest rates and fiscal austerity will impose widespread bankruptcies. This approach won't work. You don't stabilize exchange rates by killing the economy."

In a leader, the 'Jakarta Post' described the April deal with the IMF as "Our last chance." Ginandjar Kartasasmita was quoted as say-ing that President Soeharto himself had ordered that "all agreements and commitments should be honoured to the letter." Stanley Fischer was quoted as saying that the "jury was still out" on whether Indonesia would implement the programme agreed with the IMF in full and on time. He was quoted by Reuters as saying: "We have measures in place and if they are not implemented, the programme (of funding) will not go ahead. We have no assurance. We cannot have assurance, given history, that it will be done."

The fine details of the IMF April deal reflected both the determination of the Government of Indonesia to please the IMF and the markets and also its desperation. It also seemed to reflect a new approach by the IMF based on a better understanding of Indonesia's needs. The new IMF Agreement - a 117 point Letter of Intent - reminded the Government to more fully implement changes the Government thought it had made but the IMF thought it hadn't and set out a timetable for the accomplishment of reforms, old and new. It reminded the Government to implement reforms promised but so far not delivered. This time, the IMF would not be satisfied with promises. It wanted action. Its funds providers wanted action. The timetable was extremely ambitious by Indonesian standards. The fact that firm dates were inked in beside each reform was a measure of the Government's desperation as well as of the IMF's distrust. There were firm suggestions that if the timetable was not met in full IMF funds might be blocked.

The IMF's advice was now so broad and its timetable so tight that foreigners had instant doubts as to whether everything could really be carried out as planned. And, if it wasn't? Would the IMF again lambaste Indonesia, again fuelling negative media coverage? Again undermining the confidence so vital to Indonesia's recovery? Some of the items stipulated to be done the Government of Indonesia was under the impression had been done. Would the Fund ever agree? Could it ever be pleased? And if not?

The Fund's willingness to compromise with Indonesia on the timing of the removal of subsidies was now seen to be limited to October, 1998. After that, it said, subsidies on corn, wheat flour, sugar, soybean and fish meal must go. Time would tell whether this would be practical or not. If it turned out to be not practical..........?

Weaknesses notwithstanding, even critics of the IMF must surely have agreed with the Fund that, if all the suggested reforms were implemented, the 'new' Indonesian economy would indeed not only be much stronger but also much more hassle-free as a place for foreign companies to do business. The Government and the IMF now had their hopes pinned exclusively on the reputation of the IMF and the effectiveness of the reform programme being sufficient to restore that nebulous emotion known as 'confidence.' If the IMF had got it wrong, Indonesia could very well be heading for disaster. If the Government backed away from the reforms, Indonesia could be heading for disaster.

The elements still pointing in this direction were numerous.

There was the ongoing unsolved problem of the private sector offshore debt - the issue that had sparked the initial collapse of confidence. Even in April, almost a year after the crisis broke, the Government of Indonesia had still not managed to track down all the private debts. The latest report, on April 15, was that private debt had now been identified as being US$ 80.2 billion, up from US$73.96 billion; Government debt had fallen to US$ 53.5 billion, down from US$63.46 billion. Of the private debt US$ 15.6 billion were short-term with a further US$ 7.4 billion in commercial papers - a total of US$23 billion - down from US$ 35.6 billion. If previous figures were not wrong, somebody had been paying their bills. Bulk of the debt repayment was on near-standstill while all the parties involved, Government, debtors and lenders, waited for the time to come when their respective positions would be optimal to resolve the problem.

There was the ongoing problem of Indonesia's shakey banking industry, which, despite skeptics, seemed to be slowly being dragged back to proper diligence, if not solvency.

There was the ongoing and related problem of dishonoured Indonesian letters of credit, about which much had been promised but little had happened - pending IMF approval of Indonesia carrying out the agreed reforms. Even some of the help promised was sometimes highly focused and targeted and did not represent a solution to the overall problem. The LC logjam spawned a container crisis which the Government moved to solve by importing empty boxes.

There was the phenomenon of sky-high interest rates which were still said to be crippling the business sector. Care had to be taken with this. Although 80 percent of the companies listed on the Jakarta Stock Exchange were said to be technically bankrupt they seemed to be still trading. And, of course, not all companies had gone public. Many listed companies were but fragments of much larger, unlisted, parent companies. Indonesians and visitors to Indonesia could see substantial levels of business continuing, despite the gloom and doom on every side. It was known that one reason was that many companies were simply not paying their debts. Another was that there had to be very formidable sums of money outside the banking system. Still, despite the seeming continuance of business activity construction was largely stopped, new projects were halted and many factories were idle.

As the end of April neared, there were still too many negatives about Indonesia to impress foreign investors or to push the value of the rupiah up drastically. Direct investment was expected to slump by at least 40 percent while overseas investors waited for the economy to recover and for the political risk posed by ongoing student demonstrations to diminish. Portfolio investors might have an interest in bankrupt companies so long as they did not have to pay large debts and so long as the economy looked set for growth. A bankrupt company in a contracting market hardly seemed like much of a deal.

The 'Jakarta Post' quoted the Minister of Manpower, Theo Sambuaga, as warning that by March 1999, in the wake of a severe corporate shake-out, unemployment was likely to reach 13.5 million or 15 percent of Indonesia's work force of 90 million. Another 40 million people worked less than 35 hours per week - more than half the work force. Many of the workers laid-off to date had been given three months severance pay before Lebaran. In May it would run out. Then what? In its leader on April 14, the 'Jakarta Post' forecast "tough times ahead." The editorial said: "The nation is in for the roughest stretch of the reform programme over the next six months as all price subsidies for essential commodities, except rice and soybeans, will be eliminated by October. "This means that for most households the economic crisis will get much worse before it starts to stabilize and eventually recover. But higher prices for essential goods are not the only source of economic suffering. More companies may have to fold, with the consequence of massive layoffs and bigger bad debts, as the Government is required to maintain or even to further raise the already punitively high interest rates during the stabilization period." (- estimated by the IMF as requiring up to three years.) The banking industry, also, may be in for bigger jolts as the operation of more banks, battered by high interest rates and huge sums of bad loans, may have to be suspended. Cumulative inflation for the calendar year is projected at 50 percent."

Asked if he thought that the new IMF package would help the Indonesian economy, Kwik Kian Gie wrote in the 'Jakarta Post:' "Not in the short-term." Asked if carrying out the IMF programme was a guarantee that Indonesia would not suffer a similar crisis of confidence again Kwik wrote: " No." The money market didn't seem too impressed either. The rupiah rose slightly and fell slightly and was predicted to stabilize at between Rps 7,500 and Rps 8,500 to the US dollar - hardly an improvement worth talking about.

The markets were still said to be concerned about the debt hangover. Next day, while Michel Camdessus was saying in Washington that his team had at last got to the "root of the problems" in Indonesia, the rupiah fell again, to close to Rps 9,000 to one US dollar. The stock market also edged down. What was there to be bullish about? Many of the problems remained. The 'Indonesian Observer' was quoted as saying: " The sentiment was weak today. Many investors stayed on the sidelines amid uncertainties over the Government's commitment to the IMF reform package and the outcome of the debt negotiations." Continuing student demonstrations coupled with no sign of a rapid solution to the debt problem and deepening economic hardship as a result of the IMF's 'rescue' ensured that 'sentiment' stayed deeply negative - not only in Indonesia but overseas, in countries interested in Indonesia.

As April ticked away, and the rupiah failed to register any dramatic progress against the US dollar, once again, from Indonesia's point of view the IMF 'medicine' seemed not to have worked. With the economy being driven into recession, if not bankruptcy, would it ever work? Even the IMF was not optimistic. Michael Musa, Research Department Director of the IMF, was quoted by "The Indonesian Observer" as saying that "there remains great uncertainty at this time over Indonesia where it is too early to perceive when the turnaround of the economy might come." Informed speculation put it at least three years away.

With so much misery forecast and so few bright spots, it was hardly surprising to find the students pressing on with their campaign for political reform - not that any amount of reform could have solved the crisis, which still seemed to hinge firmly and exclusively on solving the country's debt problem - offshore debt, bank debt and corporate debt. Even a brand new Government was likely to paralyzed until this issue worked itself out.

On April 13, 'The Indonesian Observer' had reported the Chairman of the Executive Board of the Indonesian Muslim Students Movement, Chatibul Umam Wiranu, as saying: " If the masses want to strengthen the creation of a people power movement, my group will support them." It was unlikely that "the masses" would respond to this, unless rising prices forced their backs to the wall - or unless they were incited! Movement board member Sulthon was quoted as qualifying Chatibul's statement with another saying: "We would reject any unconstitutional political changes." More importantly, in a statement, the group

132

was alleged to have called upon Indonesia's Armed Forces to "announce where it stands."

By way of a clue, on April 14, Deputy House Speaker and ABRI faction leader, Let. Gen. Syarwan Hamid, talking to the same Islamic group in Bandung said that the students' campaign should be seen as a moral struggle. He was quoted as saying: " Feel free to express your actions as long as they do not create stability problems." The concept of the moral struggle was an interesting one which united many, many groups against the Government. Again and again we see from the record that the Government's lack of ethics was what created activists and drove them onto the streets to protest - lack of ethics in government, lack of ethics in business. It seemed that even ABRI was outraged.

In a statement on April 15, Nahdlatul Ulama's Executive Board called on ABRI to support the snowballing movement for reform. A statement quoted by the media said: " ABRI should protect and support the demand for improvement which has been brewing in society." The NU leaders said that ABRI should not try to oppose or quell the student demonstrations but should protect the students. Using the Islamic term ishlah, meaning improving or changing things that are imperfect or old and damaged, the NU said that change was sunnah or the law of Allah. "To reject reform or ishlah is tantamount to rejecting Allah's sunnah." On April 17, Amien Rais was quoted as supporting the call of the NU for ABRI to support the people's and students' calls for reform. "The NU stance was a clear signal," (to ABRI) he was quoted as saying. He added that demands for reform were a test of ABRI's claim that it was in the vanguard of the national interest. He was quoted as saying that if ABRI found that the Government was reneging on its mandate it should withdraw its support and commit to those willing to create a new, legitimate administration. He said that ABRI's actions hinged only on the words of one individual, President Soeharto. " It is not right if, as an institution, ABRI is run by one individual. It is now time that ABRI, as an institution, takes the right step (and chooses) whether to protect the interests of Soeharto and his family or to protect the interests of the nation. ABRI always says that what is best for ABRI is best for the people....now the people are waiting (for ABRI) to make its choice."

We must bear in mind that Amien had met the ABRI commanders. Some or all of what he said was almost certainly mirroring back to them what they had told him. ABRI was frustrated at being at the beck and call, not of the state, but of one man and of taking the blame for the unpopular policies and actions of that one man. Amien's statement must have touched on some very raw nerves at ABRI headquarters. Military observers generally believed that there were officers within ABRI who thought that meeting the students' demands would in no way endanger the nation. On the contrary, not meeting them posed very big dangers. Amien pointed out that if all conventional avenues to further democratization were blocked people would be forced to find "unconventional solutions."

He was quoted as saying: " The Government is adamant that anything the people's Consultative Assembly has decided should not be reviewed and that Soeharto has to be given a chance until 2003 (when his current five-year-term expires). "Meanwhile, people (facing) insufferable suffering want to limit his term. If, within one semester, Soeharto fails to overcome the (economic) crisis, it would be better if his mandate was revoked. If, within these six months, his performance improves, it's an indication he is able to handle the crisis...if not, a people's power movement could take place. Should a people's power movement take place, Muhamadiyah members, who number millions of people, would surely support it." A gauntlet had been thrown down!

According to the Foundation of the Indonesian Legal Aid Institute the number of activists still missing was now risen 11 - out of a one time total of 21. Reports said that 9-10 had returned. Those still "lost" included: Faisal Rezha, Rahardjo Waluyo Djati, Andi Arief and Nezar Patria from Gadjah Mada University, students Aan Rusdianto and Mugianto, Herman Hendrawan from Surabaya's Airlangga University. Munir, the Foundations Deputy Chairman for Operational Affairs was quoted as saying that: "If the activists were guilty of committing a crime, they should have been brought to trial, not kidnapped. All of those missing were outspoken critics of the Government. Human rights activist and lawyer, T. Mulya Lubis wrote on April 16: " It must be realized that the foundation of a law-upholding state is the responsibility the state assumes over the safety and security of its citizens and residents. Unless cases of missing people are handled seriously, people will lose faith in the integrity of a state which professes to champion the law." Had some of the people of Indonesia now reached this point? Mulya went on to make another interesting point. "Forced disappearances" he wrote were against internationally accepted conventions of the United Nations. If people were labelled "missing" he wrote: "Thus, they cannot be identified as "forced disappearances," a category of crime condemned by international human rights institutions and the United Nations."

Mulya's article made sad reading because he listed disappearances beginning not last month or even last year but with the birth of the New Order Government in the mid - '1960s, the mysterious killings of the early 1980s (subsequently admitted by the President to have been carried out by the Government), the Tanjung Priok Riots of 1984, the Lampung incident of February 1989 in which 246 men, women and children were alleged to have been shot to death in a crack down on so-called separatist rebels, the attack on the PDI headquarters on July 27, 1996 and culminating in the early 1998 spate of kidnappings of activists. The Lampung incident was complicated (as so many are) because the root seems to have been a land dispute and along the way an army captain was killed and his body confiscated by villagers, naturally to the fury of the Armed Forces. Clashes between ABRI and demonstrators are usually characterized by strong abuse of the security forces by the protesters, often involving physical violence and even deaths. Indonesians are proud and emotional people and can only stand so much abuse and name calling. Sometimes, they snap! We cannot condone or abuse human rights abuses but in many cases it has to be borne in mind that every story has two sides.

'Newsweek' of April 13 wrote that "Indonesia's college towns are turning into battlefields. Anger keeps rising over the economic crisis that began last July. Students who began by rallying against higher living expenses are now demanding nothing less than Soeharto's removal. Wage earners have begun joining the protests."

In Surabaya at the beginning of the third week of April 10,000 students mobilized themselves demanding economic and political reform; in Ujung Pandang, 16,000. There were ongoing demonstrations in Jakarta, Yogyakarta, Surakarta and Semarang. The protests spread to Medan, Padang, Lampung, Bengkulu, Jambi, South Kalimantan, Central Sulawesi, Bali and Irian Jaya. President Soeharto ordered the students back to their books. Thousands more students promptly joined the ranks of the demonstrators. During the following week student demonstrations were increasingly joined by non-students including workers, housewives, nuns and even prostitutes. During the weekend of April 18 and 19 intellectuals stepped up their support for the students, urging and encouraging them to continue with their fight for economic and political reforms. Selo Soemardjan, a professor of sociology at the University of Indonesia told 3,000 students that they should no longer tolerate the deterioration in national political ethics. He was quoted as saying: " The situation has forced them to take action since the House of Representatives has shown itself to be incapable of fulfilling its duty and acting as the mechanism for controlling the Government. Speaking in Jakarta, Amien Rais warned the Government that the student reform movement had reached "the point of no return." He called on academics and students to maintain their pressure even though the Government had shown some commitment towards reform.

The motives of some of the student protesters interviewed by the media were heartwringing. The 'Jakarta Post' quoted Dedy, a student at Gadjah Mada's School of Philosophy as saying that he was afraid of being arrested but that he could not turn a blind eye to the sufferings of so many people. He said that pedicab and meatball soup sellers he met had told him how difficult it was even to earn Rps 5,000 per day for their families in the face of soaring prices. " I don't know anything about politics. I don't have any political ambitions in joining the demonstrations. I don't know whether my involvement in a demonstration will really help reduce the prices of essentials." Dedy said that he felt proud to take part. Students, too, were suffering and the same article reported that many were forced to try to borrow money to keep up with fee payments.

Entri Sofiatun from Gadjah Mada's School of Literature explained how her school teacher parents "have had their meagre salaries cut for various donations imposed upon them by local officials. As a woman, I hear mothers complain about the prices of milk, cooking oil, flour and other essentials, while their husbands cannot earn more money. Even if I were not a student I would still join in the demonstrations. The first time I joined one I was embarrassed. I thought people were laughing at me. Now, I feel relief if I can shout at the top of my lungs during a demonstration." - Point of no return!

President Soeharto's new cabinet was slammed for seeming to do next to nothing to solve the deepening economic crisis. Political observers called even more loudly for reforms to give teeth to the legislature and control the Executive and the president. At a seminar in Jakarta, former minister, Siswono Yudohusodo, said that the 1945 Constitution allowed for the convention of an Extraordinary Session of the People's Consultative Assembly to select a new president. The Commission for Missing Persons and Victims of Violence complained on Monday, April 20, that it had still received no reply from ABRI about the missing activists, some of whom had now mysteriously reappeared - too afraid to say anything about there whereabouts. Munir, the Foundation's Deputy Chairman for Operational Affairs, was quoted as saying that an official at the defense ministry had said that the letter had been "lost." The missing activists now included: Andi Arief, Herman Hendrawan, Faisol Riza, Rahardjo Waluyo Djati, Bimo Petrus, Suyat, Yani Avri and Sonny. Three activists were now "found" in police custody, some being held on suspicion of involvement in the Tanah Tinggi bombing case. The Jakarta Legal Aid Foundation sharply criticized the police for keeping silent about the whereabouts of the activists. Meanwhile the Team of Volunteers for Humanity (TRK), an umbrella group of non-government organizations offered to provide manpower to the national Commission on Human Rights to speed up tracking down other missing activists. The TRK put the number still missing at 33. The Deputy Chairman of the Commission, rights campaigner, Marzuki Darusman, was quoted by the media as saying that he firmly believed that members of the military and police were behind the kidnappings and tortures of activists.

On Thursday, April 23, the Government proudly announced that it had succeeded in meeting the deadlines for reform set by the IMF as conditions for its "help." The IMF was presumably happy. The people of Indonesia were in tears. They were crying for help. The Government was apparently not listening. As April led into May, the people's forces seemed to be gathering and the Armed Forces seemed to be teetering between loyalty to the people and loyalty to Soeharto.

On April 24, University of Indonesia postgraduate students supported the call for an extraordinary session of the People's Consultative Assembly "in response to widely reported calls for reforms." They especially wanted the special powers given to President Soeharto to be revoked. There were warnings of civil unrest if their demands for economic and political reforms were not met. Other students heard lecturer Arbi Sanit call for ABRI and the bureaucracy to be booted out of politics. In the MPR, the United Development Party condemned Government reluctance to accept nationwide demands for political, economic and legal reform and demanded immediate action.

As April drew to a close, student demonstrations continued, involving ever greater numbers, the use of Molotov Cocktails by the protesters and tear gas by the security forces. The signs did not look good. Or, maybe they did!

CHAPTER FOUR

Pius blows
the whistle

After the April 26, 1998 revelations of Pius Lustrilanang, political life in Indonesia would never be the same again. Pius was a young
activist beaten, electrocuted and blindfolded, while being held prisoner
incommunicado for two months, after being kidnapped by an unknown
group from a downtown Jakarta street. Pius alleged that his hijackers
were armed with "military-issue pistols".

The details of his case revolted and outraged, provoking, the
'Jakarta Post' on April 29, to write in a leader: "Enough Is Enough." In
the US, Washington called the spate of disappearances of young activists "disturbing" and called for a full-scale Government inquiry. Fourteen
political activists, like Pius, had disappeared since February when students began agitating against the form of the planned March meeting of
the People's Consultative Assembly. Even after the Assembly had returned Soeharto to power for a seventh term the vendetta against the
activists continued.

The day of Pius's revelations was a day to remember. Before
the March election of a new vice-president, hopes had been expressed
that B. J. Habibie, if elected, might help steer the nation towards the
democracy it craved. On the very day of Pius's shocking disclosures
Habibie announced his master plan for the future - remarkably and de-

pressingly like the New Order's political prescriptions for the past 30 years.

Ironically, at the top of Habibie's list of reforms was human rights. This was followed by: development of Pancasila democracy and a more responsive Government attitude to rising political aspirations; development of the rule of law; development of education and, finally, equal opportunities for all. The vice president was quoted in the 'Jakarta Post' as saying that the New Order Government had always been " a bulwark of reform, manifested in various laws and decrees." Many doubted this. As much as anything else the Vice President's doubters were victims of the subjective and partisan nuances to which words can fall victim. Made at a time when the shadow of Soeharto had been removed, the same words could be made to carry a different meaning and to reflect more sincerity. With the benefit of hindsight parts of the blueprint seemed to reflect the real Habibie struggling to make himself heard, for example, in respect of accommodating popular aspirations, safeguarding human rights and a general sense of egalitarianism.

As expressed by Soeharto's vice-president, the promise to develop democracy sounded remarkably like previous hollow promises of openness, made virtually throughout the 90s. Other promised reforms, such as to human rights and the law, left people wondering whether they could really be achieved without deep-going political change. Improved education, with which everyone agreed, had been one of Habibie's hobby horses for years, especially coupled with the need to develop technology. The phrase, to be "more responsive to rising political aspirations" would later be expanded by the President himself.

The vice-president's reform plan was announced at a meeting of alumni of the Bandung Institute of Technology, which was asked to follow up. The alumni added a reform of their own: a solution to the economic crisis which had pole-axed Indonesia since June 1997. While Pius gave his statement "at the risk of death," major sectors of the economy remained on standstill, the problem of Indonesia's offshore private debt remained unsolved and even seemed to be increasing as hundreds of new debtors were discovered, the banking system was still very shaky and the spectre loomed of "massive" unemployment and, with it, of social unrest.

Students, the intelligentsia and wide swathes of the urban population had blamed the economic crisis on the New Order Government's alleged ineptitude and corruption. One commentator, sociologist, Loekman Soetrisno, in his column in the 'Jakarta Post,' had earlier called on the Government to apologize to the people.

The gruesome and horrifying disclosures of Pius Lustrilanang swept aside a veil previously screening from the people what were widely thought to be secret activities of the New Order Government. In the kidnapping and torture, Government critics thought could be perceived the same kind of moral decay they felt lay behind the economic crisis and the failure to safeguard the lives and health of the thousands suffering from raging forest fires.

In a statement on April 30, the National Commission on Human Rights said: " Based on the accounts of those who have returned, we can conclude that the abductions were carried out by a well organized group. There is now a growing perception among the public that there is a possibility that the state security apparatus was involved." The Commission called for an immediate and thorough investigation and for punishment of the culprits.

Fortuitously, at the same time that Pius was making his statement, Lieutenant General (retired) Bambang Triantoro, Chairman of the National Brotherhood Foundation, called for a special plenary meeting of the People's Consultative Assembly (MPR) to discuss political reform, especially the issues raised by student demonstrators. Having completed its work on March 11 the Assembly was not due to meet again for five years.

For decades, the people of Indonesia had lived in fear of their Government, lived in fear of speaking out, had kept their hands clamped firmly over their mouths - so long as the Government kept economic growth and incomes rising. Now, both were falling, to the point where many feared that they would soon not be able to afford to eat. Who else would speak out? And with what political consequences?

The national leadership of the Armed Forces and the police (ABRI) were prompt to deny that their high commands had ordered any abductions of civilians. But, surprisingly, Armed Forces spokesman, Brig. Gen. Abdul Wahab Mokodongan, also said that the military had no interest in questioning the returnees! Minister of Defence and Security Affairs, Armed Forces Commander, General Wiranto, was quoted by the 'Jakarta Post' on April 30 as saying: "There has been no policy or order from ABRI to abduct certain individuals in the political arena." Of course, it could well have been true that ABRI's high command had issued no orders to abduct activists. But in a force where individual officers owed their promotion to personal favouritism and selection rather than to the natural workings of the military's internal command structure, anything

140

could be possible in any combination. On April 30, the 'Indonesian Observer' reported: " However, Mokodongan has not ruled out the possibility that certain persons within the Armed Forces are deliberately attempting to discredit ABRI by kidnapping activists." The interesting part of his statement was the phrase: "attempting to discredit ABRI." Were the actions part of a plot? By whom? If ABRI's high command was discredited was someone else hoping to take over?

Subsequently, it emerged that another missing activist, Andi Arief, a member of the outlawed People's Democratic Party, had been handed over to the National Police headquarters three weeks after being kidnapped as Pius had been. He was "found" there in a cell. The police were quoted by the 'Jakarta Post' as saying that they felt there was no need for any explanation to be given about the 'find.' A spokesman for the National Police Detective Corps was quoted as saying: "You have to understand that the police could not reveal all the facts for security reasons." Were other facts also being withheld for security reasons? What kinds of legitimate reasons justified kidnappings and torture? Unknown persons, suspected of being military, handing over activists like Andi to the national police eventually fell into a pattern - a pattern deeply resented by police commanders who, like many in ABRI as a whole, wanted to act like real professionals, protecting the innocent and using evidence to bring the guilty to account.

Over the years, in the wake of protests and demonstrations and, sometimes, even without them, individuals either taking part in protests or linked to political organizations considered radical by the regime had "gone missing." Some, like the young female labour activist, Marsinah, had been killed, in Marsinah's case, in May, 1993, horribly and obscenely. She had led young women workers in a fight to earn more in a country paying among the lowest wages in the region.

On April 29, quoting from President Soeharto's memoirs: " My Thoughts, Sayings And Deeds," the Jakarta Post refereed in a leader to mysterious killings of anti-social elements in the early 1980s. Said the 'Post:' "The veil was lifted on the mystery when President Soeharto disclosed in his authorized autobiography that "the Government had resorted to the measure because the criminals had acted beyond any sense of humanity." What was the 'Post' trying to say? Were there implications, pointers?

Pius was Secretary General of what was described as a loose organization of supporters of Government critics, Megawati Sukarnoputri and Amien Rais as well as leader of the People's Alliance for Democracy. Another activist who went missing but later turned up was Haryanto Taslam, Secretary General of the Indonesian Democratic Party faction loyal to ousted leader, Megawati Sukarnoputri.

During his two months captivity, Pius met other activists held in a cell similar to his own. The activists included: Rahardjo Waluyo Djati, Faisol Riza, Herman Hendrawan of the National Committee for Democratic Struggle, a group said to be affiliated with the People's Democratic Party (PRD), human rights lawyer Desmon Mahesa and Haryanto Taslam, Yani Avri and Sonny, supporters of the ousted faction of the PDI led by Megawati Sukarnoputri.

In seeking to identify the kidnappers, one wondered how many private organizations or individuals would have access to "cells." Or who were walking around with "military-issue pistols." National Commission on Human Rights member, Samsudin was quoted as saying: "I am sure that the kidnappings were not ordered by top security policy makers." But, the 'Jakarta Post added that Samsudin said that the kidnappers methods were familiar to him because of his "experience in the Indonesian military."

For 25 years, after inheriting power in the wake of a bloody communist repression which followed the brutal murder of six army generals, the New Order Government's approach to those who held opinions about the organization and running of the state different to its own was called the "security approach." After 1988, the security approach remained, but was accompanied by a state ideology, Pancasila. The idea behind Pancasila was that Indonesians should behave politically like one big family - like a traditional village, in fact. They should identify issues, discuss them and make and implement decisions - together. There was held to be no need of and great danger in having a multiplicity of political parties.

All might have been well had the institutions of government, which Pancasila in some sense bound together, worked well - but they didn't. For traditional and political reasons, decisions seemed to flow only one way - from the top down. At the top, the ruling party exercised preponderant power, its bureaucracy seemed unchallengable. Within the ruling party the executive wielded preponderant power. Within the executive, presidential power seemed absolute. Those who reached decisions affecting the people were not always considered representative of those for whom they claimed to speak. They were not always considered the best or most able representatives. The decision making and implementing process could be skewed this way or that by the power of connections and or money. Dissenting opinion could find little redress in this process.

As the 1990s progressed, education expanded, the intelligentsia expanded, wealth increased and the middle class were soon said to account for between 12 and 15 percent of urban populations. More people wanted to behave professionally, efficiently and, above all justly. They also wanted to be treated fairly. There were the beginnings of meritocracy in the classes around and beneath the government and above the urban and rural masses. Yet the political system didn't work that way and frustrations and resentments grew. People felt that they couldn't speak out because of the risk of punishment through the "security approach." They felt that even if they spoke out their opinions wouldn't count. There developed a restless feeling that the only way that professional excellence, fairness and professional and political empowerment could be achieved was through genuine reform, with all its risks. For the most part, such feelings were suppressed and it was near universally accepted that in Indonesia politics didn't exist - only economics and development. "That's politics. We mustn't talk about that," became a familiar refrain.

The near-collapse of Indonesia's economy in 1997 seems to have forced more middle class people to say publicly that the New Order Government had glaring faults. The "common people," too, held similar opinions which they could express with great violence in private. But until April, 1998, few were willing to take to the streets for fear of the "security approach."

The "security approach" had, in reality, long ago worn out its necessity. The communists were beaten, and despite frequent reminders to the nation to be watchful, the children of the communists showed few signs of wanting to follow in their parent's footsteps - especially with the demise of the Soviet Union and the conversion of most of the old communist world, including the People's Republic of China, to market economics. Yet any who spoke up against the political realities, especially in favour of greater Western-style democracy, were often branded as communists or, at the very least, destabilizing and subversive elements.

The New Order Government's approach to politics has been unwavering. Priority should be given to economics, development and related matters; politics should be conducted only in line with the 1945 Constitution and with Pancasila. Somewhere along the line, as the alleged custodian of the one and only true way for Indonesia, the regime also seems to have decided to maintain itself in power, at all costs. Was the alleged kidnapping by the state of political activists part of this policy? The activists certainly thought so. They did not identify who their abductors were and international and domestic opinion was left to conjecture that they could have been members of clandestine military or paramilitary units or, alternatively, even renegade units.

But, times had changed. Whichever organization or whatever individual had ordered the abductions now did so in the full glare of international publicity. What could perhaps pass unnoticed amid the steamy archipelagic jungles of equatorial Asia 50 years ago, was today the subject or more or less instant international reaction and even outcry. And the people themselves were not nearly so timid and submissive as of yesteryear.

The 'Indonesian Observer" quoted Let. Gen. (ret) Bambang Triantoro as saying that the kidnappers had surely lost contact with reality. "What's happening in Jakarta can also be seen and heard in Washington and Europe." He was quoted as saying that the kidnappings had seriously tarnished Indonesia's pride. "We have no more pride as a nation," he was quoted as saying.

Pius disturbed foreign observers of Indonesia as no other activist had. He has not simply disappeared; he had not become invisible; he was not anonymous and unknown. When Pius spoke his hurt could be seen and felt; he was real. A suspicion that many foreigners, especially those doing business in Indonesia, had long forced to the back of their minds, had now been given disturbing confirmation. Pius described a clear-cut case of human rights abuse which could not be ignored. People had to take a position. Decent people had to feel revulsion.

Justice Minister, Muladi, was instantly in the international spotlight. Muladi, who is also a member of the National Commission on Human Rights, called for a thorough investigation and also for a public explanation from the military. The ambassadors of the United States, the United Kingdom, the European Union, the Netherlands and Austria all sought an explanation from him. In a strong statement from Washington, State Department spokesman, James Foley, was quoted by the 'Jakarta Post' as saying: " The United States Government deplores the practice of torture and the practice of disappearances. We call on the Government of Indonesia to conduct a full investigation into the serious allegations made by this individual." Foley added that Washington was also deeply concerned about other disappearances. He was quoted as saying ominously, "We have raised this issue at high levels with the Government of Indonesia and will continue to pursue the matter until the cases are resolved."

For years, the US had been nagging the New Order Government to improve its human rights record. As a cosmetic, the Government established a Human Rights Commission. Could anyone seriously imagine the Commission challenging the Government? Now, appalling evidence of human rights abuse had spoken out in Jakarta. Indonesia could never be the same again.

Pius received immediate invitations to visit Germany, the UK and the US. Who could doubt that he would divulge every last detail of his ordeal to all ready to listen.

In Tokyo, US Secretary of State, Madeline Albright took the US criticism of Indonesia's Government a step further. The 'Jakarta Post' quoted her as saying: " In democracies like Thailand and South Korea, newly elected governments have been able to start work (on economic reforms) with a clean slate, in a climate of openness, and with the legitimacy to call for shared sacrifice. Indonesia has had a harder time, at least in part because it lacks similar public participation in decision making. There is also a growing recognition that sound economic policies are far more likely where governments are accountable, where the press is free, and the courts independent."

Back in January, when the rupiah had crashed to Rps 17,000 to the US dollar, the British 'Economist' said in a leader: " ...the man whose 32-year rule has taken Indonesia from a scattering of unstable, poverty-stricken islands to a prosperous regional power is not credible as the man who must now take it through its next stage of development. Rigidity and autocracy may have served to consolidate Indonesia; flexibility and democracy are now needed to safeguard its unity and allow its growth to continue. If Mr. Soeharto was once the solution, he is now a large part of the problem."

On May 1 the 'Jakarta Post' had quoted Mulyana Kusumah, a member of the Indonesian Legal Aid and Human Rights Association, as saying that it was: "time for the people to take action," to form a "clean" government and to uphold democracy and law. He was quoted as saying: "People's power is needed to strengthen the student movement to demand total reform, even if it means paying a high price."

Former Armed Forces Commander in the Sukarno years, A. H. Nasution was quoted by the 'Jakarta Post' as saying that he was pleased " to see the young generation making their voices heard." He was quoted as saying: " I'm very happy. They shouldn't back down. I believe that they truly grasp what is being felt by the people." Nasution was a long-standing critic of the New Order Government and a member of the Petitisi 50 Group of mainly retired military personnel who shared his views. Other commanders were quoted as saying that debate and even dissent was only "normal" in a democratic society.

People in high places took note. To some, like President Soeharto, the student voices must have sounded all too similar to those which had been instrumental in toppling the Sukarno regime in the mid-60s with their demands for a change of cabinet and lower prices - voices which Soeharto and his supporters had promoted and encouraged to fever pitch. A switch of name and date and little seemed to have changed - except one thing - who now was behind these new voices? Who now was stirring up the students, encouraging them, facilitating them? As in the 60's, could the hand of a new generation of ABRI be detected? Time and events would tell.

Soeharto had hand-picked ABRI's senior officers, with members of his own family placed in key commands. If serving ABRI officers were backing the students he should have known. Nasution's comment was unequivocal but he was not a serving officer. If senior ABRI officers as a whole were backing the students they were being extremely careful about choosing the words they used to show their sympathies. While trying to be progressive, they had to be seen to remain loyal. Perhaps one man was suspicious, the President's son-in-law, Let. Gen. Prabowo, then commander of the elite 40,000 strong Army Strategic Reserves Command or KOSTRAD. Who knows what suspicions and concerns he may have raised at any of his many "family" meetings with his father-in-law? Did he allege that some elements serving in ABRI were overly soft on the reformers? Without doubt he did, but this was not news to Soeharto. He had know for a decade that there were elements in ABRI who not only favoured reform but favoured getting rid of him! Always, he had been able to retain control.

Soeharto had never been one of the ABRI elite and, like Prabowo after him, there were many professional soldiers who resented his rise to and clinging to power. Over the years, those who had dared voice their displeasure while serving had been shunted aside. Prabowo's rise had been meteoric and bred much resentment. Especially resented was the fact that he reported directly to President Soeharto rather than through the chain of command. Soeharto's divide and rule tactics within ABRI were doubly resented by the new generation whose credentials were not only that they were revolutionary fighters but who had passed through the military academy and therefore saw themselves as professionals.

146

Soeharto knew that ABRI contained elements that would dump him if they could, so he had to create loyal bases of his own. His strategy was to balance pro-reform elements with others, like Prabowo, absolutely loyal to him. Knowing how far to let the reformers go and to what extent to unleash the forces of repression was a delicate call. It was also a call which required the two elements, the reformists and the conservatives. If it was necessary to have power to check the reformers it was also necessary to have the reformers around to check possible excesses of those most loyal to him. The appointment of General Wiranto, a fair minded, professional, fitted this strategy exactly. In the cabinet he had appointed Muladi Justice Minister, a man highly regarded for his insights and fairness. As a progressive, Muladi was, in turn, balanced by conservative elements. Later, the two men would work closely together and be seen constantly sitting side by side, two fair-minded men, two lawyers.

From President Soeharto's point of view, despite the rising cacophony of protest, if the dialogue, opened March/April, between the Armed Forces (ABRI) and the students could lead to a channeling of student demands into the approved political process, and if the economic reforms being undertaken by the Government, improved economic conditions and prospects, there seemed still to be a chance that the New Order Government and its leader could weather the economic and political storms raging around it. Better to channel the aspirations of the reformers into patterns acceptable to the New Order than to use force to repress them. We can all too easily imagine this line of reasoning from General Wiranto. Predident Soeharto apparently saw no reason to disagree and having decided to employ guile rather than force, he waved the hard liners in ABRI temporarily behind him.

Even though President Soeharto wanted to be seen to be bending with the wind he seemed also to see a necessity for restating the political ground-rules as he saw them. Winds were unpredictable and could turn to uncontrollable storms unless harnessed carefully. On May 1, for the first time since 1968, the President summoned all political leaders and leaders of factions in the House of Representatives. Subsequent events showed that the President was intent on delivering two messages: one that political change should only be sought by constitutional means and the second that constitutional means **could** be used to prepare for political reforms - although enactment could only be substantially after 2003. Amendments to electoral laws were an exception.

ABRI appears to have been listening closely. They never took any action except by constitutional means and all their brainstormings and dialogues could be justified as a legitimate element in the process of preparing for change.

The reason for the 2003 deadline, the President was quoted as saying, was that he had been mandated in March, 1998, to carry out the latest agreed State Policy Guidelines which would only expire when his next term of office expired in 2003. Therefore, logically, reformers could only plan their changes as part of the next state Guidelines, for the period 2003 to 2008. Since this was the case, by implication, there was also no point recalling the people's Consultative Assembly. To the student demonstrators all this sounded like more of the kind of sophistry they had been fed for years. While trying to calm unrest by appearing to promise political change, the President sought to maintain the support of the bureaucracy by ordering minimum wages raised by 15 percent from May 1.

The media generally picked up only one of the President's two thoughts and the headline on a leader in the 'Indonesian Observer' seemed to sum that up best: "The President Says No." At first, the news seemed to be greeted by public silence. The President's comments were made on the eve of Labour Day weekend and, during the holiday, Indonesia's political stage seemed unusually quiet. There was next to no mention of Indonesia in the international press.

But the President was swift to act again before the silence was broken - perhaps by more student protests. As much as anyone, perhaps more so, President Soeharto realized fully the forces ranged against him, understood clearly that those forces were exceptionally and dangerously close to an expression of peoples power, perhaps an unstoppable expression. He knew that an unequivocal 'no' to political change was NOT what Indonesians wanted to hear. No fewer than two ministers were therefore dispatched to host a special press conference on Saturday, May 2, to emphasize the second of the President's points made to the leaders of political factions and organizations. A statement was also read verbatim by television newsreaders, presumably compulsorily. The President wanted to take no chances of being misinterpreted again.

Information Minister, Alwi Dahlan and Home Affairs Minister, R. Hartono told the media: "We want to straighten out reports suggesting that the President rejects political reforms until the year 2003." Minister Alwi was quoted in the 'Jakarta Post' as saying: "There is a slight misunderstanding if we observe newspaper headlines today and wire services last night. These reports portrayed the President as being opposed to any reform until 2003. Just about all reports said this. That is not the case." The two ministers were quoted as saying that the President had not ruled out political change until 2003. On the contrary, they said, extensive political change was on the agenda with the introduction of a new electoral system in time for the next general election in 2002. Constituencies would replace the current system of proportional representation and all members of the Parliament would be elected by the people. In the 1998-2003 Parliament 500 of the 1000 seats were appointed by government.

If all representatives were to be elected by the people, all kinds of developments might follow. But many questions remained. Would candidates for the House of Representatives and the People's Consultative Assembly continue to be screened by the Government? Would only the ruling GOLKAR be charged with the responsibility of organizing general elections? Would more political parties be permitted? Would presidential power remain supreme? Would the People's Consultative Assembly continue to meet every five years with no real ability to influence events or to influence or control the president or the executive. Was there any prospect of the 1945 Constitution, from which these arrangements in part flowed, being re-written?

While politicians and political thinkers might have been asking these questions the students were not impressed. Not at all impressed. On May 2, in a front page report, the 'Jakarta Post' said; "Demands for sweeping political and economic reforms have grown to a deafening pitch with students, joined by critics and noted political figures, holding rallies daily." The economy was in ruins. In the wake of Pius Lustrilanang students and society were outraged that their government was apparently so "rotten." The usually tame Parliament demanded that the Armed Forces immediately "seriously investigate" not only the case of Pius but the cases of all the allegedly "missing" activists. Pending the response, there was a profound feeling that nothing the Government said or promised could be believed. Pius's shocking revelations went far toward further poisoning overseas opinion toward President Soeharto, making economic cooperation with him less and less likely. In the minds of many foreign leaders a thread linked human rights abuses in Timor and other parts of the country with the repression of trade unions, the smothering of true democracy and freedom and the abuse and murder of activists with a regime that had become vile with immorality, greed and venality. There was a coalescence of opinion that the leader of this regime and

149

the regime's architect and chief operating officer had to be forced to step down.

May 2 was a Saturday which would mark a milestone in the course of the student demonstrations. Within hours of the President's apparent closing of the door to the immediate reforms being demanded, and virtually even as his ministers rushed to try to modify this wholly negative impression, the students turned out again to demand immediate and total reform - the People's Consultative Assembly must be recalled, the cabinet must be reshuffled, the President and Vice President must resign, corruption, collusion and nepotism must be weeded out from government and exterminated, there must be wholesale economical, political and legal reforms aimed at transforming Indonesia into an efficient, just and respected society, prices must be reduced.

Professor Deliar Noer from the National University was quoted as saying that waiting until 2003 to implement reforms was tantamount to "inviting disaster." Casting doubt directly on the Government's sincerity Noer was quoted as saying: " For example, the Government must guarantee that there will be no more disappearances of activists. This does not require a new law." Rallies were held at universities across Indonesia and dozens of students were injured in clashes with security forces. Protests were reported from Sulawesi, Java and Sumatra.

Sociologist, Slamet Soetrisno, from Yogyakarta's Gadjah Mada University was quoted as saying: "The undercurrent movements now are very strong and radical. Those who are participating in the demonstrations are now not just students but labourers." He called upon Parliament to have the courage to make the President accountable for his actions. Political commentator, Wimar Witoelar, was quoted as saying that the 1966 student demonstrations, which brought the New Order to power, were "only supported by the army" whereas today's enjoyed "greater public support." On May 4, the 'Jakarta Post' would report that alumni from 48 universities and institutions had "thrown their weight behind student rallies for reform." The alumni urged " all members of society to join the student movement in order to force the Government to initiate total reform and eliminate the causes of the crisis." With the fate of Pius and other activists fresh in their minds, the alumni also agreed to establish a network to aid families of any who might "go missing" in the future.

In Medan, especially, the protests had turned violent and on May 4, after a student demonstration, there were reports of looting and burning by non-student mobs, described by the security forces as "criminal." Under cover of the student demonstrations, large numbers of ordinary poor people had seized the opportunity to steal food, supplies and consumer durables from local shops, mainly owned by Indonesian Chinese. Many of the shops were burned. Ethnic Chinese who could afford to, streamed out of Medan across the Strait of Malacca to sanctuary in Penang, Malaysia. President Soeharto ordered Armed Forces commander General Wiranto to take tougher action. Ugly stories later surfaced of members of security forces intimidating and raping female students.

On Tuesday, May 5, after a meeting with President Soeharto, Wiranto described the demonstrations as now "bordering on anarchy" and warned that the military would crack down. At this stage it was not known whether these words were his own or Seoharto's. Over the weekend the military had already begun to take a more repressive line with rioters and demonstrators, so much so that on Monday, May 4, four major student organizations had demanded a public apology from General Wiranto for the military's handling of the weekend protests. The organizations were the Association of Moslem Students, the Association of Indonesian Catholic Students, the Indonesian National Students' Movement and the Indonesian Christian Students' Movement.

While tougher action was promised and taken against rioters and demonstrators, at the same time, the hand of New Order beneficence was extended - the President ordered Ministry of Education officials and university rectors to assist with special scholarships up to 400,000 students facing financial difficulties as a result of the economic crisis. A few days later, students were excused from paying increases in transport fares. The Association of Indonesian Moslem Intellectuals (ICMI) promptly condemned this largesse as unwanted "charity."

Markets and foreign observers smelt danger: if the students continued demonstrating and, if the security forces exerted more force, the impression created among investors would be very negative. If lawless sections of the community continued their rampages, the impression would also be very negative. In a report of a fall in securities prices on May 4, the 'Jakarta Post' said: " The President's order to the military to curb any attempt to undermine national stability suggests that the Armed Forces might use force to suppress the demonstrations." An analyst was quoted as saying: "It could worsen political tensions." Two days earlier, in Medan, the media reported that student demonstrators had been checked, using "tear gas, rubber bullets and armoured cars." Now this type of crackdown had spread to Jakarta. Observers were even more doubtful. The most likely outcome of this kind of 'check' was that the students would increase their pressure.

The student demonstrations had continued for many months, with intermittent but generally increasing intensity. More importantly, the students demands had been supported by exceptionally large numbers of lecturers, institution heads and by the intelligentsia. The message was too loud to be ignored and had prompted the President to meet with the leaders of all factions and political groups to see what could be done.

On May 5, the 'Indonesian Observer' carried a report that all the factions of the House of Representatives which had met with the President the week before, would now discuss needed political reforms. Indeed, the President was said to have encouraged them to review the five key political laws upon which Indonesia's current political system was based. Two of the laws to be discussed related to the existence of political parties and the ability of political parties to campaign in the countryside - at the moment only GOLKAR , the ruling party, enjoyed this ability. These laws had been subject to increasing criticism and attempts had been made from time to time to establish new political parties, even though this was impossible under current arrangements.

President Soeharto's invitation to the House to review these fundamental political laws was a watershed by itself. It showed clearly that the times were becoming highly unusual. It also suggested to some members that the executive was pushing a ball to their feet which hadn't been there since the inception of the New Order regime. Taking the bit between their teeth, some members sensed that the power of the House might at last be growing. Here, at last, might be a chance for Indonesia's ossified political system to be cranked into action.

Harassed and sometimes with their leaders in prison, in the political shadows continued to exist the People's Democratic Party, the Indonesian United Democratic Party, led by Sri Bintang Pamungkas, the new Indonesian National Party (PNI Baru), led by Mrs Supeni and a reborn Masyumi Islamic Party. Also in the wings and virtually offstage were the thousands of supporters of ousted Indonesian Democratic Party leader, Megawati Sukarnoputri - thousands because it is clear from the voting in the 1997 General Election that her party's losses were virtually no other party's gains. In other words there were massive abstentions. However, these ghostly electors continued to exist, continued to watch and wait.

The Government clearly hoped that, by showing the students that the President, the executive and the legislature were not only listening to their demands but had been pushed by them to take action, the undergraduates would return to their studies. In fact, on May 6, the 'Indonesian Observer' - part owned by the President's son, Bambang Trihatmodjo - said in an editorial: "As students have now gotten their way, their enthusiasm for holding demonstrations should abate. In popular parlance, they should stop pushing their luck, and get back to where they belong, the university campus, and allow legislators to review the laws." The Government could not have written this better itself.

But at a seminar in Jakarta organized by the National University, the tide of clamour for political change rolled on. If electoral laws were to be revised but other changes could only take place by constitutional means why not review the Constitution itself? The 'Jakarta Post' quoted law professor Harun Alrasid as striking at the very foundation of New Order political life by saying that the 1945 Constitution was vague and needed rewriting. He was quoted as saying: " Reform of the 1945 Constitution is needed if we want to uphold democracy, if we want a democratic government and if we want to empower all high state institutions in accordance to their function." Launching into detail, Professor Harun was quoted as continuing: " ...the Constitution should also clearly specify that all members of the People's Consultative Assembly (MPR) and the House of Representatives (DPR) should be elected. He was quoted as adding: "The new constitution should limit the presidential term of office to only two periods at the most."

National University Law School Dean, A. Dahlan Ranuwihardjo was quoted as saying: "Freedom of speech, openness, human rights and freedom of association should be respected in creating a conducive climate to uphold democracy. People should not be barred from airing their opinions, from criticizing the Government. Students should not be barred from staging rallies in the streets and from going to the DPR and government offices with their aspirations."

Referring to calls for a special emergency session of the MPR to discuss issues troubling the nation, Dahlan was quoted as saying: "During the 30 years of the New Order Government, the House has never said 'no' to wrong policies made by the Government. So, that's why it is unlikely now for the House to call an MPR special session to ask for the Government's accountability of the latest crisis. What the students are demanding in their movement can be seen as an evidence that they are taking over the DPR function."

History was not the only reason for the MPR's likelihood of saying "no". Combined with the People's Consultative Assembly, the Indonesian Parliament had 1,000 seats, 575 appointed personally by the President and 325 from the ruling GOLKAR. Only 10 percent of the Parliamentarians were even in a position to say "no".

The loud demands for total reform, not from students, but from respected professionals and university faculty showed that, in the minds of some, the definition of reform struck at the very fundamentals of the New Order Government and reflected the best Western notions of democracy. They were reforms which went far, far beyond those on offer by the Government and by the President.

The House of Representatives was becoming a laughing stock. Commencing on March 12, its members had taken six weeks leave during the worst economic crisis their country had ever faced. There were loud and frequent demands for an emergency session of both Houses. The House of Representatives had allowed leadership to pass into the hands of the students and academics. While the people suffered they were on holiday. Even had members been sitting, the public belief was that they would only do whatever the Government and the President told them.

After the long break, picking up on the President's invitation to review the electoral process, House Speaker, Harmoko, promised that members would propose swift revisions to "unfavourable" laws. The 'Indonesian Observer' quoted Harmoko as saying that the House would "actively accommodate the public's demands for (political) reforms by enacting several new laws, while doing away with any laws which are considered out of date. Earthshatteringly, he was quoted as adding: "And we'll initiate our own drafts of required laws, instead of just accommodating the drafts provided by the Government." This was reform indeed! The House was known popularly as a "lame duck" and a "rubber stamp" for the Government. Now, according to Harmoko it was going to stand up, speak out and, by implication, fight. At this stage it was not clear whether this was a rearguard action of President Soeharto's and his loyal supporters in GOLKAR, including Harmoko, or whether there was the germ of real independence. Time would tell. It looked suspiciously like a rearguard action, an attempt to defuse the protests.

An important thread running through the student demonstrations and the comments of Government critics had been the uselessness of the Parliament in the face of executive and presidential power. Could it have been that the House members were beginning to feel the hot flames of reform and perhaps even of revolution licking around their seats? Was there a growing sense that unless they went with the popular flow the flow would flood over them, sweeping them away, perhaps unpleasantly? It certainly seemed that way. The more intense and threatening the demonstrations became the more accommodating and reform minded the Parliament seemed to become.

Harmoko was also quoted as promising a review of the structure and composition of the People's Consultative Assembly and the House of Representatives, a review of the laws on political parties and GOLKAR, the floating mass system (in which citizens can vote once in five years but must otherwise eschew political activity and in which pol;itical groups, other than GOLKAR, may operate only in designated urban areas), and general elections." It suddenly seemed as if ' everything was up for grabs.' No more 'sacred cows.'

If words were to be taken at face value, what was being proposed was truly momentous. Of course, the promise was only for reviews. The culmination could be change or, depending on circumstances, a reaffirmation of the status quo. The House Speaker went on to clothe the Government's ideas about political reform in the very words used by student demonstrators. The protesters were demanding political, economic and legal reform. Harmoko had already outlined plans for political reforms. Now he added: "Economic reforms will be enacted through revisions to the anti-monopoly law, the consumer protection law and the banking law" - these were basically the demands of the IMF and really nothing radical. Harmoko went on: " ...legal reforms will be accomplished through revisions in the anti-subversion law and the anti-corruption law - corruption, nepotism and collusion being major planks of the students' campaigns.

Much of it at least sounded promising - political, economic and legal reform. But were these the wholesale, top-to-bottom reforms demanded by the protesters? Did it add up to real, substantive, empowerment of the people's freely elected representatives, under circumstances of free speech and press? Did it add up to the creation of an independent and corruption-free legal system? Did it add up to political and economic management free of corruption, collusion and nepotism? Or was it only a shadow play, a game of words?Subsequent student and public reaction would provide the answers.

While political reform was being promised by the Government in Jakarta, Pius Lustrilanang was hard at work in The Netherlands. Associated Press quoted Pius as saying in Amsterdam: "I want to campaign for international sympathy for my case and stop the kidnappings and illegal detentions that are going on." Pius said he had plans to visit the European Parliament, the US Congress and leaders and human rights officials in London, Paris, Bonn, Dublin. He was quoted as saying: " I believe that the struggle of Indonesia's pro-democratic elements will succeed. Pius was also thought likely to report his case to the United Nations Commission on Human Rights, exposing the Government of Indonesia to the possibility of a condemnatory resolution.

In the wake of Pius, the Chief of the Indonesian Intelligence Coordination Agency, (BAKIN) announced that the Government would set up a fact finding team to investigate the mysterious disappearances of political activists. Puzzleingly, at the same time, Armed Forces spokesman, Wahab Mokodongan was quoted by the 'Indonesian Observer' as saying that "the military knows who is responsible for the kidnappings but wants the National Police to deal with the matter. The police said that they could not investigate unless they had evidence...... Both military and police apparently knew of the disappearance of Pius at a very early date. The daily Indonesian language "Merdeka' said that Pius's parents had informed both organizations within a week of their son's disappearance. Up to the beginning of May, no reply had been received.

In an editorial, the 'Jakarta Post' said: "Under present circumstances, only a full, thorough and open investigation can help restore the feeling of insecurity and confidence among Indonesians, including those who feel duty-bound to express views that differ from those expressed by the Government. No less important, such measures would also effectively counterbalance any unfounded negative accusations that are made abroad against the Indonesian Government." The daily quoted a statement from the National Commission on Human Rights as saying: " ...forced disappearances are a terrible abuse of human rights. Given that the victims were taken beyond the reach of legal protection, the actions (of the kidnappers) amounted to a violation of human values. They caused suffering on the part of the victims and their families, spread fear among society and tarnished the image of the nation. In principle, a forced disappearance is a violation of civil rights and freedom, and a comprehensive and total denial of the norms and order of civilized politics. Based on the accounts of those who have, we can conclude that the abductions were carried out by a well organized group. There is now a growing perception among the public that there is a possibility that the state security apparatus was involved."

Political unrest in Indonesia had been fired by the economic crisis. At the beginning of May there was optimism in Government circles that Indonesia would meet the reform targets set by the IMF and that important doors would be unlocked once disbursements from the Fund began. But the economic crisis was by no means over. In fact, Reuters had quoted the Asian Development Bank's, Vice President, Bong Suh-lee, as saying on the last day of April that: "The worst it still to come this year for South Korea, Indonesia and Thailand. Unemployment in these countries will grow. Things will get worse before they get any better."

One of the ways in which they could get worse in Indonesia was if the Government went ahead with plans to reduce subsidies for fuel and electricity. On April 29, Minister of Mines and Energy, Kuntoro Mangkusubroto announced that this would indeed be the case. He was quoted as saying: " We are waiting for the President's approval for the price rises. I think the signal will come soon."

There were other causes of economic alarm. In connection with the Government's budget, market reports showed that the price of OPEC oil had momentarily slipped below US$13 per barrel and that Brent was down at close to US$14 per barrel. The forecast in Indonesia's state budget for 1998-99 had been that the price of oil would average US$14.50 per barrel. Any further reduction in the price of oil would be decidedly unhelpful.

Meanwhile, Finance Minister, Fuad Bawazier, announced that he expected inflation to be contained at 20 percent in the fiscal year while rising to 40 percent in the calendar year; it had risen to almost 25 percent in the first three months of 1998 alone. The expectation was that the rate would fall in the first quarter of 1999. Price increases could trigger social unrest as nothing else. Many eyes were watching the Government's next moves as well as changes in the cost of living index. What happened throughout the year might turn out to be politically cru-cial.

Markets were adopting a wait and see attitude regarding a num-ber of key questions. Despite loud and frequent Government assertions that the IMF's reforms were under way and on time, cynics continued to doubt. Progress in the banking sector was not assisted when Standard & Poor said on April 29 that Indonesia was proceeding too slowly, a statement hotly disputed by Indonesian leaders. The Agency said that at over 200 institutions, there were still far too many banks, many of them weak, including some of the eight recently released from the care of the Bank Restructuring Agency (IBRA). Standard & Poor was quoted by the 'Jakarta Post' as saying that "all Indonesian banks were dramati-cally undercapitalized, with massive asset-quality problems that were not expected to stabilize in the short-term. The Agency was quoted as describing Indonesia's efforts to reform its banking system as "lacklustre" and bedevilled by the belief that "all financial institutions should be protected, regardless of their economic viability." Fuad Bawazier, in effect, replied that in his opinion, banking reforms were proceeding very rapidly. The Coordinating Minister for Economic, Financial and Development Supervision, Ginandjar Kartasasmita added that there was no truth in the allegation that the Government was in any way reluctant to close weak banks. The Minister was quoted as confirming that there would be no "backtracking." The markets waited and watched.

Meanwhile, ahead of the May 8 Tokyo meeting of the offshore debt steering committee, Radius Prawiro, the head of Indonesia's private debt restructuring team (IDRA) revealed that up to 1,800 companies had reported offshore debt totalling US$67.69 billion, US$8.9 billion of which was owed by banks. At this stage, it was not revealed how much was short-term. Progress in solving the offshore debt issue was regarded as crucial for the solvency of Indonesia's corporates and banking system and market activity remained quiet pending the outcome of this third round of talks between representatives of Indonesian debtors and their overseas lenders in Tokyo. Analysts were not optimistic.

With doubts about the debt and the banking system continuing and fears increasing of social and political unrest arising from price hikes, despite the Government's obvious progress in implementing the IMF's reforms, there was still plenty of gloom around. It probably didn't help much when, on April 30 the IMF was quoted widely in the domestic media as saying that it had misjudged Indonesia's crisis. Bijan Aghelvi, Deputy Head of the IMF's Asia and Pacific region was quoted by the 'Indonesian Observer' as having said: " At the beginning we thought it was a pure contagion effect, which is ironic as Indonesia's problems have been much worse than other countries in the region. We thought that a strong macroeconomic programme would fix the problem."

The IMF's misunderstanding of the situation in Indonesia and its repeated recommendation of measures which provided no immediate solution to the problem of the collapsing rupiah had brought the Fund and the Government of Indonesia close to confrontation in the first weeks of 1998. When the Government seemed to be flirting with the possibility of a Currency Board to halt the decline of the rupiah, international condemnation had been loud. Eventually, the Government had caved in to international opinion and plunged into implementing the reforms suggested by the IMF - even though, despite everything, the rupiah stayed remorselessly below pre-crisis levels. Of course it would -

unless there was a solution to the problem which had triggered the problem in June, 1997 - the short-term, foreign debt. And, by May, 1998, solutions to all the ramifications of trying to defend the rupiah - such as cripplelingly high interest rates and bank and corporate insolvency.

Former Australian prime minister, Paul Keating had this to say in the 'Jakarta Post' on May 4: "Indonesia was disproportionately punished (by the markets) because a grossly inaccurate view had taken hold in some quarters in Europe and North America that it was some sort of rogue state. Why did it happen? Why have markets punished Indonesia so much more severely than other Asian countries in demonstrably worse macroeconomic shape? The main reason is that the future of the Indonesian economy became caught up in judgements about its political system."

Keating went on: " Aspects of Indonesia's own response to the crisis contributed to the difficulty. It sent out mixed and sometimes confusing messages as in the uncertainty about the Currency Board proposal. And it has backtracked on some important issues which had symbolic importance internationally. The regrettable truth is that times like these require directness and clarity rather than Javanese obliqueness. Indonesia has not been good at telling its own story.

"The result was that the international goals for dealing with the crisis, and the performance measurements against which Indonesia would be judged, were expanded and restructured to include, explicitly, wholesale economic and social reform and, implicitly, a change in the political leadership. So, the IMF's demands included not just measures to allow orderly economic adjustment but complete reordering of the Indonesian economy. It seized the opportunity to try to impose in one sweep and extensive and obtrusive programme of change. Some of the reforms it demanded were badly needed and will greatly strengthen the Indonesian economy when it recovers. But the Fund has made that recovery more difficult by changing Indonesia's political dynamics and imposing goals which were politically unachievable, and therefore delaying any restoration of confidence.

"It is important to remember that despite Indonesia's rapid growth, it remains a developing economy with serious problems of administrative efficiency - just in getting the Government's writ to run. It ought not to be surprising if it has run into difficulty implementing a complex package of reforms which I doubt that Australia, with a smaller population and better communications, could have put in place in two months."

Ironically, as Indonesia bravely drank the Fund's 'medicine,' including a potion or two of hemlock, the case of Pius raised loud voices saying that Indonesian shouldn't be given even that. Barney Frank, a senior Democrat on the US House Banking Committee was quoted by Reuters as saying of the IMF's delayed but anticipated pay-out to Indonesia: "I think it sends exactly the wrong message to the Indonesian Government and to the opposition in Indonesia." Many in the US Congress had come to feel that good money was being given to bad businessmen throughout Asia. Now it seemed to be being given to a government suspected of torturing and electrocuting its citizens to inhibit democracy. Frank warned that if the IMF's directors went ahead with payments to Indonesia it would "put in jeopardy" Democratic support for a US$18 billion top-up of the Funds depleted coffers.

Should Indonesia be condemned in this way by the US and stonewalled by the IMF, the consequences looked potentially devastating. To head off some of them, President Soeharto sent his Coordinating Minister for Economy, Finance and Industry, Ginandjar Kartasasmita, to Malaysia to request help. The Malaysian Government promised to make a bridging loan available, pending the arrival of the still officially expected IMF cash - funds the Government had been working unusually hard to secure through an energetic programme of economic reforms.

In his May 4 article, Paul Keating went on to comment on the views of cynics that Indonesia would not be able to satisfy the IMF. He wrote: " It was noticeable that, almost before the ink was dry on the January agreement (Indonesia has signed three agreements with the IMF since June, 1997) prominent voices in the United States and Europe were casting doubts on Indonesia's willingness to comply (with IMF demands). This had elements of a self-fulfilling prophecy about it. It undercut, almost immediately, the very confidence the measures were designed to restore."

More interestingly Keating went on: "Some of the commentary we are seeing about Indonesia has a chilling tone to it. Those who argue that the screws should be turned on President Soeharto and the Government because this will somehow force political change show tragically little understanding of what the consequences of widespread unrest in Indonesia would be for real people in the real world.

"The IMF has done its job with good intentions, but I agree with those who argue that it has been the wrong job. Or perhaps the right job, but in the wrong time and manner."

Many of the IMF's policies for Indonesia were irrelevant as solutions to the country's short-term crisis and some, such as the removal of subsidies and high interest rates were beggaring the people and destroying the economy.

The extent of the crisis in Indonesia's economy was deepened further on May 5 by a report from property consultant, Panangian Simanungkalit that bad debt in Indonesia's property sector could reach nearly US$5 billion by the end of 1998. He called for property projects collateralized in local banks to be taken over by an agency similar to the Bank Restructuring Agency so that they could be sold to foreign investors.

At midnight on May 5, the scenario feared equally by government and people came about. Prodded by the IMF, the Government announced step-by-step increases in the prices of fuel and electricity ranging from 25 percent to over 70 percent. 'Bus, train, ferry and airline fares were raised. "How can the people stand such increases," asked one foreign observer. No steps had been taken to prepare the public. No explanations and justifications had been given. No attempt had been made to win the people's support.

News of the price increases hit Indonesians like a bombshell. As they were announced, inflation was reported to have hit 33 percent in the first four months of 1998 and analysts predicted 80 percent in the year - double the projection in the Government's budget, vetted and agreed by the IMF. Since the start of the economic crisis the price of rice had risen 38 percent, cooking oil 110 percent, chicken 86 percent and milk 60 percent. The price of fertilizer rose 12.5 percent in April alone.

In Jakarta, workers and labour activists rallied outside the offices of the All Indonesia Workers Union Federation, demanding the resignation of the Federation's leaders, an increase in minimum wages and price reductions. Government urged profitable companies to raise workers' wages wherever possible. On the very day of the announcement of the price increases thousands of students took to the streets in protest, not only in Jakarta but in Ujung Pandang, Yogyakarta, Surabaya, Bandung, Bogor, Semarang and even Kupang in East Nusa Tenggara. In the wake of the fuel and electricity increases there was a marked new emphasis among the students on slashing prices and holding down inflation, concerns sharply felt by Indonesia's poor. At the same time they continued their campaign against corruption, collusion and nepotism, demanded the recall of the People's Consultative Assembly to discuss the crisis and called for a resolution of the presidential succession issuc.

Meanwhile, even Government critic, Kwik Kian Gie was adamant that the people would have to stand the price hikes. He wrote: " The increases in fuel prices and electricity billing rates are a must." Kwik went on: " If the Government had not raised the fuel and electricity prices, the international community would have accused (them) of not being serious in implementing the economic reform." In the same newspaper a report said: "An alternative to a drastic reduction in the fuel subsidy would be to reschedule payment of the Government's foreign debts."

The House of Representatives was not pleased with the announcement of the price increases complaining that it had not even been properly consulted about the timing. Mines and Energy Minister, Kuntoro Mangkusubroto was summoned by representatives to provide an explanation. House Speaker Harmoko said that the minister would be asked to explain why the Government had ignored an earlier suggestion from the House not to be too hasty in increasing fuel and electricity prices. Harmoko was quoted as saying: " All House factions had told the Minister of Mines and Energy to carefully consider the timing for the regulation of new fuel and electricity prices. But all of a sudden the new price of fuel and electricity was announced by the Minister."

Called before Commission V of the House of Representatives on May 7 to explain the timing and necessity for the increases, Mines and Energy Minister, Kuntoro Mangkusubroto, said he would go but that "The decision was final as far as the Government is concerned." Kuntoro is Javanese and being hauled to account by the Parliament must have been acutely humiliating. From photographs it seemed clear that the Minister's heart was not in his assignment. At times he looked close to cracking up. The parliamentarians were also eager to know why US$12.8 billion had been used to support unhealthy banks while US3.3 billion could not be found to subsidize essentials. Was the banks bailout also not a subsidy? Kuntoro did not comment saying only that the decision was political. It was also economic although, in a perfect world, perhaps not socially just. What would have been worse? Depriving ailing banks and opening the door for more to collapse, perhaps dragging the whole economy down with them? Or, asking for the people's understanding and that they tighten their belts? At this stage, presumably, the Government calculated that however vociferous the students and the "vocal critics" the mass of people would not whip up the courage to revolt.

Ministers are assistants to the president so when talking about 'government' in Indonesia in terms of final decision making one is in

162

reality talking about the President. We can guess that what had happened here was that, despite the House warnings, President Soeharto had felt pressured by the IMF to take a decision he was quite within his rights and powers to take - in consultation with his minister. But times were changing fast. While the minister had no alternative but to do as he was told - or resign - emboldened and perhaps frightened by the ongoing student demonstrations the House clearly felt that it must be seen to be on the side of the people.

Why the increases had had to be made in one go became the subject of debate for weeks to come. The IMF denied that the scale and timing of the increases was under its control. Posing a series of questions in the 'Far Eastern Economic Review' of June 4, a joint article by Michael Vatikiotis and Adam Schwarz asked: " Were certain officials seeking to hasten the inevitable?" Were the price increases too, part of a plot? Had those who wanted to topple Soeharto deliberately fed him the wrong advice, like a cup of poison from the hand of an assumed friend? Said the 'Review:' "Was Soeharto, who suffered a mild stroke last November, becoming befuddled - or simply so out of touch with reality that he was not aware of the gravity of the situation?" Habibie said on June 4, that Soeharto had become "too old to sense the mood of the people." Take your choice!

Two months earlier in the 'Review' Jakarta correspondent, John McBeth, writing together with Salil Tripathi had floated an interesting related idea. The two writers were discussing anti-ethnic Chinese riots which had flared without warning in Kadipaten, West Java. They asked: " Are protesters being incited to deflect the blame for the crisis away from the Government's policies and onto the 3.5 million Indonesian Chinese?" What has this to do with withdrawing subsidies you may ask! The writers continued: " Certainly, that would be playing with fire. But some analysts note that the heat might be useful. With the looming threat that massive unrest over price hikes could destabilize Indonesia, President Soeharto would be in a stronger position to negotiate for an easing of the International Monetary Fund's austerity measures. These analysts see the President's controversial plan to peg the rupiah to the US dollar in the same light: an attempt by Soeharto to strengthen his hand ahead of IMF negotiations over slashing subsidies on fuel and other basic goods." The writers quoted Jardine Fleming's Rajeev Malik as saying: " The compromise will be that Soeharto stays away from the Currency Board and the IMF cuts some slack (on price subsidies)." Was Soeharto really old and fuddled or was the decision to withdraw fuel and

163

electricity prices a calculated gamble?

Minister Kuntoro looked like a man called to his own execution when he duly went to the House to report. The 'Indonesian Observer' quoted the Minister as saying: " ...price rises cannot be postponed, and hopefully we can accept them as a form of sacrifice to be made by all of us in this situation." Events later showed that those called upon to make the sacrifices were dangerously unamused. And the issue of the price increases for the first time pitted parliament against president, a development which was to have dramatic consequences two weeks later when House Speaker Harmoko made a statement affecting the very survival of the President in office, let alone the exercise of his powers.

Even as Minister Kuntoro spoke, The ECONIT Advisory Group on Indonesia (German-Indonesia Chamber of Commerce) issued a statement emphatically denying that raising electricity and fuel prices was the only way to reduce the budget deficit. ECONIT pointed to greatly increased revenues from oil and gas sales as an alternative. The Group warned that the price increases would trigger high inflation which, in turn, would drive Indonesia into deep economic depression. ECONIT urged the Government to postpone the reduction in subsidies until the economy returned to normal. The Group's view was one shared by many. It would be better to take the money from almost anywhere, to borrow it even, rather than take the risk of increasing key prices.

The Government of Indonesia had been in a difficult position. The IMF had insisted that subsidies be withdrawn, although before the signing of the April Agreement it was widely believed that the Fund had agreed to more flexibility regarding timing than had been shown by the Government's announcement. It was generally believed that the Government had at least until October to withdraw the subsidies. Events seemed to suggest that the Indonesian Government was so desperate to impress the IMF that it went too far, too fast. Reflecting the pressure under which the Government of Indonesia was working, as the IMF authorized another, small tranche of funds for Indonesia, White House spokesman, Mike McCurry was quoted as saying: "The aid is in serious jeopardy if he (President Soeharto) doesn't meet the obligations he has to the IMF facility." More or less simultaneously, British Chancellor of the Exchequer, Gordon Brown, arrived in Jakarta bearing an identical message. In 1998, the United Kingdom was also President of the European Union.

The rupiah dived on fears of deepening social unrest, wiping out any gains which the Government might have hoped to accrue to its faithful implementation of the IMF reform package. Jakartans bank-hopping in the capital reported being able to see electronic exchange rate boards changing before their eyes as the rupiah slumped. Already sky-high interest rates were hiked again in its defense, to as high as 58 percent, with the prospect of further increases to come. Commercial bank deposit rates rose to 62 percent. Lending rates would inevitably soar even higher. Analysts generally believed that since the crisis in Indonesia had now gone far beyond financial or fiscal, however high interest rates went was unlikely to benefit the rupiah. Jakarta Stock Exchange dealers reported sales of shares in companies connected with the Soeharto family

Among the lower classes, there really was now a sense of the hopelessness President Soeharto had stressed constantly should be avoided. There was a sense that, however hard and long ordinary Indonesians worked they could never keep up with the price increases. There was a sense among millions more that even to get a job would now be hopeless. The fuel and energy price hike was widely criticized by students, the intelligentsia and legislators. It was predicted that up to 8 million elementary and junior high school pupils would be forced to abandon school because they could not longer afford the fees. Had they a recordable voice, the increases would have been seen to be condemned by just about all Indonesia's so-called common people. Increasing numbers could no longer afford sufficient food. Infant and maternal mortality were forecast to rise due to malnutrition. Interest rates at record levels promised new surges of massive unemployment.

The overall effect of the price hikes in the minds of the average man and woman in the street was that the Government simply didn't care about them. Whether it cared or not, to be seen by the world to be in breech of the latest IMF Agreement might have been to court international condemnation. As President Soeharto left Indonesia for Egypt on May 9, it was clear that Indonesia's master politician was only too well aware that Indonesia had sailed abruptly into uncharted waters. At an uncharacteristic airport press conference, and smiling nervously, he told the people of Indonesia that he had tried to resist the price increases but had been forced to give in to "pressure" - presumably from the IMF. He looked uncomfortable, like a man no longer in charge of his own destiny - or, perhaps, of his own country. There was something shamefaced about him, as if he was doing something that he really didn't want to do and knew would cause suffering. The President said that he had once been poor and that he fully understood the sufferings of Indonesians.

He called for unity, calm and stability in the face of the terrible economic crisis tearing at the country. On the same day, Foreign Minister, Ali Alatas was quoted as saying that Indonesia was " biting the bullet" of economic reform, despite the pain and unrest it was causing. Referring to the campus protests which now embraced the need to slash prices, the Minister went on: "We warned the world and the IMF of the scenes that you see, namely that if one removes subsidies - certain protective mechanisms that have been in place for many years - there will be social shock, perhaps strife. We hope that we will be able to overcome it, to keep it peaceful, through talking to one another, through dialogue, not through violence."

There were many who wondered about the timing of the President's departure. Did he really absolutely have to go? Or was it a calculated absence after which, if mayhem should break out, he could return, restore order and perhaps use the anarchy as the rationale for rolling back the price increases, hopefully with the understanding of the IMF but if not without it? If this was the President's calculation, the plan was destined to go badly awry.

Having failed to prepare the people but fearing their reaction, the Government now went out of its way to assure the public that the state companies providing electricity and fuel to consumers - Pertamina and PLN - would be monitored rigorously to ensure that revenues were being spent efficiently. The media shared this hope. The public mood was not improved by media highlighting of the fact that the Soeharto family and other "connected families" owned shares in two of the three companies responsible for exporting the products of Pertamina, the state oil company. The 'Jakarta Post' said in a leader: " The main question that always arises whenever the prices of basic commodities produced by state companies are raised is whether the companies - in this case Pertamina and the state electricity company (PT PLN) - have maximized their efficiency. For example, there has been a lingering question as to whether such well connected companies as Humpuss, which holds long term contracts for shipping Pertamina's petroleum, petrochemicals and liquefied natural gas, were the most competitive bidders. The Government also needs to explain a recent complaint by PLN chief Djiteng Marsudi that he has often been forced to bow to political interventions in the company's project tenders."

Concealed behind the bad news that fuel and electricity prices would rise was the good news that subsidies on rice, soybeans and basic medicines would be maintained. Although prices of even staples started to "skyrocket" the very next day, Government spokesman said that they were confident each increase would be small and that in the case of fuel and electricity specifically, the impact would inevitably be uneven and some consumers could be expected to exercise their option to reduce unnecessary use and expenditure.

On the day after the announcement of the increases the Government of Indonesia had been publicly seen to be in compliance with the IMF reform programme and its policies. Therefore, there was good news from the IMF. Fund Managing Director, Michel Camdessus recommended that bailout payments be resumed to Indonesia. Ginandjar Kartasasmita later revealed that a total of US$7 billion would be disbursed over three months from the IMF, the World Bank, the Asian Development Bank and also by bilateral donors including, Japan, Australia and Malaysia. It was hoped that bilateral donors such as Singapore and Brunei would now be encouraged to release promised funds to Indonesia.

Reuters quoted Camdessus as saying: "What I observed in Indonesia was an extremely strong commitment on the part of the authorities to stick to the programme. As far as the programme is concerned, all the signals received are for a very strict implementation." Camdessus pointedly described the programme as " the programme of Indonesia," a claim which stretched the credulity of many observers.

At the very same time, photographs appeared in local papers of President Soeharto's youngest son, Hutomo "Tommy" Mandala Putra, officially handing over all rights to his Clove Marketing and Buffer Stock Agency to Minister of Industry and Trade, Mohamad "Bob" Hasan. President Soeharto looked on, presumably hopeful that the drama of the ceremony would finally lay the troublesome ghost of his son's clove monopoly to rest. The disbanding of the monopoly as well as two others, one for plywood previously operated by the new industry minister, had been major demands of the IMF. Camdessus was right. The Government of Indonesia was leaving no stone unturned to accommodate the Fund's suggestions and restore the international confidence now so crucial for economic recovery.

Later, the IMF said that the timing of the withdrawal of subsidies had been left to the Government of Indonesia - implying wide swathes of latitude. In fact, they had stipulated that the subsidies be removed early in the new fiscal year which had begun on April 1. What did "early" mean? Presumably the first quarter! If the subsidies were still in place at the end of the second quarter they would rub right up against the IMF's final October deadline. The IMF's man in Jakarta, Prabakhar Narvekar was quoted as saying on May 5, that President Soeharto had found the decision to claw back the subsidies a "very difficult" one. Ginandjar Kartasasmita had hinted as much on April 30 when he, too, had confirmed that fuel and electricity prices would have to rise. He was quoted as saying that increasing the rates was " a very high political risk at the present time when you have social unrest." Yet President Soeharto went ahead anyway. Ginandjar made clear why. He was quoted as saying: " Indonesia will abide by its understanding with the IMF that fuel and electricity charges will be adjusted in the month of May and early June. It will show the market we're determined to repair our economy and stop the bleeding through (government) subsidies." In other words the President and his senior ministers felt that they had no time to phase in the fuel and electricity increases. It was already May and the subsidies had to be withdrawn by June. Rightly or wrongly they felt that the best way to do it was on one fell swoop.

During the first week of May, Indonesia seemed to face a combination of threats and hopes - threats from the ongoing economic crisis - hopes from IMF support for alleged solutions to the crisis as well as of the President's promise that political reforms could be countenanced. A phrase which seemed to pop up again and again in publications and in conversations was: "what will happen next?"

Would economic deprivations trigger riots - or not? Many increasingly worried observers thought they would. The 'Jakarta Post' quoted the former rector of Parahyangan Catholic University at Bandung, Pande Radja Silalhi, as saying that he thought they probably would. "The monetary crisis plus the student movement demanding political and economic reforms has already brought political stability to the brink. Now the Government raises fuel and electricity prices. This move could jeopardize political stability because it will certainly worsen the hardships faced by the majority of people.." He also pointed out that the price increases were without the endorsement of Parliament.

Would the Government's promise of political reform quieten the protesters - or not? Now that student demands for economic and political reform had embraced price reductions the answer to this was generally thought to be "no." Mistrust of the Government was now total.

Would Indonesia's compliance with the April agreement signed with the IMF be sufficient to restore international confidence in Indonesia? The answer to this was a hopeful "yes" but to the even more crucial question of whether the IMF 'medicine' would work the reply was usually: "we'll have to wait and see." Some even said a blunt "no."

It was clear from the IMF's announcement of further funds for Indonesia, that the Agency's approach remained the restoration of confidence in Indonesia in the long-term - an approach with no hope of solving immediate and concrete issues, such as bad debt. When the new funds were announced in Washington, the most that First Deputy Managing Director, Stanley Fischer, would say was that the Indonesian economy could be expected to recover "at some point" so long as it stuck to the programme agreed with the IMF to render its financial institutions sound. This sounded awfully like a hope and a prayer, rather than concrete action. Of course, the Fund had disbursed cash but what was it to be used for. According to Ganandjar Kartasasmita, only to top up reserves, already at more than US$14 billion or to help make good any unmanageable deficit in the balance of payments. The new tranche was for a little less than US$1 billion so of how much use could it be? It all came down to confidence. An important aspect of the confidence would be if governments which had promised Indonesia with its trade financing now followed through. Dishonoured Indonesian letters of credit remained as much a problem in May, 1998 as they had at the end of 1997. The problem of the shortage of containers was still said by the media to be "worsening." The markets waited for more news. Fischer now said that there were no clear criteria for the release of these bilateral funds and that donor country's would have to make their own decisions. Not helpful! Fischer added that the IMF would not hesitate to cut off funds in the future if the reform programme slowed down.

Indonesian economist, I Nyoman Moena was quoted by the 'Jakarta Post' as saying that" This (the IMF disbursement and the hope of others in the future) is a significant improvement. With those funds we can solve problems related to foreign exchange financing. like guaranteeing letters of credit opened by our importers. But this disbursement commitment does not at all indicate any returning investors confidence. To win market confidence there are still a lot of things to be done." Moena and other commentators cited ongoing political problems as likely to hold foreign investor confidence down, whatever the IMF did. A market analyst was quoted as saying: "Investors (have) ignore(d) the IMF's move as they are more concerned about the escalating political tension." This had a familiar ring to it. With the implementation of every IMF reform package market sentiment had remained stubbornly weak. Of course, market players wanted to be dealing with healthy and solid institutions and companies but their immediate concerns were all related to paying bills and solvency, and to these things happening under conditions of safety and stability.

Would the revelations of Pius Lustrilanang bring down world condemnation on the human rights record of the Government of Indonesia - or not? There were many who hoped so and many more who were shocked by the revelations. Loyal supporters and servants of the New Order became numb and depressed as news of the Government's apparent misdeeds poured out.

As had so often been the case since June, 1997, there was once again a profound feeling of waiting but, because of the price increases, a feeling of waiting tinged with mounting anxiety about the now very real possibility of a social explosion, even of civil war.

One group which couldn't afford to wait was ABRI. They had to analyze the situation, try to estimate what might happen and decide on their role. Would they continue in their role as Soeharto "enforcers" and "fire extinguishers" or was a new approach called for. At a meeting of senior officers on May 7, soon after the increase in fuel and electricity charges, the new approach won out and a Blueprint On Sweeping Reforms was drawn up and approved. First of all it was clear that Indonesia faced an unusual situation, the worst economic crisis in its history. This crisis had brought about an unprecedented and possibly terminal threat to President Soeharto. ABRI agreed that reforms were needed and could see that Soeharto would only make them with great reluctance. The longer the contest between people and president dragged on the worse it would be for Indonesia. The greater the extent to which ABRI cracked down on behalf of Soeharto the worse it would be for them. In line with its relatively long standing policy of 'enabling' the student protests, ABRI decided to back constitutional, constructive and orderly reform. Most importantly, it decided against taking any leading role in unfolding events but, instead, to play a guiding role "from the back" - a deeply Javanese concept of power. In effect ABRI had turned its face away from a coup or even a crack down and towards the reform movement. Any who dreamed of a leading role for ABRI should Soeharto fall were from May 7 on consigned to a vulnerable minority position. Soeharto hard liners within ABRI may have felt that, should the necessity arise, presidential backing would be sufficient to overturn the decisions of May 7. They were wrong. The backing never came. However, during the first week of May, it appears that such people continued to scheme optimistically. Subsequent events seemed to show that they had planned and executed a terrible drama to be enacted on the streets of Jakarta and in provincial cities.

While Indonesian stumbled under the crushing yoke of IMF demands, the President of the Asian Development Bank, Mitsui Sato, accused the IMF of "mismanaging" the Asian crisis. He was quoted as telling the Asia Society in Hong Kong: "Their prescription for these countries has been too much emphasizing the conventional prescription, by which I mean, the monetary and the fiscal." At the Society's annual conference, the Director of India's Council for Research on Economic Relations, Isher Judge Ahluwalia was quoted as saying that "the IMF needs to drastically rethink the way it operates. The IMF has not been effective in responding to the crisis. By providing some liquidity at an early stage they could have provided some countries with some breathing space. Instead they are coming in too late with some heavy structural adjustment programmes." Former Governor of Bank Indonesia, Soedradjad told the conference that the IMF needed to be "more flexible in its approach and not try to reform everything all at once." In the US, millionaire publisher, Steve Forbes, blasted the IMF for "aggravating the financial problems of Asia." he was quoted as saying: " Doctors used to bleed you. That, of course, got rid of your pain and suffering because it got rid of you." Forbes was quoted as saying that social unrest in Indonesia had its roots in the IMF's recommendation to devalue the rupiah in August 1997. He described the Fund's policies as "like telling a patient with pneumonia to go out and sit in the snow."

The role of the IMF in Indonesia will not and should not be easily forgotten. In the world at large, just as it had appeared to the leaders of Indonesia, the Fund was a little understood image - a bit like Princess Diana. Probably very few of those who urged Indonesia to obey the Fund's dictates really had even a slight understanding of what was going on in Indonesia. As we have seen, even the IMF itself admitted that in the early stages it had misunderstood the nature and depth of the crisis. Indonesia had approached the Fund at a time of extreme difficulty, believing that the Fund had answers and solutions. When it discovered that the Fund indeed did not have the answers and when Indonesia sought other ways of dealing with the economic crisis or tried to evade the Fund's long-term 'medicines,' international condemnation followed because of another ingrained international image - the image that the Government of Indonesia was inherently evil and corrupt. Most of the vociferous world seemed to think that the IMF was right and Indonesia was wrong. Indonesia did as the Fund told it because there was no choice, even taking the highly unpopular and dangerous decision to raise prices but the results spoke for themselves. The rupiah and the economy continued to weaken.

What had the IMF done in Indonesia? Primarily it had insisted on a raft of long-term, structural and often ideological reforms with little if any relevance to the crisis which Paul Keating says even an Australian government would have been challenged to implement. In Australia during the first week of May, IMF chief Camdessus blamed the Indonesians for being too slow. His comment, contrasted with Paul Keating's, seemed to show how little he knew about the size of the job he had asked Indonesia to undertake. It also showed how little he knew about the culture of Indonesia. Perhaps he and his fellow directors needed to sign up for a university course in Asian business studies! Next, the Fund had gone on to suggest its standard measures of stringent belt-tightening and fiscal prudence which quickly destroyed the Indonesian economy. The economy needed liquidity and low interest rates. The people needed low prices. Instead, the IMF limited liquidity, raised interest rates to levels which throttled even the largest businesses and lit the fuse to massive, destructive social unrest through its insistence that subsidies be removed and prices raised. Not only did it contribute nothing to solving the problem at the root of the crisis - short-term offshore debt but its policies assassinated the banking and corporate sectors and provoked widespread riots which made foreign investors think that Indonesia was further away from economic recovery than ever.

The people of Indonesia were also in the grip of a powerful myth - the myth that it was government corruption and ineptitude that had caused the crisis. This was not so. The record showed that the Government of Indonesia had won nothing but international praise for its handling of the macro-economy. What the crisis revealed, rather like a new disease striking an already sick but still mobile patient, was that, at the micro-level, Indonesia laws and regulations were disastrously weak and micro-economic management subject to all kinds of high risk behaviour, such as corruption, collusion and crony deals. In May, 1998, many people wanted the Government to pay a price for this neglect, perhaps the ultimate price of resignation. But since none of these things had been the cause of the crisis or were the cause of its continuance even new leaders and a new government might not end the economic downturn. Of course, international confidence was now seriously affected by social unrest and could not be expected to recover until the unrest abated. Even then there would still have to be a resolution of the problem of private off-shore debt and Herculean repairs to the economic havoc brought about by the policies of the IMF. Meanwhile millions of people were plunged into misery.

Writing in the 'Indonesian Observer', financial consultant, Steven Susanto said: "The IMF team should have never advised a policy that disrupts the stability of the system. The existing patterns of production and consumption should only change gradually to avoid chaos in the economic system. Unfortunately the decision to surprise and terrify people has been implemented although it has only led most Indonesians to greater misery." On April 14, the 'Asian Wall Street Journal' had said in a long editorial criticizing the IMF: " A rather more interesting question is whether the elaborate IMF package will do anything to relieve the serious hardships which afflict the Indonesian masses, and that seem likely to get considerably worse before they get better. The stage was set for those hardships last August (1997) when the Indonesian central bank gave up on trying to support its currency in international exchange markets and let it sink like a rock. Back then, when prevention of a currency crisis would have been a real option had the Soeharto Government exercised sufficient political will, the IMF did not display much concern. Indeed, devaluation has always been a favourite IMF remedy for countries suffering buffeting in the world currency markets." Actually, floating the currency had appealed to many, not just the IMF. It seemed the best way of conserving scarce foreign currency reserves. But from these comments two interesting points emerge: first that the Government of Indonesia was already following IMF advice as early as July/August and second that even this knowledgeable American publication doubted the Fund's wisdom. The leader went on to record that the devaluation "shattered the balance sheets" of the country's already weak banks. The leader concluded that based on the advice and comments of the IMF fullsomely supported by the US Treasury: " A bit of rethinking is in order for Washington, too, it seems clear." The most the "Journal' could bring itself to say about the IMF's package for Indonesia was that it had "worthwhile aims" but capable of "working no miracles."

On the eve of President Soeharto's departure for Egypt on May 9, the Association of Indonesian Moslem Intellectuals (ICMI) called for total political reform in Indonesia as the means of solving the nation's problems. ICMI's executive board slammed the Governments political reform proposals as "vague, too little and too late. The Association lent its support to demands for a special session of the just prorogued People's Consultative Assembly. Chaired by Vice President Habibie, the Association had hoped for strong representation in the seventh development cabinet. Other than Habibie, they were left out. Was there an element in this of a spurned friend becoming a dangerous enemy?

The 'Indonesian Observer' quoted ICMI, Secretary General, Adi Susano as saying: "If officials say that there is no chance of a plenary meeting or a cabinet reshuffle, then they are wrong." In a statement the Association said: " What began as a monetary crisis has since turned into an economic and political crisis. But all these crisis are rooted in a crisis or moral character; or the failure of those who should have been role models in society." Referring to the again burgeoning student demonstrations the ICMI statement said: " The lack of confidence in the Government is the source of these protests. They have widened as more and more people are feeling the burden of increasing prices of basic commodities." ICMI expressed concern that the protests could lead to violence, saying: " ...if this violence threatens peaceful protesters, coming on top of recent acts of intimidation and kidnappings, the bridge of political communication to work out solutions together will become even more difficult to build." The Association targeted corruption, collusion and nepotism, coupled with what it called the "arrogance of power" as being at the root of the country's problems. Defining the qualities the Association felt that political leaders should have ICMI said that they should meet the criteria laid down by the Prophet Muhammad: " one shouldn't lie when talking, one should fulfill one's promise, one should not betray a trust and one should not cheat."

As criticism of the Government poured out fast and furious, the Supreme Audit Body (BPK) was quoted by the media as revealing that there were "strong indications of corruption of state and provincial budget allocations" during the 1997-98 fiscal year. The agency said that it had investigated less than 5 percent of the total budget.

Outspoken former cabinet minister, Siswono Yudohusodo was quoted in the 'Jakarta Post' as calling for immediate economic and political reforms to solve Indonesia's crisis. He was quoted as saying: " Seeing the deterioration in the quality of life in the social, economic and political fields, immediate reform has become a must. There are no other alternatives. The current crisis cannot be resolved by an administration which lacks credibility and is without the people's support." Almost identical words were used by economist, Sri Mulyani Indrawati when she commented: " Unpopular policies can only be delivered by a popular government that is supported by the public." Former finance minister, Frans Seda was reported as urging the Government not to take repressive action against demonstrators which, he was quoted as saying, "would only trigger radicalism and international doubts over Indonesia."

Demonstrations of any kind posed a peculiar problem in Indonesia, largely unknown in the developed countries but familiar in those still on the road to development. The problem was this. If the Government allowed students to leave their campuses and march through cities they would inevitably be joined by members of the non-student community. Some, perhaps many, of these would be serious fellow protesters. But some, perhaps many, would be of a frame of mind in which if tempers flared or law and order seem to break down the opportunity might and probably would be taken to loot shops along the way. Students also could not be counted upon to be angels. Buildings along the route which seemed to them to represent what they most disliked were likely to be stoned. Looters often torched buildings they robbed. To allow peaceful protest was one thing. To allow looting, burning and destruction of property was another.

What course the Government should follow was not easy to determine. If they boxed up the students on campus too closely, foreign governments and observers would be critical. If they let them out onto the streets and mayhem ensued which had to be controlled by force, foreigners would be even more critical. The Indonesian people are still a largely undisciplined people. Mobs can all too easily get out of control. All Indonesians are emotional, in and out of uniform. Troop-baiting student demonstrators or mobs can provoke members of the security forces to lose control - a circumstance the Government naturally wished to avoid, so as to provide no cause for further negative overseas media coverage. But it was difficult. The students were increasingly aggressive, increasingly insulting to the security forces, increasingly tried to break out of their campus corrals and increasingly resorted to stone throwing.

Demonstrations were monitored and infiltrated by uniformed and clandestine personnel. The discovery of plain clothes agents on campuses also brought down storms of critical publicity. From the Government's point of view, if the student demonstrations got out of control, chaos threatened. Commanders felt they had to know what was going on at all times. Several clandestine security personnel were identified and beaten by students.

While corralling the students in their campuses, the Government went out of its way to try to convince them that some of the changes they were demanding were in process. General Wiranto told the students at the end of the first week of May: "We get the message." There can be no doubt that he did. General Wiranto was no mere soldier. He had diplomas in law and business administration. Until mob violence broke out in Medan, he had been in the van of the movement to dialogue with the students. Even as he departed for a state visit for Egypt, President Soeharto said pointedly that the Indonesian Parliament should listen carefully to the demands of the people. Of course, listening and acting were two different things. It was action the students and many of society's leaders wanted to see, particularly action which promised to halt what House of Representatives Deputy Speaker, Let. Gen. Syarwan Hamid, now described as impending "total collapse."

Syarwan was quoted as making a very significant statement. He was quoted as saying that the "economy had continued going downhill even with the best economic policies and management team in place...if it continues going down it will lead to our destruction." Syarwan was quoting as adding that: "There is now a wide consensus among government, legislators and the public that thorough reform, as demanded by the students through their nationwide protests, would save the nation." Syarwan was quoted as saying that the ball was at the feet of the House of Representatives. "This is a fiery ball indeed but the House could turn it into a golden ball." ABRI apparently believed the very survival of the nation and of the state was at stake.

In many parts of Indonesia, unrest had now spread beyond university and college campuses. The international media almost daily carried live and still pictures of destructive mobs and anti-riot personnel on the streets, of gutted shops and burned out vehicles. The student rallies also continued to be prominently featured. Tourism arrivals fell by 15 percent, April on April. International doubts about prospects in Indonesia were further fuelled by increasing foreign print and electronic media revelations about the Government's record in East Timor and in regard to human rights generally. Pius Lustrilanang had arrived in Washington and many Indonesians waited eagerly for the US reaction to his testimony before a committee of Congress. It was to be a long wait. Next to nothing was seen or heard in Indonesia. Presumably on 'advice' from Government, the print and electronic media had studiously avoided the subject of Pius or kept their coverage to the bare factual minimum.

Even without Pius' testimony, the United States was among the first, if not the first, government to express concern about the handling of student protests by Indonesian security forces. "We are continuing to monitor the situation very closely," said State Department spokesman, James Foley. Foley said the US understood the necessity of maintaining law and order but he urged that all legitimate peaceful demonstrations be allowed to continue unhampered.

Thousands of students repeated their on-campus demonstrations across Indonesia, even ripping up the national flag as a sign of contempt for the federal Government. Workers, professionals and even state employees were said to be joining the student demonstrators. In Medan, during three days or mayhem which began on May 5, 170 shops were destroyed and looted by lawless rioters, mostly, if not entirely, non-students. A total of 38 cars and 21 motorcycles were torched. The Army's Strategic Reserves Command ((KOSTRAD)) dispatched Battalion 305 from Jakarta to Medan to help maintain order. Fourteen kilometres north, at Lalang Panjang, 140 families of Chinese descent were forced to flee their homes as refugees while indigenous Indonesian looted their property. Press pictures showed women and young infants hauling away their possessions. There were scattered reports of other Indonesian Chinese being forced to seek shelter in the homes of officials; some fled to Singapore. Many who could not or chose not to flee mounted 24 hour guard over themselves and their property, the guards including women and girls. In Padang a mob 100,000 strong ran "amok" looting stores and pillaging banks and government buildings. In Solo 50 students were injured after a clash with security forces and "streams of ambulances" were said to be taking away the injured.

In Jakarta, 58 professors and lecturers at the privately run Trisakti University issued a statement supporting the student demonstrators. The statement said: " To save the people, nation and country, the senate and leadership of Trisakti University fully support the aspirations and demands of Indonesian students in general and Trisakti students in particular, who are calling for reform in all aspects of life right now." This commitment by Trisakti would all too soon have a tragic outcome. The senate and professors at the prestigious Bandung Institute of Technology criticized the Government's response to the calls of the people and was quoted by the 'Jakarta Post' as having "called on the rest of the nation to join in the national drive for reform in all fields." The International NGO Forum on Indonesian Development (INFID), grouping 120 Indonesian and foreign non-governmental organizations also demanded immediate reforms. INFID called for full freedom of expression, a more democratic political system, more tolerant use of force in dealing with students and an impartial inquiry into the disappearances of activists. Reported the 'Jakarta Post:' "The Indonesian Communion of Churches yesterday threw its support behind the student reform movement and called on all members of society to do likewise." The Indonesian Catholic Students Association added its voice to the demands for a special session of the People's Consultative Assembly (MPR).

By May 8, the domestic media was reporting "tens of thousands" of students demonstrating throughout Indonesia. In a leader the 'Jakarta Post' said that "....the movement for reform has reached a point of no return since so many people have jumped onto the bandwagon" From Germany, Amien Rais, leader of the 30 million strong Islamic Muhammadiyah announced a plan to establish what he called a "People's Leadership Team", to include himself, Abdurrahman Wahid, Chairman of the Nahdlatul Ulama Muslim organization and Megawati Soekarnoputri, ousted leader of the Indonesian Democratic Party. He said it could also include retired General, Abdul Haris Nasution, former Foreign Minister, Roeslan Abdulgani and prominent intellectuals and scholars. Rais was quoted as saying that his idea was that the Team should meet with President Soeharto to explore the best ways of ending Indonesia's social unrest.

Meanwhile, Minister of Defense and Armed Forces (ABRI) Commander, General Wiranto, again called on the students to halt their demonstrations and to trust the Government's commitment to political reform - a commitment he said, echoing Speaker Harmoko, that was based on the student's own demands. The 'Indonesian Observer' also quoted the General as saying: "I call on the informal figures who often speak up, just stop criticizing the Government, stop seeking a scapegoat, but instead seek a positive solution which it is possible to implement." Now the question had to be asked: was he speaking for Wiranto or was he speaking for Soeharto? ABRI chief spokesman, Brig. Gen. A. Wahab Mokodongan was quoted by the press as adding that "the military rejected calls for an extraordinary session of the People's Consultative Assembly. "Why should we hold an extraordinary session if the nation can settle the crisis and carry out the reforms by other means," he was quoted as asking. Next day, ABRI Chief of Social and Political Affairs, Let. Gen. Susilo Bambang Yudhoyono was quoted as saying: "ABRI now calls on all parties to seriously examine the proposal to hold and MPR Plenary Session." It seemed that some of ABRI's senior officers were not talking to one another!

Indonesia's political waters were decidedly murky as President Soeharto bade farewell to begin his visit to the Middle East. The impression left behind him was that winds of change might be blowing - or they might not. Or, even if they were, they might not blow the people's aspirations as far as the people themselves might wish. ABRI seemed to blow hot and cold with some statements from some officers implying the usual 'leave it to us and don't make trouble approach' while others seemed to indicate that the students and the government critics were right. It was difficult to disentangle which of ABRI's statements were from Soeharto and which were, in effect, their very own, reflecting an approach to Indonesia's economic and political crisis entirely different from their commander's. Then there was the matter of the price hikes. Would the people stand for them? Did they have any choice? Reformists sensed that the 32-year-old- tree of the New Order Government had begun to shake. Perhaps it could be pushed over!

As the price increases filtered throughout the economy, at first, people reacted with numb disbelief. Then there was bewilderment. Then there was a questioning and searching for answers to the question: How can we live? There was a new, deep, sense of total hopelessness among Indonesia's millions of poor. Not only was there no bright dream to follow but, with business declining on every side and prices rising on every side, there was a realistic fear that even the costs of daily necessities could in future not be covered. "Where can the people of Indonesia turn now? Where can we go? These were typical sad comments. The simple people whom the crisis had turned into lawless looters were often quoted as saying that they were "hungry." There was a strong feeling that the end of a road had been reached - a dead end! Manpower Minister, Payaman Simanjuntak announced that unemployment was likely to rise to 13 million by the end of the year with underemployment of Indonesia's 90 million strong workforce reaching 45-50 percent.

In Cairo, President Soeharto warned leaders of the Group of 15 Developing Countries (G-15) that Asia's economic crisis would have negative ramifications far beyond the region. Within the region, the President warned of rising unemployment, spreading poverty increasing crime and political instability - eventualities all already occurring in Indonesia. President Soeharto blamed the crisis squarely on "external factors" because, he said, all the affected southeast Asian countries were generally accepted as having "sound fundamentals" and had pursued policies opening their economies and liberalizing trade and investment.

Events in southeast Asia had clearly brought about a major change in the attitude of developing countries to globalisation and liberalization. Opening the G-15 meeting, Egyptian President, Hosni Mubarak set the tone when he said that "The liberalization of our markets must be gradual." He also drew attention to the "social costs" of over-rapid globalization - the one thing the IMF had seemed to ignore completely in Indonesia. Egyptian Foreign Minister, Amr Moussa warned that although their were benefits from globalisation G-15 countries should be sure that World Trade Organization policies (WTO) did not damage their interests. "Rapid liberalization may have negative impacts which we should bear in mind," the Minister was quoted as saying. A few days earlier, in Singapore, IMF chief, Camdessus, admitted that Asia's crisis had shifted attention away from the benefits of globalization towards "the many ways in which countries can reduce their vulnerability to its risks." Camdessus argued that the surest defence remained strong banking and financial systems. Meeting in London, the G-7 finance ministers agreed a series of measures aimed at strengthening the architecture of the emerging world financial system the need for which they said had been highlighted by the crisis in Asia. The plan was little different from the recommendations of the IMF, except that it specified the need for greater cooperation and collaboration among international financial institutions. The weakness of this developed countries approach was that it failed to take into account the special needs of developing countries. In Cairo, some of the developing countries had taken note.

Government critic Amien Rais had now returned from overseas and, on Tuesday, May 12, was quoted by the 'Jakarta Post' as saying that he doubted if the New Order Government was capable of the reforms demanded by the people. Speaking metaphorically about the Government, he was quoted as saying: " Just as water stagnates in a sewer, that's how we are now. Being stagnant like that, the water only collects disease. That's why it has to flow." To help the water flow, Rais announced that on or after May 20 up to "30 or 40" public figures from various elements of society would come together in his People's Leadership Team to press the Government to hasten and deepen political reforms. In addition 45 Government critics, grouped together in a group known as the October 28 Group also called for a national committee to coordinate all pro-reform forces. PNI Baru leader, Mrs Supeni, speaking on behalf of the Group, said that she and her supporters rejected President Soeharto's accountability speech at the March General Session of the People's Consultative Assembly (MPR). They also rejected the Assembly's decision to reappoint President Soeharto and to appoint B.J. Habibie as Vice President. Ali Sadikin, a retired marine corps lieutenant general and former governor of Jakarta, speaking on behalf of the Petisi 50 Group of Government critics was quoted as saying: " The two decisions are not valid since the MPR members do not truly represent the people. Only a small number of the MPR members elected through the general election last year are valid." The Petition of 50 Group was formed in 1980 by public figures who claimed that the New Order Government had abandoned many of its founding goals. Sadikin was quoted as saying that his group supported the student movement for reform, including new national leadership, because the New Order Government had "too long abused the state ideology, Pancasila, and the 1945 Constitution. He was quoted as saying: "In 1967, Soeharto launched a total correction against the Old Order government under the late president Sukarno and now students demand total political, reform toward violations against the Constitution. Among the October 28 Group's supporters was former secretary for development operations, Solichin, a retired army lieutenant general. He was quoted as saying that he supported the Group because: " We have carried out the development programme for 32 years and all natural resources have been exploited for it, but many people are still living below the poverty line and many others are still poor. The Government has failed to bring prosperity to the nation while we have spent a lot of our time and resources for the government-planned development programme. We should not let the state leaders, who have failed to perform their duties well, continue their service. Reforms should be made immediately by an extraordinary session of the People's Consultative Assembly." Scholar, Dr. Nurcholish Madjid, called for the holding of a new general election. Roeslan Abdulgani, the 83-year-old former foreign minister, launched a book defining total reform. He blamed the current crisis on "greedy governance," crony capitalism and past chronic moral transgressions on the part of Indonesia's rulers.

The Government's intelligence services recommended extreme vigilance. According to testimony given in September by Armed Forces Intelligence Agency (BIA) chief, Maj. Gen. Zacky Anwar Makarim, the agency had been recommending extra alertness since April and were especially concerned about the day of action planned by Amien Rais on May 20 - a day they knew all about because senior officers had met with Amien at a hotel in Yogyakarta.

On May 12, the 'Jakarta Post' quoted retired senior military officers and Government critics as calling on the Indonesian Armed Forces to join the growing movement for political reform. Let. Gen (ret) Solichin was the spokesman. He was quoted as saying: "Almost all sections of society, except ABRI, have agreed on the need for thorough political reform in the country. Such thorough reform is extremely urgent because it could quickly lift the nation out of the crisis. Therefore, the student calls for immediate and total reform should be fully supported. It is appropriate that ABRI become part of the reform movement." Little did he know.

Way back on March 21, the 'Jakarta Post' has observed in an editorial: " The obsession to make the MPR General Session a success had virtually forced all the political factions to work according to a prepared script. The few attempts to deviate from this scenario were quickly quashed. In the process, they have virtually cut themselves off from the rest of the nation. The MPR sessions may go down in history as one of the smoothest. Its success, if it could be called that, however, must be discounted by the breakdown in communication between the political elite on the one hand, and the people, as represented by the students, on the other."

The meeting of the People's Consultative Assembly in March 1998 really represented the culmination of years of preparation by President Soeharto to ensure his re-election for a seventh term and to ensure that every political threat to the continuance of the New Order Government and its policies had been neutralized - perhaps neutered is a better concept. With family and friends appointed to high places and with enemies routed, the stage was set for what happened - a sterile confirmation of the status quo. At another time and place President Soeharto might have got away with it. This time, beyond the windows of the Parliament building passions and even the country itself were in flames. Revolution was in the air. It was time to go to the barricades. It was time for people to take sides - and to be seen to be doing so.

CHAPTER FIVE

Tragedy at Trisakti

On Wednesday, May 13, when it seemed as Indonesia teetered on the very brink of civil war, Indonesians awoke deeply shocked. The previous day, four students had died at the culmination of a day-long confrontation with security forces outside the campus of Jakarta's Trisakti University. Within 48 hours another would die - heroes of the reform movement. Thirteen others were injured and 17 were "missing." Students said that the deceased were shot inside the campus by the security forces.

Piecing together media reports it seems that 5,000 students attempted to breech ABRI's order not to leave their campus and began to try to march on Parliament. They were successfully turned back by riot police using a formula that one row of students would back up for every row of police who did so. According to 'Newsweek' of May 28: " As they retreated back through the school gates, a suspected undercover intelligence agent sang out, "Chicken." It was a fateful taunt. Students began beating the agent and police retaliated...."

Said 'Newsweek:' " They (the police) used real bullets, not rubber, and shot to kill. With sniper rifles and automatic weapons, officers fired from a freeway overpass outside the Trisakti gates, and from positions just inside the wall. Tear gas swirled in the air as at least six students fell dead. Others fled in panic and those who tripped were kicked and beaten. Bullets shattered plate glass windows of the administration building and two students fell dead on the front steps amid bits of flesh and brains."

An eyewitness report in 'Time' magazine of May 25 described police giving up respecting the integrity of the campus and pursuing students inside the university ground and even buildings. One policeman was quoted as yelling at a student: " Get inside, you dog." 'Time' said police were seen on the campus firing as they went. There was mention of one officer doing nothing but collecting spent shells. The police were seen to enter a building and drag out and away two blood smeared young women. How had they become blood smeared? Why were they being dragged off the campus? After the slaughter, 20 people were found to be 'missing.' Later, when an investigation was commenced, the National Commission on Human Rights reported that "eyewitnesses had been threatened by unidentified people forbidding them to give testimony."

The Dean of Trisakti University's School of Law, Adi Andojo Soetjipto, a former justice dismissed for blowing the lid off legal corruption, was quoted as saying: "It's very cruel. It's very sad and it makes me very angry. We'll immediately send a strong protest to the national police chief and to the minister of defense. There was no warning. The students were already heading home. But they were shot down like pigs. That's why Soeharto has to go." At Sumber Waras Hospital, reporters saw the dead students with gunshot wounds to heads, necks and lower abdomens.

Said 'Newsweek:' " The name of Trisakti now takes its place alongside Tiananmen as a code word for martyrs to the cause of Asian democracy."

City police spokesman, Lt. Col. E. Aritonang who was said to be present at the campus, was reported by the 'Jakarta Post' as insisting that there were no deaths. Or, if there were, "the victims were possibly trampled to death by their fellow protesters" while being dispersed by security forces. There was said to be no response from Jakarta Military Command spokesman, Lt. Col. DJ Nachrowi.

Later, controversy would boil around the shootings. There was an allegation that the "police" firing from the overpass had been soldiers wearing "borrowed" uniforms. More than two months later, following a staff investigation, 'Asiaweek' would report in its July 24 issue that four officers fired from the overpass and that, athough dressed in police

184

uniforms, they may have been soldiers masquerading as police. Police commanders remained adamant that their officers had not been issued with live ammunition. The magazine reported that a week before the incident four police officers, their uniforms and their motorcycles "disappeared." Who would have dared to do this? What kind of people would be capable of planning or have a motive for shooting the students?

On the day of the tragedy, human rights lawyer, Desmond Mahesa, became the second returnee to speak out. Like Pius Lustrilanang, Mahesa had been detained for two months and like Pius he had been tortured. He had chosen to speak out, he said, because of the slurs cast upon Pius by the authorities. Some spokesmen for the security forces had tried to suggest that the person who had spoken out in Jakarta wasn't even Pius. Mahesa removed every last vestige of doubt. Not only were his experiences the same as those of Pius but Pius was "brought to the detention camp 10 days after I arrived."

On Wednesday, May 13, at the Tanah Kusir burial ground over 3,000 students rallied to pay their last respects. Female students wailed and even fainted with emotion; male students fought for the honour to carry their colleagues' coffins. There were shouts of Allah Akbar (God is Great) from the thousands of students and observers. Some hummed the tune Gugur Bunga (Fallen Flowers) traditionally sung for heroes. Boy Bagus Yoga Nandita, the father of one young man said tearfully: " I'm letting go of my son Elang as a martyr because we are convinced that he has been chosen by God. And I'm convinced that the cause he fought for will be continued by others." Gede Mahendra from the University of Indonesia said that the four students had given the last drops of their blood to the struggle for reform. The students were "martyrs" killed in a holy war, he said. "They died while fighting for justice and truth." In a leader the 'Jakarta Post' said: " The death of four students at the hands of unidentified gunmen during a demonstration at Trisakti University in West Jakarta on Tuesday is a national tragedy. Those who sprayed bullets on the mass of innocent and unarmed young people deserve world condemnation. The authorities should quickly investigate the incident and bring the guilty parties to justice."

In a joint statement 12 non-governmental organizations called on ABRI to never again use weapons or bullets to threaten, torture or kill people. "We pray that the students died as martyrs. We state our full support for calls for total reform that the students, intellectuals and other elements of society have been demanding." More than 100 researchers at the state-run Indonesian Institute of Sciences demanded the "resignation of President Soeharto as a requirement for reform." A statement by 109 scholars condemned what they called the "massacre" by security personnel. Legal and advocacy associations, artists and intellectuals and religious groups formed a long line of individuals and groups publicly condemning the killings. The Indonesian legal Aid and Human Rights Association called for a week of mourning with flags flown at half mast. The Deputy Chairman of the National Commission on Human Rights, Marzuki Darusman was quoted as saying that there was" "No justification whatsoever for these killings. In this case somebody must be held politically accountable for the security forces. There should be no more excuses, no defensive statements from the Government blaming it on the situation or even blaming it on their subordinates."

Two hundred and fifty University of Indonesia professors and lecturers had filed a petition with the ABRI faction in the House of Representatives (DPR) demanding an immediate, full and transparent response to student demands for total reform. Delegation leader and former minister, Emil Salim, was quoted as saying afterwards: " The House is now racing with time to decide necessary measures for reform. The longer the House takes to decide the worse the economic crisis will become." Salim called upon the House to immediately exercise its "legislative initiative."

At the same time Ali Sadikin praised Armed Forces Commander, Wiranto, whom, he was quoted as saying, had brought a "new atmosphere to ABRI's security approach." He was quoted as urging General Wiranto to "respond positively" to the student movement. Ali also urged President Soeharto to take the first steps in initiating political reform. " It's better to be late (than never) for the President to take the initiative for reform," he was quoted as saying. Commentators such as Marsilam Simanjuntak, a founder of the Forum for Democracy were not optimistic. He was quoted as saying that: "The reforms planned by Soeharto are quite different from the ones being pursued by the students." If the chasm between the students and the Government was really so wide what was the solution? "I think Soeharto has to step down first, by whatever means acceptable, to give way for the nation to disentangle the power which has thus far been too centralized and embodied in the President and to formulate a new system of Government. To guarantee that the planned new system is democratic, citizens must be given operational sovereignty and power to establish the system of their own government and to reserve the ability to change it again if there is any demand for improvement."

At Trisakti University on Wednesday, ousted PDI leader, Megawati Sukarnoputri had told thousands of students assembled to commemorate the deaths: " What the students have been demanding is the same as what the PDI has been demanding. Let us build unity among students, the people and ABRI to continue reform." She was quoted as adding: " The actions of the security forces in shooting their own people cannot be condoned. ....I call on the security forces not to hurt their own people." Poet W.S. Rendra told the gathering: "Don't let the students die for nothing. It is now time for everybody to move together for reform." Amien Rais renewed his call to ABRI to decide which side it was on, the people's or the Government's. He was quoted as saying: "Whoever shot the students committed crimes against humanity. The troopers have used their weapons and armoured vehicles, bought with the people's money, to oppress the people. I am calling on the soldiers not to shoot. I am calling on students to continue demonstrating until the goals of reform are reached."

In an editorial on Thursday, May 14, the 'Jakarta Post' said: "Today's crusade for reform has gained support from people of all segments of society. There is no previous example in the country's history showing a fight for reform enjoying such huge public backing. Demonstrations for reform have spread to all major provincial cities throughout the archipelago." The cards were on the table. The demand facing the New Order Government had escalated to a call for total democracy - NOW. Student demonstrators appeared at campus demos with banners reading "Reform or Die."

At Jakarta's Attahiriyah Islamic University, student leader, Rahmatullah L.N. was quoted as saying: "We will continue our rallies until President Soeharto steps down and total political and economic reform has been properly implemented." Other student leaders spoke of being "frustrated" and "skeptical" about the Government's promises of change and of having "lost faith in the constitutional process." Said Anita R, a student at Trisakti University: "For many years, they (the Government) never listened to the people."

After the mid-term break, tens of thousands of students now resumed their demonstrations, in some cases kicked-off by their own rectors - people who had been told by the Government earlier to keep the students at their studies. Protests were reported in Jakarta, Yogyakarta, Surabaya, Surakarta, Purwokerto, Semarang, Bandung and Medan. In Semarang demonstrators took over the state run Radio Republik Indonesia, forcing the radio station to air their demands. Later the provincial governor's palace was stormed. Student numbers had now risen to the hundreds of thousands.

In the wake of the shootings at Trisakti the nation was in shock - the second in a few days, the first being the unimaginable increase in the prices of basic goods. The nation was figuratively and literally crying. A television female interviewer taking questions and opinions about events at Trisakti wiped tears from her eyes on camera. Government critic Kwik Kian Gie said he had cried when he heard the news. Some people called for a minute of silence at noon on Thursday, May 14. Universities declared classes suspended for three days in tribute to the "martyrs" of Trisakti. Everywhere there was a profound sense that elements of the security forces had gone too far, that the crisis had gone too far. Everywhere there were pictures of people crying. The country now felt itself to be in an economic and political straightjacket from which there was no way out but revolution. Would the President try to block it? Would he assist? Would he meekly step aside and allow the democratic juggernaught to roll forward to its destination - true merdeka or freedom for the people of Indonesia - with all its consequences, good or bad, stable or unstable?

The students were clamouring more loudly than ever for a moral and caring government - the very thing even the poorest of the poor craved too. The price increases seemed to show the poor that the Government didn't care about them - despite President Soeharto's airport remarks to the contrary. In their minds the Government cared only about helping the rich, especially certain ethnic Chinese whose speculative developments swept away urban kampongs and rural farmlands. The shootings seemed to show that far from caring for the people the Government was even prepared to kill in its apparently stubborn defence of the economic and political status quo. The students had raised the slogan "Reform or Die" and as Wednesday slipped into Thursday the call found a ready response in many hearts. Megawati Sukarnoputri, popular among the labouring classes and the poor had said that the student's struggle was the struggle of the PDI. The struggle of Megawati was also the struggle of many of the common people. The ingredients were coming together for a massive social explosion.

ABRI was also in shock. They had held dialogues with the students, had tried to treat them as partners in development, had been photographed hugging student leaders. Now some had died, apparently at their hands! One can all too easily guess that, in the face of the public outcry, urgent meetings were called within ABRI to find out exactly what had happened and how the high command should best explain - and apologize. According to 'Newsweek' of June 1, the top ABRI brass did indeed meet. They were indeed shocked. While the impact of the slayings had been bad enough there was also the worrying question of who had ordered the student shootings? Whoever it was had gone too far. Had the President ordered such a thing? Which units of ABRI would carry out such an order? Was Let. Gen. Prabowo involved? Was it a covert operation that was not supposed to be discovered?

As with the kidnappings of activists, when the media had screamed 'Enough is enough" now there was once again a feeling that certain behaviour of the state had become unacceptable.

Said 'Newsweek:' "The (ABRI) brass decided that Soeharto had to go." Did this mean that they did indeed suspect the Indonesian President of ordering the shootings? Or did it merely reflect a belief that the reform movement could not now be stopped unless President Soeharto quit? One thing was certain. Mainstream ABRI genuinely was very sorry about the deaths of members of the flower of Indonesia's new generation. On Wednesday, senior ABRI officers attended the funerals of the slain students and apologized personally to bereaved parents, among them Jakarta Military Commander Maj. Gen. Sjafrie Sjamsoeddin and the chief of the regional military police Col. Hendardji.

As the funerals of the students proceeded and, while some people nursed grief and others shock, still others wanted revenge. The students had fought for political and economic reform. The apparent response from Government had been a hail of bullets! On Wednesday, outside Triskati University droves of young high school students rallied to offer their support to their senior brethren in exacting retribution from the security forces. The students stayed on campus but their younger 'colleagues' - with an unenviable reputation for brawling among themselves - had soon taken matters into their own hands and quickly joined by mobs of other young people from the vicinity triggered a rampage of violence and looting until the area around the university was said to look like a "war zone." "Kill, kill" and "destroy, destroy," they were heard to scream. 'Newsweek' quoted young men in the crowd as saying: " Come on students, join us. Let's get revenge on the police." One international newspaper quoted a rioter as saying: " We were so angry that our neighbours got shot. Another said that recent price increases and inflation at more than 30 percent had made people desperate. "None of us go to shopping malls or eat at Macdonalds. Life is a hardship for us lower class people. We want changes."

189

According to 'Asiaweek,' quoting a "high-ranking military officer," : " Some time between 4 and 5 PM Wiranto ordered Jakarta military commander, Maj. Gen. Sjafrie Sjamsoeddin to send troops to control the spreading violence. Sjafrie did order some troops onto the streets. But, he allegedly did not deploy them with dispatch, send them to the areas where they were most needed or give them clear orders. Troops barracked in the western part of the city were commanded to go to the east and those in the east to the west. Prabowo urged Wiranto to let him bring his special reserve units into the capital but Wiranto refused. At about 7 PM Wiranto checked with Sjafrie and was not pleased with the response." While the public clamoured to know who was behind the Trisakti killings Wiranto wanted to know who was behind his own back - was it friend or foe? The weak response of Sjafrie 's units to the spreading anarchy rang loud alarm bells in the commander's mind! Prabowo's offer of "help" probably rang them even louder!

There was a public clamour to know who had ordered the police to shoot the Trisakti demonstrators - not to mention who had issued them with live ammunition. These were questions that would not be answered easily - or quickly. If the shooting had been deliberate what was the aim? Could it have been to provoke the students into rampaging off the campuses? Were those "high school students" and others who had urged the students to get their revenge on the police genuine or provocateurs? Could it have been designed to embarrass those elements within ABRI supporting the students? Not only to embarrass them but to snatch control of the students from them? If the students got out of control someone close to President Soeharto might feel that the President would welcome the services of a strong man who could put them back in their places. Public and media opinion generally thought that this strong man was Prabowo although that officer consistently denied most allegations made against him. If the students could be induced to run amok, those ABRI commanders who had backed them would be struck down. Men willing to crack down on the students and preserve the status quo would replace them. Such a man or men might even have known of the plot by other officers to work with the students to bring Soeharto down. In retaliation, they may have hatched a plot of their own. If Trisakti had been a provocation it would have been aimed squarely at thwarting the anti-Soeharto plotters. If it was a provocation, it is unlikely that Soeharto knew of it. Manifestly, the organizers of the provocation would hope that the shooting and subsequent rampage would be taken at face value so that an offer to rescue the President and the state would seem

190

genuine.

The students did not respond to calls for revenge, although the mob, including the ubiquitous high school students, certainly did. The numbers of rioters grew quickly from hundreds to thousands and their activities spread like wildfire to north and west Jakarta where there were concentrations of ethnic Chinese shophouses and shopping malls - people and businesses quietly hated by jealous and frustrated mobs of urban have-nots, a resentment wittingly or unwittingly inflamed over the months by even senior military officials who sought either to link them with anti-government groups or to blame them for food hoarding and price hiking. The mobs were not intimidated even when police fired warning shots and the rioting and looting continued unabated even after dark. The rupiah slumped to Rps 11,000 to the US dollar and the stock market fell.

In Jakarta's urban kampongs the poor were simmering. The economy was in a mess and the Government was to blame. The country's leaders had wallowed in corruption, collusion and nepotism instead of doing a good job and safeguarding the welfare of the people. President Soeharto had even left the country. Rising prices were putting basic necessities out of reach. Joblessness was on the increase. Even those lucky enough to have jobs could not earn enough to keep up with prices. Malnutrition and sickness were rising. Begging and crime were on the increase. More and more people were hungry and hurting. The student demands for economic reforms and for a new government to implement them seemed to offer the 'little people' their only hope of survival. But the students were apparently being pushed back. If the students lost the people would lose too. Now, a Government widely perceived as corrupt and incompetent, was apparently even killing students rather than clean itself up, institute reforms and restore normal economic life. And the killings came in the wake of a long series of mysterious kidnappings and tortures apparently designed to silence political opposition to the Government. Fury built up in the kampongs. Emotions ran murderously high. As night fell on Wednesday there were mutterings of the need to take "revenge."

In the wee hours of Thursday morning, the fury of the mob broke out again at Tangerang, in West Jakarta, an area of regular worker unrest against low pay as well as Muslim protests against the presence of bars and discotheques. It was an area of rock bottom poverty. Across the road from the glittering, new, Daan Mogot shopping Mall people literally lived in shacks in the dirt, with poverty and disease as companions. As darkness turned to dawn and dawn to day, as if in time to some silent, invisible signal, the mobs flooded from their poverty stricken kampongs and urban alleys to join in the 'therapy' of a mass amok - their targets once again the symbols of wealth and the wealthy - shopping malls and the ethnic Chinese thought to own them, primarily in north and west Jakarta, and corporate and physical symbols of the Soeharto's and their cronies - Timor cars and showrooms, the Social Affairs Ministry headed by the President's daughter, offices and supermarkets owned by his sons. One of the Jakarta homes of long-time Soeharto crony, Liem Sioe Liong, was burned to the ground and his portrait publicly desecrated. 'Asiaweek' of May 29 quoted Tanah Abang looter Santoso as saying: " I just want to take some of the fruits of development." Most of the business he and his friends targeted were Chinese owned. Said Santoso: " Who owns the offices and the high-rise buildings? Are there many pribumi businessmen.?" 'Asiaweek' quoted another rioter as saying: " It is time for the Chinese to pay their bill and time to get even with the troops for what they did to me." In these quotations we glimpse all the motivations which drove the mobs onto the streets - jealousy of the Chinese, a deep sense of being left behind and of not benefiting and resentment and frustration at being kicked around by men in uniforms.

The areas in which the Jakarta riots took place were mainly ones where the gap between rich and poor, have and have not, pribumi and ethnic Chinese and, for that matter, Muslim and Christian, was at its most stark. In the 'Chinatown" area of the city it was very noticeable even to a complete stranger that all the shops at street level seemed to be run by ethnic Chinese and all the 'coolies' seemed to be pribumis. The shops were tantalizingly full of products the poor could rarely, if ever, afford to buy. In the new shopping malls there was more of a mixture, with shops and offices sometimes owned by pribumis.

In the reaction to the appointment of Mohd "Bob" Hasan to Soeharto's last cabinet, while the West had fulminated against cronyism, some Jakartans and other Indonesians had muttered dangerously that the real problem was that he was Orang Cina - i.e. ethnic Chinese. President Soeharto had long been thought to be a champion of the Chinese, to the objection of pribumis large and small. Perhaps, thought the analysts, the appointment of a Chinese as minister of industry had lit the fuse of popular hatred of Indonesia's ethnic Chinese. Such hatred was alarmingly intense. After the Thursday riots it was not difficult to find people forecasting with relish that the next week they were going to "burn Sudirman" - a major business street full of ethnic Chinese owned businesses. Spontaneous or provoked the anti Chinese fury had found fertile social ground in which to grow.

As the rioting spread, many property owners swiftly displayed signs saying either that their property or business was "Muslim" or "indigenous owned." Not all were saved. Eventually the looting and lawlessness became random and the mob went after anything and everything. Banks, shops and offices closed down, transport stopped and barricades went up in Chinese neighbourhoods. Many people displayed signs on their homes and businesses saying "We support reformation."

Under normal circumstances, Indonesia's 'little people' would never dare institute such havoc. But with the Trisakti killings something seemed to snap in their minds and once the barrier broke between obedience and disobedience there was no stopping it. They were hurt, they were frustrated, no one seemed to be listening to them, no one seemed to care about them. Their frustration was as palpable as it was hysterical. At first the mobs stoned the symbols of what they had never had and perhaps never could have, the money and the good life represented by banks and shopping malls; then their fury turned to those they deemed to be always rich, the ethnic Chinese. Finally they foraged for symbols of the hated Soeharto's, the family blamed for all their current miseries. Uncontrollable mobs surged along most major streets from Glodok in the north to Tangerang in the West to the area around Trisakti University, leaving behind a trail of smashed and burned buildings. Fury seemed to feed fury until stoning turned to looting, looting turned to burning and as they went girls and women, mainly ethnic Chinese, unfortunate enough to be found and caught were stripped, groped, forced to dance naked in the street, and occasionally raped. Later 468 such cases would be reported to Dr. Rosita Noer. The strippings and gropings seem understandable if reprehensible. The rapes are a different story.

In the case of the rapes, according to media reports, in many cases the rapists entered houses and apartments. Mobs of young men moved from house to house, in apartments forcing families to flee to higher and higher levels until they had nowhere else to go. Families of rape victims claimed that some of the outrages were committed within earshot of security forces. Victims alleged that in places where they were raped, such as vans, they glimpsed folded military uniforms. In the city of Solo there had been allegations of rapes of ethnic Chinese girls and women and in Medan there had been allegations of the rape and harassment of female students by security forces. Later, sickening allegations of rapes by military personnel would also be reported from Aceh, soon to be dubbed Indonesia's "killing fields" and later still from East Timor. While there was no firm evidence of military involvement in the mass Jakarta rapes, nevertheless, revelations from Aceh and East Timor revealed that rape was a not uncommon practice among members of certain units of the Armed Forces. The trade union activist Marsinah had been raped before she was murdered and, although the culprits have not yet been punished, evidence again pointed to members of the security forces.

Nearly 180 wives and daughters of ethnic Chinese men were said to have been raped, sometimes by whole gangs and sometimes in front of husbands and fathers. There were grisly stories about a raped and pregnant woman being thrown several stories from a building and about another discarded and raped female being flung into the flames of a burning building. A third needed hours of restorative surgery after foreign objects were forced into her vagina. Some had their vagina's ripped open to the anus. A raped and sexually abused nine-year-old died subsequently after a rescue dash to Singapore. Another died in her own blood after being raped and stabbed repeatedly. Her mother, aunt and sister were also raped.

According to 'Asiaweek' the rapes were both random and organized with those organized taking place in 10 places in the city and undertaken by groups of men moving in an organized manner through houses or apartments.

It was not until two months later, on July 10, after a public outcry, including from overseas, that the Government as a whole seemed prepared to admit that the rapes might even have taken place and measures were taken to identify and assist the traumatized victims. Few victims were willing to come forward to the security forces and the police said they could do nothing without "evidence". Of course, rape cases are notorious for the fact that victims are usually unwilling to come forward, even in countries where the rule of law applies let alone in situations where it doesn't and the victims lives have been threatened if they speak out. Even three and four months later, the security forces and the Government stuck to their guns that there was no evidence of the rapes. The military even went overseas to Australia and Singapore to check at foreign hospitals but said they had failed to find evidence of even a single case.

A group called the National Body for Communication and the Development of Harmony among the People (Bakom-PKB) headed by Dr. Rosita Noer received complaints from 1,286 ethnic Chinese victims of the riots including "rape victims of all ages." The information was mostly given to Bakom-PKB on condition of confidentiality if not outright anonymity. Dr. Noer said her data would be passed to the United Nations once the Indonesian Government signed the UN Convention Against Torture and other Cruel, Inhuman or Degrading Treatment or Punishment. In fact, it had been signed but not yet ratified. There was no reason to doubt the statements of Ms Rosita Noer, a medical doctor and a reputable business woman.

On June 23, the State Minister For The Role Of Women, Tutty Alawiyah, said that the Government possessed no accurate data on the rapes. On July 10, she said that the Government was convinced that rapes had taken place but, later, in August, she would echo ABRI's complaint that there was no firm evidence capable of leading investigators to the culprits. To make sure that there never would be, concerned agencies working with the women said that many victims had received anonymous telephone calls from men warning them not to report what had happened to them to the authorities. In some cases the callers showed they knew every move the women made. In Aceh, after military rapes, the pattern had been the same. Even officials of investigating agencies claimed to have received calls warning them to halt their inquiries. In some cases their own daughters were threatened with rape.

On July 15, President Habibie had met 25 concerned women for two-and-a-half hours to discuss the riots and rapes. He must have been very convinced because next day, he regretted and condemned the violence expressed during the riots, particularly against defenceless women.

Elsewhere in the Government the search for evidence went on. Who might these rapists have been? Were they members of ABRI? Or were they forces brought in and encouraged by certain elements of ABRI, acting without the knowledge of the high command.

In August, 'Asiaweek' revealed that criminals and hoodlums were routinely used by the military in East Timor. Over the past four years, hundreds of Jakarta's miscreant street youths had been rounded up and subjected to supposedly corrective military training. Had some of these now been called back to do the dirty work in Glodok - not only fanning the mob's interest in looting but in raping as well? The victims were too frightened to say but, according to rumour, elements of the military or brought in by the military were the prime suspects for some of the apparently organized rapes. Perhaps significantly, on August 10, writing in the 'Jakarta Post,' Hermawan Sulistiyo said: " The Indonesian people mostly regard military personnel as criminals or armed hoodlums." The unsavoury side of ABRI's activities was consistently denied by the high command but as Hermawan pointed out: "Such plots usually come from intelligence units." By their nature such units are near impenetrable and ABRI is honeycombed with them, watching suspects, watching each other, in many cases, according to 'Asiaweek's Jose Manuel Tesoro, with "their own command lines direct to Jakarta." Such units could easily operate outside the main ABRI command structure and even without the knowledge of senior officers. Of course, someone, somewhere had to be giving the orders!

Various media implied rather than stated the identity of an ABRI officer who might have resorted to instigating both the rapes and the riots as a whole. Said 'Asiaweek:' " Prabowo is ambitious and he certainly had the means to instigate the riots. He had at his call thousands of reckless young men, may of them members of paramilitary organizations known to foment trouble. Hoodlums, gangsters, paramilitaries, youth groups- call them what you will. Some, like Pemuda Pancasila, are well established and led by retired officers. Military sources suspect that other organizations involved in the riots are no more than local rackets headed by thugs recruited in the provinces and set loose in the capital."

In some of the rapes there seems to have been not only a pribumi-Chinese hatred but a Muslim-Christian hatred as well, a hatred which had been boiling in recent years with the burning of churches in East Java and other areas. The moral outrage against the Soeharto Government was felt most keenly by Java's Muslims. Some of the activities they most disliked, such as the operation of bars and discotheques, were undertaken by ethnic Chinese. Ethnic Chinese were often associated with selling illegal narcotics. Marsinah was said to have been murdered after ethnic Chinese entrepreneurs bribed elements of the security forces. The ethnic Chinese were perceived to be as much the root of bribery and corruption as Soeharto himself. Many Chinese would say that they were forced to resort to bribery to protect themselves and to achieve objectives which would otherwise be denied them in Indonesia's maze-like, bumpy, playing field. In addition, many ethnic Chinese seemed to despise the often poor pribumis. A chance to rape women and girls who were seen to represent Chinese, Christian, arrogant, immoral and corrupt beliefs and values may have been irresistible to the weak minded among the have-nots. A number of bars and discotheques were destroyed, their facades daubed with the word "immoral" in huge letters. Conversely, during the May riots there were examples of concerned

Muslims rescuing naked ethnic Chinese girls from the mob. Subsequently, Muslim leaders went out of their way to condemn the violence and to call for ethnic and religious tolerance and harmony. No one suggested for a moment that such crimes had been conceived or ordered by any responsible member of any religious community. If they occurred, they occurred during a time of uncontrollable or orchestrated mob passion. And, incidentally, if media reports are true, some of the rapists and provocateurs were brought to Jakarta from Christian areas of eastern Indonesia and so were not Muslim at all.

At first, on Thursday, the rioters had the streets to themselves. General Wiranto was in Malang, East Java, according to 'Time' magazine with "the entire top brass of two, three and four-star generals." A military analyst was quoted as saying: " There is little doubt that they were discussing their next moves in the crisis." Presumably, the next stage of the crisis had been thought to be May 20, not Thursday, May 14! There was much to discuss. What had happened at Trisakti? Who was to blame? What should be ABRI's response? What point had the student movement reached? What would happen if Amien Rais and the students came together on May 20? How should ABRI handle such a monster demonstration? If allowed, where might it end? Could ABRI control it? And if ABRI lost control what might happen to life and property in the path of the protesters? But there was also a more pressing issue - if that can be imagined.

Why had Maj. Gen. Sjafrie Sjamsoeddin's efforts in Jakarta been so ineffective? What could be done about it? Most of the troops in and around Jakarta were commanded either by Sjafrie or Prabowo. For the moment, did these officers control the capital? Were they deliberately letting the mayhem get out of control? Was one of them fomenting it? What could the ABRI high command do to restore its authority and order in the capital? The answer was to send fresh troops, loyal to the high command, to Jakarta from Central and East Java. But the journey took most of a day and during that day the mobs rampaged.

The police and military adopted such a low profile that by nightfall on Thursday the lawless mobs who had commenced their rampage at Daan Mogot in the early hours of the morning seemed to be in control of the city. The headline in one newspaper actually said: " Mobs rule streets as riots rock the city." Throughout the day on Thursday, it had seemed that the Government side, whoever that was now, had given up. Chaos more or less reigned under the now largely benign gaze of security forces. Who could guess at the battle raging within ABRI itself, let alone on the streets! A life or death battle the outcome of which would seal the fate of Soeharto and also the future of democracy in Indonesia.

The Jakarta Military Governor, Sjafrie Sjamsoeddin, later described as "ineffective," was widely perceived to have failed to take firm action to halt the riots. Had he, like the intelligence services, really been taken by surprise? Later, he said that he had been and that the riots flared up too quickly for effective action to be taken. Media reports claimed that he had 23,000 men at his disposal plus 160 armoured vehicles. It was hard to believe that he did not have enough troops? Could they not have been mobilized faster? Were they really outnumbered? Was there really little that they could do? On Thursday night Marines were deployed to protect foreign embassies in Jakarta, at the direct order of General Wiranto. Later Sjafrie would tell investigators into the riots that he had mobilized 11,200 of his troops during the Thursday riots, but mainly to protect "vital places" such as the Armed Forces headquarters, the state palace and the state water company.

By July, quoting military officers, 'Asiaweek' stripped naked the Jakarta garrison commander's duplicity. Said the magazine: "At about 2 am (on May 14) the regional military command, headed by Prabowo's friend Sjafrie, began issuing radio instructions to groups on the streets. Throughout the day, people in Sjafrie's HQ were overheard ordering men where to go next. Eventually, the frequency was jammed; only KOPASSUS special forces and army intelligence can do that."

"Just after dawn, says another military source, gangsters from Lampung in south Sumatra were escorted into town by KOPASSUS troops, the force Prabowo commanded from 1995 to February this year. A civilian who works with the military said that in the week before the riots, hundreds of young men trained by KOPASSUS were brought from East Timor to Jakarta. He says that they were flown from Dili to Yogyakarta in chartered planes. They travelled from Yogyakarta to the capital by train.": (Maybe some of them stayed behind in Yogyakarta to stir up the mayhem there!)

Some people said that police in Jakarta stayed off the streets because they were afraid of reprisals for the Trisakti killings. This is likely to be true. On Thursday, the police had apparently been ordered to stand-by at their barracks. As the riots developed, an additional explanation for police absence may have been that the situation had progressed beyond the scope of the police and now required the very different approach of the military. But, with much of the city on fire, fire services, too, were inexplicably ordered only to stand by.

Images of rampaging non-student mobs, torching buildings and vehicles, flashed across television screens worldwide. Eyewitnesses spoke of being afraid for their lives and of mobs "possessed with the devil's spirit." During the daytime on Thursday, troops were seen apparently standing idly by as looters broke into shops and hauled home their prizes. 'Asiaweek' said: " ...many soldiers secretly sympathized with the people....many just stood by and watched the action. Troops who were called to secure Indofood's Jakarta distribution centre even helped the looters. Staff member, Lukman, watched from his office on the second floor as the soldiers asked rioters to line up for merchandise." Troopers were quoted as saying: " Once you've got enough, please go outside and give other people their chance." Later, intelligence services chief Maj. Gen. Zachy Anwar Makarim added that troops in Jakarta were "tired and depressed" after having been on alert not only since the March meeting of the People's Consultative Assembly but since the general elections of 1997. Faced with tens of thousands of murderously angry rioters, perhaps this was a battle they saw no point in fighting. Did the troops sympathize with the people? Were they tired and depressed? Or, had they been ordered to take no action?

With the whole nation now seemingly ranged against the President it was easy to imagine that ABRI had decided that it was time to take sides - or at least to become more neutral, pending the outcome of events. Just as ABRI had not wanted to pit itself against the students it seemed that now it was not ready to pit itself against the people. As the students and the mob advanced ABRI seemed only to watch and wait.

The media seemed to favour a conspiracy theory for ABRI's low profile. Was there a conspiracy by certain commanders to deliberately allow the riots to get out of control so that when Soeharto returned martial law would have to be proclaimed and General Wiranto removed as chief of the Armed Forces? Had these commanders had a hand in the student killings and in fomenting the riots and encouraging the rapes? Was there calculation by such a group that, since mainstream ABRI was controlling the students, the mob would have to be incited or encouraged. What better way to do it that by provoking them with a few student killings, choosing the right moment when crippling price increases had just been announced and then inciting hatred against the number one enemy of the poor - the allegedly wealthy ethnic Chinese, people who were thought to own owned too many businesses and who were suspected of being clever enough to find some way to benefit even from the price increases.

In another scenario, ABRI may only have been awaiting new orders. General Wiranto was a new commander. His boss was away. He was subject to blistering criticism for the alleged actions of members of the security forces at Trisakti. Parliamentary support for the reform movement was growing, including among organizations affiliated to the governing GOLKAR. In this situation the commander could be forgiven for not wanting his forces to make any more mistakes. His television address suggested that his heart was with the student demonstrators. He wanted an army loved by the people, not one feared, hated and despised. In other cities, too, ABRI had not opposed the students, merely accompanied them as they demonstrated - even in Semarang, where students had stormed the Governor's palace and occupied the Government radio station.

Another reason for the military's low profile may have been that the security forces really were outnumbered. Indonesia's security forces total fewer than 500,000 out of a population of 202 million. Almost 200,000 of these were police. On May 15, the 'Jakarta Post' quoted a "senior officer" as saying: " We're totally helpless and outnumbered." It was not hard to believe because while ABRI knew what the students were doing no one had forecast mass riots. As a result, ABRI generally may have been genuinely taken by surprise. Of course, if one really wants to do nothing probably the best course is to claim to be outnumbered and helpless!

It is easy to imagine that with the whole city apparently in revolt or on fire it was difficult to effectively apply military tactics. Where defensive lines could be formed, for example, in east Jakarta, a number of important ethnic Chinese areas were effectively protected, Mangga Dua, for instance, and Kelapa Gading (where, nevertheless, large sums of money were reportedly paid to the security forces to ensure public safety). Residents in ethnic Chinese areas eventually took protection into their own hands, built make-shift barricades of barbed wire and metal drums and armed themselves with iron bars, sticks and clubs.

Much later the truth would out! Quoting military sources, 'Asiaweek' of July 24 reported that when soldiers had asked their officers for instructions they had been told: " If you are stoned by rioters, respond with a smile. I order you only to smile, that is all. Others making reports were told simply to stand by. The magazine reported allegations of persistent "unclear orders."

There could no longer be a shred of doubt. The riots had been deliberately allowed. But had they also been planned and fomented and, if so, by whom?

As Thursday wore on, to Indonesians and expatriates alike it seemed that nobody's security could any longer be guaranteed in the capital. US Ambassador, J. Stapleton Roy was quoted by Canada's 'Globe and Mail' as saying: " It was clear as the rioting got worse on Thursday that the police were no longer able to provide any protection. Some of our citizens have been threatened and some of their homes have been looted. The situation has just spiralled out of control. In the same report, Chinese American, Andy Tan, was quoted as saying: " As long as you look Chinese you want to think twice about staying." US, Canadian, British and thousands of other foreign nationals were either advised to flee the country or began doing so on their own initiative. On the way to Soekarno-Hatta International Airport on Thursday and Friday many had to run the gauntlet of mobs of boys demanding money from drivers using the toll road. All toll booths had been abandoned. To ensure payment, the mob banged on the cars with fists and sticks. Injury, death, rape, looting and arson now stalked Jakarta's lawless streets. Anyone could be a target, anywhere, anytime.

On Thursday afternoon, as the riots threatened to reach their peak, in a special television broadcast, looking sad and sincere, Armed Forces Commander, General Wiranto apologized for the deaths at Trisakti. Clearly, still more occupied by Trisakti than the escalating riots, General Wiranto was quoted as saying: "ABRI is really concerned and regrets Tuesday's incident (at Trisakti University) It should never have happened. We should like to express our sympathy for the students reform movement," adding that ABRI had not intended to "stand opposite the students."

He announced that ABRI had established a special team to investigate the shooting and welcomed participation by the National Commission on Human Rights. He promised an "honest probe" into the incident and legal action against security personnel found to have violated laws and procedures. Firing live ammunition at protesters was a clear prima facie violation of military procedures. There were plenty of shells as evidence. Indonesians awaited the results of the investigation eagerly. ABRI's political fate could hinge on it. Of course, General Wiranto had to put as much distance as possible between ABRI and Trisakti and with the security situation in Jakarta out of control he needed to mobilize public opinion against those within the military who might be found responsible for Trisakti and who were even now obstructing ABRI in the capital.

Turning to the rioters and looters, Wiranto said that It remained the duty of the Armed Forces to protect lives and property and that they would do this using all force necessary. General Wiranto had said: "I call on the rioters and other parties taking advantage of the chaotic situation to stop. ABRI will not hesitate to take serious measures against those proven to have violated the law."

By Thursday night the situation in Jakarta looked very different. General Wiranto had drafted into Jakarta troops he could rely on, especially Marine units from Surabaya, and the city was under firm military control. Marine detachments were very much in evidence. Former Marine commander Ali Sadikin was a prominent member of a group of Soeharto oppositionists, the Petisi 50 Group. Sidelined by Soeharto, Marine memories of his sidelining may have been longer than thought. Perhaps now the time had come to regain some of the limelight. Later, Marine officers would be prominent in their support for the party of Megawati Sukarnoputri.

From Wiranto's point of view, if any kind of control of the situation was to be maintained the mobs had to be snuffed out. General Wiranto's nightmare was made plain in a quotation of his which appeared in the 'Bangkok Post on May 18. He said: " ABRI is not ready (not equipped) to face crisis points with crowds all over the country. ABRI in Jakarta is not designed for such unrest." Significantly, the General was quoted as saying that ABRI would "treat demonstrators differently from rioters and looters." One difference was that on Friday, May 15 some of the looters had been made to march without clothes through Jakarta's streets singing "We will not steal any more." Armed troops willing and able to impose order were now plentiful to help them keep their resolve.

If Prabowo had been making a bid for Wiranto's job, he had lost! In restoring order Wiranto was doing what Soeharto had ordered! What more could any commander do? While public order was restored, pro-reform protests were allowed to continue as before.

Describing Wednesday and Thursday's riots in a report on Friday, May 15, the 'Jakarta Post' said: "Thick black smoke covered the Jakarta sky as hundreds of shopping centres, supermarkets, automobile showrooms, state and private banks, discotheques (regarded by many as immoral), hotels, bookshops, offices, cars, trucks and motorcycles were set ablaze at dozens of different locations.... At least four police stations...were set on fire. Two police vehicles were also burned." Nearly 1,200 people were burned to death in the flames, many only recognizable to relatives from a watch or a ring on their charred re-

202

mains. Scores more were "missing" or known to have been injured. Three soldiers had also been killed and many injured by flying stones. Destroyed to date were 6,000 buildings, including shops, malls, banks and gas stations, 3,800 kiosks and a hotel, 2,000 cars and 500 motorcycles. Damage ran into millions of US dollars. As if unemployment was not severe enough, 14,000 people were reported by the Manpower Ministry to have lost their jobs - almost certainly a conservative estimate. A month later the figure was put at 100,000.

By Friday, the military had established a pervasive presence throughout Jakarta. More than 15,000 troops, (fewer than Sjafrie had at his disposal on Thursday) backed by tanks and armoured vehicles were deployed at key locations. Whether because of this or not the mobs stayed at home and the wreckage-strewn streets were quiet. In fact, they never came back. Granted that in the wake of the fall of Soeharto there was sporadic lawlessness around the country as people sought redress of alleged grievances, stole food because they were hungry or could sell it for money, took back land of which they claimed to have been wrongly dispossessed and, at the political level, took to the streets on unprecedented numbers of days to try out their new democratic freedoms, but, the riots did not return. More riots were feared and there were intermittent rumours. ABRI said that it was sure that there wouldn't be any more. And they were right. But how did they know? State Intelligence Coordinating Board chief Moetojib said it was because they were "following every single movement, every single day."

Throughout Friday and Saturday it was very clear that a military 'smile' campaign was under way. General Wiranto and other ABRI commanders were photographed smiling and shaking hands with ordinary and law-abiding people; soldiers were carried shoulder high by students. Was it a 'smile' campaign or was it more? Was it a 'hearts and minds' campaign? Had ABRI decided that even neutrality was not enough? Had it decided that its constitutional role as a partner with civilians in government precluded armed repression of the very people it was supposed to be representing and helping? If it had decided this, was the President now largely alone or were there still forces he could rely on - the Army's Strategic Reserves (KOSTRAD) commanded by Let. Gen. Prabowo, for example? It was KOSTRAD with its unique, discrete, network of links to other units, which President Soeharto had used as the headquarters from which he restored security and order in the wake of the alleged communist coup attempt in 1965.

The riots had traumatized Jakarta's ethnic Chinese and made

forcigners and Indonesians anxious about their safety if the riots should be repeated and spread. In the wake of the orgy of destruction, Jakarta's famous rumour mill went full steam ahead. Some people were doubtful if Indonesia's so-called "little people" would have whipped up the courage to riot, rape and destroy - unless they were led and egged on by as yet unknown organizers or provocateurs. How quickly the trouble had subsided! Was this because the suspected provocateurs had been ordered off the streets?

Could it have been the case that the hand that had pulled the triggers at Trisakti and urged the students to seek revenge on the police had also had a plan either to escalate the unrest through vengeance seeking or, if that failed, to provoke unrest by inciting have-nots to attack the ethnic Chinese? Trisakti was a private university attended by many ethnic Chinese. Had the hope been that it would be ethnic Chinese who would be shot? Could it have been the case that, as a follow up to Trisakti, provoking widespread civil unrest was the guarantee certain parties needed to ensure that President Soeharto would be forced to declare martial law and appoint new, more ruthless, ABRI commanders?

In a special survey, Catholic priest, Sandyawan Sumardi found that residents in all five of Jakarta's mayoralties had seen high school students being bused into the riot-torn areas accompanied by men with "crew cut hair." The residents said that the gangs incited riots and then moved on. It was also reported that figures in the crowds had been seen and heard to urge on others. Some of these 'leaders' were said to have sported military style crew cuts. Many of the buildings torched had been swarming with looters and cynics felt it unlikely that the robbers would have set themselves on fire - or, for that matter, known how to do it or possessed the means. Sandyawan also reported that he had interviewed young men trained as provocateurs.

Eyewitnesses to riots around Indonesia had several times said that they thought they saw plain clothes or off duty security personnel among rioters. Trucks seen to drop off groups of over age "high school students" around Jakarta sported out of town number plates. There were suspicions of similar incitements in Medan and Solo. In Bali, the Balinese had succeeded in turning back truck loads of outsiders bound for Denpasar, suspected of aiming to foment mayhem in the provincial capital, thereby robbing Bali of its crucial income from international tourism.

According to 'Asiaweek' at the ethnic Chinese owned Lippo Karawaci Mall remote cameras recorded six truck-loads of men arriving at the mall, breaking into banks, cash dispensers and silversmiths, then inviting in thousands of looters. The report by Father Sandyawan Sumardi found that: "The story was the same in other places." It added that military looking men leading the mobs "screamed anti-Chinese slogans."

In August, Jakarta Governor, Sutiyoso would tell a Government sponsored fact finding team investigating the riots that, in his opinion, the riots had been organized. On August 28, the 'Jakarta Post' quoted him as saying: "They were organized." There was no elaboration, then or later. Members of the fact funding team were quoted as saying that the had discerned a pattern to the riots which "would have required a certain level of skill to organize." A team member added pointedly: "It is easy for people to burn a car but not all people can burn down a high-rise building."

'Asiaweek' of July 24 left no doubts. The magazine published eye witness reports of the activities of military vehicles dropping off groups of men and of organized groups, sometimes carrying petrol cans, attacking and firing buildings and then inciting the mob. Witnesses saw some of these men armed with pistols and radios.

Just as there had been an ABRI plot to force the retirement of Soeharto using constitutional channels through the MPR and by condoning the students, had there been another plot to keep Seoharto in power by discrediting the reformists and provoking a martial law crackdown? As the 'Far Eastern Economic Review' had suggested back in March, was this Soeharto's own plot - to foment unrest to enable a crackdown and also to roll back the IMF? And was there yet another plot? Even if Soeharto fell and the Vice President became head of state, might he not be as likely as Soeharto to proclaim martial law and to call for the services of a hard liner? Wasn't Habibie like an adopted son to Soeharto? Wouldn't he be likely to favour officers related to Soeharto for the post of Armed Forces commander, in place of Wiranto? Were any of the Soeharto favourites perhaps dreaming of becoming president themselves? Let. Gen. Prabowo perhaps! Some international magazines had already speculated that Prabowo was positioning himself for the presidency in 2003.

Doubtless the riots did include a major element of the spontaneous outpouring of long pent-up frustrations and jealousies? The 'Far Eastern Economic Review' argued in its edition of May 5 that some New Order officials had fuelled these jealousies, particularly against ethnic Chinese. It said: "There is no proof that the Government has directly instigated any of the dozens of riots that have hit Indonesia since the start of the year. But Human Rights Watch, a New York-based non-governmental organization, charges that it deserves at least some of the blame.

"In February, the group accused senior government officials of fanning resentment among the population - in particular by failing to explain that high prices and food shortages are not the fault of individual retailers. These same officials, it added, have failed to state explicitly that the ethnic Chinese are a valued and important part of Indonesian society.

"Diplomats, meanwhile, point to signs of rising anti-Chinese sentiment in segments of Indonesia's powerful military. That criticism is echoed by Human Rights Watch. In a report, it says that former Armed Forces commander, Gen. Feisal Tanjung, new army strategic reserve chief Lt. Gen. Prabowo Subianto and the leader of the military's parliamentary faction, Lt. Gen. Syarwan Hamid, have incited racial tension with statements hinting that " any shop-owner who refuses to sell at pre-crisis prices or who closes his or her shop for fear of violence is deliberately making goods scarce to keep prices high.

"During a February 9 meeting with the Indonesian Ulemas Council, a key Islamic body, Soeharto himself accused "certain business people" - most Indonesians take that to mean ethnic Chinese - of triggering the crisis through gambling and speculation. Given that the Soeharto family had what one regional magazine described as a "smorgasbord of business alliances with Indonesian Chinese, here was loyalty indeed! Of course, from the point of view of many pribumis, the crisis that gripped their country was a debt crisis of the conglomerates. And who mostly owned the conglomerates? Ethnic Chinese! The fuel for a major fire was present; it only needed someone to light a match! A day later, the Council dutifully declared a jihad against speculators and hoarders of staple commodities. Such practices, it said, violate Islamic law. In a 'Jakarta Post' column of February 20, the director of the Indonesian Society for Pesentran and Community Development, Masdar Mas'udi said that he feared that the latest string of attacks - such as in Kadipaten and the nearby towns of Jatiwangi, Losari and Brebes - were staged in response to the Council's call."

Sofyan Wanandi, Chairman of the Gemala Group, was quoted in Singapore's 'The Straits Times' of Saturday, June 27, as saying that he " and many Government opponents believe the riots were abetted by a military faction led by Let. Gen. Prabowo, a long-time critic of the role of Chinese in the Indonesian economy. The 'Straits Times" said: "They (the critics) cite as proof ABRI's failure to mobilize and stop the violence at once."

Three weeks earlier, some other, strong evidence, emerged in the media. Returned "missing" activist Rahardjo Waluyo Mahesa testified before the Commission for Missing Persons and Victims of Violence that after being kidnapped and taken into captivity he was quizzed about his involvement with the National Committee for Democracy, a group supporting Megawati Sukarnoputri. The 'Indonesian Observer' of June 5 went on to say: " ...his captors had also tried to indoctrinate him with their anti-Chinese rhetoric. Djati said: " I was interrogated about my involvement with the group. They also asked me if I had received financial support from Sofyan Wanandi - allegedly implicated in an anti-Government bomb plot. I told them that we were barely able to support ourselves and that I had never heard Wanandi's name before. They also told me that the Group's activity was causing suffering to the people and to shift our focus (from the Government) to burning Chinese-owned stores, which was shocking to me."

Had there been a carefully thought out campaign to whip up popular sentiment against the ethnic Chinese - not to topple Soeharto but by fomenting unrest to strengthen his hand in negotiations with the IMF? Had it been a plot of Soeharto's to enable him to crush his opponents? Is this why the President had requested special powers at the March congress at which he was re-elected for a seventh term? So that, whatever happened, he could step in, enforce order and dictate terms.

Or was an anti-ethnic Chinese campaign a naked plot by officers loyal to Soeharto or loyal to those with links to Soeharto to make sure the President stayed in power by bringing about civil war between the pribumis and the ethnic Chinese across Java and perhaps across the archipelago? That the whole incident was an orchestrated and carefully planned anti-Chinese campaign there can be no doubt. Trisakti had been a university favoured by ethnic Chinese; torched shopping malls had been carefully selected as owned by ethnic Chinese - other than when the mobs got out of hand and went their own way; provocateurs had roused the mobs with anti-Chinese slogans. Were the riots a crude attempt to draw Muslim officers within ABRI away from the student movement and thoughts about democracy and to rally them to the status quo by playing the Chinese card as a means of creating havoc?

Was the solution to the havoc to have been a Soeharto rescue or a rescue by hard-liners on behalf of Soeharto or, as the Indonesian Observer' speculated on May 27, were the events of May 14 designed only by one man "to embarrass Wiranto with a view to pushing him out of his post." And was that one man Let. Gen. Prabowo?

What went wrong? If the intention had been to consolidate President Soeharto's power how come the reverse had occurred? Had reformist elements in ABRI seen a chance to get rid of him and seized it? Had Prabowo's bid for power over the armed forces been so resented that mainstream ABRI had decided to take him on and get rid of him too?

ABRI was resentful at the way it had been treated by Soeharto but maybe, by May, 1998 ABRI had also lost all confidence in the President's ability to lift Indonesia out of its economic mess. Maybe, like many others in the reform movement, ABRI now realized that Soeharto had become part of the problem, an obstruction to continued assistance from the international community. Maybe ABRI resentment was also fuelled by constant presidential interference in its affairs, including its business affairs. Maybe it resented the pervasive power of the Soeharto family as much as the community as a whole. Maybe hithertoo loyal elements of ABRI were tired of doing Soeharto's dirtier work and being blamed by the public. Maybe they were simply fighting too many wars - in East Timor, Aceh and Irian Jaya and now, increasingly and alarmingly, against the suffering and frustrated ordinary people of Indonesia. Maybe Muslim officers were tired of killing their own in Aceh and seriously depressed that the main opposition to Soeharto was coming from fellow Muslims. How could they go against Muslim brothers? ABRI could certainly benefit from an incident with which to threaten Soeharto. Maybe the riots provided it!

On August 21, Armed Forces commander, Gen. Wiranto would admit that "its soldiers were involved in the kidnappings, the mid-May rioting and the deaths of the Trisakti University students." On July 23, the 'Far Eastern Economic Review' published a report alleging that no fewer than four separate military commands had been involved in the abductions alone - we might guess that three of them were KOPASSUS, KOSTRAD and the Jakarta Military Command. Missing activists were suspected to have been held at KOPASSUS headquarters at Cijantung, outside Jakarta. When investigators arrived there on the trail of the activists they found that a KOPASSUS Group 4 detention centre had been "levelled about a month earlier." Ironically, this KOPASSUS Group 4 was the military's anti-terrorism group! The ABRI commander apologized for violations of the law and human rights during the events of May that had claimed lives. He was quoted as saying: " To prevent such procedural mistakes from recurring, ABRI is determined to modify its ethics and doctrines." He added that ABRI had also decided to clarify its operations in Irian Jaya, Timor and Aceh.

Some of the mysteries seemed almost solved. Ninety days after the May riots it did indeed look as if there had been a plot by Soeharto loyalists which had misfired, and a plot by mainstream ABRI which had succeeded. Indonesians eagerly awaited more details. Just how badly the pro-Soeharto plot had misfired and who might have been behind it was perhaps revealed by the fact that on September 4, 'Asiaweek' said that Soeharto had cold shouldered Prabowo when he turned up for his 77th birthday. "Asiaweek' described Prabowo as " an outcast within this family of outcasts." But, why? Why was Soeharto angry with him? What had he done wrong? Could it be that he had lost Soeharto the presidency!

On Friday, most Jakartans took no chances with their safety and stayed home. Some stayed there until the following Monday, by which time they had run out of food and money. In all sensitive areas of the capital there was a heavy military presence, including armoured cars and light tanks but there was no curfew. Over 100 task force units were deployed to keep order. Throughout the day and on into Saturday hundreds of those either caught looting red handed or identified as looters and arsonists were rounded up by the secretary forces as a warning to all. Ultimately 1,000 arrests were made.

Television reports throughout Friday revealed widespread dismay at the "anarchy" and "disintegration" which had characterized the orgy of burning, stoning and looting in Jakarta on Thursday. Religious leaders from all faiths condemned the violence. So did Megawati Sukarnoputri. A leader in the 'Jakarta Post' screamed: "Stop the rampage." Most offices and factories were closed, most shops were closed, most public transport was stopped. People were too afraid to go out. Some were forced out by the need for food, especially for babies. To find an open supermarket required cross-city travel and waits of up to four hours in long lines of other desperate people. Thanks to the mobs, ordinary people could not go to their jobs at shops and offices, service workers either chose to stay home or had no customers. The entertainment sector was shut tight. As if making a living wasn't hard enough, as if the prospects for Indonesia's economy weren't bleak enough, now mindless mobs - not students - had brought a reign of terror to city streets. During their amok they had destroyed huge quantities of increasingly scarce imported goods, which since they could not be replaced quickly, promised to create problems for weeks or months to come. Ironically, even demonstrating students were prevented from leaving their campuses for fear of the marauding mobs. The students and their supporters wanted political, legal and economic reform. The mobs seemed to want anarchy and loot.

In reality why the mobs appeared and why they did what they did was a lot more complicated than simple "mindlessness." Asking why the rampage occurred after 32 years of stability the 'Jakarta Post' said: "This (the stability) was achieved only by burying feelings of anger, injury or injustice that have slowly, but surely, been building up in society. Unfortunately, in the prevailing environment of relative prosperity, such ...... warnings were more often than not ignored by the authorities concerned. Under the circumstances, one could be inclined to agree with those who see the present flare-up of social and political unrest as a direct consequence - an explosion as it were - of those long pent-up feelings and emotions."

It was easy to talk about 'mobs' but who were these mobs if not the people - people who nursed a deep sense of injustice, a deep sense of having been forgotten, a deep sense of being irreversibly poor while others, especially Indonesia's ethnic Chinese, seemed destined always to be rich and favoured. The mob's frustrations had everything to do with dollars and cents and little with the student demand for freedom. But the student demand for economic reform had everything to do with dollars and cents. Like the mob, the students, too, were the victims of long pent-up emotions. The apparent breakdown of law and order provided an opportunity for long suppressed resentment and jealousy to explode. The sight of the students demonstrating and dying may have provided a match to light the passions of the poor. Many of the looters reportedly welcomed the freedom of the pro-democracy movement because they thought it gave them a new freedom to steal and even-up life's perceived injustices. Some of them were heard to shout: "Long live economic reform."

The wealth gap had caused their hurt but there was no more a quick fix for income disparity than there was for the rupiah. The City of Jakarta declared the beginning of a new wave of make-work programmes on May 25 but the programmes were not designed or funded for the millions who now needed them and funding had in any case been cut by 35 percent due to the crisis. Nationwide US$125 millionh had been earmarked for similar purposes.

Whatever the Government of Indonesia did was now being watched around the world. The United States immediately deplored the student deaths and called for moderation on all sides, including that of the looters and demonstrators. On Friday, the campuses were quiet, in mourning for the student martyrs. Indonesia's cities were also quiet and flags everywhere flew at half mast. Like frightened children, the mobs had run for cover, waiting to see the consequences of their fury. Places that were suddenly strangely busy were ports and airports as expatriates and Indonesians of Chinese ancestry rushed to escape further violence. Toll gates along the expressway to the airport had been abandoned and those fleeing had to run the gauntlet of mobs of youths armed with clubs and sticks, trying to extort tolls of their own. They banged and tore at vehicles whose owners were uncooperative, frightening the occupants. Despite the risks attendant on fleeing, foreign governments had little choice but to advise their citizens to leave and embassies and corporations began evacuating their employees. In Jakarta, hotels as yet undamaged by the mobs were crammed with Indonesian Chinese, wealthy refugees seeking safe havens with their families. The economy to which President Soeharto would return was in tatters. The country was now quite literally at a standstill.

Following the student deaths and the mob riots, the rupiah shot downwards to between Rps 11,000 to Rps 12,000 to the US dollar. Market analysts predicted it could fall to Rps 15,000 or below - with disastrous implications for the price and even the availability of imported goods, upon which Indonesia's modernizing economy was heavily dependent. The stock market had also plummeted, especially companies in which the President's family held shares. Two of the eight foreign investors said to be interested in buying into the soon-to-be-privatized state firms, withdrew their plans. Analysts predicated that foreign investors had probably bought themselves one-way air tickets out of Indonesia.

From the offshore private debt talks in Tokyo nothing conclusive had emerged except strong hints of an impending solution to the problem of offshore interbank debt. Another round of talks was scheduled to take place beginning May 26 in Frankfurt, Germany, focusing primarily on offshore corporate debt. One of the wrangles in Tokyo had been at what rate of exchange corporate debts could be repaid and who would make good any forex losses. A new and darker question mark now hung over this.

From the banking sector there was more bad news. Sky-high central bank rates were tightening the squeeze on credit as never before, threatening bank and corporate solvency as never before. Analysts argued that however high interest rates were raised, they could never rescue the rupiah now that market response was increasingly dominated by non-economic factors, such as the student and mob unrest. Bank Indonesia Director, Miranda S. Goeltom, defended the central bank's policy arguing that at least it limited the rupiah's drop. Bankers and businessmen wanted only to see a return to what they called "normal business activities" and seemed now not to be so concerned about propping up the currency. One analyst called on Bank Indonesia to simply let the rupiah float on the grounds that, under circumstances of acute political unrest, nothing they could do could save it. Even Bank Indonesia Governor, Sjahril Sabirin seemed disappointed with the performance of the rupiah in the wake of three successive increases in the banks benchmark SBI rates. He described the fall of the rupiah as a "problem of confidence" and said that without political and social disturbances he would have expected the currency to have risen to the level of around Rps 8,000 to the US dollar.

But there WERE social and political disturbances. High interest rates had brought business to its knees; now high prices had brought the people to their knees and forced them out onto the streets. The now almost forgotten Professor Steve Hanke was quoted by the 'Indonesian Observer; as saying that the IMF's austerity prescription for Indonesia was not working and attempts to push through economic and political reform were ill timed and would trigger more unrest. "The whole thing is going to blow up. I thought it was going to take three to four months but its is going to be sooner."

This second collapse of the rupiah would have serious implications for the state budget, already recalculated three times. A budget deficit was forecast. Economist, Sri Mulyani Indrawati also forecast that a shortage of cash in government coffers would have severe consequences for poor provinces largely dependent on the central government, such as, Bengkulu, East Nusa Tenggara and Maluku. There could also be political implications because parts of Indonesia had long ago dreamed of independence. Perhaps some still did. Some analysts now predicted negative growth of up to 8 percent and inflation of over 100 percent.

By mid-May, as had been the case for the past nine months, the priority for the Government remained the stabilization of the rupiah. With the IMF satisfied with Indonesia's economic reforms and with IMF-supplied or brokered funds beginning to flow one set of factors important for the recovery of the rupiah was at least positive. Yet steps needed to be taken with which the IMF might not agree. Then, even this last positive prop to the rupiah would be removed.

In mid-May it seemed clear that the first and perhaps unavoidable step needed to calm the passions of the people was to reintroduce all the subsidies taken away at the insistence of the IMF - totalling around US$3 billion. This would enable prices to be reduced and 'normal' life to resume.

For 'normal' conditions to return to business, the central bank's benchmark SBI rates, kept high at the insistence of the IMF, needed to be pushed down significantly. Of course, for this to happen under present circumstances, required other changes conducive to a resurgence of confidence in the currency, otherwise people would simply unload rupiah. Decreased interest rates would restore the liquidity that banks and corporates had needed for months but which had been squeezed out of the economy by the policy of high interest rates. Time deposits at private banks showed a strong upward trend in the wake of Bank Indonesia's beginning-of-May hike in interest rates to close to 60 percent. Bank reports suggested that the increase in private deposits was as high as 30 percent in the first quarter. At state banks, generally regarded as 'safe', the increase in the first three months of 1998 was over 60 percent. But this increase in time deposits did nothing to help the rupiah, the banks or the economy. If anything, it made the situation even more desperate.

In line with IMF recommendations, the money supply needed to continue to be strictly controlled to avoid hyperinflation. Also in line with IMF recommendations, tough measures were needed to speed up the largely stalled process of bank mergers until only the strong survived.

A roll-over had been agreed for interbank offshore debt. If the same could be agreed for the foreign, short-term, corporate debt, markets fears about corporate solvency would be considerably relieved. Of course, this was under no one's control other than the lenders and would inevitably take more time. Roll-overs were in everyone's interest. They would enable business to continue to function, providing Indonesians with vital jobs, They would enable economic activity to continue. They would ensure that, eventually, creditors would get their money back. The problem, as always throughout the crisis was largely one of confidence. Would lenders get their money back or, armed with the Government's new bankruptcy law, should they press for immediate resolution through the sale of assets?

The value of the rupiah against the US dollar was now also largely a matter of confidence. Some analysts felt that Indonesia had little alternative but to peg the rupiah against the dollar at a reasonable rate, the Rps 6,000 agreed in the state budget, for example. Indonesia had operated such a peg for 25 years. This would enable banking and business to function again and would also assist with repayment of the troublesome offshore debt. What was the stumbling block to this rosy picture? The answer - money.

If the subsidies were reinstated, where would the US$3.3 billion come from? If the rupiah was pegged and there was an immediate rush for dollars, where would the dollars come from if the Government's US$14 billion reserves proved inadequate? - which they almost certainly would. If, as a result of the crisis, the state budget was in deficit, where would the money be found? There was really only one answer - sovereign loans. In mid-May total foreign debt stood at US$133 billion of which less than US$60 billion was public debt.

The likelihood of a currency peg or a currency board, however, seemed remote. On May 18, Bank Indonesia Director Miranda Goeltom said categorically: "Please do not misunderstand that the Government has a plan to peg the rupiah against the US dollar and will bail out private sector debts."

But, with the capital aflame and the prospect of more demonstrations, if not riots, to come, with the threat of more pro-democracy demonstrations to come, if, for some reason, the IMF withdrew, who would agree to lend the Government of Indonesia the money it needed? - a Government unpopular with the people and likely to be unpopular with the IMF if it tried to please the people by defying the IMF. Even if the Government kept on with the damaging policies recommended by the IMF, given the political situation, would the Fund, especially its US supporters, continue to approve the release of new tranches of the US$43 million bailout package agreed in 1997?

Money is usually the cause and salvation of all situations but in Indonesia's case it was not. There was another factor, the political factor. Market analysts were now agreed that it no longer mattered what interest rate was set by the central bank in defence of the rupiah because the one big factor pushing the currency down was the political factor.

Popular demands had escalated. They had begun with moral outrage coupled to the key demand that President Soeharto step down. Then they had rolled on to violent opposition to the withdrawal of subsidies and subsequent swingeing price increases. Finally, they had culminated in a fury of opposition not only to President Soeharto and his family but to the entire new cabinet and even the entire new parliament.

By mid-May the demand from students, the intelligentsia and many community leaders was for total political reform - not only political but legal, economic and social. On the eve of Amien Rais's day or protest on May 20, the Day of National Awakening, it looked as if nothing could stop the pro-reform juggernaught, other than new elections for a completely new government and head of state. This alone would restore tranquility to the streets and campuses - if coupled with decreased prices and interest rates. This alone would restore international confidence in Indonesia. This alone seemed likely to restore confidence in the rupiah. If confidence returned to the rupiah many things would become possible. There really would be light at the end of what had become a very dark and long tunnel. One man stood in the way, President Soeharto.

When asked what would be the response of business if President Soeharto did, indeed, step down, economist Sri Mulyani said: " It would raise hopes and enthusiasm for a rapid leadership succession, but would receive a mixed reaction from the business community, which would fear uncertainty during the transition." Even at this late stage the business class was still quiet leaving the noisy protests to religious and academic leaders and to students, all of whom had little in common with the mob.

Of course, foreigners, too, would watch the transition carefully. There would be no stampede of foreign investors back to Indonesia until the political situation settled down and safety and some element of predictability could be restored to economic activity. Or even of such domestic players as the Indonesian Chinese, many of whom had fled the country in fear of their lives.

One of the measures a new government might take could be to make Indonesian Chinese equal citizens in practice, as opposed to theory - with achievable equal opportunities to be educated and to take part in even the highest levels of the military and government. In May 1998, their activities were in practice restricted only to trade. Whenever things went wrong with the economy their lives and property were the first to be threatened by other Indonesians, the so-called indigenous Indonesians - meaning non-Chinese. It would not be an easy decision. The poorer classes resented the apparent wealth of the ethnic Chinese but all classes resented the ease with which they seemed always to be able to negotiate special facilities from the Government. Many felt the relationship between the ethnic Chinese and the New Order Government was little different to the relationship the ethnic Chinese had with the Dutch colonial power. To make matters worse, the ethnic Chinese liked

215

to stick together, working with their own, employing their own, doing business with their own. Not a few adopted rough and insulting tones to pribumis taking little trouble to hide the fact that they despised them. On their side, many even middle class indigenous Indonesians resented the apparent favours enjoyed by ethnic Chinese and the way the ethnic Chinese seemed to have of favouring their own and looking down on pribumis. They particularly resented the feeling of discrimination they had, for example, whenever they asked at a bank for credit - most private banks were ethnic Chinese owned and seemed to feel that many pribumis were bad credit risks. Clearly, there were faults on both sides. If the indigenous Indonesians wanted to make the ethnic Chinese more equal as citizens they would have to be more welcoming. If the ethnic Chinese wanted to be treated as equal citizens they would also have to be more welcoming. Out of the compromise might spring hope. From a relationship of often mutual contempt needed to be forged genuine compatriotism. Two peoples less alike and less likely to be able to get on with each other can hardly be imagined.

Indonesia's middle class had been shaken by the riots. From what Sri Mulyani had said, some of them might have been glad to see the President return, bringing with him at least the promise of the restoration of law and order. Some may have begun to wonder at the wisdom of changing leaders during the country's worst crisis for decades. Many of Indonesia's leaders have said many times that Indonesia is a difficult country to govern. A sprawling far-flung country, Indonesia is home to many peoples, cultures, religions and political views, any element of which can become highly dangerous to sovereignty or stability if allowed to become exclusive. The lesson of the Sukarno years had been felt to be that Indonesia could only be held together by a strong leader. Now large sections of the population were saying that they wanted a strong leader no longer. There were clear dangers, massive dangers.

Nevertheless, Government critics pressed ahead with their campaign to force the resignation of the President. President Soeharto has been known to say often that he felt that there was no other leader to replace him as president. Suddenly Indonesia seemed to be full of leaders. Amien Rais and 43 other critics formed the Council for the People's Mandate on the Thursday night of the riots. Its first act was to call upon President Soeharto to resign. Earlier, supporters had called upon the House of Representatives (MPR) to invite the President to resign and to establish an interim government. More or less simultaneously a second group of Government critics banded together to form the Indonesian

Working Forum. This group received the backing of Abdurrahman Wahid, chairman of the 40 million strong Islamic Nahdlatul Ulama. Amien Rais was also numbered among the supporters but did not attend the founding meeting. Other visitors to the Parliament building were leaders of KOSGORO, a mass organization affiliated to the ruling GOLKAR party. They called upon the President and Vice President to return the mandate they had been given in March and backed the calls for an extraordinary session of the People's Consultative Assembly. Canada's 'Globe & Mail' daily newspaper quoted one KOSGORO leader as saying: " If he (Soeharto) won't step down peacefully, then we must force him to leave." Fifteen retired senior military figures who had fought alongside Soeharto in the independence struggle 50 years ago also urged the President to resign. A statement said: " It is of the utmost importance that President Soeharto immediately carry out his own statement (allegedly made in Cairo) to resign from the office of president/head of state." The statement was signed by "Officers of the Armed Forces Generation 1945." Several were members of the Petition of 50 group. The President promptly denied that he had offered to resign. In so many words he had not. Assuming that, in fact, he had, the Association of Indonesian Intellectuals (ICMI) welcomed the President's apparent willingness to make way , for someone else.

Among foreign commentators former Australian foreign minister Gareth Evans seemed to sum up best what most were thinking, even it they didn't put it into words. He was quoted as saying: " Soeharto's time has come. The First family's time has come. The only question now is whether a transition can be managed without too much more chaos and bloodshed, or whether it can be done reasonably smoothly."

On Friday, in Surabaya, mobs went on the rampage, also in Surakarta and Bandar Lampung. Tension was high on Batam Island and in Pekanbaru, Riau, Bengkulu and Semarang.

Students were shocked by the activities of the mobs. One was quoted widely as saying: " If this is what people meant by the reform of their choice, then maybe we shouldn't have reform at all. Please differentiate student demonstrations for reform from the rioting where people ransacked and looted properties." The students mainly confined themselves to campuses for fear of unleashing a further round of mob violence.

Public figures and religious leaders deplored the mob violence. Amien Rais told an audience at a packed Jakarta mosque: " There's not a single verse in the Holy Koran that justifies the looting of Chinese houses..... Looters must bc clobbered." One terrified mother of three was quoted as saying: " It's just so scary to see those looters. It's as if they were possessed by Satan. From the television we can watch how happy and innocent they look as they loot, burn and throw stones. I think it would be OK for security forces to shoot at them." Jakarta Governor Sutiyoso said that he was scandalized by the behavior of the mobs. "As a governor and people's leader I am really ashamed that my people's behaviour is like that...."

Fear had continued to spread among expatriate households and neighbourhoods and throughout the weekend commercial and charter flights ferried thousands of non-essential employees and women and children to safety, often with Singapore as the first stop. Between May 14 and 18, approximately 100 charter flights hauled away an estimated 40,000 expats. Almost 60,000 had left after the collapse of the rupiah in January. During the next few days another almost 85,000 foreigners would leave together with 75,000 Indonesian Chinese, at this stage widely thought to be fleeing for their lives. The IMF team in Jakarta fled with them. One of those who arrived early in Singapore was 16-year-old, Danielle Townsend. She said gratefully: "We made it alive out of Jakarta."

Japan, Malaysia and Taiwan sent military transport planes to pick up fleeing refugees. Two Taiwanese warships were on stand-by off Bali. Taiwanese factory owner, Chen Lao-an, arriving at Taipei after fleeing Jakarta was quoted as saying of the rioters: " They are not human beings." A US battle fleet consisting of the navy helicopter carrier Belleau Wood and two support ships carrying 2,000 marines, hovered off the coast of Java, north of Jakarta. A US diplomat had been quoted in the press as saying that the US was concerned that Indonesia's police were "incapable of protecting foreigners in Jakarta." Twenty-four hour task forces to monitor the situation had been set up within the US Embassy, Jakarta, the Pacific Command and the State Department.

President Soeharto cut short his visit to Cairo returning to Jakarta at 4 am on Saturday morning, May 16. While in the Egyptian capital it had seemed that there was a possibility that the President had now "got the message" the students and the people were so eager to give him. On May 14, he had been quoted in the media as saying that if the people of Indonesia no longer trusted him to lead the country it would not be a "problem." He was reported to have said that he would not use armed force to stay in power. The President expressed his deepest condolences for the deaths and injuries at Trisakti University. As President Soeharto had flown home precipitously from Cairo, the nation wondered what his first words to the public would be. From the media it seemed clear that the words either had to be: "I resign" or "I hereby promise to implement all reforms and with immediate effect rescind the decision to withdraw all subsidies as agreed with the IMF."

On May 12, the House of Representatives had rejected the fuel and electricity price hikes, demanding that they be rolled back. The stage seemed set for the first ever confrontation between executive and legislature - a measure of the seriousness of the crisis. All these men and women had been "screened" by the Government and emerged with the check-mark of loyalty beside their names. Now even the chosen were rebelling. On May 15, KOSGORO, one of the organizations affiliated to GOLKAR, had urged the President to "take the initiative" in calling a special session of the People's Consultative Assembly at which it was expected that he and Vice President Habibie would return the mandates given them only 60 days earlier. Loyal Soeharto supporter, GOLKAR Chairman and House Speaker, Harmoko, was under mounting pressure to "respond positively to the people's demands - especially from ABRI's faction in the House." Parliament, the intelligentsia, academia, the students and the mob - all were lined up against Soeharto as he arrived back home.

While Indonesia burned, in Seoul, South Korea on May 12, the IMF's Asia and Pacific Director, Hubert Neiss praised Indonesia for implementing the reforms agreed with the Fund. He was quoted by Reuters as saying: " One important element (in Indonesia's recovery) is that the economic reform programme is on track, that all the measures that were agreed upon are implemented fully and on time.. I should say that, so far, this has been the case. All measures agreed to....have been implemented." He was quoted as adding: "There is of course political risk to the programme. That everybody knows and we all have to live with." He did not mention social risk. Tens of thousands of Indonesians were deciding that there was no way they could live or even survive the social consequences of the IMF's policies. Appearing to distance himself from the price increases, Neiss repeated that the "precise timing" of the fuel and electricity price increases had been left to the Government of Indonesia. While Ginandjar had said at the end of April that Indonesia and the Fund had agreed to the fuel and electricity increases in May and June, Neiss said that the Fund had recommended the first half of the new fiscal year - meaning any time between April and September. Somebody was confused somewhere! Neiss confirmed that the precise measures taken to increase prices had been agreed with the IMF.

Even by Thursday night it had been clear that President Soeharto certainly wouldn't be flying home to offer his resignation. From Cairo, Foreign Minister Ali Alatas explained that the President had no objection to stepping down, provided he was asked to do so by constitutional means. In other words there would have to be a recall of the People's Consultative Assembly and a majority of the delegates would have to withdraw the support given to him in March. Since the President's own party, GOLKAR, dominated the Assembly this appeared to be a challenging task. And if the President could not be dislodged constitutionally............. Indonesia and the world waited.

As President Soeharto stepped off the plane at Halim Military Airport on Saturday morning, May 16, he looked more hunted than in charge. Those around him seemed more to be watching him than to be with him. In some of their eyes seem to be a fear that Soeharto would somehow find out that, behind his back, they had been talking about the political situation, about alternative scenarios, even plotting, maybe! Everyone present knew that the demands for the President's resignation had reached fever pitch. Had some of the President's top advisers and state servants discussed the possibilities amongst themselves, for example, Habibie, Wiranto and Feisal Tanjung? Ginandjar, too, maybe? Perhaps the time had come or even passed when back-up plans had to be in place! If President Soeharto really was toppled there had to be a contingency plan, soundings had to be taken, alliances tentatively pencilled in place, others firmly ruled out. In Tokyo, on May 13, Ginandjar Kartasasmita had been quoted as saying that the Government must "take notice of the student protests." He did not elaborate but he could have meant many things.

The President cut a lonely figure. What would he do? What would his supporters do if he remained unpopular? If the mob was coming for Soeharto it would also be coming for them! Should they encourage him to step down? Would he be amenable to this? Should they try to give him a nudge? Could they be successful? Or should they wait and see? Better still, should they develop a contingency plan while they waited. The airport faces bore very much the expression of people who had been talking among themselves and were afraid to be caught. No one wanted to be on the receiving end of presidential anger. But suppose the President stepped down? Or was forced down? Who would take over? The Vice President? The military? Someone as yet unknown? These matters had to be discussed! Few would have been surprised if all those around the President at the airport had not at least discussed the issue of constitutional succession and taken appropriate soundings. If the baton of power passed to Habibie would he accept it? Would the people accept that he had accepted it? Could ABRI accept Habibie? So may crucial questions as Soeharto returned to his burning capital.

More than 100 armoured vehicles were deemed necessary to escort Soeharto to his home in the central Jakarta suburb of Menteng. Once there, the President went into emergency mode. Predictably, he instantly summoned security leaders. As some were doubtless hoping, he wanted to set up a special emergency committee. He was commander of the Armed Forces and in March he had been granted emergency powers for just such an eventuality as this. What were the assessments of the intelligence agencies? What really was the public mood? Who was "the public"? What were the opinions of his law enforcers? Could there be a crack down? Against whom? Would ABRI be united in carrying it out? Would it be accepted?

This meeting was dangerous because it directly pitted against each other those who wanted reform and Soeharto's ousting and those who wanted to defend the status quo. It was vital for mainstream ABRI that Wiranto and his men dominate these discussions. They would have wanted to exaggerate the threat of revolution while playing up the difficulty of ABRI going against the people. The status quoers would have sought to downplay the revolutionary threat and talk confidently about ABRI's ability to crack down. Between the two groups, Soeharto was faced with a dangerous gamble. Either way he risked losing the presidency. If he failed to crack down, he might be swept from power. If he cracked down, he might still be swept from power by a possible wave of reaction. The discussion must have been tense. Forcing the pace was the spectre of new mayhem on Wednesday, May 20, when Amien Rais was threatening to bring a million of his followers not only onto the streets of Jakarta but on 'long march' to Freedom Square and to the State Palace.

The President would have been extremely angry over the riots and mayhem. Surely, he would have told Wiranto to do a better job. Subsequent 'stern' statements from Wiranto indicated that this was indeed the case. While he may not have agreed with Soeharto he had no choice but to obey orders. In Hong Kong, the 'South China Morning Post' appeared on May 18 with a screaming front page headline reflecting Soeharto's anger: " Soeharto may dump military chief." Wiranto, aiming to support the students but having to please the President, was treading on eggs. Fortunately, he, too, agreed that the riots and mayhem must stop, and he told the rioters so in firm terms. The mobs were no part of any plan ABRI may have had. Would the mere restoration of order be enough? Said the 'Post:' "His (Wiranto's) removal could dramatically increase the already substantial power of Mr. Soeharto's son-in-law, Let. Gen. Prabowo, who has been much less conciliatory with protesters."

If Wiranto had any aces, one might have been that he was able to reveal to the President and to the media and people of Indonesia that live ammunition had indeed been used by what he described as indisciplined individuals or forces at Trisakti University. Soeharto knew that it was these killings which had triggered the public outburst. While he may have wanted a crack down how could this be done in the current tense atmosphere. Reluctantly, he might have agreed with General Wiranto that though order must be restored it could be done in a firm but conciliatory way, without the use of undue naked force. If the President had indeed agreed, from this moment on the hard-liners would have been on a losing wicket. The circumscription of Government ability to use excessive force or, perhaps any force, was underlined by a new statement from Amien Rais who was quoted as saying: "Soeharto will be held responsible by the people if more killings take place." If Soeharto had not known about the shootings at Trisakti, and it seems unlikely, we can only guess his anger if he knew the real culprit, especially if his hope had been to return from Cairo and crack down on those who could be portrayed as being against the state - subversives, in other words.

Wiranto's crack down was good humoured but over the weekend hundreds of arrests were made and on the streets there was a heavy military presence. President Soeharto said pointedly but without specific reference to the ethnic Chinese, that the lives and property of ALL Indonesian citizens would be protected. Why should he not? For years ethnic Chinese had been his close business associates. Sensing the economic and even diplomatic danger of a large and sustained exodus of ethnic Chinese, military leaders went out of their way to assure them that it was safe to return to their homes and businesses. But, even weeks later, many of the damaged businesses remained firmly shuttered, their owners still overseas. Eventually, most would return. Indonesia was their home after all. But the businesses often remained closed. Who would pay for the restoration?

By Saturday afternoon, people were generally beginning to feel safe enough to leave their homes, some public transport resumed and a few shops were open. The military appealed to everyone to get back to normal. There was an intensified smile campaign by the security forces. News commentators in the electronic media repeated constantly that the situation in the capital was returning to "normal." The hope was that on Monday it really could be business as usual. Sarwono Kusumaatmadja was quoted as saying: " The people are banking on the Armed Forces to save themselves and the country and for General Wiranto to be the man of the hour." He did not mean that Wiranto should take over. Merely that he should help push Soeharto aside. The country had no stomach left for any kind of military rule. A coup would have resulted in civil war. University of Indonesia political scientist, Arbi Sanit, was quoted as saying that the Trisakti killings had only hardened the resolve for civilian rule.

Within hours of his return, the President ordered some small cuts to fuel and electricity tariffs. The price of premium gasoline would be reduced by Rps 200 per litre and the price of automotive diesel from Rps 600 to Rps 550 per litre. Before the price hikes each respectively had cost Rps 700 and Rps 380 per litre. Only the price of kerosene, widely used for household fuel, was returned to its former level of Rps 280 per litre. Announcing the reductions the hapless Minister of Mines and Energy, Kuntoro Mangkusubroto said: " I apologize if the cuts are not as much as people had hoped for, but it is the best we can do." To implement even these small cuts Coordinating Minister for the Economy, Finance and Industry, Ginandjar Kartsasmita, had felt obliged to discuss the move with IMF chief Camdessus who told him that the cuts would not be regarded as breaching the IMF agreement. It seemed as if the drastic price hike had not, after all, been part of a deliberate Soeharto plot to cause mayhem and roll back the demands of the IMF. After the riots, the Government seemed as fearful as ever of offending the IMF.

The 'Indonesian Observer' said in a leader: " If anything (scrapping the fuel subsidies) illustrated again and again how inept some ministers are in foreseeing events - and how weak a grip they have on the harsh realities of the small people." (It was President Soeharto who authorized the price increases and, later, President Habibie would describe Soeharto as old and out of touch). "Did they really think that the people, most of whom are poor and unemployed, would accept yet another blow in these difficult times, and do nothing about it?" The President's unprecedented airport briefing as he departed for Cairo showed that he was by no means out of touch on this issue. He guessed very well the sufferings of the people and perhaps even feared their reaction. But the IMF bully left Indonesia no choice. The risk had to be taken. The President had appealed for calm and patience and identified himself with the people's suffering. In Egypt he had apparently concluded that the people no longer felt that he was doing a good job and allegedly offered to stand down. From Soeharto's point of view he had done the best job he could in the worst economic situation ever faced by Indonesia, a job the IMF had at one and the same time both improved through recommended reforms and hindered by stubborn ideological commitment to free exchange and capital movements.

Having ordered the immediate restoration of public order, President Soeharto's next major concern was what might happen on Wednesday, May 20 if Amien Rais and the students carried out their threat to march and keep marching until he stepped down. The September 19 issue of 'Detektif and Romantika, quoted Yusril Ihza Mahendra, a lecturer in law and government at the University of Indonesia as saying that President Soeharto even discussed with General Wiranto the possibility of shooting Amien Rais! According to the magazine, Rais was reputedly scared enough to say good-bye to his wife and family. Later, Yusril denied the statement attributed to him. Wiranto doubtless counselled finding out what the students really wanted and seeing if they could be accommodated. How much future had a state which shot down those who opposed it!

On Saturday, May 16, President Soeharto had met a nine-strong delegation from the University of Indonesia, the key institution whose students had said that they would march on Parliament the following Wednesday. The delegation was led by Rector, Asman Boedisantoso. President Soeharto asked them what exactly the protesters wanted and, more importantly, what they thought he should do. It was not clear why he selected these advisers or why the briefing excluded his staunchest critics, such as Amien Rais and Megawati Sukarnoputri - unless, of course, the meeting was designed to be mere political window dressing. Nevertheless, the exercise was an extraordinary one for a leader who, until now, was not often seen to take advice in this way and about these subjects. Even more extraordinarily, the President was quoted as saying after the meeting that he hoped to receive more advice from other universities. The 'Indonesian Observer' commented: " For once, the process of openness has started to roll like a gust of fresh wind, cleansing the archaic and obsolete measures that have hampered progress. This process will provide a way out of the present untenable situation." Was it a process of openness or was President Soeharto, as always, searching for ways out of the current predicament that would leave his power intact? Was the desire to protect his power the reason why Amien and Mega were cold shouldered? If he asked either of them what he should do, there could only be one answer!

When greeting guests, the President was normally seen to be very much the confident host. When chairing meetings he was very much in command. If not matters of record, his speeches were didactic. Reprimands flowed easily toward those Soeharto felt had more to learn from him than vice versa. On the occasion of meeting the representatives from the University of Indonesia he looked embarrassed, almost like a child who knows that it has done something wrong and now expects to have to take the medicine. Clearly, he disliked having to take advice in this way. He looked much the same when greeting former US Vice President Walter Mondale, another visitor whose advice he felt he did not need and should not be forced to take.

There can be no doubt that the University of Indonesia team had told the President that some members of his cabinet were hugely unpopular and that the public felt that only fresh general and presidential elections could lift Indonesia out of the current crisis - a crisis which most people agreed was even more serious than the events of 1965 when the economy was also in ruins and 500,000 people were killed in an anti-communist bloodbath, including many ethnic Chinese with suspected links to Maoism. Whether the group told the President bluntly that he had to step down is unknown. It is possible that they did not, since a second group of advisers who met the President a few days later had to be specially primed by ABRI to pop the question.

A Saturday night announcement from President Soeharto seemed to reflect what he had been told by the academics. To head-off the clamour for political change, the President announced an impending cabinet reshuffle. Few were impressed. Former Environment Minister, Sarwono Kusumaatmadja was quoted as describing the announcement as a "tactical maneuver to buy time. As a former aide of his, I will be sad and I pity him for his own interests because we already know that he's becoming part of the problem." Economist Mari Pangestu asked: "The big question is: Is a cabinet reshuffle enough to restore confidence in the Government? Will the entry of new persons in the cabinet really put the people's faith back in the Government? The Chairman of the Interparliamentary Cooperative Body, H. Zamharir A.R. warned that the new ministers must not act solely as "yes men." he was quoted by the 'Indonesian Observer' as saying: " Pak Harto is the central figure, but he is not superman. He needs qualified assistants to handle the economic

225

crisis. I hope that the new members of the cabinet will be capable persons." The new ministers should be competent, hard working and respected at home and abroad, he said. With President Soeharto still in power public reaction to the promised reshuffle was understandably mixed and, in some cases, cautious. While Soeharto held power it could still be dangerous to speak out. Mirroring these mixed feelings, the Chairman of the Muslim Youth Association, Syaiful Anwar was quoted as saying: " It is a positive step but it does not meet the people's aspirations for political reforms."

In the aftermath of the student deaths and the mob rampages, people at home and abroad weighed up the prospects. World leaders were cautious in their comments. Perhaps the 'New York Times' summed up best what they seemed to be thinking: " It is now clear that recovery (in Indonesia) cannot begin as long as President Soeharto remains in power. He can spare Indonesia further turmoil by yielding office to a government that quickly sets a date for free and fair elections." The 'Jakarta Post' said in a leader: " What the national leadership has been trying to do so far is to simply keep what it sees as destabilizing forces at bay. This is not only exacerbating the economic crisis and political instability, but is also increasing the costs of the eventual and inevitable leadership succession, now seen by most analysts as the only way out of the present national crisis."

The 'Post' also said: " Not a single economic measure, however sound it may be, seems to matter anymore, as Indonesia descends into near chaos and a number of foreign governments contemplate evacuation of their citizens from the country. The country is moving inexorably towards a black hole as more and more worried entrepreneurs, both Chinese Indonesians and foreign, move their capital out of the country, this despite the painful reform measures which have been introduced. Until stability is restored, no new money will flow in. Even the next installment from the second tranche of IMF aid and assistance from other multilateral agencies and country donors are now at risk of further delay."

Writing in the 'Indonesian Observer' on May 16, Keith Loveard wrote: " For the time being Indonesia must forget about economic recovery. Recovery from the past few days will take a lot longer than the two or three years that might have been required before the Trisakti killings and the rule of the mob which followed. What is needed now is sweeping political reform, reform that also allows the Chinese minority some place in the official order and the administration of the country.

The military also has to accept that Chinese Indonesians can make soldiers just as good as the pribumi (indigenous Indonesians). Collusion, corruption and nepotism must go. The economy must be steered, however slowly, in a direction in which small people can feel they are part of the game."

As the day of action on May 20th approached, Indonesia seemed poised on the brink, not of anarchy, but at least of political change, if not of democracy. If change could be achieved, a storm of freedom might roar through Indonesia. Not only would people be and feel politically empowered. There was hope, too, that in their workplaces bapakism (paternalism) might give way to empowerment and meritocracy. If the aspirations and energies of a free people could be set free within a framework of socially acceptable rules and responsibilities Indonesian might be transformed. If change could not be achieved, the country seemed to stand on the brink of war.

In Washington the IMF and the US State Department denied that the Fund had caused the appalling problems being suffered by Indonesians. Literally, this was true. But had there recommendations not prepared the ground from which the riots sprang? In Kuala Lumpur, Malaysia, asked about the impact of the IMF's policies on Indonesia, Prime Minister, Mahathir Mohamad commented: "I think the IMF can see on CNN what happens when we pull subsidies too quickly from people who depend on subsidies. Even if they want to pull (the subsidies) back they have to do it gradually. When people become poorer and you pull back the subsidies then, of course, you are deliberately agitating the people, almost wanting them to revolt."

Had this been the name of the game all along? Had there been a carefully conceived Western plot to topple President Soeharto? Or had those who wanted to achieve this objective seen their chance as the economic crisis deepened? It was noticeable that in the same way that US President Clinton was warm and friendly to Thai Prime Minister, Chuan Leekpai (who was an IMF dream PM) to President Soeharto he was austere. All other developed countries, especially the G-8 Group, meeting in Birmingham, England, followed the US lead. Had President Soeharto's critics and reformers within ABRI decided to jump on the bandwagon while the going was good. Had Soeharto loyalists tried to thwart them all with a risky plot of their own, involving shootings, riots and even rapes?

The IMF said blandly that its recovery programme for Indonesia "is still very much appropriate for the Indonesian economic situation and for restoring confidence and bringing about a resumption of economic growth." US Democrat Senator, Thomas Daschle was quoted as saying that it was not the IMF reforms which had sent Indonesia up in flames. "In fact it may be just the opposite. It may be the leaders' unwillingness to recognize the importance of these reforms that has led to all this disruption."

However it had come about, as the week of May 18 opened Indonesians awaited political developments fearfully yet optimistically. Perhaps the only event which would really depress them was if the President refused to resign!

CHAPTER SIX

" I Quit"
says
Soeharto

The atmosphere in Jakarta on Monday, May 18 was curious. After the amok, in which hundreds had died or been injured and trillions of rupiah worth of property destroyed or damaged, people seemed in a happy and relaxed mood - as if the orgy of destruction had purged their systems of the boiling frustration which had been there previously. In Jakarta and Medan "thousands" of people reportedly were overcome with guilt at what they had done and began returning stolen property to its owners. Suddenly news from the electronic media, especially television was all relatively good. Few realized that the Government had introduced strict new rules for reporting social unrest and had been instructed to emphasize that everything was returning to "normal." The security forces joined in the campaign.

In reality, the atmosphere was still far from normal. Foreigners and ethnic Chinese were flocking to Jakarta's international airport in even larger numbers in anticipation of more havoc during Wednesday's day of action called by Amien Rais. In many government offices even less than usual seemed to be happening, pending news of the cabinet reshuffle and, more importantly, pending the outcome of the massive protest planned for May 20, National Awakening Day. But everyone was relaxed, as people are when all the usual rules and constraints seem temporarily to have dropped away. It was a time, one could say, of nervous laughter. In the supermarkets there were long queues of people stocking up with buggies brim full of supplies. Banks had opened for the first time since the preceding Thursday and people were also stocking up with money. They were expected to close again next day. The more "normal" the media said things were the less normal they really seemed.

Some hotels, especially near the airport, were booked solid - in effect, with refugees. Others were doing better business than they would normally - thanks to the rush of ethnic Chinese and foreigners to get out of the way of the massive pro-democracy demonstrations expected to roll through the week in an attempt to force the resignation of President Soeharto and his Government. Convoys of cars moved incessantly towards the international airport, bearing away capital, purchasing power and skills so badly needed in Indonesia. Wednesday was clearly 'D-Day.' Those who could, escaped.

Those who elected to stay behind and who felt threatened turned their homes into personal fortresses and avoided non-essential travel. Barricades were up in ethnic Chinese neighbourhoods and the men were as armed as it was possible to be - sticks, bats, golf clubs, iron bars, machetes. Schools, universities, shops, offices - all were to be closed from Wednesday onwards. Everyone was extra vigilant.

Amien Rais had said he would bring millions of pro-democracy activists onto the streets. The students had said "We're going to march." The capital was anything but 'normal.' On Wednesday, 'the people' were coming - With whom would they stop? Where would they stop? With what would they stop? What would it be like? What would the targets be? Would it be just speeches? Or would an angry, throbbing, frenzied human tide seek to tear down the President and the Parliament and install a provisional president and assembly in their stead? Would the military stand back? Or would they resist the tide? Could there really be a second Tiananmen Square in Jakarta?

In the House of Representatives, Government leaders were under intense pressure from all sides. Demands for a special emergency session of the MPR flooded in. Traditional supporters of the ruling GOLKAR threatened to withdraw their support if the session was not called immediately. In 32 years, the House had virtually never asserted its independence from the Executive about anything. Now, society was demanding that it lead, in effect that it confront the President and uphold society's demands. All factions condemned the price increases but now even the Government's most loyal supporters could see that the people would not be satisfied now with even price reductions. They were fed up. They were angry. They were sick to death of President Soeharto and his family. The economy was in ruins and with it the lives of millions. In the public mind President Soeharto and the corruption and incompetence of his New Order regime was to blame. It began to look as if anyone supporting the President would soon be doomed to be swept away.

Calm had been restored to the battered streets of the capital but, otherwise, nothing had changed. Merely restoring calm offered no solution to the terrible sickness of the economy, a sickness Government critics believed was brought on by President Soeharto. A sickness that could not now be cured if he remained in office.

ABRI's strategy was to work toward the resignation of President Soeharto by using constitutional means. On May 18, the 'Bangkok Post' quoted as Western military attaché as saying: " ABRI has short, medium and long-term concepts for reform aligned to the University of Indonesia package calling for political, economic and legal change. But ABRI has decided that it will do all of its change through the ABRI faction in Parliament and this means that ABRI is attempting to avoid any form of overt use of force to achieve change."

It seemed that even at this eleventh hour Soeharto continued to see the possibility of staying on, or, at least, not to have admitted to himself that he must finally go. ABRI decided to turn up the heat by using its adopted tool, the MPR, an institution that was, in any case, ripe for its intervention because of anger with the Government for proceeding with the fuel and electricity price increases without consultation and dismay at the activities of the students and the mobs. At the same time the volume of noise from the universities was also turned up.

On Monday night, reflecting the gravity of the situation and the deep sense of threat felt by the New Order regime as a whole, Speaker of the House of Representatives, Harmoko, a hitherto loyal Soeharto disciple, made the bombshell announcement that all factions of the House of Representatives, including the Armed Forces, had agreed to ask the President to resign. One of Harmoko's houses had been partially burnt by the mob and, it was rumoured, that his hands shook when he read the announcement. Perhaps it was anxiety about what Soeharto might yet do to him if the call to resign went unheeded and the President found some way to retaliate. Significantly, at the close of Harmoko's announcement, Armed Forces faction leader, Let. Gen. Syarwan raised his fist in the air to indicate that he, and ABRI, were on the side of reform. Harmoko undoubtedly found ABRI's support highly reassuring. It is more than doubtful if he or anyone else would have dared to call for Soeharto to step down without the unequivocal support of the Armed Forces. Indeed, was ABRI supporting an initiative of his or was Harmoko supporting an initiative of ABRI's? Picking up the faction leaders' call, media reports added that President Soeharto and his family should also surrender all their wealth to the nation. The 'Indonesian Observer' of May 27 said that President Soeharto had been "shocked" by the defection of Harmoko, " his main sycophant."

The people and the media could hardly believe that Harmoko had made such a statement. Only two weeks earlier he had flatly rejected calls for a special session of the MPR. The 'Jakarta Post' reflected the amazement on May 19: " The wind of change is blowing through this country at unbelievable speed and nobody appears to be able to stop the very force of this phenomenon. Yesterday's decision by the House of Representatives leadership to support popular calls for President Soeharto to step down is one of the greatest surprises in the course of our nation's struggle for complete reform. The decision was, of course, somewhat unbelievable since many members of the legislature have close connections with the President. The fact that House Speaker, Harmoko, who announced the decision, had been a staunch opponent of the type of reform called for by the student movement and that the House has long been branded a rubber stamp legislature are noteworthy when viewing the sudden decision. Many Indonesians, astounded by the swiftness of events, are now joking that the mice are jumping from the sinking ship."

As might be expected, the riots and associated capital outflow coupled with a temporary moratorium on international aid had had a devastating affect on the economy. On Tuesday, May 19, headlines screamed: "Economy at the crossroads." The 'Indonesian Observer' quoted currency analyst Theo Toemion as saying: " The economy is practically dead now and the impact of last week means that it will not recover until the national leader is changed." A financial consultant was quoted as saying: " The Government's credibility is eroded and the abduction of Pius Lustrilanang and several other activists has made things worse for the economy."

With little, if any, capital entering Indonesia and billions of dollars flowing out, Toemion called for the urgent imposition of capital controls through the introduction of a two tier exchange rate. He was quoted as saying that Indonesia now needed more than just the IMF rescue package. "We can no longer afford to become the IMF good boy. The problem is now not only the economy but social unrest." Much later, writing in the "Far Eastern Economic Review' of October 1, 1998, Henry Sender would note that: " Many bankers believe that Indonesia should have been the last candidate for the IMF's "cookie-cutter" approach to the currency crisis." What a wonderful thing is hindsight!

On Tuesday morning, with Harmoko's ultimatum ringing in his ears and the rupiah down at Rps 17,000 to the US dollar, President Soeharto sounded out nine public and mainly Muslim leaders at the Merdeka Palace. Others at the meeting included General Wiranto and the chief of the Army Strategic Reserves Command, Lt. Gen. Prabowo. There was also constitutional law expert Yusril Ihza Mahendra. Some of the leaders pulled no punches and said that the demonstrators' definition of reform meant the President's resignation. Later, in August, President Habibie would say that Soeharto had been told that his resignation was the only way to save the state, the perception which had driven the MPR to call for the President's resignation. If Soeharto refused to quit the entire regime was at risk! Unknown to the President, one of the academics, Nurcholish Madjid, had already met with ABRI's chief of Sociopolitical Affairs, General Bambang Yudoyono. The General encouraged Nurcholish to be blunt in asking Soeharto to resign. Nurcholish and the others did exactly that. Even as they met, Standard & Poor lowered its credit ratings on 11 Indonesian corporates with all ratings on CreditWatch with negative implications.

Following the meeting, a breakthrough seemed to have been made. President Soeharto told a press conference that he was quite willing to resign - "I've had it with being a president," he was quoted as saying - but, he said that it should not be at once, for fear that the nation disintegrated in chaos. Instead, he proposed that there should be a fresh general election "soon" followed by new elections for president and vice president. He was emphatic that: "I don't wish to be nominated again for president." Meanwhile, a reform committee would be set up comprised by public figures to draw up new laws on elections, political parties, the MPR and DPR and other political reforms demanded. The unpopular March cabinet would be reshuffled and named "the Reform Cabinet." Tourism, Art and Culture Minister, Abdul Latief resigned immediately rather than await the reshuffle. The hand of General Wiranto could be discerned behind these new initiatives.

The President explained that although he wanted to resign he did not think that it should be immediately because a) this would not be the correct constitutional procedure and b) the vice president would have to take over. Sensing that the protesters would feel Habibie was a Soeharto man, the President was quoted as saying: " Would this solve the problem. There'll be more protests for him to resign, and this will go no and on." Habibie was apparently not amused by being written off so peremptorily. According to 'Asiaweek' of July 24: " Habibie called on Soeharto that night, fearing his political career had ended prematurely that morning. Soeharto had pledged to hold elections rather than hand over to his vice president. Habibie, say colleagues, was hurt. He promised Soeharto a dignified retirement, and warned that others might not be so reasonable." Pleading that the 1945 Constitution be respected, Soeharto was quoted as saying: " If we don't hold on to the Constitution, what will become of our country? ...It can lead to a bigger conflict, bloodshed and possibly even civil war." Holding to the Constitution was in fact what everybody was doing. ABRI was doing it by working through the MPR. Habibie was doing it by signalling his willingness to take over. If he resigned, even Soeharto would be respecting the Constitution!

Some of those at the Tuesday meeting were shocked that Soeharto had not, in fact, agreed to resign immediately. Others, for example, such as Abdurrahman Wahid supported the gradual approach to change, citing the problem of finding a successor to Soeharto. Abdurrahman was quoted as appealing to the students to call off their demonstrations because, he was quoted as saying: " Our goals have already been achieved." Environment Minister, Juwono Sudarsono clarified that President Soeharto intended a comprehensive reform of electoral laws within two months and parliamentary elections within three to six months. Muslim intellectual, Emha Najib told the media that he believed the consensus at the meeting with Soeharto favoured elections within six months. Muslim scholar, Nurcholis Madjid, was quoted as adding that presidential elections might take place as early as March, 1999 - a vastly more rapid timetable than that to be proposed later on and presumably reflecting the urgent pressures of the day.

The students and Government critics who had not attended the meeting thought Soeharto was up to his old tricks, playing for time, promising much and likely to implement precious little. Soeharto seemed to make concessions to the reformers while playing on fears of civil war. He bowed to the demand of the Parliament - but not immediately. At the same time he conspicuously sought advice and, by implication, backing, from Indonesia's Muslim community, theoretically the dominant group.

By agreeing to step down and promising many of the reforms being demanded, President Soeharto may have believed that Parliament's ultimatum could be defanged, that the students might go back to their studies and that the planned mass protests could as a result be called off. About the mass protest ABRI agreed. They supported the students, not the mob. This would explain ABRI's insistence later in the day that mass demonstrations planned by Amien Rais for the Day of National Awakening be cancelled. ABRI had previously signalled their support for Amien Rais's efforts to force Soeharto to step down. Now they were afraid that his mass rally would again inflame the mob. Soeharto could not have known that his dismissal of Harmoko's demand that he resign would merely prompt ABRI to renewed efforts in the House. By agreeing to step down - but not right now - Soeharto was also bidding to split and weaken the reform movement, dividing it between those who wanted immediate change and those who feared immediate change and would prefer a gradual transition. In fact he made the reformers all the more determined.

As the critics said, the President's statement changed little. Left to his own devices, he would remain in office to serve out his term, unpopular cabinet members would be sacrificed and steps would be taken towards political reforms to be implemented in five year's time. Once again this was not what many people wanted to hear. Whether he could or could not have split the reform movement, those who wanted immediate change held the floor - the vocal critics and the students.

Amien Rais, Soeharto's most fiery and persistent critic, slammed the President's latest offer as another bid to buy time. He was quoted as saying: " His statement shows that he is not willing to step down and that he is ignoring the aspirations of his own people. Government critic and former minister, Emil Salim, was quoted as saying that Soeharto's statement indicated that he intended to retain power and dictate what political change could taken place at what time. He said that Soeharto should resign and hand over to Vice President Habibie whose task would then be to prepare for an extraordinary session of the People's Consultative Assembly "within three months, to elect a new president and vice president."

The students were not fooled. 'Asiaweek' of May 29 quoted one University of Indonesia student as saying: " He is playing a game of words. Soeharto must go. Full stop."

Commenting on the President's offer, the 'Far Eastern Economic Review' of May 28 said: " The grounds for disbelief are obvious. Soeharto, who has always treated elections as a symbolic rather than an active expression of democracy, will now be in charge of restoring political pluralism in Indonesia. It tests credulity that this same man can now fashion laws to allow real political parties to replace the sycophantic GOLKAR, create a framework for the first fair election since 1955, and attack the corruption and nepotism that Indonesians in all walks of life have finally mustered the courage to reject. Many Indonesians doubt that he intends to try."

The forces ranged against the President on the Day of National Awakening were potentially awesome. President Soeharto had become a figure of near universal hate. The country would not be satisfied until the man they blamed more than anybody for the economic crisis stepped down. Some wanted more than that. Amien Rais was quoted as speaking of the need for an apology to the people and accountability for "corrupt" administrations.

From Soeharto's point of view what looked like an increasingly desperate bid to hold on to power may have had another motivation. There had long been unease about a missing letter from Sukarno allegedly transferring power to Soeharto. Soon there would be allegations that Soeharto had known about the plot to kill army generals back in 1965. There would be allegations that there had never been a communist coup attempt. There would be inferences that Soeharto had, in effect seized power. There would be talk about the involvement of foreign intelligence agencies. There would be new questioning of the way Indonesia's first president had died. Had Soeharto clung to power so long lest such dark secrets be brought out? Had he clung to power so long because he feared for his own safety if such allegations could be proved?

Even as Soeharto had outlined his willingness to step down at some time "soon" and unveiled his plans for reform, elements of the security forces departed dramatically from their on-campus policy and allowed more than 30,000 students to storm the Parliament building, even taking up positions on the roof. Signs appeared saying ominously: "Kill Soeharto." Some of the buses used by the students were thoughtfully provided by the Marines after permission was said to have been granted for the parliamentary protest by Gen. Syarwan Hamid, Deputy Speaker of the House. ! Other banners read: " Thirty Two Years Is Enough" and "Return Sovereignty To The People." On the campuses troops were seen exchanging high fives with students and giving them the thumbs up sign. According to 'The Straits Times' of Singapore, one

20-year-old sergeant commented: "The students are showing the world the real situation in this country where there are a lot of problems of nepotism and corruption and Soeharto needs to be replaced. Today, we are not intimidating the students, but allowing them complete freedom. We support them 100 percent. They are fighting for what we too want to fight for."

Just as President Soeharto had used students to topple Sukarno, now someone, was allowing, if not using, a new generation of students to bring down Soeharto. That someone, of course, had to be those elements in the military high command, almost certainly the majority, who had long dreamed of getting rid of Soeharto and his ways. Seeing their chance at last, for weeks Wiranto and other senior officers had given uncharacteristic approval of the student's right to protest. Security forces can always stop protesters if they wish. In this case, clearly, they didn't wish. There were scenes of open and frequent 'fraternization' between certain troops and demonstrators - but not the special forces commanded by the President's family and his military friends. They were photographed by the media at the Parliament building looking thoroughly disapproving and threatening.

'Time' magazine of May 25 quoted Yogyakarta's Gadjah Mada University professor of political science Afan Ghaffar as saying: " The military has decided that what's good for society is good for the military, and what is good for the military is good for society. I strongly believe that the military will take the side of the students as the crisis continues." Amien Rais thought the same thing. On the very next page of the same magazine, Rais was quoted as saying that the military "share my ideas of change. Many of them have told me that they share my views and ideas almost completely." Asked what the President might do Rais responded: " He will try his best to hold onto power, but I think he is playing a losing game. He is not sharp any longer and no longer understands the situation. We have come to the conclusion that the situation will deteriorate and get out of control. The only way to stop this move toward anarchy and chaos is for Soeharto to step down. There is no alternative. All the demands for change have boiled down into one single demand: Soeharto has to step down." While they had apparently not told Rais as much ABRI had reached exactly the same conclusion and were using the students to step up the pressure.

For weeks the students had been allowed to demonstrate but kept on campus - a standing and growing threat to Soeharto. Now, in the face of the presidential shilly-shallying they were suddenly let loose

- and under threatening banners saying: "Kill Soeharto." 'Newsweek' of June 1 revealed that ABRI was indeed behind the students. At the meeting of top brass following the massacre at Trisakti 'Newsweek' quoted human rights activist and former GOLKAR legislator, Marzuki Darusman as saying: " They (ABRI) decided to allow the students to keep the pressure on Soeharto in public protests and to activate a constitutional and legislative process that would remove him from office." Concluded the magazine: " Soeharto was caught in a vice."

At the Parliament building, student demonstrators were soon joined by over 1,000 labour activists from the Federation of All Indonesian Workers Union. A potentially dangerous link had now been allowed between the students and organized labour. Who knew how far such links could go? Was this the beginning of people's power? Was it meant to look like such a beginning? Even as ABRI officially called for the demonstration of Amien Rais to be called off, units continued to facilitate the students. The message of the demonstrators at the Parliament was uncompromising:- they would occupy the building until Soeharto - and Habibie - stepped down.

The media carried endless quotes from people from many walks of life calling on President Soeharto to resign. Young professionals demonstrated outside the Jakarta Stock Exchange with banners demanding Soeharto's ouster. The Petisi 50 group of mainly retired generals, many of them sidelined by Soeharto, pledged support for the students. Retired generals could say what serving generals could not - even if they thought it. General Abdul Haris Nasution called on ABRI to support the aspirations of the people. He reminded ABRI that "soldiers must fight for honesty, truth and justice" - something by implication it was clear he meant that Soeharto had not done.

Despite ABRI's admonition against mass demonstrations, in Yogyakarta on National Awakening Day, Sri Sultan Hamengkubuwono X was expected to lead an immense rally of over 200,000.

At home and abroad, it was hard for President Soeharto to identify anyone who supported him. The clamour for his resignation was near total. According to the student banners some wanted him to hand over any wealth he had amassed, others wanted to see him put on trail, some wanted him dead! Despite the bleak and uncomfortable future the students seemed to have planned for him, still, Soeharto clung on, pondering his options.

Throughout the remainder of Tuesday, Minister/State Secretary Saadilah Mursjid and his staff worked to contact the people nominated to the new reform Committee, due to be set up on Thursday, May 21. This time its members were to include Rais and Megawati together with 43 other academic, religious and community leaders. When potential members of the Reform Committee were contacted, most refused to serve.

From overseas, Soeharto found little encouragement to stay on. US Secretary of State Madeline Albright called on him to "preserve his legacy" by permitting a transition to democracy. Cynics wondered if she knew all there was to know about his "legacy." 'The Straits Times' of Singapore revealed that since 1995 the United States Government had funnelled US$26 million to non-government organizations which opposed Soeharto. The organizations included the Indonesian Legal Aid Society. The money was given by the US Agency for International Development (USAID) and former senior counsel, Peter Galbraith was quoted as saying: " The idea was to send a message that the US was concerned about something other than the banks and the economic issues, that we thought about the ordinary people of Indonesia, and to prepare for a possible transition from Soeharto to what we hope will be a more democratic and stable system." As late as June 14, three weeks after Soeharto's departure, Malaysia's 'New Sunday Times' said that 88 Indonesian legislators protested to the US Government against the use of funds to be used to interfere in domestic affairs. Despite the fact that the funds had been aimed at supporting opposition to Soeharto, the legislators were quoted as saying that the deployment of the funds was not in Indonesia's "national interest." Indonesians could still remember other US interference in the 1950s and '60s, interference which some suspected had helped bring Soeharto to power in the first place.

In Washington, even Democrat senators were pressing President Clinton to demand Soeharto's resignation. Within the US Congress there was no sympathy for fresh IMF payments until President Soeharto stepped down. Congressmen suspected that a portion of the funds would simply find their way into the pockets of the Soehartos and their business allies. The role of the Soeharto family had been on Washington's mind since the start of the year. State Department spokesman, James Rubin said he thought it was unlikely that the IMF would go ahead with its June 4 payment of US$1 billion to Indonesia until the political situation became clearer. One international banking official, based in the US capital, was quoted in January by Britain's 'Daily Telegraph' as saying: " What we are dealing with in Jakarta isn't just a financial and economic crisis but a 76-year-old autocrat under pressure from his relatives to stay put and protect their interests," The World Bank announced the postponement of loans worth US$1.2 billion to Indonesia quickly followed by the postponement of another US$2.5 billion from the Asia Development Bank. In a related development, leading international banks postponed further discussions on rescheduling Indonesia's offshore private debt. Members of the US Senate Foreign relations Committee called on President Soeharto to reform or quit. The Governments of Britain and Australia urged President Soeharto to resign.

Despite its concerns about human rights abuses in Indonesia, President Soeharto received no shrill condemnation from President Clinton. Singapore's 'The Straits Times' US Correspondent, Lee Siew Hua wrote in the May 23 issue that one reason may have been that it looked to the White House as if Soeharto would fall without any additional help. Washington's silence was nevertheless interesting. Jakarta's rumour machine had said for years that it was possible that President Soeharto had come to power with the help of foreign intelligence services, maybe the CIA or the British. Both had been or were fighting communism in Vietnam and Malaysia. Sukarno seemed to favour the communists. Malaysia was additionally threatened by Sukarno. What more natural than that the US and the UK should welcome a change in government in Indonesia away from the left leaning Sukarno and in favour of the right wing Soeharto. Could Washington's silence be construed as that of an old ally not wishing to offend an old friend. Who knows. It is always dangerous to place any reliance on rumours. Still, if one reads his autobiography, for a relatively junior officer, Soeharto was remarkably confident. Just as he was to become the master dalang of so much that happened in Indonesia had there been a dalang or two behind him?

The 'Far Eastern Economic Review's' Michael Vatikiotis and Adam Schwarz seemed to think so when they wrote in the June 4 issue: " On September 30, 1965, six generals and a lieutenant were murdered by members of the presidential guard and their mutilated bodies thrown in a well. Mystery still surrounds this incident. Many Indonesians wonder why Soeharto was left off the list. As commander of KOSTRAD, the Jakarta-based strategic reserve, he was in charge of the only active fighting force in the capital.

"Soeharto has always maintained that he was only informed of the murders early on the morning of October 1, and moved quickly to crush the coup. But now, one of the ringleaders, Colonel Abdul Latief, now aged 72, has said that he told Soeharto about the plot on the eve of the generals abduction.

"Whether Suharto conspired or was simply reluctant to act, the murders were used to attack the Communist Party of Indonesia and discredit President Sukarno because of his patronage of the communists."

On November 30, one of Sukarno's wives, Dewi, supported Latief's allegation saying that, as far as she knew, Soeharto had known about the planned killings of the military top brass the day before they were scheduled to happen. Showing letters to her from Sukarno, she said that the President did not know the fate of all of the generals until October 3, two days after the killings - impossible if he had commissioned them. She was quoted as adding that the slayings were not even the work of the Communist Party of Indonesia as Soeharto had always alleged. "It was not the PKI. It really wasn't" she was quoted as saying. Soeharto, she said, just made them a scapegoat.

Some of this had a familiar ring to it. During the Jakarta riots, Jakarta-based military units had seemingly decided not to intervene! There was something very Sherlock Holmesian about this tactic. It was not what was done that was important but what wasn't done! As Holmes would have said it was not that the dog barked that was important so much as the fact that it didn't bark.

When Wiranto left the meeting at the State Palace on the morning of Tuesday, May 19, it seemed to the general public that Soeharto still regarded him as his loyal commander, a man, like Soeharto himself, caught up in the flow of events, a man still willing to obey presidential orders. If anything, Prabowo and his associates had been made to look ineffective throughout the riots, not Wiranto. Perhaps Soeharto still felt that he could trust Wirantro, a former adjutant, to a greater extent than his ambitious and hot tempered son-in-law - a man whom he had probably been told now had dark shadows hanging over his head, a man who had bid for supreme power in the armed forces and lost! As a loyal commander the General went directly to ABRI headquarters. He soon appeared on television screens to say that the call for President Soeharto to resign from the House of Representatives faction leaders had "no legal basis" because they represented only themselves and not the Parliament. He called for planned mass demonstrations to be called off. The public was confused. Whose side was ABRI on? It looked as if Soeharto's time was up and as if ABRI supported the reformists but here was the ABRI commander apparently defending him!

Wiranto's comment could be taken two ways:- first, that he backed the President or secondly, that he was pointing the way to mak-

241

ing constitutional what for the moment wasn't. House members from the dominant GOLKAR faction, including ABRI, assumed the latter and promptly called for a special plenary session of the MPR to remove Soeharto. Harmoko told Soeharto: "Resign by Friday or be impeached."

Wiranto knew that ABRI wanted to avoid seeing the President being impeached at a special session of Parliament, a possibility which they judged would be certain to follow if he failed to heed the faction leaders demand that he step down. Had he been asked by Soeharto at their earlier meeting, Wiranto might have hinted or even said outright that it would be better for the President to step down rather than await impeachment or try to fight what seemed a losing battle. Impeachment would have been humiliating for a president many of them knew well and had served loyally. It would have been humiliating to ABRI to have one of its generals called to account in this way. In addition, it would be difficult to control the accounting process. Cupboards might be opened which, in the national interest and certainly the regime's interest, might best be left locked. Impeachment could also bring a searing spotlight to bear on ABRI at a time when the Armed Forces were already exceedingly low in the public estimate.

General Wiranto favoured the reform movement from the outset. He was not alone. There were many others who fully realized that the writing for Soeharto was on the wall. Within ABRI there were officers more loyal and officers less loyal to Soeharto but doubtless majority shared the view that political change could no longer be prevented. Soeharto himself seemed to realize this but by the time he had climbed aboard the reform bandwagon, as he himself would say later, he had completely lost the trust of the people. There was probably a coalescence of opinion within ABRI that since the people were clearly and loudly rejecting him, what was needed for President Soeharto was a graceful constitutional exit toward a dignified retirement, after which he would be duly protected by the military. Clearly, there also had to be a level of deterrence to ensure that the protesters were not allowed to carry their campaign to the point where the entire New Order Government and the stability of society as a whole was threatened.

As a soldier, Wiranto and those who thought like him, could not easily go so far as to directly ask his Commander-in-Chief to resign - especially if there were still elements in the high command loyal to President Soeharto under any circumstances. General Wiranto was in a difficult position. Soeharto was still President as well as Commander-in-Chief of the Armed Forces. He was in direct communication with his son-in-law, with tens of thousands of troops under his command. Let. Gen. Prabowo could rely on the loyalty of other commanders. Nothing could be taken for granted until it happened. Soeharto was still president until he resigned. For the time being, either he must be obeyed or the disobedient officer must risk the consequences. At this stage, had Wiranto acted in any way outside the limits of his power by requesting the President to step down or acted unconstitutionally, it would still have been possible for President Soeharto to fill his shoes with someone more loyal to him. Said 'Newsweek' on June 1: " Wiranto denounced the Parliamentary leaders' demand for the President to resign as unconstitutional and threatened to crack down if unrest continued. Wiranto's strategy bought the military leaders time - and prevented Soeharto from sacking them or replacing them with Prabowo and declaring martial law." Ex GOLKAR legislator Marzuki Darusman commented in 'Newsweek: " Wiranto simply couldn't let Soeharto know that there was a plot against him. He had to keep his distance from his prime movers to keep the appearance of independence." Had Soeharto known about the ABRI plot the consequences could have been dire. There must have been many occasions during these crisis hours when Wiranto and some of those around him feared for their lives.

For months ABRI had been dialoguing with the students and mingling in the community. Perhaps, better than the President, isolated by sycophancy and by his lonely position at the top, ABRI knew the mood and aspirations of the people. It was also a golden opportunity for which the ABRI mainstream had waited for years. In his book: ' Indonesian Politics Under Soeharto', John Vatikiotis argues that while ABRI did not want to be seen to go against the constitution some of its leaders relished the occurrence of an 'incident' which could be used by ABRI to assert its power and even to topple Soeharto. The tension between ABRI and the Executive would finally be resolved - in ABRI's favour.

Public criticism of ABRI, especially because of the Government's eviction of Megawati's PDI from its Jakarta headquarters on July 27, 1996, the recent spate of kidnappings of activists and, now, the killings at Trisakti, had not only reached fever pitch but had reached a peak of unacceptability to ABRI. Mainstream ABRI wanted to be the people's security force, not feared, hated and reviled. Later, when Soeharto had finally fallen, 'Newsweek' quoted a Lieutenant Misyanto, assigned to guard the National Monument, as saying: " We didn't want a Tiananmen Square in Jakarta. We're protecting the people and we're also part of the people. We didn't want to fight our own people."

After Harmoko's announcement and the student occupation of Parliament, Soeharto would have known that the Armed Forces had joined the other elements of GOLKAR and the other factions of the MPR in demanding his resignation. He would have known that ABRI was behind the students. Wiranto had been a presidential adjutant and, like many others, knew President Soeharto well. But, in this situation of acute crisis, friendship could not be allowed to obscure the political realities or lose the political opportunities. The people wanted Soeharto to go. Parliament wanted Soeharto to go. ABRI had wanted Soeharto to go for a decade. Now was the moment! Wiranto had been hand-picked by Soeharto and promoted out-of-turn but in his heart he was a career soldier with a clear perception of a professional security force accountable to a democratic state which it was sworn to protect. It is hard to imagine how the two men could have continued to mee1t and discuss once President Soeharto realized that ABRI had switched sides. Indeed, some of the press photographs seem to portray Wiranto looking inscrutable but Soeharto peering intently with glittering eyes as if he would look into the General's very soul.

During his televised address, Wiranto had harsh words for rioters and protesters, words that we can all too easily imagine President Soeharto instigating at the meeting at the Cendana residence. He warned that many people knew that more unrest was planned for later in the week, commencing on Wednesday, May 20, and was quoted as saying: " ....ABRI, as a stabilizing force in society, asks that all people continue to abide by the prevailing law because any other course of action will only exacerbate the situation. ABRI warns the certain parties to stop anarchic actions if they do not want to face military force." One of the "certain parties" was Amien Rais and rumour had it that he was called to ABRI headquarters and told that if he went ahead with his planned day of action on Wednesday, he and his supporters would risk an Indonesian Tiananmen. Around 40,000 police and military personnel would be available in the capital alone. Of course, if the protests went ahead the pressure on President Soeharto to resign would be magnified. In warning against the mass demonstrations, ABRI only drew attention to the terrible danger more forcefully and frighteningly. Not a few living in Jakarta were convinced that revolution was about to break out.

On Tuesday night, President Soeharto summoned all four of the Government's coordinating ministers - for political affairs and security, for economy, finance and industry, development supervision and people's welfare. President Soeharto wanted the fullest information about the economy and social conditions as well as about the ongoing protests and security. Quite obviously all these elements were now dangerously linked. As head of state, he could not afford to take too narrow a view.

ABRI's advice or the advice of certain officers within ABRI had to be weighed against economic and social developments. For example, a crackdown, though theoretically possible, would risk destroying the unity of ABRI and might subsequently bring down the economy by eroding even the last vestiges of investor and market confidence. There is little doubt that even at this late juncture President Soeharto favoured a last stand in his bunker. As late as the night of May 19, according to the Indonesian language 'Berita Buana' of September 11, Soeharto allegedly ordered that if Amien's demonstrators reached Monas, General Wiranto's forces should meet them, not with rubber bullets, but with live ones! He was adamant that the demonstrators should not be allowed pass. What Wiranto decided about the bullets order we can only guess. We know that he did indeed go ahead with preparations to seal off Freedom Square (Monas) but in typical Javanese fashion, other steps were afoot to ensure that the marchers never reached the military barricades. According to 'Detektif & Romantika' magazine, President Soeharto had earlier allegedly asked Attorney General Soedjono to arrest Amien on charges of subversion. The Attorney general refused on the grounds that there was insufficient evidence.

The message from the all-important market was now very clear: Soeharto and his policies had become the problem. If he fought to stay on the problem would remain and the economy would deteriorate further. Soeharto doubtless had to fight with himself. He wanted to stay on, yet everything pointed to the desirability of him quitting.

The Tuesday meetings which had proceeded throughout the day at Jalan Cendana resulted in more bad news for the President. Led by his new Coordinating Minister for Economy, Finance and Industry, Ginandjar Kartasasmita, now a key player in the bid to save Indonesia's economy from total collapse, 12 ministers resigned from the cabinet. Their common view was that peace could not be restored to the streets until the President resigned and that until he did so all measures aimed at salvaging the economy were doomed to failure. They warned that the economy would collapse in less than a week unless he stepped down immediately. Better than anyone else, Ginandjar would have known that the IMF and the US felt that new money would be wasted on Indonesia until President Soeharto stepped down. The letters of resignation were

245

written at the offices of the National Planning Board in Menteng. Their letters delivered, they gathered at the house of Vice President Habibie, stung by Soeharto's dismissal of him and now more prepared than ever to take over.

Presumably not knowing they were there, Soeharto rang Habibie to ask him to persuade the ministers to reverse their decision. At this stage, such a thing was impossible and, equally presumably, Habibie told this to Soeharto. Habibie, Ginandjar and his colleagues were now of a mind, ABRI and the MPR were of a mind. Wiranto and Ginandjar are both nationalists and must have shared a great deal of common ground. Ginandjar was also ex-ABRI, formerly having been an Air Marshall. Habibie, Ginandjar and Wiranto were now firmly and inextricably allied. Those who would have to sort out the succession issue, should President Soeharto resign, had agreed their game plan. It is also certain that they had agreed that President Soeharto could be thrown no life lines. He would have to go!

The President's options were diminishing quickly. With the ABRI faction in the House backing or even pushing Harmoko, support from the Armed Forces was now more than extremely doubtful. All other faction leaders in the House of Representatives, including his most loyal allies, had called for him to resign and were ready to start impeachment proceedings if he failed to heed their call. Key ministers had resigned. No one would serve on his Reform Committee. Like the economy, his Government was crumbling around him. A succession of visitors to Jalan Cendana urged him to resign.

Even on Monday, a leader in the 'Jakarta Post' had said: "Support for the idea of total and peaceful political reform is pouring in from people of all ages and all walks of life. These people's voices are being clearly heard above the boisterous mayhem and worsening economic crisis gripping the country. They speak for the nation in demanding total political reform because changes that include no less than a changing of the guard would fail to heal the country's wounds. The call for reform is now even supported by the ruling elite, some of whom had staunchly opposed the idea before."

If President Soeharto still harboured even shreds of the thought that he was in control of the situation, in reality, the initiative had passed into the hands of others. Of course, the President could try to resort to force but, even had this been possible, it seemed that his will for a shoot-out over the presidency, at least, was lacking. President Soeharto had said several times recently that he would not use force to cling to power. And he must have realized that the use of force in his defence would only have made his position so much less tenable. The use of force in this way would have made civil war a real possibility.

ABRI felt that it had the students under some sort of control and it didn't want a repeat of the previous week's riots if Amien Rais went ahead with his demonstration. ABRI seemed determined that if Rais went ahead his supporters would be sent packing. For the reformists, the risk and consequences of another Trisakti on a mass scale must have been daunting. And there was every reason to believe that, despite the kid glove treatment of students by pro-reform elements in ABRI, a mass Trisakti or even a Tiananmen Square could take place. By late Wednesday the streets of Jakarta could be running with blood.

In the early hours of the morning of Wednesday, May 20, the day of action, Amien Rais had driven around Jakarta and seen tens of thousands of security personnel and their equipment moving into position for the expected protests. Tanks and armoured cars rumbled onto stations, barbed wire barriers were being thrown across streets, dark-clad troops were fully armed for combat. Most of the troops were from the Jakarta Military Command, led by Sjafrie Sjamsoeddin, a loyal Soeharto appointee, the Marine Corps, the Air Force Special Squad and the Army's special force, KOPASSUS, until recently led by the President's hard-line son-in-law, Prabowo. A ring of steel was being thrown around all state or sensitive buildings, especially Monas, where the rally was planned to conclude in the large open space, close to the presidential palace. Ostensibly, it was an ABRI operation yet some suspected that once again the deployment reflected the tug of war between Soeharto hard liners and ABRI reformists.

Rais was quoted as saying: "The security made me think of a world war. In such a situation, I'm afraid there would be people - civilian or military - injured for nothing (and this) would only damage our campaign for reform." Rais had made his tour after a meeting with members of ABRI earlier in the day. He did not reveal which members. He was quoted as saying: " An Army general (told me) he doesn't care at all if a Tiananmen accident...takes place in Jakarta this morning. I was shocked to hear that."

As a result of what he had seen and heard, at the last minute, Amien Rais called off his planned demonstration. The cancellation of the day of protest was historic. In Indonesia's power centre of Jakarta, the riots had badly frightened the upper and middle classes. Nobody wanted a repetition. In Yogyakarta on the Day of National Awakening the demonstration went ahead drawing an incredible 600,000, three times the number expected. The crowd was reportedly primed and ready for a second Jakarta but the Sultan persuaded them to remain calm and, after speeches, return home. Demonstrations also went ahead in Surabaya, Purwokerto, Medan, Semarang, Bandung, Bogor and Unjung Pandang, involving crowds up to 150,000 strong.

Nevertheless, at Jalan Cendana, Day of National Awakening or no Day of National Awakening, President Soeharto could see that he had finally run out of options. Mass demonstrations and bloodshed had been averted but Parliament's ultimatum still stood. He could leave quietly, be impeached or continue to risk being pushed from office violently. The mobs had been contained and dissuaded but the students were still there, still focused on his ousting, still as determined as ever, still transparently supported by the ABRI high command. To make use of his son-in-law and his military allies could only lead to war. The economy was already close to collapse. War would leave the country in ruins. Troops ringed the presidential residence at Jalan Cendana. Were they protectors or captors? On Wednesday night, General Wiranto arrived to say officially that the Armed Forces could no longer support him! As expected, he added that ABRI would not wish to see the President impeached.

Since Saturday, overwhelming forces had been marshalled against the President. Wiranto's argument that it was impossible to go against such a weight of public opinion now carried the day. ABRI's high command took the decision to ask President Soeharto to resign. Wiranto and his men were safe. The Soeharto/Prabowo loyalists were finally finished. According to Singapore's 'The New Paper' on Friday, May 22, "Let. Gen. Prabowo reportedly said that he would accept the decision of the leadership." There was no other sensible choice.

President Soeharto agreed to go. At 9 am on Thursday, May 21, 32 years after coming to power, one of the world's longest serving leaders announced: "I quit." He had seen, he had taken advice, he had pondered, he had tried to cling to power but, by the early hours of Thursday morning it must have been clear that his remaining could now lead only to the total destruction of his country - along the lines of the denouement of a James Bond movie. The prospect was for more riots, more destruction, more bloodshed and unspeakable suffering for jobless, penniless and hungry people. Around his birthplace villagers were already dying of starvation.

In his resignation speech, referring obviously to the fact that no one would serve on the Reform Committee, to defections from the cabinet as well as the public position of ABRI and Parliament, Soeharto said that it had become impossible for him to carry out his state duties. No one wanted to work with him. At the end, he had talked to constitutional experts about the succession. Who would take over? Those who would be involved in doing so had prepared their ground. Constitutionally, he was told, the vice president should step up. To President Soeharto's surprise it must have also been indicated that ABRI would support this. ABRI was no friend of Habibie's. With his strategic industry concept Habibie had taken over lucrative ABRI companies and with the purchase of the former East German Navy he had muscled in directly on military terrain. Later, it would emerge that the deal between Habibie and Wiranto was that ABRI would support Habibie provided he committed to a programme of reform, provided that Wiranto remained armed forces commander and provided that Prabowo could be transferred away from KOSTRAD.Clearly, Prabowo's influence and command of KOSTRAD was feared but Prabowo's influence may have been less than outsiders assume. Prabowo had only recently been appointed to KOSTRAD in February 1997 - replacing Wiranto. Wiranto would certainly have left his mark on the force and Prabowo would have had little time to eradicate it. The main point was that Prabowo was the former president's son-in-law.

In a brief ceremony at the Merdeka Palace, Soeharto handed the reins of power to his Vice President, B.J. Habibie. He shook hands with the new president and at the moment of doing so he must also have realized that Habibie knew this was going to happen, that his staunchest and most loyal supporter, his adopted son, had, like Brutus, finally turned against him. Habibie tried later to talk to Soeharto but he was never forgiven and every approach was rebuffed.

General Wiranto publicly declared that ABRI was united in its approval of Soeharto's resignation and of the constitutional hand-over of power to Habibie. The use of the word "united" pointed to a final defeat for Soeharto loyalists. Some observers and analysts felt that General Wiranto had had a chance to take power during these tension-packed crisis hours. Certainly he had. But two weeks later Wiranto was quoted by Singapore's 'The Straits Times' as saying that he did not want to be president. Wiranto was quoted as saying that his duty was merely to uphold the Constitution and create stability and the rule of law, views which President Habibie would repeatedly echo.

Within 46 hours, Prabowo would be removed from his command of KOSTRAD and moves would be set in train to replace others influenced by Prabowo including KOPASSUS commander, Maj. Gen. Muchdi Purwopranjono and Jakarta garrison commander, Sjafrie Syamsuddin. In August, Sjafrie would be appointed to the House of Representatives, thus removing him from the limelight and from awkward questions. Sjafrie had also been a presidential adjutant. The implication of his removal seemed to be that the commander had perhaps been led astray or felt that he could not say no to possible hints and requests from a senior officer close to Soeharto. Within weeks Prabowo would be under investigation, according to Singapore's 'The Sunday Times:' accused of "ordering the shootings of students in demonstrations ... and the disappearances" (of "a number of political activists." According to 'The Sunday Times' US Ambassador to Indonesia J. Stapleton Roy had met personally with Prabowo to "express Washington's anger over the disappearances and to request that he try to secure their release." Why with Prabowo? What did he suspect? Even if it was accepted that Prabowo was behind the kidnappings the questions still remained: Had he been involved in the shootings of the Trisakti students? Had he stirred up the looters? Was he behind the alleged rapes of ethnic Chinese women? Whether he was or he wasn't, the activities of renegade ABRI personnel had brought disgrace on ABRI. Disgrace is one of the things Indonesians find most hard to take. Wiranto and the reformists must have been galvanized as never before by the kidnapping, shootings, riots and rapes. These immoral and horrifying acts must have made them implacably determined to weed out the poison within, to reestablish their image as a professional force at the service of the people. If Prabowo had been trying to help Soeharto he had only succeeded in bringing him down. If he had been trying to further interests of his own he had guaranteed failure. On August 24, 1998 he was dismissed from the Armed Forces.

Ironically, just as Soeharto had tried to close the door to political change by insisting that it must always be constitutional (Soeharto controlled every facet of the constitutional channels) ABRI had all along agreed with him while using the constitutional channels to bring him down. You can imagine the two men standing face to face and agreeing that political change had to be constitutional - Soeharto meaning that in this way he could cling to power; Wiranto meaning that in this way he could be forced out. The General added that ABRI would protect the "safety and dignity" of the former president and of his family. To the extent that Soeharto loyalists remained quiet, it was true that ABRI was united. A page in Indonesia's history had been turned. Civil war and anarchy had been avoided. The constitutional process had been proved to work. ABRI had stood guard over the Constitution and its workings regarding presidential succession. Vice President Bacharuddin Jusuf Habibie was sworn in to take Soeharto's place, ostensibly to serve until the year 2003, the 'normal' time for the next five-yearly general elections. At the swearing in, General Wiranto stood nearby, his presence a loud statement that those who challenged Habibie challenged ABRI.

This was potentially another dangerous moment for General Wiranto and for Indonesia. Soeharto was not without supporters, including in the military where many of the senior officers he had hand picked and which included even his own family. Even if Soeharto himself chose not to make a fight of it were there officers who would fight rather than see him step down? Were there officers who perhaps nursed the dream of becoming president themselves? Could such an officer seize power on the pretext of rescuing Soeharto and restoring law and order? Such a scenario defied belief. The people would never stand for it and the military's reputation and standing would be destroyed. But in this situation, if people felt desperate, who could tell what might happen!

Fears were fuelled when, that night, May 21, Prabowo turned up at the presidential palace, armed with a pistol and accompanied by truck loads of "special forces troops." 'Asiaweek' reported on June 5 that he "ringed the palace and presidential office with troops loyal to him." He demanded to see the new president but Habibie refused. Later President Habibie would say that he was afraid he was going to be killed. That night, for safety, he moved to the state guest house, adjoining his presidential office.

According to 'Asiaweek' Prabowo and Habibie had discussed what might happen if Soeharto stepped down. "He wanted to force B.J. Habibie to honour an alleged deal made months earlier that he would be made armed forces chief." Habibie was now in no position to honour such a promise. Unable to win backing from his now powerless father-in-law and unable to meet the new President, Prabowo was left with no options except rebellion. This he chose not to take and, presumably seething, sent his troops back to barracks and went home himself. To have chosen the path of rebellion would have meant taking on the whole ABRI chain of command not to mention all its units, with far more troops than he had at his own command. Next day, at his home on Jalan Cendana, he is alleged to have told General Wiranto that he would accept his new posting and on Monday the ceremony went ahead and was duly photographed for posterity by the media.

Elsewhere on Jalan Cendana the former president was also at

home. Said 'Asiaweek' of May 29: " Soeharto remained in his private residence, surrounded by troops. For most of his rule the President had maneuvered the military for his own purposes. Now he was at their mercy. Talk of a split in the army, of a coup, of a massacre, of civil war, was all over Jakarta. Indeed, all had been a possibility. But for now, ABRI had arrived at a position where it could influence the choice of the next president, reduce its political role and become real professionals." No more dirty work! How sweet the victory of ABRI's reformers must have seemed!

Actually, there had been civil war of a kind in Jakarta but all played out in typically Indonesian, or perhaps Javanese fashion. Dark shadows had moved behind screens, there had been covert meetings, clandestine plots, things had been left unsaid, glances had been exchanged, tension had filled the air, hands had rested menacingly on pistols. At the end of the play the audience realized that they had witnessed a dangerous duel between two martial leaders, each taking advantage of the people's noisily expressed aspirations and actions to fuel their respective purposes, the one, a black prince of evil, the other a white knight who made the people's needs his own. The 'fighting' had been serious and to the death yet, in reality, it had been limited to a few days of noisy extras rushing to and fro across the 'set' with their arms laden with undreamed of booty.

In the hours after Soeharto's dramatic and sudden resignation there was hysterical jubilation among the student demonstrators. There were also continuing demands for Habibie to also step down. Some students said that they were adopting a wait and see attitude and would give the new government "three to six months" to prove itself. The new president was seen very much as a Soeharto crony and a man far too tarred with the Soeharto brush to be likely to be able to introduce the reforms demanded. The momentum of the reform movement was still in place and, while they had the chance, some leaders said that, by itself, the President's resignation was not sufficient - there should be a recall of the People's Consultative Assembly, the election of a new president and vice president and the appointment of a completely new cabinet untainted with even the remotest links to Soeharto. Whatever the record of cabinet ministers and parliamentarians, the student view was that, since they had been appointed by Soeharto, they should quit, too. Almost nobody wanted to wait until 2003! There were calls for a presidium or government of national unity to be set up to manage the transition between the dissolution of the old Soeharto Government and Parliament and the election of a completely fresh team.

The 'Jakarta Post' summed up the mood in its editorial of May 22. "Finally, President Soeharto bowed to his people's demand and resigned. This astonishing decision was unthinkable until the beginning of this week. Three days ago, despite the mounting public pressure for his resignation, the President was still doing his utmost to keep his position. He failed to realize that Indonesians were weary of his maneuvering. On Wednesday, he was forced to realize that he had lost his people and, at the eleventh hour, his Armed Forces, who had staunchly supported him in the past.

"The procedures of Soeharto's resignation and the appointment of Bacharuddin Jusuf Habibie as the new president are constitutional in nature. (There was debate about this because the swearing in of a new president should have taken place at the Parliament, still occupied by students.) The question now is, will the new man in command be able to implement the popular demand for total reform in order to heal the country's ills. The answer seems to be negative.

"Habibie is part of the old, entrenched system and is not far from authoritarianism, cronyism, collusion and nepotism. Reports have said that he and his family own major conglomerates. Habibie is not particularly popular among any segment of society. Despite his inarguable intellect, he is well known as intolerant of ideas which differ from his own; until recently he had openly opposed the public demand for complete reform, especially the convening of a special meeting of the MPR to discuss the regime's record.

"For these reasons, it is hard to believe that he will be able to realize what the people want. Tomorrow does not bode well for a better situation, as most signs point to more suffering of the people as the economy continues to deteriorate."

Amidst the raging political storm it was momentarily easy to forget that what had sparked the protests was not political factors at all, but the state of the economy, especially prices increased in line with the latest agreement with the IMF. As Soeharto stepped down, prices, the money supply and inflation were rising, banks and markets had ground to a halt, bankruptcies and unemployment loomed more menacingly than ever, foreign trade was still paralyzed, the IMF and associated agencies such as the World Bank announced further delays in the disbursement of funds and May talks aimed at rescheduling Indonesia's private offshore debt were postponed. Foreign investor interest in Indonesia hovered around zero as they awaited the outcome of political events. The last thing needed now was more instability.

The hand-over of power to Vice President Habibie, while unacceptable to some, was nevertheless firmly in line with the 1945 Constitution. It promised legality, legitimacy, continuity and, above all stability. In the heat of the moment of Habibie's appointment the clamour for his removal remained loud. But hour by hour, it seemed that powerful forces were or came to be behind the Republic's new president. ABRI had said from the outset that it welcomed the constitutional process and would respect and obey Habibie as president. This commitment was of major importance. ABRI had had many disagreements with Habibie in the past and cannot have been deliriously happy about his elevation to Vice President. But the constitution was the constitution. No precedent could be allowed for disobedience. From the swearing in onwards, whoever challenged Habibie challenged the military. It didn't mean that ABRI would side with Habibie come what may. Only that his constitutional rights would be protected until such times as he no longer had them. No one could say when that time would be. It might be 2003 or it might be in three months or six or a year. Plenty of people were still clamouring for new presidential and even general elections. Habibie was generally regarded as transitional and, therefore, bearable. As calm returned to the streets of Jakarta, more and more voices were heard saying that the economy must be given total priority and that its rescue depended on a respite from chaos. ABRI's attitude to street disturbances suddenly became more businesslike.

The day after Soeharto's resignation, remaining students were moved easily from the Parliament building by armed security forces. Before they left, about 1,500 Muslim students staged a rival demonstration at the parliament calling for full support for President Habibie, a Muslim himself and a man seen, since his leadership of the Association of Indonesian Muslim Intellectuals (ICMI), as something of a champion of Muslim interests. Later, Muslim organizations would indicate their support for ABRI against anarchic elements. Perhaps Habibie could build a power base after all! Pro-reform students continued sporadic demonstrations around the country, welcoming Soeharto's resignation but frequently demanding an investigation into the wealth of himself and his family and a special session of the People's Consultative Assembly so that new elections could take place.

Other than the students, fear of the mob was still fresh in everyone's minds. Whatever reforms were wanted by critics, other than the hard core students, were from now on to be called for from behind closed doors - not on the streets. This was a major change in mood and tactics. Other than Amien Rais and Muchtar Pakpahan, most previously vocal critics of the Government - religious, community and intellectual leaders - now said that Habibie should be given a chance as a transitional president, "at least for six months" until, fresh elections could perhaps be held. The business class virtually to a man said that they hoped business could now get back to normal. World opinion welcomed Soeharto's decision to step down as a step towards democracy and neighbouring countries expressed the hope that it would now be possible for the Habibie Government to give urgent attention to the economy.

The response of Asia's leaders was sharply practical; the response from the West idealistic.

The West wanted to believe that there had been the equivalent of the Philippine peoples power movement in Indonesia; it wanted to believe that all the freedoms the West associated with democracy were in the air; that revolutionary political reform and change would now gush through the flood gates. This was a misconception on the grand scale. There had been articulate middle class critics of the Government, there had been students and there had been the mob. When the mob went home that left the critics and the students. Within a day or two, the students were urged to return to their studies. That left the critics, now comparatively muted by the promise of the reforms they had been demanding. There had been no peoples power. That is not to say that there were not at least demands for democracy. Certainly there were, from among the academics and students especially. Both groups had demanded the repeal of five political laws restricting popular participation in politics and defining what was or was not subversive. Some critics also called for an end to the dual function of the military in which it was both a security and legislative force. The people as a whole were noticeably silent about democracy. Their concern before, during and after the unrest seemed only to be governed fairly and to have rice bowls filled at a reasonable price. Business simply wanted to get on with business. The vested interest of business in stability and the people's silence on questions of politics left a wide margin of discretion for those in charge of reforms. Most had been appointed by Soeharto. How radical could they be expected to be?

Prices had been fundamental to the Jakarta riots. One step best taken at once was the rolling back of the price increases which had fuelled the violence. In fact, the prices had been reduced somewhat by President Soeharto in the hours before he stepped down. Fuel prices had been slashed by around 20 percent the previous week after hikes of up to 71 percent and now land, sea and air transportation fares were reduced accordingly. Certain fare increases were wisely delayed.

Soeharto had been brought down and the military had played a key role. 'Time' magazine said in its June 1 issue: " The military was the key to the entire process. Walking a tightrope between its loyalty to Soeharto and its realization that the longer he stayed on, the worse the economic crisis would get - and the greater the risk of renewed violence on the streets." Asked to comment on happenings in Jakarta during the fateful month of May, 1998, Singapore elder statesman, Lee Kuan Yew was quoted by 'Newsweek' as saying: "This was a controlled exercise. Right up until the shooting of the six students, the government, army and police were in complete control. They allowed the demonstrations to carry on in a controlled way. Then, somebody did something not in the script and that triggered it (the riots) off."

In June, while still in command, Jakarta Military Commander, Maj. Gen. Sjafrie Sjamsoeddin had been quoted as saying that the Jakarta riots were "spontaneous acts," although he was alleged to have added that "some of the riots were sporadically organized by small groups in certain areas of Greater Jakarta." What else could he say? There had been too many witnesses! He was said to have stressed that these groups had no links to each other but had also become spontaneously involved in the mayhem. The riots were widespread and, whoever started them, swiftly got out of control. Security units had been conspicuous by their absence. Yet, apparently it was possible to say quickly who had done what. On the other hand, within ABRI, a closed and disciplined community where it should have been even faster to identify the hands behind the kidnapping of activists and the Trisakti killings than it had been to identify the organizers of the riots, research and findings seemed painfully slow and inexplicably difficult. Did Wiranto continue to face formidable opposition? Was he beginning to be concerned about the need to protect ABRI's morale by not confessing to too much too soon?

After persistent detective work by the media, firm evidence eventually emerged of involvement in the riots of organized groups. The task of these groups was to incite the riots. They were also suspected of following up by providing the skills and wherewithal to set fires which cost hundreds of lives. A macabre twist to the groups' brief in Jakarta may have been a mini campaign to rape and terrorize ethnic Chinese women. Trucks with out-of-town number plates were spotted disgorging provocateurs, sometimes older men dressed incongruously in high school uniforms - a threadbare attempt to pretend that there was a link between the riots and rapings and students. Few, if any, would have believed that, at least not in Jakarta. In Solo, where curiously synchronized riots also began on Thursday, May 14, mysterious groups incited students to leave their campuses, quickly turning into a destructive mob which looted and torched hundreds of buildings. The damage was so great that, in August, Solo was the first Indonesian city to receive rehabilitation funds from the central government - US$457 million. More than 300 buildings had been torched and gutted, 75 percent of them owned by ethnic Chinese, 20 people were killed and 11,000 were rendered jobless.

Truck loads of potential troublemakers from East Java were detected trying to enter Bali but were decisively turned back to Java by the wily Balinese, determined to save the island's and Indonesia's tourism industry. Whether the groups were active in Yogyakarta or not it, as yet, unclear, but mayhem was spared when, on June 20, the Sultan went among crowds of potential rioters and successfully appealed for reason and calm. Almost three quarters of a million people went quietly home. Yogja was saved.

In retrospect, if the riots had been orchestrated by a pro-Government group, the effect was not to enable the Government to crack down but to push the army closer to backing the calls of the protesters for their main target, the President, to resign. The riots dealt further heavy blows to the economy while making the possibility of political upheaval more certain. The immediate effect of the outburst was to paralyze trade and industry and send people and money fleeing overseas.

If indeed there was a plot to push back the reform movement it backfired in a big way. There was no student uprising following Trisakti and therefore no need for a military backlash. The destruction brought about by the riots was so terrible and horrific that instead of taking emergency measures against the people reformist elements in ABRI felt the time had come to work with the people rather than against them. ABRI had no future in opposing either the students or the people. The reformists had won. The conservatives had lost.

CHAPTER SEVEN

Full Circle

There were ironies in Soeharto's withdrawal from the presidency. Just as he had encouraged students 32 years ago to help push Sukarno from power, so, today, students had been encouraged to push Soeharto from power. Just as Soeharto had used the incident of the murdered generals to crack down on perceived enemies so the incident of the May riots was used to bring him down. There would have been a double irony if, in fact, Soeharto had been planning to use the riots for a crackdown of his own against the New Order's perceived enemies of the 1990s. As it was, it seems they were part of some hair-brained scheme of his son-in-law's.

Another similarity between 1998 and 1965 was the way in which in 1965 government had been a balancing act between president, ABRI and the communists. In 1998 it was still a balancing act between the President, ABRI and the people, as represented by the reform movement. But, while ABRI had advanced its power into civilian areas of government in the aftermath of 1965, by 1998, ABRI was being pressed not only to scale back its activities but to withdraw from the civil sector and concentrate on becoming a professional security force. Another wheel was turning.

Even as the years had passed and President Soeharto took to referring to the 1950s and 60s as "long ago," some people remembered

258

the events as though they had happened yesterday. Some, especially those languishing in prison, still suffered from them. Even as Soeharto stepped down, 1965 would rise up again! What had really happened?

President Soeharto had long schemed to stay in power. In the run up to the 1997 general elections he had sought to destabilize and neutralize the PDI and to remove Abdurraman Wahid, a persistent critic, from the leadership of another potentially powerful opposition group, the Nahdlatul Ulama. He had cracked down on known anti-regime elements and sought to identify others as yet unknown. The crack downs had only made heroes of his enemies!

The plan to crack down on pro-democracy reformers, some, if not many of them, pro-Megawati - whosoever the plan really was - by kidnapping and intimidation backfired when Pius Lustrilanang told all, not only to Indonesians but to the world. By July, Pius was given a hero's welcome back to his home country where he vowed to continue his fight for justice for himself and for other kidnap victims. On July 20, the 'Jakarta Post' quoted him as saying: "I believe that there are more institutions involved (than KOPASSUS) and from the beginning I've believed that Soeharto knew a lot about this case because without political support no military unit would dare to do such a silly thing." Pius said that he suspected that at least five of the still missing activists were dead.

Following GOLKAR's predictable victory in 1997, Soeharto had sought to pack its governing committee with family and cronies to ensure his re-election in March 1998. He had rigged the military high command to ensure family and friends occupied key positions. The scenario for the March once-in-five-years meeting of the People's Consultative Assembly was that there should be no discussion other than on topics and in ways agreed previously. ABRI, with Soeharto's friends in charge, had been commanded to make sure there were no disruptions. President Soeharto had turned the screws tighter than ever during the elections of 1997 and '98 to stifle not only criticism but even debate about the problems facing the country.

But the new Parliament and the new cabinet were instantly and widely despised either for their links to Soeharto, their corruption or their lack of ability other than to act as New Order yes men. Indonesians felt that Soeharto had made them a nation of political prisoners, their views and sufferings ignored, ruled by the corrupt and mediocre in the interest of the First Family and its hangers on. Frustration with what threatened to become an Indonesian version of a totalitarian dictatorship reached boiling point.

Back in 1996, Soeharto's plan to retain power must have looked like plain sailing through well charted waters. Then, in June, 1997, the currency crisis broke and swept over Indonesia in a tidal wave that quickly and remorselessly led to an economic crisis and then to the political crisis which destroyed all Soeharto's plans and hopes. He threw out a desperate hand to the IMF, but the Fund not only failed to save him but its policies made his fall even more certain. The IMF rescue had not worked and public fury had turned on the very people he had chosen so carefully to support him - family and cronies. The rigging of the political process and the clamp down not only on dissent but on debate during the worst economic crisis in Indonesia's recollected history led to a degree of public outrage which shook ABRI and undermined his support from ABRI. By May 1998, instead of being at the centre of Indonesian political and commercial life, as they had planned with such obvious confidence, the entire Soeharto clan had become what one magazine termed "outcasts".

Perhaps Soeharto's biggest mistake had been the unseating from the leadership of the Indonesian Democratic Party (PDI) of Megawati Sukarnoputri, the daughter of Indonesia's first president. President Sukarno's image had a strong following among the lower classes and just by being the great man's daughter Mega commanded wide loyalty and support - loyalty and support which remained with her even after her ousting and could be seen clearly in massive abstentions during the 1997 general elections. Informed society felt that Megawati had been treated badly and that her treatment formed part of the New Order's long history of covert interventions in Indonesia's political life and of the use of intimidation and violence to achieve dubious ends. The feeling emerged that "Enough Is Enough." The more Soeharto discriminated against Mega, the more sympathy and support she attracted. The fall Soeharto had planned for Mega turned into his own.

By the end of July the wheel of politics looked as if it was turning full circle. Megawati's supporters undertook a "spontaneous" reoccupation of the former PDI headquarters in Menteng, Jakarta and even the party's Medan headquarters was recovered for her faction - Medan had been the location of the Government sponsored congress to unseat her two years earlier. There was no opposition from security forces or from the new government. Quietly, without causing fuss, instigating mass demonstrations or firing a shot, Megawati was positioned to occupy the highest moral ground in the public mind and to present almost a cult alternative to Soeharto. In the days, weeks and months ahead, as Indonesians experimented with the closest thing to democracy they had had recently, support for Mega's PDI grew steadily. Megawati never lost sight of the fact that she regarded herself as the legitimate leader of the PDI and one of the first requests President Habibie would receive was one to reinstate her as leader of the one and only PDI. He refused. Mega was unhappy. The reformers were unhappy. Students were unhappy. The public was unhappy. In the general elections of 1999, would Habibie, too, fall to Mega's silent revenge? A poll in 'Merdeka' on July 3, 1998 showed that if elections for president were held then Mega would win!

The New Order Government had been famous for its iron fist, security approach. Sometimes there had been too much iron in the fist and massacres had occurred, such as in Dili or at Tanjung Priok, which would never be forgotten. In 1998, years after the events the families of victims would still be asking for justice. Justice was wanted, too, for the hundreds of people who had simply gone "missing" after altercations with the security forces. Names thought long forgotten - Tanjung Priok, Lampung, Dili, Marsinah - had been covered over but never forgotten. With the fall of Soeharto relatives of victims began demanding justice.

Throughout the 1980s and '90s the security approach had created a number of 'incidents' about which the Soeharto Government had tried manfully to close the files. With the fall of Soeharto several of the most notorious cases exploded again. The National Commission on Human Rights called on the Government to reopen the case of the 1984 Tanjung Priok riots in which many died and 400 were still missing. Relatives of the victims formed a group called National Solidarity for the 1984 Tanjung Priok Affair and pressed for an investigation. They demanded that military commanders of the time be held accountable. Later, a protest rally of an incredible 15,000 people would be held at Tanjung Priok.

The wheels kept turning. Old ghosts refused to be buried. Events long forgotten suddenly popped back into view. Clocks were turned back. Farmers, sometimes led by students, were resuming land which they had been forced to sell to government backed developers at derisory prices. Vegetables were planted on golf courses. Even parts of the former presidential ranch at Tapos were resumed by farmers.

The problems of East Timor, Aceh and Irian Jaya exacerbated, if not created, by the unitary concept of the state President Soeharto had inherited and espoused, also refused to go away. The more ferocious the crack down in these provinces, the more resentment built up locally and the more condemnation Soeharto's Government attracted

261

from human rights activists. Ironically, the very same problem of autonomy for the regions had been on the political table when Soeharto became president. Little had changed. The wheel had simply turned full circle. Inflexibility had bred dislike. Regional autonomy was once again top of the agenda. This time, instead of being welcomed as defenders of the nation, in the regions, ABRI found itself vilified and hated and sensed that genuine nation building was as far away as ever.

The feeling was strong that the days of the security approach should be over. Attempts at Government justification were generally treated as laughable by the critics. Informed Indonesians wanted to break out of the New Order political straightjacket, to live free from fear and most of all wanted to join the modern world and be genuinely free. It was no accident that students occupying the Parliament building in Jakarta in May culminated their victorious campaign with hysterically tearful cries of "Freedom."

Soeharto represented the darkness and fear of the security approach, for control, for restriction, for stern punishment. Plus, he had been in office too long, for the whole of some people's lives. For most of the last ten years of his long rule, he seemed more interested in clinging to power and protecting his family interests than in giving the nation the changes it wanted and needed. What Indonesia's new generation wanted was light, fresh air, openness, empowerment, democratic freedoms enjoyed under an impartial law. Above all they wanted economic efficiency, free from the corruption, collusion and nepotism which seemed to have brought the economy to its knees. To make the change from darkness to light, the king of darkness had to go. Soeharto had to resign.

President Soeharto's ultimate problem was that significant sections of the Armed Forces agreed. ABRI was tired of presidential intervention in its appointments, tired of being shackled, not to the state but to Soeharto himself, tired of doing the President's dirty work- and getting the blame, tired of fighting losing battles in Irian, East Timor and Aceh. ABRI thirsted to be a proud, ethical and professional force ready to defend Indonesia and Indonesians at the legitimate behest of a legitimate government. The New Order under Soeharto had lost its legitimacy. As if these were not reason enough, President Soeharto had by no means been considerate to ABRI, slashing the number of seats they held in the Parliament, attempting to keep their candidates away from the vice presidency, resenting their criticisms of the activities of his family and generally rolling back military influence. Since Soeharto's base was the military this was perhaps his biggest mistake. Even under Gen-

262

eral Wiranto, the military take their dual function in Indonesia very seriously and show no signs of being willing to see it reduced. ABRI believes that it can be a force for good in society and the nation and was working hard to be given another chance.

President Habibie and others have said that Soeharto had grown old and out of touch. Perhaps so. Certainly he underestimated the strength of the forces ranged against him in May. If his gamble really was to return from Cairo and become a national hero by restoring law and order in the face of popular anarchy the scheme badly and terminally misfired - most of all because the anarchists were really democrats. His belated efforts to go with the political flow failed when they were received for what they really were - ploys to cling on to a power which many now knew had been abused royally.

To the end, it was members of his own family who helped bring him down - Let. Gen. Prabowo's suspected and assumed dangerous bid for power leading to an orgy of destruction which brought down the President and threatened to bring down the country. Prabowo was only the tip of the First Family iceberg. When the decision had been taken in the mid-1980s to give the private sector its head, the First Family had seen its chance to get rich, many chances, in fact, and had ruthlessly trampled on anyone and everyone to take them until they were gorged with opportunities and money.

Aside from presiding over a regime of greed and corruption, throughout his long 32-year rule, Soeharto committed the ultimate philosophical mistake - he went against the flow. Instead of changing as society changed he tried stubbornly to maintain concepts which over the years became dead, fossilized and useless. Perhaps dark secrets of his past, especially the manner in which he had come to power, could never have withstood the bright light of truth. Perhaps this was why the lid always had to be clamped tight on democracy. Perhaps this was why so many still languished in prison. When the plug was removed by the May riots the flow overwhelmed him. In its wake was the hope of justice for old abuses and the dream that at last Indonesia might stand on the threshold of genuine Merdeka. For the realization of this hope all eyes looked to President Habibie.

Indonesia would now need time to reassess President Soeharto and to reassess the achievements made during his long rule. While it was clear that Indonesia was glad to see him walk off quietly into retirement there were those who felt sad that his role in eliminating communism from the islands and in bringing about continuous economic development and rising living standards might now be buried beneath scandals about how he came to power in the first place and beneath the political and economic wreckage that Indonesia had become in 1998.

Others felt that the economic and even social policies pursued during the Soeharto years were no more than skin deep and will 'o 'the whisp. Critics felt that the New Order Government had failed to adequately develop and exploit its resource and agricultural sectors, had failed to build an appropriate and viable industrial sector for the long term, had failed to adequately educate the workforce, had failed to put in place solidly based, uncorrupted and well run institutions. They felt that democracy, personal empowerment and intellectual life had been stifled by the New Order and that this was a wheel of change Indonesia must begin rolling again if there was ever to be the proud, talented, self confident and self reliant Indonesian and Indonesia that the independence fighters had dreamed of more than 50 years ago.

CHAPTER EIGHT

The Habibie Government

Under President Habibie there were strong signs of life returning to Indonesian politics. Even pessimists were optimistic about the
future. But no one took anything for granted. The kind of political, economic and legal changes proposed and their pace were being watched
carefully. With the best will in the world President Habibie was a New
Order man. Many of his cabinet colleagues were New Order men. While
the pressures for change were many, there were also pressures to protect vested interests, if not past ways. The need to balance the old and
the new within the New Order perhaps forced President Habibie to proceed more slowly than he otherwise might. Many felt that deepgoing,
wholesale change would not come about until after the general elections of 1999 when the people were expecting genuine representatives,
free from the ghosts, dogma and vested interests of the Soeharto years.

One of the policies inherited from Soeharto was his decision,
albeit an understandably reluctant one, to cooperate fully with the IMF.
President Habibie had promptly signalled his support for the Fund. But
what had the press headlines been saying at the very moment this recommitment was made? "IMF blunders through Asia, leaving disaster in
its wake," said a headline in the 'Indonesian Observer' of June 7. Writer,
Mark Weisbrot, said: " It is now widely recognized that the International

265

Monetary Fund has actually worsened the Asian economic crisis; in fact, it is difficult to find an economist outside the government (presumably the US government since the article was first published in Los Angeles) or the IMF payroll who will defend its recent actions. As the misery and frustration spread throughout the area expressions such as "IMF riots," "IMF survival crimes," and IMF suicides" have become a part of the regional vocabulary. In Indonesia would the buzz phrase become "IMF Indonesian debacle?" The new Government of Indonesia hoped not.

The most urgent task facing President Habibie was the need to appoint a government, President Soeharto having dissolved the Seventh Development Cabinet. It was difficult to craft. Clearly, ministers widely despised would have to go. Perhaps competent ministers could be retained and their numbers augmented. The new President naturally preferred to select people he knew and could trust but he had to watch over his shoulder constantly to avoid fresh charges of cronyism. The additions would have to include not merely competent people but some on the economics side and others on the political side, to take into account current economic needs as well as the demands for political reform. There was little chance of making everyone happy but Habibie did his best. Making as many people as possible happy seemed to become the hallmark of his early stewardship. By no means everyone was amenable to his attempts to forge something akin to national reconciliation. His association with the old New Order had been too close.

Another difficult task was convincing Indonesians that he could do the job they wanted. Many suspected, and feared, that Habibie would be no more than a Soeharto puppet, his strings pulled daily by the wily old master dalang (puppeteer) at his residence on Jalan Cendana. And having been part of the New Order leadership for a quarter of a century as well as having responded to Soeharto as if he had been an adopted son, was Habibie really likely to be serious about stamping out corruption, collusion and nepotism? Were the people around him, still largely figures from the older version of the New Order, likely to be serious about stamping out a sickness they had tolerated and perhaps even participated in for years? As usual in these situations, only time would tell. But, the faster he moved, the better for all concerned. During the first few days he HAD to move fast. The public would not have accepted anything less. And he had to move fast to change policies of his former leader's which the public disliked but which he had once supported or, at least condoned. No politician could hope for a future merely by proclaiming business as usual minus Soeharto. The public expected substantial change. The public wanted a leader who would be different from Soeharto, a leader whose policies would be as different from Soeharto's as night was to day. The more political distance that President Habibie could put between himself and Soeharto, the better. President Habibie picked up the challenge. He was faced with a daunting task. Yet, from his jaunty smile and confident demeanour it seemed one that he actually relished. He had almost certainly begun relishing it even before his friend and mentor stepped down. There was a great deal to do. The man who could do it would feel enormous satisfaction. The man who could do it might have the brightest of bright prospects.

As far as ordinary people were concerned there was an increasingly urgent hope that the new head of state would be successful in quickly restoring health to the economy, restoring value to the rupiah and restoring jobs, money and basic necessities to homes across the archipelago. It was the rapid destruction of the fruits of three decades of development which had stoked public anger against Soeharto. The destruction had also stripped bare the wealth gap and, especially in urban areas, had shown part of the 'fault' to lie along ethnic lines. Action seemed desirable to calm and reassure the ethnic Chinese while at the same time improving the lot of the largely indigenous have-nots. With the advice of the IMF, much was already being done to reform the economy. President Habibie and his team placed much of their faith in this 'medicine.' They were also working assiduously to get as much as possible of the private offshore debt rescheduled, an infinitely more immediate and practical policy which, at a stroke, would help quench the demand for US dollars and relieve the pressure on the rupiah. If, as a result the rupiah appreciated, interest rates could be brought down, with highly favourable implications for corporate functioning and for debt resolution. Even the future of the banking system was tied to the resolution of this single problem of the rupiah.

Then, there were the political problems. Some of these appeared to have been solved merely by the act of Soeharto stepping down. Many Indonesians felt that at long last the New Order's straightjacket had been thrown off. With their new freedom, everybody seemed to want to speak up. At the lower levels, some took the opportunity to take back property alleged to be theirs or even to steal from some of those deemed to have too much - especially foodstuffs. It seemed that there could be no going back. Empowerment was in the air. Everybody seemed to have tried to empower themselves in some way or other whether it was legitimate or not. At higher levels old structures broke up and new ones formed, expressed in an explosion in the formation of new political parties, within 100 days to reach almost 90. The students and other critics of Soeharto and of the New Order regime wanted solutions to such long standing problems as political empowerment, political accountability and the role and actions of the Armed Forces, problems which would require a substantial overhaul of the entire political system. These problems led into others concerning civil rights and rights abuses.

The winds of change gusting through Indonesia were not only aiming at reforming existing structures and policies but, in some important respects threatened to change the structures. In East Timor, Irian Jaya and Aceh rights abuses and, in some cases, economic injustice, fuelled discussion about the possibility of Indonesia breaking up. Popular disquiet in East Timor and Aceh, if not yet in Irian Jaya, needed as much attention as all the other pressing problems if the Republic was to be kept intact. The new freedom sensed in Jakarta was also sensed by latent or actual separatists. To separatists, empowerment meant only one thing - separation.

Rebuilding the economy, rebuilding the political system, holding the nation together - these were the formidable tasks confronting President Habibie.

President Habibie took office amid continuing gusts and swirls of civil unrest, of student demonstrations, of reformist's criticisms. Gradually, these swirls and gusts became eddies and the eddies mere, barely discernible breezes until finally, for a while, much of the criticism evaporated. Of course, this evaporation was vigorously encouraged by ABRI and, soon, by the new Government itself. What other sensible course was there? During President Habibie's first weekend in power, Brig. Gen. Abdul Wahab Mokodongan, articulated ABRI's position when he called on Indonesians to create and maintain a secure and peaceful situation. He said that the new President was well aware that Indonesia had only a short time to "shake off its bankruptcies and food shortages." Nevertheless, he said, while concrete steps must be taken to improve conditions in Indonesia, reforms generally would be carried out in stages. KADIN said much the same thing, calling for concrete measures and a realistic timetable for their implementation as a means of re-establishing business certainty.

One piece of useful advice given in 'The Singapore Straits Times' on May 23 by Umar Juoro, a senior researcher at the Centre for Information and Development Studies, Jakarta was that: "He (Habibie) should not pretend to be a strong man like Soeharto. He should listen more to the experts, particularly in economics and finance." There were many signs that President Habibe agreed.

Habibie's new cabinet was announced on Friday, May 22, one day after the changeover at the Merdeka Palace. It was named the Reformation and Development Cabinet. Out of a total of 36 ministers 20 were retained from the cabinet appointed by Soeharto. Some of the ministers hoped that the new cabinet would continue until 2003. Others favoured elections. The reform movement and politically conscious elements of society was also split. Some continued to demand immediate elections while others saw the benefit of a period of stability to allow the economy to recover. At some stage President Habibie would have to decide which way to tilt. When he first inherited power, like everyone else, he seemed to have assumed it would be for the short-term only. The former president thought so, too.

The new cabinet noticeably excluded the governor of the central bank and the attorney general, probably to underline a new independence for these offices from the Executive. It very noticeably included politicians from the United Development Party (PPP) and Soerjadi's faction of the Indonesian Democratic Party (PDI) - a potentially clever move at a time when some people were demanding a government of national consensus. Members of Soeharto's family and Soeharto cronies were left out of the new cabinet. The Secretary General of ICMI, a staunch critic of Soeharto, was also included. Any disgruntlement the Muslim organization may have felt about having been left out of Soeharto's cabinet seems to have been removed by Habibie's appointment.

Foreign governments and agencies generally welcomed the new Government although local opinion was, as usual now, divided between those who wanted a totally new cabinet and those prepared to let Habibie have his chance. Amien Rais said he was neither for nor against. Foreigners, including spokesmen for the World Bank and the Asian Development Bank, found the new team "impressive" while some local people agreed and others denied it.

The staunchest opponents of the New Order regime, for example, Megawati's faction of the PDI criticized the new cabinet not only for including too many from the Soeharto era but for including a number of figures thought to be die-hard conservatives. A number of these were from ABRI. Habibie was in a difficult position. He had no power base of his own and was distrusted and even disliked by many in the elite. He was in power because, constitutionally, that was his right and because, practically, General Wiranto and ABRI had agreed he could be. It was hard to imagine that, at this time, Habibie could go against the Armed Forces.

Most damning of all, the new cabinet included no reform figures. For example, Kwik Kian Gie had allegedly been invited to become Finance Minister but had declined. Virtually to a man, the reformers felt that President Habibie's Government was just a revised edition of the old New Order and preferred to keep their distance. When elections were called, it would be better to have preserved their independence. And elections might be called faster if reform groups withheld their operational support and collaboration with President Habibie. The perceived danger was that the more help they gave, the longer the new government might stay in power.

If Habibie had to depend on ABRI's support, in some important respects it was by no means onerous. Habibie was said to enjoy a good relationship not only with General Wiranto but also with former Armed Forces commander, Feisal Tanjung, in his new cabinet, the Co-ordinating Minister for Politics and Security.

Within less than a week of Soeharto's ousting, ABRI's Chief of Sociopolitical Affairs, Let. Gen. Susilo Bambang Yudhoyono was quoted as saying: "ABRI is aware of the fundamental weakness...violations of procedures involving all sectors and elements of society. ABRI's official position was that political reforms were badly needed and, surprisingly to some at that time, Habibie had let them know he agreed. Together, a civilian president supported by the Armed Forces would move Indonesia closer to democracy. ABRI had promised to give Habibie a year. Habibie had accepted. It was a trail marriage.

Economically, Habibie got off on what those who wanted to please the IMF thought was the right foot. The revolution to unseat Soeharto had been about economics. If Indonesia's economy had not been torpedoed by the withdrawal of investor confidence Soeharto might still have been in power. The fight now was to regain that confidence. The key to doing this was stability and the right approach. Many in the nation understood this. General Wiranto had already guaranteed stability. Now, on the day after his ascension to power and in his very first public statement President Habibie promised to faithfully implement Indonesia's latest agreement with the IMF as the means of "dragging the nation out of its economic crisis." "I'm keenly aware that this is an enormous challenge," he said. To help him with it he had retained the services of Ginandjar Kartasasmita. Among Ginandjar's first statements as a member of the new Government was that the IMF should help

Indonesia by making a thorough and quick assessment that would lead to the disbursement of the promised bailout funds. After meeting Habibie's economic team on his return to Indonesia after the riots, Hubert Neiss was quoted as saying: " This is a very good economic team and we are happy to work with it. It is the best team you could wish for. They are excellent."

Not only was President Habibie prepared to go all the way with the IMF but he was even quoted by the 'Asian Wall Street Journal' as saying that he would "gladly sacrifice" his controversial high-tech projects for the sake of the nation's recovery - including state aircraft manufacturer PT Industri Pesawat Terbang Nusantara (IPTN). He was quoted as saying: " I'm not responsible for IPTN or high-tech any more. I'm responsible for the whole people of the Republic (and I have) different priorities." Habibie pledged ongoing "gradual and constitutional" reform in all sectors and appealed for the support of the nation. While his willingness, under IMF pressure, to ditch IPTN seemed sensible, to some, the phrase "gradual and constitutional" sounded remarkably like the old Soeharto foot dragging.

The markets seemed pleased with the presidential changeover and on May 23 the headline in the 'Indonesian Observer' said: " Stock mart soars, rupiah stabilizes on new cabinet." Events were to show that whatever really prompted this "soaring" and "stabilizing" the markets would soon realize that nothing regarding Indonesia's fundamental economic problems had changed. After the fall of Soeharto and the ascension of President Habibie, there were as little grounds for optimism about Indonesia's corporate and national balance sheets as there had been while President Soeharto retained power.

Just as he had been Soeharto's economic supremo, Ginandjar Kartasasmita held the same position under Habibie. Just as the policy had been to please the IMF under Soeharto, so it remained under Habibie. But Ginandjar seemed to believe that the thoroughgoing reforms needed could not be made accept by a completely new leadership. On May 23, the day after Habibie's maiden speech he was quoted in the media as calling for elections "as soon as possible." he said: " One thing is for sure, we have to have a new government with a new mandate from the people."

According to the 'Far Eastern Economic Review' of June 4, Habibie saw Ginadjar's statement as a pre-emptive strike. It was thought that Ginandjar had his own presidential aspirations. The 'Review' said that Habibie was infuriated but noted that Ginandjar's statement "forced him to make a commitment to elections as soon as possible himself." Many agreed with Ginandjar so no harm was done. The longer it took to carry out prerequisite reforms and to hold elections, the longer it would take for investor confidence to rebound, the uncertainties were too great.

Habibie aide, Ms Dewi Fortuna Anwar, appealed for a resumption of international aid to pull Indonesia's economy back from the brink of collapse. Just as the IMF First Deputy managing Director, Stanley Fischer had announced suspension of aid the week before, pending the outcome of political developments, now, as President Habibie spoke, IMF Managing Director, Michel Camdessus, confirmed that there could be no immediate resumption of IMF brokered assistance. Fischer had said that the economic assumptions underlying the package would have to be reviewed again. The IMF's Washington office announced that Hubert Neiss was being sent back to Indonesia to make the review. Foreign investors generally were making reviews of their own. Until the smoke cleared, the chances were slight of the massive funds injection Indonesia needed.

Michel Camdessus seemed to go out of his way to stress that the IMF had not caused the upheavals which had brought down Soeharto. He was quoted by the Singapore 'The Straits Times' as saying: " The political turmoil and all the developments have not been caused at all by our efforts to restore a solid basis for economic development. If you have doubts about that, read what the students were asking for. They were asking for an end to corruption, collusion and nepotism." Of course, it was obvious to most people that the reason for these demands had been because the economy had seemed badly managed, resulting in the economic crisis, the IMF's nasty tasting 'medicine' and the price increases.

In Hong Kong, under the heading "Bailout bungle" the 'South China Morning Post' said in an editorial: " ....it will now be difficult to rebut the increasing perceptions that the IMF has failed in Asia. Malaysia's Prime Minister, Dr. Mahathir Mohamad, explicitly blamed its action for provoking the rioting in Jakarta. Although the US continued to loyally defend the IMF yesterday, it is probably only a matter of time before other Western nations, such as Australia, break ranks and push for alternative remedies. In any event, even the IMF can hardly describe as a success a programme that is partly responsible for such bloodshed and one which cannot now even be implemented."

The Government of Indonesia had long ago reached the conclusion that it had no choice but to implement the IMF's policies. At least this would bring in increasingly badly needed foreign funds and, hopefully, relieve some of the pressure on the rupiah. Under the new macroeconomic conditions the funds were urgently needed to help ensure that the people would not lack access to basic necessities. Presumably, in the back of the decision makers' minds was the thought that if the IMF programme didn't work it had to be clearly seen to be the fault of the IMF and not Indonesia's. After this, other options could always be pursued - capital controls, for example.

President Habibie announced the retention of the Economic Monetary and Resilience Council set up by former President Soeharto. Its members would include respected older-generation economists Widjojo Nitisastro, Ali Wardhana and Frans Seda. Widjojo was appointed chairman with the State Minister of National Development and Planning and head of the National Development Planning Agency (BAPPENAS), Boediono as his deputy. Radius Prawiro, head of Indonesia's Debt Restructuring Team, IDRA, sat on the Council as well as KADIN chief, Aburizal Bakrie.

At ABRI headquarters, on Friday, May 22, no time had been lost in moving Soeharto's son-in-law, Let. Gen. Prabowo from his command of the Army's Strategic Reserves (KOSTRAD) and posting him to ABRI's Staff and Command College in Bandung. Prabowo was a field officer with a reputation for being a tough and able commander. During the transition of presidential power it had been clear that he favoured a less conciliatory approach to demonstrators. Worse still, he had been a dangerous loose canon as the presidential hand-over took place, being spotted at Jalan Cendana and later even turning up armed at the office of the new president, whom he failed to meet. And he hadn't gone alone. According to 'Asiaweek' of July 24, he turned up with "truckloads of special KOSTRAD troops, who had stripped off their regimental markings."

Even though, according to the 'Review', Wiranto had succeeded in gaining Soeharto's approval to remove Prabowo, "in the last hours of Soeharto's presidency," there were fears that Prabowo might either follow a new agenda of Soeharto's or perhaps that he had one of his own. At any rate, the reformists within ABRI clearly felt it unwise for him to continue in command of large numbers of troops. 'Asiaweek' of July 24, quoting a "senior military officer" noted: " Prabowo was obsessed with his belief that the only way to govern Indonesia was by military stratagems and that he could take power in exactly the same way as his own father-in-law wrested power from Sukarno." Said "Asiaweek: " The officer claims Prabowo wanted to create such chaos that his rival, Armed Forces chief, General Wiranto, would be unable to restore order. Soeharto, in Egypt at that time, would have had to declare martial law. As chief of KOSTRAD (which Soeharto had himself headed in 1965), a key combat -ready unit, Prabowo would have been the only one able to take charge (just as Soeharto had been the only one able to take charge in 1965.) Asiaweek' said that another theory was that Prabowo simply wanted to impress his powerful relative by creating chaos and then proving he could control it - presumably with a view to promotion. This was never likely because, according to 'Asiaweek' former armed forces commander, Feisal Tanjung had already warned that "Prabowo was too dangerous a man to lead the army." Presumably Soeharto agreed. Why else promote Wiranto?

Even before Soeharto had stepped down, but sensing strongly that this was imminent, Prabowo had tried to intervene in the process of discussion between Soeharto and the ABRI high command by turning up uninvited at the home of Army Chief of Staff, Gen. Subagyo, whom he knew had met the President earlier to discuss affairs of state and ABRI matters - including perhaps himself. The 'Far Eastern Economic Review' of June 4, quoted an official who learned of the incident from an eye witness as saying: "It was like a raid." Even after Soeharto had resigned, Prabowo appealed to his former boss to reverse his transfer to Bandung. According to the 'Review' Soeharto and other members of the former First Family advised him not to make trouble. Nevertheless, from there he went straight to President Habibie's home in Kuningan on the same mission.

Prabowo had come to occupy an unenviable position. After Soeharto's resignation, understandably, the former First Family, did not want to be seen to be causing trouble. According to the 'Far Eastern Economic Review' of July 23, the day after his resignation Soeharto had testily branded Prabowo a "troublemaker." Perhaps because of his suspected hand in the train of events which had led to Soeharto's ousting - the kidnappings of activists, the killings at Trisakti and, finally, the carnage of the riots. Ironically, according to the 'Review,' Soeharto also "criticized the young general for not ending the student occupation of Parliament, which became a powerful symbol of the reformist struggle around the world." Had Soeharto not ordered the rounding up of activists after all? Was it simply that Prabowo had gone too far? Was this part of the trouble he had caused? Or was it his alleged involvement in the Trisakti killings and involvement as an instigator of the riots which led the former president to brand him a troublemaker? According to the "Review' Soeharto would have preferred him to clamp down on the students, presumably without doing anything else, such as stirring up mob riots. If the students could have been pushed back to campus and there had been no mass riots, was Soeharto thinking that he might still be in power? From Prabowo's point of view, he had wanted to deal firmly with the students but he was in a difficult position. He was up against Wiranto and the high command. To deal with the students he would have to disobey orders. More importantly he might have to fight members of other units, notably the marines under whose benign escort the students had arrived at the Parliament. Whatever the former First Family might have thought and hoped Prabowo had always been on a losing wicket. When Soeharto took action from KOSTRAD headquarters in 1965 most of the army's high command had been wiped out or rendered ineffective. In Prabowo's case, ABRI's command was intact and, given the climate of the day, the reformers firmly and decisively outnumbered pro-Soeharto elements. Prabowo did try to wrestle with his situation, especially by trying to extract from President Habibie, execution of an alleged promise to make him Armed Forces chief, the only way he could act lawfully. But the forces ranged against him were too senior and too many to overcome. In the end, inscrutable and tight lipped, he had no choice but to obey orders - or suffer the consequences. The orders could never have involved the crackdown Soeharto wanted and therefore could never have led to saving Soeharto.

On Monday, May 25, General Wiranto took the trouble to personally brief 10,000 low, middle and high ranking officers from the Jakarta garrison. In a 60-minute address he denied that there was or had recently been any disunity within ABRI. The danger point seemed to have passed; ABRI had made a commitment and had been seen to make a commitment, but events had moved quickly, perhaps too quickly for entrenched loyalties to adjust. It was essential now to show and prove quickly that the entire ABRI command was behind the Habibie government and behind reformation.

Almost simultaneously the commander of the 6,500 strong KOPASSUS, Maj. Gen. Muchdi Purwopranjono, and the head of the strategic West Java, Siliwangi Military Command were replaced. For Prabowo or anyone else in the military to have their own agendas really still required the involvement of Soeharto but there was no sign that the old general was prepared to fight again. On the contrary, according to people who knew him, bitter at being abandoned, the former president seemed to have gone into virtual seclusion, except for Friday prayers at various military mosques. Thus, any residual pro-Soeharto/Prabowo forces which may have existed were deprived of a vital rallying point. Before 30 days had elapsed the commander of the Jakarta Garrison, Maj. Gen. Syafrie Syamsuddin, Prabowo's good friend, would be removed along with other commanders with ties to the Soeharto family including also the commanders of the navy, airforce and police. By the end of June key commanders appointed by Soeharto and any suspected of being influenced by or loyal to Prabowo had been reassigned leaving General Wiranto in firm command of the security forces.

Reinforcing the sincerity with which he had earlier apologized over the Trisakti killings, Wiranto called upon the troops to enter the campuses, mingle with the students, commit to a mutual fight for reforms and, most importantly, to " apologize to all of the students for all that has happened to their friends." This was to be the beginning of a long term campaign to change the image and policies of ABRI, to convert swords into ploughshares. Soon, in place of terror, torture and death, ABRI would be seen hard at work not only helping students, but helping the poor with essential foods, helping farmers, building infrastructure. There was no other way. ABRI had become widely distrusted and even despised. Especially to safeguard its special position in the political process ABRI had to work hard and fast to recover the respect and even love of the people.

Within hours of Soeharto's ousting, reform groups, parents and relatives began demanding the release of political prisoners, some said all, others said only the non-communists. The Soeharto Government had built up a dark record of stifling free expression, intimidating opponents and cracking down harshly on all anti-regime elements, including intellectuals and writers. There was hope now that many lids would be ripped off many previously tightly sealed boxes. In some quarters there must also have been a fear that cupboards, too, would be opened and skeletons come tumbling out.

The murdered Trisakti students had by no means been forgotten. Parents and reformists now began pressing ABRI to make public the outcome of its investigations into the identities of the perpetrators, especially their units in the military or the police. The National Commission on Human Rights said that the state police had not used live ammunition at Trisakti, leaving the finger pointing at the military. Outgoing Jakarta police chief, Maj. Gen. Hamami Nata was quoted as saying pointedly: "It is time to separate ourselves from the Armed Forces. Too much pain. Too much slander." Stories began to emerge that several witnesses to the Trisakti killings had been threatened by "unidentified people forbidding them to give testimony."

On May 26, General Wiranto was quoted by 'The Straits Times', Singapore as saying that 14 members of ABRI may have been involved, including six officers. He was quoted as saying that they were "suspected of encouraging unprocedural and undisciplined actions. Intriguingly, Wiranto was quoted as saying that the results of investigations into the Trisakti killings "would be coupled with the results of other inquiries" - into the earlier kidnappings of activists, for example? Or the riots and associated rapes? The public waited with baited breath. By June 3, the number of military personnel likely to face court martial had risen to 19. General Wiranto had won high marks for his support of the student reformers and for his overall handling of the crisis which had brought down Soeharto. The public was impressed again with the speed at which an investigation into Trisakti seemed to be being conducted and with the fact that the National Commission for Human Rights was involved.

Students around the country, albeit now in comparatively small numbers, continued to demonstrate for "total reform" - meaning new elections but the movement was clearly fizzling out. Overcoming the clamour for immediate new presidential and vice presidential elections had been a major hurdle. As the new cabinet had been formed, even the powerful Coordinating Minister for Economy, Finance and Industry, Ginandjar Kartasasmita, had said that he favoured elections as soon as possible. Only hours after he was sworn in he was quoted as saying: " We need to have a new government with a new mandate from the people. Economic recovery cannot be achieved without a conducive political climate." This had also been the basis of his rebellion in leading the group of key ministers to resign from Soeharto's last cabinet. He was quoted as saying that he and the other ministers in the new cabinet had accepted their jobs because they felt that someone had to take care of the economy while the country worked toward reform. Should the people wish for a different government, he said, he was willing to stand aside. He added that he and the other economic ministers had no intention of remaining in office until the year 2003. Ginandjar represented a faction in the cabinet that dominated thinking about the economy as well as one that reflected popular demands for political reform.

The reformists were doubtless expecting, with great naiveté, rapid and dramatic change in the wake of Soeharto's unexpected fall from power. But the new President needed time to understand and get a firm grip on the situation he had inherited. He needed to meet as many people as possible, then he needed to reflect Finally, he needed to explore the limits of his new power in terms of what would and would not be acceptable to those around him. President Soeharto had given orders, military style, and they were obeyed. It is likely that Habibie would have to tilt more toward consent than command. From the outset this seemed to be his position as he was seen consulting and taking advice, here, there and everywhere, being careful to give the leadership those around him felt was needed but not getting very far in front.

One of the reform leaders who was given an early meeting with him was Amien Rais. Habibie said he welcomed proposals for political reform. Afterwards Rais told the media that President Habibie had promised elections within six to 12 months. Rais quoted Habibie as saying: " How can I stay until 2003? I am only staying to prepare for the election of a new MPR/DPR, which is truly chosen by the people and after that I'm done." Also present at the meeting were Emil Salim, former cabinet minister Rudini, scholar, Nurcholis Madjid and lawyer Adnan Buyung Nasution - all vociferous critics of President Soeharto. On the night of his meeting with Habibie, Rais's organization of reformists, the Council of People's Mandate, called for "clean, fair and honest elections." While the reformers accepted the promise of elections, clearly, they were worried that they might not be open and fair.

The issue of the timing of elections was a major one. One school of thought was that the political, economic and social dislocation of recent days should be repaired before elections took place. Another school of thought was that the longer it took to hold elections the longer it would be for investor confidence to return. Of course, if investors thought that elections would be held soon they would almost certainly delay their decisions pending the outcome. Most remembered the violence of the 1997 election, even under tight controls. Now the elections were presumed to be free and open with a plethora of new parties competing. Would this mean more fighting on the streets? Worse still, would it result in an unstable government? Instead of firm government could there be a shaky coalition? There were many questions and, as yet, no answers.

A sign of the direction in which the ruling GOLKAR might be headed in free elections was given as early as May 27, when one of its founding organizations, Musyawarah Kekeluargaan dan Gotong Royong (MKGR), led by former minister, Mien Sugandhi, announced that it would form a separate party. Mien indicated that many individual members of

GOLKAR affiliated organizations had long felt Soeharto's political straight-jacket gripping them too tightly.

Direct investors in mega-projects were adopting a wait and see attitude. Few large investors were pulling out of Indonesia but most were in a holding pattern and few newcomers could be expected until the situation was seen to be stable over a reasonable term. On the Jakarta Stock Exchange the story was the same. The 'Jakarta Post' quoted fund manager, Viola Tam of BT Fund Managers (Hong Kong) Ltd., as saying: " We don't know if (Habibie) has the will to carry out the reforms of the IMF and we believe the situation is still pretty risky." Commenting on the new cabinet, Robert Barker, fund manager with National Mutual Funds Management (Asia) Ltd., was quoted as saying: " This is a change of face rather than a change of system. We need to see more of what Habibie will be proposing and the types of policies he will introduce." Surprisingly, the number of projects involving foreign investment held up well. During the whole of 1997 there had been 790 projects and only until mid-August there were already 629. The Investment Coordinating Board was quietly confident that the 1997 total could be exceeded. of course, in dollar terms the investment total was down by around 60 per cent - until August 15. Many of the new projects were in the primary or secondary sectors, including food and resources, but not large scale. Despite the mayhem, it seemed that there were still investors willing to jump in while the chances were good. Such investors realized that the mayhem was unusual, short term and often limited to a few urban centres, especially on Java and in Jakarta.

Those who wanted Habibie to step down shared the view that the Habibie Government was a Soeharto government in disguise. Habibie and Soeharto had been close and good friends for years. Habibie was the former president's protégé. Might Soeharto not simply be pulling Habibie's strings from his residence at Jalan Cendana? President Habibie faced an urgent challenge to prove that he was his own man and not merely a puppet. And then there were the 20 ministers appointed by Soeharto. Were these not remnants of the old and detested system which should be swept away? While they remained in office was there really a chance of the full reforms demanded by the activists? And what about the House of Representatives and the People's Consultative Assembly? Were their members not all approved or appointed not so much for their abilities and skills but because they had been thought unlikely to rock the Soeharto boat? Should these not all be swept away, too, in new general elections? There were plenty who believed that most of

Indonesia's most able people had been deliberately excluded. Seeing which way the winds were blowing the 'Indonesian Observer' of May 27 noted in an editorial that "scores of members of parliament have voluntarily decided to hand in their resignations in a move to reject nepotism...." Media reports linked 200 MPR appointments with nepotism.

On June 2, reflecting vociferous popular clamour, Attorney General Sudjono Atmonegoro, appointed by former President Soeharto, announced the commencement of a probe into the former President's wealth. In June, Forbe's magazine's rankings of the world's richest men claimed that Soeharto had US$4 billion with stakes in about 3,200 companies. Soeharto continued to say he had nothing but his pension of Rps 15 million-a-month. Demonstrators demanded that Soeharto be tried for corruption and critics suggested that a portion of his alleged wealth be returned to the state. Economist Christianto Wibisono was quoted as saying that not only Soeharto but all those who had amassed wealth illegally should return at least 55 percent to the state in exchange for an amnesty. Not much more was heard of this! There were demands to subject all of Soeharto's foundations and companies to rigorous investigation.

Attorney General Soedjono was quoted as saying that his office was preparing to recommend independence from the government and he announced the commencement of an investigation into corruption across the board which, he added somewhat depressingly, "would take time." Appointed by Soeharto, some people thought Soerdjono was deliberately keeping his investigations at a slow pace. President Habibie seemed to agree because within two weeks, Soedjono was replaced by ABRI's chief auditor, Maj. Gen. Andi Muhamad Ghalib. After the sacking, Coordinating Minister for Development Supervision, Hartarto, said that the Government planned "fast and consistent steps" to wipe out "corruption, collusion and nepotism." Cynics wondered whether Soedjono had been going too fast! Minister Hartarto enjoyed public respect and his statement seemed to quash fears that Maj. Gen. Ghalib's appointment was, in fact, aimed at helping ABRI keep its promise to protect the former president. ABRI spokesman, Wahab Mokodongan went out of his way to stress that the military's promise to protect Soeharto was not the same as protecting his alleged wealth. Both ABRI and President Habibie were quoted as saying that that the law must be allowed to take its course and that they would not protect the fallen leader from legitimate corruption charges.

Cynics found it impossible to believe that officials with close links to Soeharto and the New Order were really going to honestly and thoroughly investigate the former president. They said that many of those linked to Soeharto feared that a thorough Soeharto probe might rattle skeletons in some of their cupboards. On June 17, political observer Arbit Sanit from the University of Indonesia was quoted as saying that the switch of attorney general may have been part of ABRI'S promise to protect the former president. Even Megawati Sukarnoputri had called upon the public to leave the former President alone. "Is it right that once we have pressured him into stepping down we should continue to hound him?" The Sukarno's had been hounded by Soeharto. Now, apparently, they wanted to occupy the highest moral ground. A vice president of the Government Funded Human Rights Commission said that it was right for people to be told if bad and illegal things had happened but that after that it was better to "forgive and forget." The sighs of relief around Indonesia's power centres were almost audible.

Investors were concerned about Indonesia's relationship with the IMF. The IMF still enjoyed so much prestige and implied power that investors were convinced that only by following its recommendations to the letter would Indonesia's economy recover. In fact, as each letter had been put in place by the Government of Indonesia the economy had deteriorated further and the market response had been even more nega- tive. The liquidity squeeze had put business flat on its face and the price increases and removal of subsidies had unleashed a destructive fury. President Habibie would have to make up his mind fast whether - or not - the IMF was killing Indonesia with its prescriptions for a return to eco- nomic health. One can easily imagine that the new President and his cabinet were terrified of upsetting the IMF and calling down on their heads another round of international condemnation which would surely kick the bottom right out of the economy. The day after the announce- ment of the new cabinet the Government's position was made clear.

Ginandjar Kartasasmita had said that the new Government re- mained committed to the IMF programme. He was quoted as saying: " The programme itself is good and still valid. We need to continue imple- menting it." The policy of tight liquidity was to be maintained. Whether he really meant this or was simply playing to an audience remained to be seen.

IMF Managing Director, Michel Camdessus, was quoted as say- ing in Canada on Monday, May 25, that IMF-brokered funds would be forthcoming for Indonesia but only after yet another review of Indonesia's economy. Naturally, investors and markets now wanted to wait for this new review. Asia Pacific Cooperation Forum (APEC) finance ministers were meeting in Alberta. In a unanimous statement they said that IMF assistance to Indonesia should not be delayed "unduly." "Everybody wants to ensure that when the funds are advanced they will have the maximum effect," Canadian Finance Minister, Paul Martin, was quoted as saying. This statement seemed more based on hearsay than fact. Did the APEC ministers really know in fine detail what the IMF's funds were for? Or were they simply parroting the commonly held view among Western leaders that the IMF must be obeyed? Or did Martin's comment simply reflect the common fear in the West that too large a chunk of any funds given would find their way into the wrong hands and pockets? Were the ministers aware that none of the IMF's disbursements (US$4 billion to date), its reform measures and its macro policies had achieved anything beyond the beggaring of the economy? Presumably the answer to most of these questions was 'No.' Soeharto was gone so there could no longer by any suspicion that the West was using the IMF to get rid of him. Whatever actual and potential donors to Indonesia knew or didn't know, the Habibie Government clearly and understandably felt that no risks should be taken. "We're going to be good and do as we're told," in effect it told the Fund. "Next time you give us a scorecard you'll be even more pleased." Maybe. But would the markets care a hoot?

In his statement from Alberta, Camdessus had given no indication of any new IMF initiative likely to address Indonesia's fundamental problems - the chronically devalued rupiah and the liquidity crunch. All he said was that the new review would be to take into account the latest realities and reassess macroeconomic targets. Surely, any competent member of the Indonesian Government's economic team could have done that! To cynics, what anyone expected the IMF packages to achieve was increasingly mysterious.

Over the weekend of May 23 and 24, the Indonesian Chamber of Commerce and Industry (KADIN) had made its position clear. The Chamber called on the new Government to carry out the programmes agreed with the IMF, to adopt a concrete programme to restore the economy and to take steps to reduce the wealth gap between indigenous people and Indonesia's ethnic Chinese. KADIN called on people to give President Habibie a chance. Almost daily, some organizations echoed this view while others rejected him. No one spelt out how all these things were to be brought about.

The line up against Habibie for president had included: the Coalition of Indonesian Environmental Lawyers, the Coalition of Indonesian Women for Justice and Democracy, the Alumni of the University of Indonesia and the Indonesian Legal Aid and Human Rights Association. Their most major complaint was that Habibie had been a long serving and loyal ally of the deposed President. One implication was that he was unlikely to favour the wholehearted and wholesale reforms demanded by pro-democracy activists. Indeed, his statements following his election as Vice President in March had been strictly in the Soeharto mold - gradual change within existing structures. Habibie had promised the further development of Pancasila democracy and a more responsive Government attitude to rising political aspirations; development of the rule of law; development of education and, finally, equal opportunities for all. There seemed nothing revolutionary in any of this, except, perhaps, bringing about the rule of law. Of course, there could have been. The outcome would depend on how these broad promises were interpreted and applied. With Soeharto in power the promises didn't look much; with Soeharto out of power they could mean a lot more. Nobody knew. Despite the appointment of Muladi, few thought that the law in Indonesia would ever take precedence over the government. So, without evidence to the contrary, during his first days in power critics continued to brand Habibie as a Soeharto man.

There were other issues, resentments and complaints whirling around the new president. One issue among the public at large was Habibie's alleged profligacy while heading up the state aircraft manufacturer, IPTN. Complaints included the manner in which he had allegedly persuaded President Soeharto to use money for IPTN from the state reforestation fund - one of those soon to be selected for compulsory audit by the IMF. Among the security forces, resentments included the way he had been put in charge of strategic industries including arms industries and the way he had intervened to insist on purchasing the old East German Navy - military matters all. Then there were charges of nepotism. Several relatives held senior posts in state industries and agencies. His brother promptly quit as head of the Batam Industrial Development Authority. The resignation coincided with a positive stampede of wives and children of ministers and senior officials to surrender their posts. Nepotism had become a very dirty and dangerous word. The share prices of Soeharto family linked companies continued to fall and there were growing calls for privileges and contracts granted to all family businesses to be investigated, reassessed and, if necessary withdrawn.

Among the political public, the weight of opinion fairly quickly fell on the side of those willing to give the new Government a chance. Habibie helped them by demonstrating a proper sense of urgency and a proper distancing of himself from his former boss. No one but a political lunatic could imagine being able to continue in the old and discredited ways. Soeharto's successor could hardly stand up and say "No" to reform. The demand was for the long closed doors and windows of the house Soeharto had built to be flung open. Either he had to give the people the reforms they were demanding or step out of the way. The people were in no mood to be fobbed off with a halfway house - the old regime plus a bit of tinkering. They wanted total reform. Habibie seemed to quickly decide that he would be the man to do it. He would show that he was not a Soeharto puppet. He would show that he was his own man with his own policies. He would show that these policies were sensitive to past and present injustices and the muzzled aspirations of the people. He would lead the reform movement. In doing so, he would also automatically halt a witch hunt of the entire New Order.

At his first cabinet meeting on Monday, May 25, he announced that his Government would be free from corruption, collusion and nepotism and he ordered his ministers to instigate reform in all their sectors of responsibility. In case people were already concerned about it, he said he was committed to limiting presidential terms to two. Policies to rescue falling living standards and the economy generally would include boosting agriculture and agribusiness, exports and tourism, implementing in full everything agreed with the IMF, controlling the state budget and inflation, seeking to stabilize the rupiah exchange rate, accelerating bank restructuring, resolving the problem of the offshore debt overhang and generally restoring confidence in the Government and in the economy. He also took the bold step of ordering the dismantling of all special facilities and privileges granted to "certain people or business groups." The speed with which this last instruction was followed up defied all cultural traditions. It was no sooner said than in process. Again it prevented a wider witch hunt. But some of his broader promises, which sounded so positive at the moment of hearing, such as seeking to stabilize the rupiah exchange rate and accelerating bank restructuring were to prove to be problems as intractable under Habibie as they had been under Soeharto.

Tacitly endorsing Habibie's approach, ABRI Chief of Sociopolitical Affairs, Let. Gen. Susilo Bambang Yudhoyono was quoted as saying: "ABRI feels that fundamental reform is the answer to all crisis which have hit the country." In his final official meetings with President Soeharto at Jalan Cendana, while Soeharto seemed to want to cling on, this was the policy General Wiranto was sworn to implement. However, Let. Gen. Susilo cautioned that reform should not be over hasty.

ABRI's internal politics during 1998 will doubtless one day be the subject of a book in their own right. One thing we can be sure about is that there was heated debate and that during the debates not everyone agreed. Writing in Singapore's 'The Straits Times' on July 2, Derwin Pereira said that ABRI commanders normally broke down into two - merah-putih or red and white secular officers and hijau or green Muslim officers. In the instant of toppling Soeharto we can guess that both groups agreed, albeit for different reasons. The hijau officers might not have liked Soeharto's sidelining of Muslims and the apparent favouring of ethnic Chinese. The merah putih officers probably favoured a secular, professional army, standing above politics and performing only legitimate military duties as required by the state. The obstacle to both groups was Soeharto. They could agree that he had to go. Beyond that, divisions almost certainly persisted. Within the hijau group were loyal Soehartoists who may have wanted to back the old leader as long as possible before transferring allegiance to someone else, not necessarily Habibie. There was doubtless a fourth group of fence sitters.

The challenge Wiranto had faced in mid-May lay in neutralizing the loyal Soehartoists/Prabowoists while maintaining unity in all other respects. Events showed that he was able to achieve this. The next challenge lay in the nature and pace of reforms to be instigated by a new government. The reformers within ABRI seemed to favour faster rather than slower change, so long as it was constitutional, orderly and peaceful. Events showed that they got their way. President Habibie's timetable for a special session of Parliament and general elections fell exactly within the time frame of one year he had been given by ABRI when he accepted power. Within ABRI, within the cabinet and among civilian, non-government reformers, there was a widespread and undoubtedly correct view that the longer the electoral reform process and the longer it took to actually stage elections the longer it would take to restore confidence in the country.

While ABRI had become a driving force behind the reform process it also faced a major problem - its past actions. Whatever might be blamed on Soeharto loyalists or on Prabowo in regard to kidnappings of activists, the Trisakti shootings and the May riots, the fact of the matter was that ABRI as a whole had been engaged in what many now identified as horrendous abuses, especially in the provinces of Timor, Aceh and Irian Jaya. Even the kidnapping of activists had been going on long before May 1998. The objective was sometimes to obtain information and sometimes to intimidate. There seemed a careless disregard for the lives of people who fell into ABRI units' hands. General Wiranto contritely apologized for abuses committed by troops in the field and coupled his apology with a promise to reform ABRI's ethics and field behaviour. For many of the general public a mere apology from ABRI was insufficient. They wanted to see the culprits rooted out.

This must have posed General Wiranto with his final challenge. To root out officers responsible for past mistakes and excesses might mean taking on powerful officers with loyal followings. It might involve risk. As Gen. Wiranto told President Habibie on June 23, such action would take time. At the end of June the public and President Habibie were pressing ABRI for the truth about its past activities, especially those committed in May. The Deputy Chairman of the National Commission on Human Rights, Marzuki Darusman was quoted as saying on June 23: " ..we are now beginning to understand that the resolution of the (mystery of the) missing people, the Trisakti incident and the riots are strongly related to ABRI's internal consolidation." In other words ABRI's reformers needed time to consolidate their grip on the Armed Forces. Presumably they also needed time to work out how to emerge reasonably honourably from the debacle without the friction which might be engendered if too many of their senior officers had to be reprimanded.

By August 24, ABRI's policy was clear. Officers suspected of involvement in the kidnappings, the Trisakti shootings and the riots were retired or had their careers frozen. More formidable punishment might have provoked their supporters - loyal troops, perhaps - and it might have dangerously divided ABRI. As it was ABRI's decision was reached by consensus. ABRI had to hope that it would not ignite passions within its ranks and would at the same time satisfy the reformers and the victims of its misguided officers. ABRI had taken another step along the road to decency and professionalism. Meanwhile, internal investigations continued, particularly in regard to the killings at Trisakti.

Even with its internal consolidation over, ABRI still faced problems. As General Wiranto was to say in September, not all ABRI's activities were illegal; in other words ABRI had acted in response to clear Government orders. It was with these orders that the public should take issue, not with ABRI. If ABRI identified and punished those of its members guilty of what the public regarded as excesses, not only recently, but for years past, such actions could severely undermine morale and disrupt unity. Therefore, General Wiranto questioned the fairness and appropriateness of demanding such retrospective action. Even though the General must have known by September who was responsible for what during the May riots ABRI's willingness to identify the culprits seemed limited. It seemed that its action against senior officers and its identification of other officers alleged to have been responsible for the Trisakti killings were deemed to be as far as ABRI should, or perhaps could, go.

Many observers, especially overseas, seemed to think that ABRI was obsessed with its political role and that this obsession formed the basis of possible divisions of opinion within the force. Certainly, it was a matter for heated discussion but equally certainly mainstream ABRI was ready to accept a lesser political role, although perhaps not no political role. There was a feeling that ABRI had been given too much power and that it would benefit from improved control and guidance by a properly motivated government. Soeharto loyalists might have objected to this but even for them the writing was on the wall. Once elections were held and a new government elected no longer hand-picked by one man, ABRI could have no boss other than the state and if the public was to be respected the new state's functionaries should give no place to corruption, collusion or nepotism and especially not to the 'dirty tricks' the Soeharto Government had apparently commissioned the security forces to carry out in support of a single group. Henceforth ABRI would serve and protect the nation as a whole. As the weeks slipped passed, in the wake of the fall of Soeharto. statements that perhaps ABRI should have no political role were modified by actions rather than words - actions which implied strongly that ABRI looked forward to at least a role in social, economic and political affairs.

Derwin Pereira said that ABRI had drawn up a concept paper reflecting a month of brainstorming about political issues. The paper, said Pereira, included such objectives as: transparency in decision making, separating the executive and judiciary, modifying the election system to broaden the base of participation, encouraging a multi-party system of only three to six parties to prevent a single majority from appearing and also preventing uncontrollable numbers of smaller parties emerging, preventing government interference in the activities of political parties, revising press laws and subversion laws and eradicating corruption, collusion and nepotism. No wonder Amien Rais said the military had no disagreements with him! Rais would have said much the same things. Finally, the paper said that ABRI should indeed continue to play at least some political role, with seats in the MPR, for example. But it stressed that from now on this was a strictly non-partisan involvement. Many Indonesians would agree with that. ABRI was needed for the cohesion and stability it brought. It wasn't needed for its abuses. With the election of a new government the door would be open for ABRI to turn a new and hopefully shining page in its history as a true partner with the people in their evolving concepts of development and stability.

The United States had publicly taken a very low key approach to the change of president, insisting that the succession was basically a matter for the people of Indonesia. However, it was well known that Washington was strongly critical of aspects of Soeharto's iron fist approach to government and, since the onset of the economic crisis, strongly critical of the corruption inherent in his Government.

As President Habibie was chairing his first cabinet meeting Singapore's 'The Straits Times' quoted 15 "top US lawmakers" as writing to President Habibie: " We respectfully suggest that there are a num ber of preliminary steps you could take that would demonstrate publicly your commitment to serious reform." Said the 'Straits Times: " The suggested steps include freeing political prisoners, establishing a clear timetable for free and fair elections, repealing repressive laws and initiating dialogue on the political status of East Timor and Irian Jaya." There can be little doubt that the White House would have concurred completely. Indonesia now had a political IMF on its hands.

The Habibie Government had now been set a new test, been given a new list of reforms to carry out. President Habibie's first actions showed that the was keenly aware of this. Aid and political reform were now tightly linked. Apparently as a gesture of goodwill the US Export-Import Bank announced that it had made available US$1 billion in trade financing.

Just as Ginandjar Kartasamita had known that the IMF and the White House would never continue to support Soeharto, General Wiranto knew that Washington would no longer tolerate abhorrent civil and human rights abuses in Indonesia. If Indonesia's civilian and military leaders wanted help from the US and its allies the message was very clear: "Take to the road of decency and democracy. Put you political and economic house in order. Then, we will help you with all our might." If this approach had been publicly low key, behind the scenes it had been powerfully convincing. It was not always low key. Almost exactly a year befor his downfall, the US State Department had said that Indonesians had been deprived of their ability to change their government through democratic means. Was 1998 a replay of 1965 in other important respects? Just as Soeharto appeared to draw confidence from hidden sources, did Wiranto and his fellow reformists draw a similar confidence from a source across the Pacific? Was it the same one but at a diffent time and for dif ferent reasons?

General Wiranto would also have felt the chill blast of US displeasure on other issues, for example, the cancellation of F-16 fighters and the opening of negotiations with the Russians for Sukhoi jets as well as new helicopters for KOPASSUS. Soeharto had also cancelled joint US-ABRI training exercises. There can be little doubt that Washington was pleased to see Soeharto go. Even before his seat was cold the deal for Sukhoi fighters and choppers was cancelled.

Within a month of Soeharto's fall, the United States announced that it would resume support for international lending to Indonesia by such agencies as the World Bank and the Asian Development Bank. On June 22, the Bank announced that it was considering a US$1 billion policy support loan for Indonesia to help pay for reforms to the banking sector, improve corporate governance as well as mounting urgent social needs. USAID promised an extra US$50 million in the form of food and loan guarantees. The agency had already provided US$151 million. On June 18, Japan's Exim Bank, provided a new US$1 billion trade financing facility. With Soeharto gone, doors were beginning to open.

CHAPTER NINE

One nation united

Among President Habibie's first initiatives was a trip to Jakarta's so-called Chinatown, badly damaged in the riots of early May. The riots were estimated to have caused about US$1 billion worth of destruction. Many Chinese were terrified and traumatized by the riots. After the may hem, tens of thousands of ethnic Chinese had fled Indonesia taking with them as much as an estimated US$20 billion. Those who fled overseas elected to remain there as long as possible. Those who stayed in Indonesia were tense and fearful. For days after the riots some continued to be terrorized by gangs of high school students, their faces painted frighteningly to resemble the war paint of KOPASSUS troopers.

Ethnic Chinese were important members of the business community. They were strong in the critical field of distribution and also in bus transportation, banking, construction, coffee plantations, forestry, the production of alcohol, textiles, pulp, paper, electronic products, jewelry and cigarettes. In distribution, ethnic Chinese operated around 12,000 businesses, some of them handling rice . By August, the breakdown of the rice distribution network coupled with drought induced scarcity would deepen scarcity and push up prices to critical levels.

While they might not dominate small business and the informal sector, up to 70 percent of large companies were thought to be ethnic Chinese owned. But numbers can be deceptive. According to one leading pribumi businessman companies worth over US$1 billion per annum were controlled by only 13 families and firms worth over US$500 million were controlled by 15 families owning 2,348 companies. The same man estimated that 68 percent of Indonesia's GDP was accounted for by these large companies. The wealth gap was painfully obvious.

Other statistics showed that, in terms of turnover, only 10 conglomerates accounted for 30 percent of GDP. In turnover terms, a total of 300 conglomerates accounted for nearly 50 percent of GDP; their assets accounted for 76 percent of GDP. The largest conglomerates operating in mega projects with mega dollars were cited as being the Salim Group, the Soeharto family and Barito Pacific, controlled by Soeharto crony Pangestu. At the end of 1997, these three companies were said to have been operating with foreign investments of over US$11 billion. It was to be hoped that this really was investment and not debt. Christianto Wibisono, Director of the Indonesian Business Data Center revealed at the end of 1997 that publicly listed companies affiliated to the conglomerates generally had a combined debt of around US$80 billion. Wibisono concluded that Indonesia's economy was therefore "greatly influenced by the ups and downs of the conglomerates." Knowing these figures gave new meaning to the reform slogan that Indonesia's 200 million were hostage to 200 families. Once foreign debt became identified as destroying Indonesia's economy it is easy to see why Indonesia's reformers felt that Soeharto and his cronies had to go.

In Java, where majority of Indonesians live, majority of the people are Muslims. President Habibie is a Muslim and many Chinese wondered how much he would really do for them - especially since it was Muslim moral outrage against the New Order as well as their profound sense of having been politically sidelined and economically left behind, that drew many Muslims into the fight to topple Soeharto. While Indonesia's government and security were firmly in indigenous hands, many Muslim's believed that Soeharto had favoured the ethnic Chinese, while appearing to discriminate against Muslims. His family empire had been built in collaboration with ethnic Chinese, one or two of whom had come to be numbered among the world's richest men. Worse still, from the point of view of the ethnic Chinese, only three months earlier,the pro-Government Indonesian Ulemas Council had called for a jihad or holy war against speculators or hoarders, provoking riots and attacks on shopkeepers, some of whom were ethnic Chinese.

Two years earlier, in April, 1996, Abdurrahman Wahidhad made a milestone speech in Yogyakarta in which the topic of Muslim sidelining was his major theme. There were two aspects to his concern: one that Muslims felt intimidated and afraid about even trying to participate in national discusssions about social change and secondly that Government was not behaving in ways consistent with the teachings of Islam. In an apparent sideswipe at the Association of Indonesian Muslim Intellectuals (ICMI), chaired by Minister B.J.Habibie and long thought to be a Soeharto tool, Abdurrahman said that it was "unfortunate" that "Muslim scholars have even joined the group who have resigned and adjusted themselves to the situation, helping to preserve the status quo." After the fall of Soeharto, the Muslim leader sought to redress the balance by abandoning his long held policy of eschewing politics and taking part in the formation of a new political party. Since its leaders included former vice president, Try Sutrisno and Edi Sudradjat there was an impression that the party might be GOLKAR with morals, rather than anything radically new.

In October, 1997, hundreds of worshippers at Jakarta's Al Azhar Grand Mosque had heard imams say that recent disasters were a divine warning and called on the nation to repent. They said that forest fires, economic turmoil, fatal air crashes and social disturbances were all warnings. "We are calling on the Government to remember that power is a mandate from Allah that has to be accounted for, now and in the hereafter. No matter how great and strong a power is, Allah will some day take it back." Soeharto had been listening but he didn't appear to believe it. Muhammadiyah leader, Amien Rais had spoken at the same meeting and also concluded that the Government wasn't listening. Appearances, however, can be deceptive. Soeharto had taken note and, as we know, had instigated steps to push Gus Dur aside. Amien Rais said that the disasters referred to by the imams should alert everyone to the fact that there was "something very wrong" in the country. But, he had added, " The biggest disaster, however, is the fact that some of the leaders of this nation, have become immune to those various disasters." There could be no doubt that Muslims expected better things of Habibie and, if not received from him, then from his successor.

Hundreds of thousands of Muslims rallied in Surabaya during the first weekend of Habibie's Government under banners reminding him that reform must continue and that government should be accountable. Muslim's had increasingly high expectations of the new Government. There was talk of indigenous business taking over from any Chinese who had quit the country. Nevertheless, President Habibie's message during his walkabout was and had to be: "In Indonesia, we do not recognize racial or religious differences among people. We will not tolerate it in any form." People close to President Habibie say he is no exclusivist and that, in any case, the Muslims around him are not fundamentalists.

In practice, the ethnic Chinese had not been treated as equal citizens under the New Order. President Soeharto had favoured a few ethnic Chinese while keeping the broad mass firmly toeing the New Order line. And, if he had favoured his ethnic Chinese cronies by blocking off opportunities to pribumis and Muslims, they were few compared to his broad support for the Muslim majority. In fact, far from favouring the ethnic Chinese as a whole, President Soeharto had used some of the conglomerates to advance family business interests and had squeezed them to pay for any privileges they may have been given. Several times, the owners of the largest conglomerates had been summoned to his Tapos ranch or to the State Palace and told to help pribumi-run cooperatives or to give a portion of their profits to help smaller, pribumi businesses. The attitude seemed to be that the Chinese could be allowed to do business in Indonesia but they should always stand ready to pay the piper. The ethnic Chinese naturally resented this.

But, among the people, these were not the perceived realities. Indonesia's ethnic Chinese as a whole felt discriminated against, not favoured; Indonesia's Muslims as a whole felt sidelined, not favoured. The ethnic Chinese thought that the pribumis were Indonesia's number one people; the pribumis felt that this position was occupied by ethnic Chinese. The ethnic Chinese felt insecure; the pribumi's felt jealous. President Habibie had to walk a narrow line, between reassuring the ethnic Chinese and pleasing his Muslim constituents. If his praise for the ethnic Chinese was too fulsome he risked provoking the anger of indigenes. If it wasn't fulsome enough, he risked provoking the anger of the ethnic Chinese. A clue to his sympathies seemed to come in late July when he was widely quoted as saying that even if many of Indonesia's ethnic Chinese fled abroad: " Do you really think that we will then die? If they don't return their places will be taken over by others." Was this a reflection of where his sympathies lay or was the President just being realistic. Of course, objectively it was true. How could a nation grind to a halt and die because a few tens of thousands of people chose to leave? If he was being brutally realistic and if he was sincere in his one nation promise many ethnic Chinese wondered about rights? Were the ethnic Chinese in future to share equal rights with pribumis?

Despite President Habibie's attempts to reassure, according to comments made on June 8 by Christian Wibisono, Director of the Indonesian Business Data Center, Indonesia's ethnic Chinese face "more than 20 existing regulations, which are discriminatory in nature." On June 10, the ethnic Chinese-owned 'Jakarta Post' said that Chinese feel they have been "practically shut out of all other fields except business" and that their success in business has made them targets."

In Jakarta, on June 12, city authorities decided to remove from local identity cards special indications that their holders were Chinese. Officials were told not to rip off Chinese applying for new cards. The cost was Rps 1,000 but officials sometimes bled the Chinese of Rps 200,000 or more. Bleeding the ethnic Chinese for money had seemed to be one of the national pastimes. Compared to the alleged 20 discriminatory regulations it was a small concession.

Sixty days later President Habibie would be quoted by 'Business Week' magazine (August 3) as saying that "It would be very, very sad if an economy of 211 million people depended on just one ethnic group." Indonesia's ethnic Chinese took this as more evidence that they were not really wanted in Indonesia and that in reality the Government's cares about their plight since May were skin deep at the most.

The magazine printed other material which pointed firmly in the direction of a lower profile for ethnic Chinese in the new Indonesia. Said the magazine: "Instead (of depending on one ethnic group) Habibie is rebuilding the distribution system using pribumi companies and forcing out Chinese ones. Already, the Government has taken away contracts from hundreds of ethnic Chinese distributors of state-subsidized foods, even though they had remained in the country. The state logistics agency, which distributes rice and cooking oil, instead gave millions of dollars worth of contracts to pribumi." Promised new anti-monopoly laws would affect the conglomerates most of all and 43 out of the 50 listed on the stock exchange were ethnic Chinese owned. There were even people calling for the nationalization of Chinese assets and their redistribution among pribumis. One media report included the advice to ethnic Chinese who had fled the country that they should remain overseas and continue any businesses they had in Indonesia on the basis of foreign investors.

During his visit to Jakarta's 'Chinatown,' President Habibie stressed that the Government of Indonesia cared about all its people and would protect them. If they doubted it he said that they were welcome to form self protection groups. Many of his listeners did doubt it and self protection groups were formed. Subsequently, ethnic Chinese traders complained to the media that after years of paying protection money to the security forces, during the riots, they had been left to their own devices. There was little sign of any rush to return among those who had fled overseas, especially to Singapore and Malaysia. It was easy to promise security but would it really be available when needed? Habibie was quoted as promising that "all possible ways" would be sought to assist riot victims. Later he spoke about the need to introduce a Bill of Rights for all Indonesia's 200 million people, regardless of race.

Ethnic Chinese political scientist, Christianto Wibisono was quoted by 'Business Week' as saying of the May riots: " It was a marriage of convenience between latent racist masses and agents provocateurs." Habibie also faced this latent racism, an expression of a rivalry which in some parts of the archipelago was generations old. Officially the Government steered the only way possible, the middle way, offering equal rights and protections to all its citizens whatever their race. In practice the latent racism referred to by Wibisono persisted in raising its head. Later, one ethnic Chinese commentator would blame the slow resolution of the foreign private debt problem on the fact that the Government seemed to have little sympathy with ethnic Chinese debtors. Plenty of hopeful commercial vultures were lurking around, waiting to pick at the carcasses of any conglomerates which might become defunct. The Government and many others would say that this was simply the reality of business. Whoever wanted to pay some one else's debts! The bottom line was that the ethnic Chinese felt far from loved and needed.

On Friday, June 5, a group of young ethnic Chinese launched a new political party, the Indonesian Chinese Reform Party - but not to make any kind of fight with the majority of Indonesians. The organizers said that its objective was the promotion of harmony between ethnic Chinese and other Indonesians and its leaders announced that anyone could join. Nevertheless, the formation of the party was a sign of the times. The ethnic Chinese felt badly treated and some of them had decided to create a political vehicle to advance their interests within the framework of reform, together with others who agreed with them.

On Tuesday, May 26, the first of Soeharto's political prisoners had been released - Sri Bintang Pamungkas and labour leader Muchtar Pakpahan. The release took place one day ahead of a visit by US Congressman, Christopher Smith, Chairman of the Congressional Subcommittee on International Operations and Human Rights. Cynics hoped that the release would turn out to be more than a "cosmetic" arranged to please the US. Smith presented a petition calling for the release of 12 leading political prisoners. After the visit there was a promise of more releases and, indeed, on Thursday, May 28, two more were released - Nuku Suleiman, Chairman of the human rights group, Pijar Foundation, and Andi Syahputra, an activist from the Alliance of Independent Journalists. Upon their release Bintang and Pakpahan both immediately vowed to continue the campaign for total reform. Considering how dangerous they were supposed to be both men were subsequently strangely quiet.

In the prevailing atmosphere of total reform there was also a feeling that a government really committed to total reform would immediately release all political prisoners and not just one or two. On May 28, the 'Jakarta Post' had said in a leader headed "Free them all:" " A job half done is a job undone. Debatable as such a statement may be to some, many people would agree that this holds true in the case of the release of political prisoners in Indonesia. Amid the current demands for total reform and the correction of the wrongs and injustices done under the recently departed regime, the release of these opposition leaders has naturally been greeted by the public as one of the most significant so far.

"The release of the two, however, is not enough. Unless the Government follows up their release and honours its promise to free more prisoners, and fast, an impression could easily arise that Bintang's and Pakpahan's release was no more than a cosmetic step aimed at assuring Indonesians and the world that things have changed in Indonesia.

"Indeed, given the current climate of total reform, even the promise of more releases in the coming weeks - with the condition that those freed were not involved in the 1965 communist coup and still show a faithful adherence to the Pancasila national ideology and the Constitution - may not satisfy the multitudes of Indonesians seeking to correct the wrongs of Soeharto's New Order regime.

"An unconditional release of political prisoners would certainly do much to restore this country's poor human rights reputation, tattered further in the past months by reported abductions and torture of student and political activists, the forceful repression of student demonstrations and the fatal shootings of students in Jakarta.

"Of no less importance is the fact that the Government needs the full support of all Indonesians if it is to conquer this country's protracted crisis. Now is the time for the Government to start working toward a national reconciliation involving all segments of society. For this purpose, we can imagine no better gesture than the indiscriminate and unconditional release of all political prisoners."

It was widely expected that others of the estimated 200 political prisoners would be released soon. Justice Minister Muladi said that the cases would be reviewed as a prelude to a gradual and selective release. He said that former communists or those involved in the 1965 coup attempt would not be released. The Government said that jailed East Timor independence fighter, "Xanana" Gusmao was among those not likely to be released since he had been found guilty of criminal activities. East Timor would very soon be back in the headlines as separatists there sensed that there time had at last come. At the same time, United Nations Secretary General Kofi Annan called on Indonesia to release "Xanana."

On May 26, Manpower Minister, Fahmi Idris had announced that workers were from then on free to form and join trade unions of their choice.

Throughout Monday and Tuesday, May 25 and 26, President Habibie gave his attention to political reform. A Working Group was established consisting of ministers and activists to draw up the reform concepts. The basic issues were changes to the laws within which the electoral process operated and the timing of new general and presidential elections. House Speaker Harmoko said contemporaneously that the legislature must be consulted about the time table for elections and about electoral reform. On timing there was the now familiar disagreement, with some advisers arguing for early elections and others arguing against. Those against seemed to carry the day because clearly it would take time not so much to decide what to do about the old laws as to properly formulate and promulgate new ones. The implications of proposed new enactments would need lots of time for mature and comprehensive consideration. More conservative elements thought that, as President Habibie had said earlier, reform of the electoral law could not be achieved except within six months to a year, certainly not within three months, as some people were suggesting. There were suggestions that for its new electoral system Indonesia should study the Philippines, South Korea and Thailand - the latter two constantly held up as models by the IMF and the US - as well as invited experts from the USA.

While the political discussions went on animatedly and exhaustively, IMF Asia-Pacific Director, Hubert Neiss had arrived in Jakarta to undertake the Fund's latest review of Indonesia's economy. One of his first comments was to deny emphatically that the IMF had dictated the timing and scale of the price increases which set off the recent riots. However, no one had forgotten that the removal of subsidies had indeed been part of the IMF programme, about which so much fuss and uproar had been made to be sure Indonesia stuck to it to the letter. Observers could draw their own conclusions. One of the first people he met with was former finance minister Arifin Siregar. One of the first things Siregar and others told him was to leave the subsidies alone! Malaysia's 'New Straits Times' quoted Siregar as saying: " I have told him (Neiss) that the IMF should reconsider the lifting of food subsidies" scheduled for October 1. "The lifting could only cause more suffering to the little people." One of Neiss's more insightful comments upon arrival, as quoted by the 'Indonesian Observer' was that the Indonesian economy "needed attention." Wow! That was advice really worth paying for! He was also quoted as noting that: "The (recovery) process will be an enormous task." Thanks again!

On the eve of Neiss's arrival, economist, Mari Pangestu, from the Center for Strategic and International Studies was warning of economic contraction of up to 20 percent, inflation at up to 100 percent and unemployment of up to 16 million. The riots had driven the rupiah down to Rps 11,000 to the US dollar. While he seemed to be greeted as a returning saviour, Neiss stressed that he was only in Jakarta to review the macroeconomic assumptions made earlier. Nothing else. A favourable review, he implied, could see the release of a dribble of additional money from the US$43 million package the Fund had put together in 1997. Being asked, he ventured the opinion that it was important for the trust of the Indonesian people to be restored in their government and for the confidence of investors to be restored on the basis of continuing stability. He emphasized that the presence of these conditions was essential to the efficacy of the IMF's programme for Indonesia. IMF critics would argue that the Fund's policies had gone a very long way to undermining the confidence Neiss said must now be restored. And all too obviously he had come quite bereft of any new policies likely to encourage such a return. Only more prudent bookkeeping! Recovery, he said, cheerlessly would "take time."

Neiss met with a group of prominent Government critics including Emil Salim, Amien Rais, Megawati Sukarnoputri and Nurcholish Madjid, to get a feel for the new developments gripping Indonesia. As Neiss's boss had said recently in Alberta, hopefully not tongue in cheek, the IMF did not feel that it was "obsessed by political considerations" but had to be assured that there was sufficient stability for its programmes to work. Nevertheless, it seemed clear that continued IMF funding and advice was firmly dependent on political reforms being of a kind and extent which the IMF judged acceptable. As he departed for the US, after a flying visit, the media hung on his words and were pleased to be able to report that the IMF representative felt that "there had been progress" in the political situation. Hope revived!

After the meeting with Neiss, Nurcholish was quoted as saying that he thought that the Fund was delaying disbursements pending the setting of an exact date for new presidential elections. Emil Salim was quoted as telling Neiss that the Fund should not "interfere in Indonesia's internal politics." He was also quoted as urging the Fund to make new and long promised disbursements. Incredibly, but interestingly, Amien Rais was quoted as saying that Neiss had asked him whether he felt that IMF loans to Indonesia were still necessary! There were a growing number of people who failed to see how the meagre IMF disbursements had or could rally the economy. Did this group now include the IMF itself? Surely not! Later Rais refused a second meeting with Neiss because, he was quoted as saying, such a meeting "won't have any result."

Former Organization of Petroleum Exporting States (OPEC) Secretary General Subroto also met Neiss and Malaysia's 'New Straits Times' quoted him as reflecting the frustration of Indonesians by saying: " We suggested to the IMF that if they cannot disburse funds, at least they should not object if other sources provide help." The old tension with the IMF was still there - Indonesia desperate for a solution to its economic crisis, the Fund following an agenda of its own while at the same time fuelling international condemnation of Indonesia if it tried to sidestep even one clause of the agenda.

Between the reported comments of Neiss and Salim one could see the nub of a problem which would now characterize the IMF's entire relationship with Indonesia. Emil was speaking for those who, if they didn't believe in the IMF's magic, knew its backers and its power. To regain confidence, people who thought like this believed that further disbursements from the IMF were crucial, irrespective of what they were used for or what good they did. The point was that the world and the markets would be impressed - hopefully. Then, there was a second group, ones who couldn't see that the disbursements could possibly lead to economic recovery. Somewhere in between those who felt the IMF should be obeyed and those who thought it was useless were the views of people like labour leader Muchtar Pakpahan, who also met Neiss and asked him to withhold further payments on the grounds that "the funds will only go to corrupt men within the Government."

Ex central bank governor Soedradjad confirmed later that the IMF had been asked to be more "adaptable" in its approach to the problems in Indonesia. On May 31, Malaysia's 'New Sunday Times' revealed that the Fund had agreed to ease the reform deadlines proposed on Indonesia. Neiss was quoted as saying: "When it does not make sense to stick with certain deadlines, we have to be pragmatic and relax the deadlines. Deadlines are never absolutely firm, they are always adjusted given evolving circumstances and new possibilities." This is hardly the message Indonesia had been given previously, not only by the IMF but by leaders of the world's top economies. Hadn't absolutely all the fuss been about Indonesia's alleged failure to stick to deadlines?

As Neiss continued his soundings the 'Jakarta Post' ran a feature with a banner headline: "IMF may not offer all the answers." Actually, if anybody would have noticed, the article would better have appeared before the new Government was sworn in. Basically, what its Australian authors advocated was that the Government of Indonesia should abandon the IMF.

Peter Sheehan and David Ray, from Melbourne's Center for Strategic Economic Studies wrote on Friday, May 29: " It is essential that the Government (of Indonesia) consider at this time its options for dealing with this (economic) crisis, rather than immediately recommitting to the existing IMF reform package or to negotiations with the IMF on a new package. In particular, recommitting to the existing IMF package will soon lead the Habibie Government back into the economic and political problems of recent months.

"The current IMF package seeks a number of long-term objectives within the context of a floating exchange rate and open capital markets. It provides little in terms of restimulating the (otherwise healthy and dynamic) real economy in the short run."

The writers poured scorn on whether the IMF's package had really worked elsewhere, citing ongoing economic reverses in South Korea and Thailand.

In Thailand, at the end of May, the country was said to have been plunged into "megagloom." The IMF had administered 'medicine' near identical to Indonesia's - high interest rates, budget surplus, legal and regulatory reform. Like Indonesia, the Thai Government had been reluctant to carry out all the measures the more its economy collapsed.

Like Indonesia the markets were skeptical about the commitment to reform and prudent business practices. Like Indonesia, Thailand had pleaded with the IMF not to impose such harsh measures. Nevertheless, as in Indonesia, in line with IMF advice insolvent banks and financial institutions had been wound up or strengthened and insolvent companies declared bankrupt. Doors had been opened or opened wider to foreign investors although few could be enticed to enter. The result was economic contraction and unemployment which Thai analysts said looked likely to produce a long-term recession. By August 'Newsweek' could talk about "great numbers" of Thai and South Korean businessmen committing suicide in the teeth of the depression. In 1998-99 alone the Thai economy looked set to contract by at least 8 percent.

In Malaysia on June 1, where elements of the IMF's favourite 'medicines' had been applied, minus the IMF, high interests rates were said to have sent the economy into a "tailspin."

South Korea was said to be headed firmly into recession and facing a contraction of 7 percent. As in Indonesia and Thailand, loans to Korea's conglomerates weighed down the politically influenced banking system. Also, the conglomerates had borrowed recklessly offshore. When international market confidence crashed, the currency went after it, intensifying problems throughout the economy. The stock market had plummeted, bankruptcies were at record levels, companies were downsizing or closing, unemployment had doubled to 1.4 million, hundreds of thousands of workers had taken to the streets in protest and there were complaints familiar from Indonesia's experience that high interest rates and other IMF recommended austerity measures had brought South Korea "more pain than gain." Inflation was rising. 'Newsweek' of June 8 quoted displaced worker Song Chul Won as saying: " The IMF agreement is killing us." As in Indonesia the South Korean Government and the IMF haggled over whether banks should be closed. The IMF said they should. The South Koreans preferred to try saving them and the economy.

Said Sheehan and Ray: "The new Government has the opportunity to put in place a reform timetable which is more realistic and more achievable that that dictated by the IMF in its various packages, and which can garner international support for such a revised timetable."

These simple paragraphs were laden with messages. Was the IMF just experimenting with applying free market forces in Indonesia? Had the Fund any idea how its policies would really turn out? While nobody disagreed that most of its recommendations were helpful and perhaps necessary at some time, were they of the slightest help now? If the free and open market approach was the wrong one and the IMF reforms irrelevant in the short-term what should be done?

Sheehan and Ray argued that to stabilize the rupiah there should be a fixed exchange rate and perhaps duel exchange rates for trade transactions and capital flows and that capital controls should be introduced. At the same time they proposed a sort of Marshall Plan within which investors from friendly countries would pump large amounts of capital into Indonesia. Obviously, if the IMF was out, large amounts of new capital would have to come from somewhere. Where better than countries worst affected by Indonesia's economic collapse such as: Australia and Singapore. Optimistically, the writers added the US and Japan to their list. Other analysts mentioned the APEC countries as a whole. The short-term objective of this investment would be the stimulation of the real economy. The writers suggested that major international banks whose loans to Indonesian private companies were in jeopardy might have a vested interest in this process. In any case, they said, a resolution of the private debt overhang was a vital precondition for economic recovery.

The writers urged President Habibie's new Government to listen solely to the IMF and its backers and supporters no more but to draw also on influential and respected figures from outside Indonesia, who had been critical of the IMF, including: Joseph Stiglitz, Chief Economist at the World Bank, Professor Jeffrey Sachs from Harvard Institute for International Development and the Governor of the Reserve Bank of Australia, Ian Macfarlane. They might also have mentioned Professor Steve Hanke.

As we have seen, virtually the first economic move of the Habibie Government was recommitment to the IMF. As far as cynics and growing numbers of Indonesians were concerned the jury was still well and truly out! So far the result of following the IMF's advice had been largely mayhem. Could there be more to follow if the economy drifted further downhill under the weight of some new IMF deal?

Malaysian Prime Minister, Mahathir Mohamad was quoted by Malaysia's 'The Star' newspaper as calling on the IMF to "stop its delaying tactics and release badly needed funds pledged to Indonesia." Australia's Foreign Minister, Alexander Downer was quoted as warning that Asia's economic crisis could be prolonged if "international bailout packages promised for Indonesia, Thailand and South Korea are delayed and if the Japanese economy goes into recession." Indonesia had already fallen victim to problems in Thailand, had felt the aftershocks of the collapse of the South Korean Won and now was being warned about the possibility of collapse in Japan!

As June prepared to open and Indonesia continued to sink beneath the waves of economic adversity there was a barrage of local criticism of the IMF. Outgoing Philippine President, Fidel Ramos said that in Thailand and Indonesia "IMF conditionalities had worsened their suffering." He said that the IMF's formula for "stabilizing an economy" - tight money policy - "might have unwittingly worsened Thailand's problem by accelerating the rate of corporate and banking failures" _ Indonesia's too! And he added: " ...in Indonesia, the raising of fuel prices required by the IMF triggered the Jakarta riots that forced President Soeharto to step down."

Malaysia's 'The Star' on June 11, would quote Isher Judge Ahluwalia as saying: " By providing some liquidity at an early stage, they (international lending agencies) could have provided some countries with breathing space. Instead, they are coming in too late with heavy structural adjustment programmes. Noordin Sopiee, a member of the executive committee of Malaysia's Economic Council was quoted as saying: " The IMF was the only doctor in town, but this doctor believes in bleeding very much in a way that ancient medieval doctors in Europe cured many diseases by bleeding the patients."

The Singapore-based Pacific Ecomomic Cooperation Council (PECC) said in a report issued on June 2: " With hindsight it appears that alternatives to closing errant banks should have been explored."

Tan Sri Ramon Navaratnam, writing in the June 6 issue of the 'New Straits Times' of Malaysia linked the IMF's programmes to discussions with Organization for Economic Cooperation and Development about a new Multilateral Investment Agreement. Tan Sri Ramon accused that the OECD was made up of representatives from the richest and most developed countries who, he said, were determined that national status should be extended to companies doing business in another country, regardless of whether that country is rich or poor. He wrote: " Understandably, there has been resistance from developing countries against the takeover and economic domination by the rich countries. Nevertheless, the IMF, has managed to insist on national treatment as its conditions for providing financial aid to Korea, Indonesia and Thailand." Tan Sri Ramon said that he believed that powerful vested international interests were trying to discredit Malaysia because of its resistance to the IMF and he concluded: " We should continue to resist the IMF to prevent

303

its kind of bungling especially in Indonesia and Korea." Not a good press for the Fund!

On May 28, a week after Habibie came to power, the new Government announced its timetable for political reform and for new elections. House of Representatives Speaker Harmoko said that a special session of the 1,000 seat People's Consultative Assembly would meet "later this year or early next year." This would be basically the same parliament which had re-elected Soeharto back in March.

Government critic Amien Rais immediately slammed the plan. He was quoted by Malaysia's 'New Straits Times' as saying: " We have to remember that the 1,000 members of the present (parliament) were hand-picked by (ousted president) Soeharto and...is just a creature of the ancien regime of Soeharto." When it was revealed in August that Rps 10 billion (US$1.1 billion) would be needed to pay for it critics and foreigners alike were signally unimpressed. Rais said that rather than hold another meeting of Soeharto's rubber stamp parliament a better idea would be to hold the open and democratic elections the students and other pro-reform leaders had demanded. Following Harmoko's comments President Habibie told CNN that he expected a new president to be elected at the end of 1999.

Some reformists were disappointed; others could see the sense of it. All the laws relating to parliament and to the political process would have to be thrown open for discussion, conclusions reached, drafts made, agreement sought and new laws formulated. All would take time. An election by itself was perhaps relatively straightforward but extreme care would have to be taken in changing the number of political parties which could contest polls and altering the basis of parliamentary representation.

Let. Gen. Susilo Bambang Yudhoyono had been quoted on May 29 as saying that ABRI "will no longer play any political position." What would that mean? ABRI occupied 75 appointed seats in Parliament. Would these now be sacrificed? What would be the implications for ABRI's historical dual function, providing security as well as taking part in the government of the country? A month later General Wiranto himself confirmed that the "ABRI-GOLKAR relationship will not be continued." He added: "ABRI wants to maintain the same distance from all sociopolitical elements in the country." He did not talk about the withdrawal from politics hinted at by Susilo. Perhaps something was merely lost in translation.

As part of its efforts to clean up its image, on May 29, it was also announced by ABRI that 18 members of the security forces would face court martial for their role in the shootings at Trisakti. Also, that week, the absurd case against a group of mothers who had demonstrated against increases in milk prices was dropped.

The new Information Minister, Yunus Yosfiah met members of the media and provided some replies to their queries which would have been unthinkable a week earlier. Yunus was a former army lieutenant general. The Minister said that he supported the creation of alternative media organizations - in line with the policy to free trade unions - that he would review controversial press and broadcasting laws which in the past had been used to close down anti-regime publications - the last occasion in 1994. Two of the magazines banned then 'DeTik' and "Tempo' vowed to be back on the newsstands within a few weeks. The minister concluded the meeting by telling the media: "I'm on your side.

There was a sense of euphoria in the media at the apparent suggestion of the new Information Minister that he intended to restore press freedom in Indonesia. Commented the 'Jakarta post' on June 1: " ...we sincerely hope that it means the revocation of all laws and regulations which curtail all basic freedoms. Since press freedom is inseparable from other freedoms, such as freedom of expression, of association, from fear and freedom to dissent, the Government should also guarantee the freedom of the legislative and judicial branches from administrative influence. This nation suffered beyond words during the oppressive regime of President Soeharto, which only tolerated a "don't-touch-the-regime type of journalism during the last 24 years of his 32-year rule."

As good as his word, within a few days, Minister Yunus issued decrees removing ministerial ability to arbitrarily withdraw publishing licenses. He was quoted as saying: "The logic behind this is that we want to give a proper share (of press supervision) to the Court of Justice and not just to the Information Ministry. However, the Minister could still suspend publications which "violated their publishing permits" for " a period of time." The reforms were still a giant step away from best democratic practice and while welcomed, were greeted warily. Later there would be protests against the retention of the Government's power to revoke publishing licenses and against its new plan to license journalists. This looked like even less press freedom then before. Now the papers and the journalists would have to stay on good behaviour or risk their licenses withdrawn. The journalists' licensing proposal was opposed by both The Association of Indonesian Journalists and the Association of Indonesian

Publishers.

To his credit, Yunus was quoted as arguing that the Ministry of Information was a heavy drain on the Government's budget "doing work that mostly obstructed the flow of information." He was quoted as saying: " We feel that the state has spent too much money for the operational and salary costs of civil servants (within the ministry of information), while on the other hand it has in reality so far only restricted the flow of information to society." When he took over Yunus said that he encountered a backlog of 90 applications for publications licenses dating back up to seven years. He said he had granted 20 permits in two weeks and found the backlog "astonishing." The ministry had been formerly headed by Harmoko. There were allegations from the public that to obtain a license quickly or to get one at all officials requested large ex gratia payments. One publisher in southeast Sulawesi received his license from Yunus after an incredible 13 year wait.

On June 23, Minister Yunus said that he could envisage his department being scrapped altogether. Some thought he meant it literally but a careful study of his comments made it clear that what he had meant was that the ministry might not be needed in its present form and certainly not at its present over-staffed size. The Ministry employed 51,000. He held out the prospect of TVRI and RRI becoming financially independent. Later, in August, after staff protests, he would confirm that his hint that the ministry could be closed was not meant to be taken literally.

But things really were different. 'De Tik' appeared again as 'De Tak' and publications across the board seemed free to reveal or say more or less whatever they liked. After the June honeymoon, in July and especially August, there would be reminders to journalists and editors to stick to the facts, not to rely on rumour and not to exaggerate - especially if in doing any of these things helped project an unjustifiably negative image of Indonesia or promoted instability.

After President Habibie's first week in office, praise was beginning to roll in, not just from organizations within Indonesia but from the all important US, Europe, Japan and neighbouring countries in the region. Arbi Sanit perhaps summed up President Habibie's position in his column in the 'Jakarta Post.' He wrote: " He (President Habibie) is now building his popularity by demonstrating his openness and flexibility to accept proposals from various parties. If he succeeds in leading the democratization of the country, he will be acceptable to compete for the next presidency. Otherwise, he will have to retire."

The last week of May, 1998 had been an incredible week in the modern history of the people of Indonesia. A man now widely regarded as a tyrant had stepped down. As man widely regarded as an anti-reform crony had stepped up and shown promise that he was more than the man people thought him to be. The promise of genuine reform was in the air. The promise of democratic freedom was in the air. Indonesia had embarked on a road of unprecedented change. Each new day produced its new excitement as old groupings broke up and new ones formed, as long repressed demands, complaints and emotions bubbled to the surface, sometimes in ugly riots, such as those in North Sumatra and South Sulawesi on May 28.

Some of the protesters demanded improved morality, others faster political reform. In many parts of Indonesia the protests, riots and Soeharto's resignation had visibly emboldened people. There was a new confidence, a new aggressiveness, a new sense of: "Don't think you can push me around." Hopefully the new confidence and aggressiveness would be channelled constructively and not into significantly higher levels of mayhem. While the promise of reform looked like coming to reality in, at least, a realistic time-frame, dark clouds still hung over the economy, blackening with every passing day. Foreigners said that they had little else to do in Jakarta but sit in their offices "watching the economy go down."

On May 29, Indonesia's new president himself declared that he planned to hold free and democratic elections in 1999. He was quoted as saying that about six months would be needed to draw up new election laws during which time new political parties could be formed " as long as they are not against the state ideology, Pancasila, or the 1945 Constitution." He was quoted as saying: "If we want to do something we must do it as well as possible. It will be better than achieving something rapidly but in ways which are wrong. We are truly carrying out reform programmes, total reform, but not anarchic or violent reforms." He confirmed that the once loudly demanded extraordinary congress of the People's Consultative Assembly could be held late in 1998 or early in 1999. Subsequently the date was confirmed as November 10. After this, a date would be set for the new general elections and after that a date for new presidential and vice presidential elections. The general election was expected to be in May, 1999 and the presidential and vice presidential elections in December giving Indonesia a completely new government with which to enter the new millennium - if the millennium was really important to anyone.

By December 1998 the Government aimed to revise three political laws - on elections, on the composition of the House of Representatives and the People's Consultative Assembly (MPR). In January 1999 new political laws would be enacted. The period January 1999 to mid-1999 would be used to socialize the new political laws, to form and endorse new political parties and to prepare for the May general elections. The December 1999 MPR meeting would draw up the State Policy Guidelines and elect a president and vice president.

The government confirmed ongoing work on the laws on subversion, corruption, press and broadcasting, monopoly and competition and ratification of the United Nations conventions against racial discrimination and torture.

The election plan was immediately condemned by leading reformers. On June 25, Emil Salim was quoted as saying: " The Government should hold the general election as soon as possible since this is the only thing which can return business to its normal capacity. Daniel Sparringa from Surabaya's Airlannga University was quoted as saying that Government procrastination over holding a general election was "killing the economy." Gus Dur, soon to participate in the leadership of a new political party, said elections should be held within seven months of the GOLKAR congress planned for July

Neither the flames of political passion aroused among the intelligentsia and students nor the flames of economic unrest lit among the lower classes were easy to put out. Despite changes in the composition of the Government criticisms continued. In Jakarta, if not riots, rumours of riots sent people scurrying for cover. In business and workmen's circles there was a fear that the clamour for political reform was overshadowing the more dire need to fix the economy and get business and labourers back to work. Indonesian Chamber of Commerce Chairman, Aburizal Bakrie was quoted as reminding the Government to "keep a tight focus on restoring the country's economy. On May 29, he was quoted as saying: " Try not to be too enchanted with political issues only; the economy is very vital because it involves the lives of many people. Many people cannot afford to buy food, millions have lost their jobs, business can no longer operate, (more) malls and offices will be closed. Abrurizal said that the country was still in dire straights and needed considerable funds to finance the recovery process. The same day Habibie had said that he had been told by ordinary people that they didn't care who was president or vice president so long as they could earn money in peaceful conditions.

Even Amien Rais agreed. Over the end of May weekend he called for an end to protracted political wrangling about reforms and concentration on the economy. He appealed for President Habibie's legitimacy to be respected and for the new Government to be given a chance. He was quoted as saying: " The administration, even though it is a transitional one, still needs both domestic and international support in order to be able to carry out programmes to deal with the crisis. He stressed that the campaign for political reform and the urgent need for effective measures to rejuvenate the economy should proceed side by side but not with political reform at the expense of economic recovery. He called on Indonesia to forgive Soeharto but said that the former president should return any illegally obtained wealth to the nation. He backed calls for any illegal acts of Soeharto's children to be investigated and, if necessary, punished. Megawati Sukarnoputri added her voice to calls to stop the denunciation of the ex-president. Even East Timor's Bishop Carlos Belo said that the condemnation of Soeharto should stop. All three said that Soeharto had done Indonesia "great service."

Mines and Energy Minister, Kuntoro, announced happily that one of the first companies with Soeharto family connections to be probed would be the state oil giant Pertamina. It was subsequently found that no fewer than 120 Soeharto related companies were involved. Had this been why the price of fuel had been so high? Had this been why its price to consumers had to be subsidized? Pertamina would later appear on the IMF's list of agencies to audit - along with the reforestation fund and the logistics agency BULOG.

In the wake of the fall of Soeharto, investors in politically linked companies were said to be reviewing their options. Indonesia's largest bank, Bank Central Asia, had to be taken under the wing of the Bank Restructuring Agency (IBRA) after liquidity support exceeding 200 percent of the Bank's assets. BCA is 70 percent owned by Liem Sioe Liong and, in the last week of May, public fears that, as a Soeharto linked company, the Bank might fail, led to an unprecedented run. The remaining 30 percent is owned by the former president's daughter, Siti Hardiyanti Rukmana and by his son Sigit Hardjojudanto. Subsequently, to halt the run, Liem announced that he would buy out the Soehartos. Other domestic and foreign investors were said to be thinking along the same lines.

While there was an understandable urgency in getting the economy back on track the floodgates opened by the fall of Soeharto continued to discharge new opportunities and demands.

Another GOLKAR affiliate, MURBA, announced that it, too, would break away and exist as a political party in its own right. Blaming GOLKAR Chairman Harmoko for the fall of Soeharto and the break up of GOLKAR, senior members demanded a special congress to unseat him and to try to save what was left of the organization. Harmoko said that they were within their rights and that is such a congress was held he would not stand for re-election. An affiliate of the PPP, Syarikat Islam, announced that it would strike out on its own. Some community leaders welcomed the move; others drew attention to the potential danger of religion based political parties. At the end of May an Indonesian Women's Party was formed. There were daily rumours of others from around Indonesia.

On June 2, the new Government announced that it would ratify the International Labour Union convention on freedom of association and protection of workers rights. Earlier, ratification had been demanded by all 13 members of the Government approved Federation of All Indonesian Workers Union as well as by the Indonesian Prosperous Labour Union led by Muchtar Pakpahan. On June 5, the President had duly ratified the International Labour Organization (ILO) convention on the Freedom of Association and Protection of the Rights to Organize.

Students were told that their on-campus affairs would no longer be controlled by their rectors. However, the new President quickly expressed the thought that the students might soon return to their books. Flushed with their new freedoms, thousands of students in Ujung Pandang and Jambi, central Sumatra, occupied their respective provincial legislatures in imitation of what their colleagues had done in Jakarta, protesting against corruption, collusion and nepotism. Hundreds of students, sometimes joined by workers, continued to demonstrate against corruption and irregularities in Semarang, Purwokerto, Surabaya and Medan. There were more calls for governors and regents to resign. Meanwhile, back in Jakarta, thousands of high school and university students, Megawati supporters and members of a women's group turned up at the national parliament to demand an extraordinary session of the People's Consultative Assembly and also that the former president be put on trail for alleged corruption.

CHAPTER TEN

Many lids of
many boxes

The National Commission on Human Rights now received requests to investigate Irianese claims that an Armed Forces unit has engaged in vandalism and killings between December 1996 and October
1997 at Irianese villages in the Mimika area. This was a time when Government forces were cracking down on Irianese separatists who had
made international headlines with a series of kidnappings, even of foreigners. The Commission also announced that it planned to investigate
the deaths of an incredible 39,000 Acehnese and the detention of 1,000
others in connection with anti-separatist operations carried out in the
province by Indonesia's military during the last decade. Detainees were
said to be serving jail sentences of between eight and 20 years for alleged separatist activities. Most of these 39,000 were men. Most left
behind widows and children. Some of those on the military's wanted list
were alleged to have been recently repatriated to Aceh from Malaysia.
The public wondered about their fate. More than 1,000 were said to
have been detained. Thousands more were alleged to be "missing." The
Commission said on June 4 that it planned to ask ABRI to withdraw
security forces from Aceh and revoke the status of the province as being
on a war footing - together with East Timor and Irian Jaya.
     ABRI spokesman, Brig. Gen. A Wahab Mokodongan was quoted

in the 'Jakarta Post' as saying that "even simple logic" suggested that it was impossible for the military to kill so many people. He was alleged to have admitted that some people might have died because they were caught in "crossfire" but he was quoted as saying that "none were shot at deliberately".

In August the National Commission on Human Rights said that it thought that less than 800 people had been killed in Aceh although 3,000 women were widowed. General Wiranto was quick to point out the inconsistency. The Commission said that 15,000 to 20,000 children had been orphaned and 368 people tortured. An official, meaning Government, team later found that 760 people were missing or believed killed, 600 women had lost their husbands, 10 women were raped and 1,960 children had been orphaned. Clearly, there could be great debate about such statistics and equally great disparities in circumstances where people were afraid to report truthfully and fully. It seemed that there had been killings but that investigators were still some distance from knowing accurately how many. Meanwhile allegations in the aftermath of the fall of Indonesia's strongman and his policies continued to be rife.

Victims and relatives of victims in Aceh spoke about practices which must have sounded all too familiar to Pius Lustrilanang and other activists. There were allegations of kidnappings, "sadistic killings," warnings to victims to keep their mouths shut on pain of death and even of rapes of the wives of those abducted, arrested or killed. It was alleged that sometimes, for those lucky enough to be given a proper burial, widows were made to pay for it.

The Commission's usual backlog of unsolved cases and complaints was now growing rapidly . Dating from 1998 alone, it was still not known who individually was responsible for all the student killings at Trisakti University.

As early as June 1, Jakarta Military Police Chief, Colonel Hendardji had announced that 18 military officials, all police, would go on trial for violating procedures which led to the deaths of the students at Trisakti. The 18 included one lieutenant colonel, seven lieutenants, six sergeants and four privates. Until September only two lieutenants had been convicted. The two police officers were found guilty of ordering their men to shoot at the students and jailed for 10 and four months respectively. Their defence was that they had been provoked and attacked by the demonstrators. Defence lawyers called for the charges against most of the 18 to be dropped after it was found that the police had had no live ammunition while the students had been shot using real bullets.

No explanation had yet been given of the whereabouts of 14 other still-missing activists kidnapped around the same time as Pius Lustrilanang. There were plenty of unsolved "disappearances" from 1997. Now here were new complaints from Irian Jaya, new revelations from Aceh.

Indonesia had basically been at war for years in Irian, East Timor and Aceh. Now there was hope that these long running disputes could finally be solved - or at least the national government's handling of them made more humane and effective.

In his book 'The Armed Forces of Indonesia,' Let. Col. Robert Lowry, an Australian who graduated from the Indonesian Army Command and Staff College, Bandung, says of the military's operations in Aceh, Irian Jaya and Timor: " Comparing and contrasting these three examples of large-scale internal security operations, one concludes that Irian and Timor had similar experiences in the initial stages of occupation/invasion in that they were both regarded as foreign lands in which victory meant rewards for the occupying forces. Consequently troops confiscated moveable assets and sold them or returned them to home bases, the government took over ownership and profits of fixed assets regardless of any claims the local people may have had and outsiders assumed almost all administrative posts. Aceh, by contrast, was part of Indonesia from the beginning and suffered the indignity of being deprived of its provincial status and losing administrative posts to non-Acehnese and traditional rulers who had been ousted during the revolution - the latter only serving to heighten local and political conflict." Lowry describes this behaviour of ABRI as characterizing the initial stages of its activity. Many in the affected provinces said that such behaviour was typical throughout.

President Habibie issued a strong statement about East Timor saying that there would be no change to Government policy " no matter who the president is." He stressed that there could be no question of secession although he offered East Timor autonomy. This was rejected by pro-independence activists and activists and human rights campaigners urged the Government to hold a free, and fair referendum. Aceh had also been given special status but in practice it had meant little more than symbolism.

On June 11, the military cleared 700 East Timorese protesters from outside the Foreign Ministry complex in Jakarta. A similar demonstration was held in Dili, capital of East Timor. On June 16, according to

'Asiaweek' of June 26, a youth was shot outside the capital "seemingly for no apparent reason." Next day demonstrations were held again in Jakarta. The demonstrators were demanding a free referendum on the province's future. The protesters carried banners saying; " East Timor is not part of Indonesia." Malaysia's 'New Straits Times' quoted one demonstrator as saying that "Soeharto's invasion of East Timor has killed more than 250,000 people." The total population is only 840,000. In its July 4 edition, 'The Economist' of Britain put the number killed at 100,000.

On June 24, less than a week later, after a meeting in Jakarta with Bishop Bello, Habibie promised a gradual reduction of troops in East Timor.

During the following week students at Dili's Timor Timur University continued to conduct free speech forums demanding self-determination for the people of East Timor and a referendum to ascertain their view once and for all. On Monday, June 15, Foreign Minister, Ali Alatas ruled out a referendum saying that it was "inappropriate to the majority of the people of east Timor" and " fraught with all kinds of risks."

At the end of June in Dili one person died and five were injured when security forces fired on a crowd surrounding a vehicle in Baucau, East Timor, escorting three European ambassadors on a visit to the territory. Reflecting a widening strand of public opinion, the 'Jakarta Post' said on June 30: " Ultimately a free referendum - and a wholehearted acceptance by Indonesia of whatever results that may bring - could prove to be the best and most honourable way to settle the problem for good."

Two days later, writing in the 'Jakarta Post' political scientist Arbi Sanit wrote what at least some Indonesians thought. Commenting on President Habibie's offer, he wrote: " The offer, according to most Indonesians outside East Timor, is more than adequate. However, I think the East Timorese will not be satisfied if the offered status is similar to that already given to Yogyakarta and Aceh because they feel that they should not be under Indonesian rule. I think we'd do better by giving the East Timorese a chance to decide their own fate. If the East Timorese want independence what is wrong with that? Why do we force them (to be part of Indonesia)? If they are just a thorn in our flesh by demanding more money than other provinces while giving us nothing. They are just disturbing us." Earlier in his article Arbi had noted that East Timor had been enjoying "luxury budgets" from Jakarta for years but that "steadily improving prosperity" had been overshadowed because "their political rights have been under pressure for decades."

In his book, Robert Lowry asks what might be the reasons for Indonesia's refusal to let Timor go. He writes: "Indonesia's original reasons for seeking to incorporate East Timor included fear that an independent socialist state there might attract communist-bloc support and perhaps support insurgencies elsewhere in the archipelago. But the demise of communism as an ideological threat raises the question of why Indonesia should remain intransigent on the issue of self determination for East Timor. Among the possible reasons for this are: the lives and resources that have been poured into pacifying the province and developing its infrastructure; the geographical location of Timor and a desire to maintain tidy boundaries; the underlying insecurity of the Indonesian state and residual fears that allowing East Timorese to choose whether or not to remain part of Indonesia might set a dangerous precedent for other regions; the concern that an independent Timor might be inherently unstable and that its problems might spill over the border; the possibility of oil discovered in East Timorese waters; the vested interests of ABRI; probably the most important, the intransigence of the President and the absence of strong international pressure for a referendum."

At the end of June, 'The Economist' magazine of Britain wrote that: "It is an historical fiction to claim, as Indonesia does, that East Timor voluntarily agreed to annexation in 1976. The evidence of the streets suggests that it is equally untrue that only a minority of the east Timorese oppose integration with big brother." Another article in the same July 4 edition said: "...the pro-integration camp seems surprisingly small; even many Timorese civil servants want independence." The article added: ..."the longing for independence had been nurtured by the brutality of Indonesian rule."

At the end of June, 1998 the vox populi of East Timor seemed to be saying loudly and clearly that the province wanted to breath the fresh air of freedom. The national government in Jakarta was saying that this was impossible. But President Habibie had promised a reduction of troops and would later define the political and economic parameters of the new "autonomy."

The Armed Forces had many preoccupations at this time. There was the question of replying to demands for information about missing people and, more importantly, giving justice in the cases of alleged military abuse of power, cases which stretched back for a decade. From the high command's point of view the unity of the armed forces must have seemed an equally, if not more, pressing priority. On May 29 General Wiranto called senior commanders together for a briefing about the progress of political reform. Presumably also, the commanders weighed up the security situation and the safety of the new president and of his government. Were protests likely to die down or flare up was probably one of the burning issues. Army, navy, airforce and police commanders were all present. Such were the rumours about possible disunity within ABRI that it had been necessary for General Wiranto to prove by his appearance that he had not been assassinated! Significantly, one of the commanders present at the headquarters briefing had been Let. Gen. Prabowo. In leaving the meeting soon after he had opened it Wiranto seemed either very confident that he was in charge or taking a calculated risk to prove that he was.

Meanwhile, Yahya Muhaimin, head of Gadjah Mada University's Center for Security and Peace Studies, was quoted as saying that ABRI should end its dual function and especially its security approach to politics. Some expert observers thought that ABRI should be allocated no seats in the House of Representatives but should instead fight elections like all other candidates. Indria Samego from the National Institute of Sciences (LIPI) was quoted as saying: " To be a House Member one must be elected through polls." Law draftsmen, working with President Habibie, were thought to favour the retention of 50 seats for the military.

ABRI had committed its support to President Habibie on May 21 and this support was renewed on June 5 when ABRI called on Indonesians not to continue to question the legitimacy of the new government and to focus on finding a solution to the economic crisis.

Since the election of B.J. Habibie as president the students had fallen noticeably into disarray. Thousands of students were still demonstrating in Jakarta and elsewhere in demand of a provisional people's assembly to run the country pending fresh elections. In Jakarta, students said that ABRI would be welcome to take part in the assembly. But a clear division had emerged between those demanding that Habibie step down and those willing to give him a chance. Many felt that with the ousting of Soeharto their job was done and only a comparative minority continued to clamour for the resignation of the entire New Order Government and preparations for immediate fresh national elections.

Of course, President Habibie was not the only target for the demonstrators. There were deep feelings against KKN across the country. On June 8 in Bali 20,000 protesting students forced the 46 strong provincial legislature to resign. As in Bali, students elsewhere kept up pressure on local administrations and officials deemed to be corrupt. On June 11, 3,000 students demonstrated outside the Jakarta Parliament demanding the establishment of a transitional government. The rising cost of living was also a critical concern. From the Greater Jakarta Students Forum students said that the Government had a moral obligation to lower prices and warned that "choking prices" and unemployment could drive people to "anarchy."

On June 12 President Habibie appealed to the nation to have patience while reforms were worked out. He pleaded that hastily conceived and implemented measures would only make the country more chaotic. Also, he asked Indonesians to believe that he was only a transitional president, his aim, to steer the country along the path of reform and towards general elections in May, 1999 and a presidential election in December. He stressed that he himself had no intention of standing for re-election. Earlier, ABRI commander Wiranto had said that " continually questioning the president's legitimacy is a waste of time." Wiranto had also quite sensibly said that people had to accept that the reform process should be orderly and subject to reasonable level of control less the whole process fell short of its targets. In fact, by mid-July, protests, demonstrations and criticisms had died down to such an extent that the press began to say that the Habibie Government appeared to have lost sight of the fact that Indonesia was in deep crisis.

The exception was public security. Reformists and rioters were full of a new confidence and there were attempts to take over land and generally redress perceived wrongs inflicted by the old government. These seemed to be allowed. Tapos included. Crime was naturally frowned upon but those taking commodities or food to survive seemed to be able to do so. Security was often so low profile that many people felt there wasn't any. Habibie confirmed that the security approach had been abandoned in favour of the open, democratic approach.

In the wake of the riots, rapings and shootings of students, President Habibie clearly felt that Indonesia needed to take urgent steps to improve human rights - especially in the eyes of international observers. On June 9 he announced that Indonesia would begin a five year National Action Plan on human rights in an "attempt to improve its much maligned international image." The campaign would include the ratification of several UN conventions. For example, Indonesia had signed the UN Convention Against Torture and Other Cruel, Inhuman or Degrading Treatment or Punishment but not yet ratified it. Two other conventions waiting to be signed were The International Covenant On Economic, Cultural and Social Rights and the International Covenant On Civil and Political Rights.

There were many in the country, in the Government and even within ABRI who felt that these measures were long overdue. Over the years, as abuses mounted, they had kept quiet for fear of reprisals from Soeharto. Now he was gone. Fresh air swept through the corridors of power. Those close to President Habibie described him as an open, approachable and fair man, as willing to take advice as criticism. President Habibie knew that the country was hungry for openness, transparency and justice and he moved quickly to show that he understood this. He had to. Otherwise he would have been perceived as merely another Soeharto and kicked out. Nevertheless, On June 9, he clearly regarded himself as no more than an interim president whose mission was to brush away cobwebs and open doors so that through the proper constitutional channels a new Indonesia could emerge from the wreckage of the brutal and corrupt New Order. While forging ahead with reforms, President Habibie confirmed that he did not intend to be president after 2000. At this time he and the people were one in thinking of him as purely transitional. On June 10, it was announced that 16 more political prisoners would be released, 15 from East Timor.

While these laudable grand designs were going forward, those harmed in the May riots or harmed by covert ABRI operations wanted information, explanations, apologies and punishments. Investigations had either not been wholly commissioned or appeared to be progressing slowly - too slowly for informed Indonesians and concerned foreign observers alike.

On June 11, President Habibie called for a thorough investigation into the causes and perpetrators of the May riots, especially any "organized groups" which may have incited them or taken part. ABRI's 'conservative' elements were now warned that they were under attack from the highest level. He met 151 senior ABRI officers at the State Presidential Palace. He was quoted as telling them: " I particularly ask the Armed Forces leadership to reveal the truth over allegations that an organized group was seen inciting people to burn and loot buildings in several areas where disturbances occurred."

Two weeks later the President was quoted as having told members of the National Commission on Human Rights that he realized that the credibility of his government depended heavily on solving the Trisakti shootings, the disappearances of activists and the riots. But, he was quoted as saying: " Give ABRI an opportunity to complete its internal consolidation." Clearly, Wiranto was still not convinced that he was master in his own house!

On July 4, 'The Straits Times' Singapore revealed that ABRI had announced that 40 soldiers had been arrested in connection with the kidnappings of activists. The announcement followed a June 29 admission by the ABRI commander that military personnel, from KOPASSUS, had been identified as the culprits.

Despite the police convictions, there had been rumours that the killers were not police at all but from an "elite military force." This was denied by investigating military police. Media reports immediately after the killings had conjectured that soldiers from a rogue element of ABRI had donned police uniforms and posed as police in order to undertake the fatal shootings. The 'Indonesian Observer' of June 3 noted: "...students from Trisakti who witnessed the killings have been threatened not to testify or come forward with any information." To whom did these voices belong?

On June 12, new members were added to the Supreme Advisory Council, a body which exists under the 1945 Constitution to advise the president. The new members included former home affairs minister, Yogie SM, the man who had opened the Soeharto Government sponsored PDI Congress in Medan and also the leader of the Government sponsored PDI, Soerdjadi . A few days later, Mochtar Buchori reflected reformists reactions when he wrote in the 'Jakarta Post:' " What puzzled the public was that the body (the Supreme Advisory Council) includes many personalities from the Soeharto regime. In the public's eyes this is entirely contrary to the spirit of true reform and the explanation given by the Government is very unsatisfactory. It was only stated that the presidential decision in this case was based on recommendations by the House of Representatives, which in most people's eyes is politically defunct, and also on recommendations from the three political groupings, that is the United Development Party (PPP) GOLKAR and the Indonesian Democratic Party's Soerjadi faction. It is widely known that these three political parties are nothing more than instruments of the old regime, and, as such, their commitment to the reform movement is at best suspect. And the public wonders why not single representative from the reform camp, that is groups who have consistently supported the students in initiating and sustaining the reform movement, has been included in this body. Has the Government ever asked people like Amien Rais, Emil Salim, Arifin Panigoro or Kemal Idris to join this body? It is these unanswered questions that make people fear, rightly or wrongly, that Soeharto forces are now making a political comeback. Some people have even concluded that the reform movement has come to a halt and that counter reform forces are on the ascent."

General Wiranto seemed to have made it clear that Soeharto himself would not be permitted to regain power. Subsequent measures against the family's political role confirmed this. But there were deep fears that the Habibie Government was only the New Order minus Soeharto and that the reforms yearned for by the informed public would not be forthcoming quickly and might not be forthcoming at all.

Although demands that Soeharto be tried had died down there were continuing calls for him to be stripped of all residual powers, including his post of chairman of the patrons of the ruling GOLKAR and also that the wealth of himself and his children be returned to the nation. Despite early rumours there was only ever the slimmest chance that Soeharto could make a come back. By mid-June General Wiranto felt obliged to issue a statement saying that ABRI would not permit any return of "old political forces."

Regarding his wealth, other than the ongoing probe of the new Attorney General and the seizure of the capital of his foundations, the Government made little response. Later, it would have to dramatize this investigation in order to calm public agitation.

Behind the scenes Wiranto seemed to be trying to ferret out who was to blame for the kidnappings, riots and rapes but even by June 23 still said that he needed time. One of the problems was that ABRI units sometimes reported directly to the President. Another was that intelligence units often seemed to function in world's of their own. Yet another was the way in which some orders could be more suggestive than specific, leaving wide latitude to unit commanders to make their own interpretations. Soon, it would emerge that the kidnappings fell into the latter category. When orders were vague, over-zealous commanders could also exceed their instructions. It was thought that Trisakti fell into this category. There were clear suggestions that the kidnappings and shootings were by the same hand. Whereas the kidnappings were designed to nip in the bud opposition to the New Order the killings at Trisakti seem to have been aimed at driving a wedge between the students and ABRI. It was clear that elements of ABRI, including General Wiranto, favoured the students. If ABRI could be seen to harm some of them, maybe they would turn against the security forces, triggering a crackdown led, perhaps, by the man thought to have ordered the kidnappings. As we know, this didn't happen and the shootings made ABRI even more determined to be seen to support the students. In respect of these matters, Wiranto's hand may have been strengthened when the US called for a full inquiry into ABRI abuses. Gen. Wiranto said that he needed time but, in fact, time was something he had little of. When new elections were held it seemed likely that the New Order would be swept away and the doors to its vaults full of secrets finally torn off.

On June 29, Gen. Wiranto was quoted by the media as admitting that "ABRI had identified several of its personnel who were allegedly involved in the kidnapping of activists. They have acted beyond their authority." The General said that those responsible had "acted individually and not under official orders." Later, he said that the cases involved "some military personnel who have acted outside procedures." The country wanted to know which personnel? There was cynicism about the possibility of soldiers acting without orders. If there were orders, who had given them? In late September the nation was still waiting for the full details and especially for information about activists still missing.

As early as July 18, Prabowo had admitted his involvement with the kidnappings of activists which he said, along with other actions taken by him and by subordinates, were dedicated to the "safety and prosperity of the nation." He was quoted by the 'Jakarta Post' of July 18 as saying that he was ready to take responsibility for the kidnappings of activists but only of the nine who had returned home safely. Others were still missing. A month later, on August 10 an Officers Honour Council investigating the kidnappings would say that "Prabowo had reportedly acted on his own initiative and had been given autonomy by his superiors to maintain stability with whatever means he deemed necessary. It was Prabowo's own interpretation (of his orders) which led to the decision to kidnap activists." On August 12, Prabowo himself admitted that he had misunderstood his orders. According to media reports Prabowo's orders could have come from General Feisal Tanjung, General R. Hartono or General Wiranto. Of course, they could also have been given by the supreme commander, General Soeharto. On August 24 Prabowo was dismissed from the service. Investigations into the possible role of other commanders continued.

Prabowo, of course, had not acted alone. He had been a commander with troops at his disposal. It was they who had physically done his bidding. Who were these soldiers? Where were they? 'Asiaweek' magazine of July 24 speculated: "A source close to the military says that as of early July, 74 KOPASSUS soldiers were missing from their barracks. He believes they are on Jakarta's streets, collecting information and covering their tracks." Father Sandyawan had been warned with a live grenade to end his investigations into the rapes of ethnic

Chinese. What kind of people possess grenades? In September a group of 10 men, some wearing military uniforms, would be spotted carrying out various robberies in the city.

Wiranto also said that ABRI investigators had visited people said to have been raped during the riots but " none admitted that they had been sexually violated or that they had told anybody that this had been the case." Human rights, womens and social organizations were busy accumulating horrifying evidence of rapes and sexual abuse. Among the statements were many that the victims had subsequently been warned to say nothing about their ordeals. Wiranto also said that none of those admitted to hospitals had complained of being raped or molested. Emil Salim pointedly called for the setting up of an independent commission of inquiry.

At the end of May, he economy was in ruinous state. Some observers gave it three months before total collapse. Despite "punitively high" interest rates, the rupiah stubbornly refused to appreciate, reserves had fallen to US$14.5 billion against a short-term debt obligation of US$14.2 billion and a monthly import bill of US$4 billion. Capital inflows had virtually ceased. Bankruptcy seemed to loom. Prices were rising, inflation was thought likely to reach 80 - 100 percent in the year. With their high import content, exports had failed to snowball although in the last fiscal year there had been a welcome trade surplus of US$15.10 billion. The cessation of trade finance had also harmed exports. The economy was predicted to contract by at least 10 percent resulting in 20 million unemployed. On the bright side the World Bank released a small sum, US$225 million, to help alleviate poverty. Hopes of more funds from the IMF failed to impress markets. On June 10, Minister of Education and Culture, Juwono Sudarsono announced that all state school fees would be abolished. Without such a move the drop out rate threatened to become huge and Indonesia's future prospects correspondingly dimmed.

Per capita income had crashed from US$1,100 to US$300. On June 10 the rupiah slipped below Rps 13,000 to the US dollar because of perceived ongoing political uncertainties and further economic deterioration. The rupiah and stocks were also badly effected by the plunging Japanese yen and Chinese yuan. Two days later the rupiah had tumbled to Rps 15,000 to the dollar, allegedly due to "weak regional markets, persistent political problems and a sudden rising demand for dollars by domestic commercial banks. As part of a deal soon to be reached in Frankfurt, commercial banks were required to pay their interbank debt of approximately US$ 9 billion and US$1 billion in trade finance areas by June 11 - the demand for dollars pushing down the rupiah. During the third week of June the rupiah seemed headed for Rps 18,000 to the US dollar. Debt repayment, the fall of the yen and political uncertainty in Indonesia were said by some analysts to indicate possible further falls of up to Rps 25,000 to the dollar. PT Chandra Asri's, President and CEO, Peter Gontha was quoted as saying: "If the rupiah continues to remain weak against the dollar no single company will be able to survive.

After having completed his post-riots review, on the eve of his departure from Jakarta, Hubert Neiss expressed the hope that Indonesia "wouldn't have to wait too long" for the disbursement of another tranche of US$ 1 billion promised as part of the US$43 billion bailout.

In Frankfurt on June 1 talks involving 13 creditor banks got under way to try to restructure Indonesia's US$ 80 billion private offshore debt. The talks had been postponed from May 26, due to the Jakarta riots and change of government. The aim was to cover bank debt, corporate debt and trade financing. On June 4, agreement had been reached to establish an Indonesian Debt Restructuring Agency (INDRA) administered by Bank Indonesia and backed by the Government. INDRA would provide exchange rate risk protection and assurance as to the availability of foreign exchange to private debtors wanting to reschedule their debt. Participation in INDRA would be voluntary. INDRA participants would be able to buy US dollars at the best real 20-day average exchange rate. The private corporate debt of around 2,000 companies could be repaid over eight years with a three year grace period. Indonesian bank debt was to be rolled over for four years. This would help the banks and Indonesia's balance of payments. Total private debt now due in 1998-99 had fallen to US$20 billion for the corporate and US$ 9.2 billion in foreign bank debt. Ginandjar Kartasasmita was quoted as saying that Indonesia had been given an important "breathing space." Outstanding trade credits (LCs) amounting to US$1,085 billion were to be guaranteed by Bank Indonesia.

The agreement looked positive for Indonesia's banks and for trade financing but analysts had doubts about whether the voluntary nature of the mechanism to resolve private corporate debt problems would really work or work quickly enough. Also, doubts persisted whether lenders had really been told all there was to tell about the true position of Indonesian banks and corporates. There were allegations that some of the players had lied, that debt had been understated and assets overvalued. At any rate, some progress appeared to have been made. Euphorically, but perhaps temporarily, the Jakarta stock market rose on the news.

The IMF's Michel Camdessus was quoted as saying: " The corporate debt scheme provides a framework that not only reduces scheduled Indonesian external payments over the next few years but also gives corporations substantial initial cashflow relief, thus providing them breathing space to recover from the current crisis. Because it reduces exchange rate uncertainty and restructures the debt, the scheme should be attractive to both debtors and creditors."

A few days later, on June 8 Minister Ginandjar Kartasasmita said that private debt totalled US$ 29.2 billion - corporate debt US$20 billion and the non-trade liabilities of commercial banks US$9.2 billion. Had it been necessary to pay it back immediately the sum was twice that of the official foreign reserves so the rescheduling was very welcome. Ginandjar said: " The immediate benefit from the debt rescheduling agreement is that our balance of payments, which has been under severe pressure so far, will be given a chance to breath."

Two weeks later, on June 26, Indonesia would begin talks with foreign banks to roll over the US$9.2 billion in bank debt. The initiative had been agreed in Frankfurt. New loans would be guaranteed by the central bank over two, three or four years with maximum interest of 3.5 percent.

The Frankfurt debt deal was just in time. The Government, through the central bank, had already poured US$ 12.4 billion into banks facing chronic problems of liquidity. The banks needed funds but business was demanding that interest rates be lowered. A large delegation from KADIN told President Habibie that more had to be done not only to stabilize but to revive the banking industry. The delegation was not only concerned with the payment of debt but with bank ability to cater to normal business needs for credit, currently non-existent. It was hard to see how the President could help them.

On June 5, former cabinet minister and Government critic Emil Salim accused President Habibie and House Speaker Harmoko of lacking a proper sense of the crisis faced by Indonesia. He cited the decision to have elections spread out throughout 1998 and 1999. Emil was quoted as saying that to restore business confidence and predictability what was needed was for general elections to be held before year's end with presidential elections by February, 1999, before the next annual Muslim holiday. To do otherwise, Emil was quoted as saying, merely prolonged uncertainty. "Habibie has said that his Government is transitional in nature., that means it must be brief. It must not exist too long because the market is wondering when the government which is not transitional will come." Simultaneously, the US said that it "wanted" President Habibie to establish a clear timetable for holding general and presidential elections.

The IMF said that it would mount a further review of Indonesia's economy starting June 8. And the World Bank said that the Consultative Group on Indonesia, which it leads, would meet on July 29 in Paris to decide what level of funding could be committed to assisting Indonesia, particularly to meet social shortfalls. Virtually every year since 1992 the Consultative Group on Indonesia (CGI) has allocated about US$5 billion to Indonesia, usually for development purposes. In 1998, such funds might be vital in making good an expected budget deficit.

News from the banking system was grim. More than US$12 billion had been disbursed by the central bank as part of its policy of guaranteeing all bank deposits and liabilities. By mid-June, non-performing loans reached 25 percent and the central bank poured money into wobbling banks to prevent a crash, albeit at punitive interest rates and against corporate and even personal assets. Credits to ailing banks were subject to 150 percent of the average Jakarta Interbank Offering Rate (JIBOR) , overnight rates on the first day, and 500 percent of the JIBOR rates on the following days. Bank Indonesia Governor, Sjaril Sabirin was quoted as saying: " The higher rates will discourage the banks from using the credit for expanding their business and encourage them to find alternative sources before coming to BI for new funds."

On June 22 a group of business people grouped themselves together in the Reformed Entrepreneurs Forum to reschedule their debt to private domestic banks. They planned to ask for a grace period of five to eight years. A few days later Tanri Abeng, State Minister for the Empowerment of State Enterprises said that restructuring private domestic debt was crucial for economic recovery.

On June 11, Lippo Group Chairman Mochtar Riady blasted BI's policy because he said it was now only propping up insolvent banks which should be closed and adding to inflation. In its leader on June 11 the 'Jakarta Post' summed up. "Recapitalization seems now the quickest and most effective way of restructuring the ailing banks. But not a single domestic investor is capable or likely willing to invest in the crippled banking industry since most large business groups, which are themselves major shareholders in most banks, are being overburdened with foreign debts. Foreign capital inflow or a return of Indonesian capital, which fled overseas after the recent riots in Jakarta and other areas, is not a prospect either. The outlook is quite grim indeed. As the capital base of most banks erodes and with a virtual stop in new lending, more banks will eventually be forced to enter IBRA care, which is now tending to more than 45 distressed banks. Given the severe banking crisis and the blunt fact that its resolution is crucial for the stabilization of the rupiah at a reasonable level, it is high time for both the central bank and IBRA to act firmly and quickly on insolvent banks. Allowing them to stay afloat with additional liquidity credits not only makes it more difficult to strengthen the whole banking industry but also risks wasting a huge sum of public funds and further hyperinflation."

The Government was in a difficult position. If the banks were closed the Government was still committed to meet their liabilities. Perhaps it was better to keep them in business and avoid spreading panic among he public and in the market. On the other hand, how far could the Government go with bad debt rising at an alarming rate. Its reserves were by no means limitless.

On June 19, to reduce the pressure on the banking system, Finance Minister Bambang Subianto announced that minimum bank capitalization of US$16 billion would only apply to newly formed banks. The capital adequacy ratio was also lowered to 4 percent by the end of 1988, 8 percent by the end of 1999 and 10 percent by the close of the year 2000. Bambang was quoted as saying: " This is part of the overall effort to revive the economy and the banking sector in particular."

In line with IMF advice high interest rates were still being used to shore up the rupiah - in the teeth of opposition from the House of Representatives. On July 16, DPR legislator, Indra Bambang Utoyo was quoted as saying: " We persist with our demand for lower interest rates. " The DPR argued that high interest rates had not stabilized the rupiah but instead were killing the banking sector, driving more businesses into bankruptcy and creating more unemployment. Governor Sjahril responded: "I'm certain that if the interest rate is reduced now the rupiah will fall further." The central bank governor added that he had no plans to reintroduce a managed exchange rate system.

Lippo Group Chairman, Mochtar Riady was quoted as saying that the IMF and the World Bank had "made many mistakes" and between them "destroyed (Indonesia's) economy. David Malpass, economic adviser to Ronald Reagan and George Bush praised currency boards as a way of stabbing currencies and blasted the Fund for encouraging

Thailand to float the baht. He warned that Asia's regional crisis threatened the world economy.

From Hong Kong, Morgan Stanley said that persistent high interest rates exposed the failure of IMF regional programmes. Analyst Tim Condon was quoted as saying: " The crisis economies need lower real interest rates. The lack of a framework for monetary policy (adjustment under the IMF programmes) means that there is no credible means for reducing nominal interest rates without exchange rates in these countries gapping down. For this reason we consider it likely that real rates will be reduced by means of an acceleration of inflation. Monetization of a larger fiscal deficit will deliver the high inflation." Condon expected that regional exchange rates would continue to fall against the US dollar.

The Hong Kong-based analyst said that: " ...the stabilization of currencies in the IMF supervised countries has crushed economic activity." Condon said that Thailand and South Korea were both experiencing deflation. He explained: " A sharp drop in the velocity of money is terribly destabilizing to economic activity. The IMF programmes have caused the drop in velocity." He went on: " The IMF programmes are failing, in our view, because they underestimate the time it will take for foreign capital to flow back into the crisis economies."

What then was the answer? "Inflation," said Condon. He claimed that "Indonesia had shown the way" by letting its inflation rates rise, even as credit remains tight.

Condon said: " Higher inflation - not hyperinflation - need not be catastrophic. High inflation has been part of the recapitalization process following financial crisis in many emerging markets. Asia has long been an inflation resistant region, and we do not forecast any country moving into destabilizing high inflation."

It was an interesting theory. But with the growth in money supply controlled in Indonesia by limits agreed with the IMF its realization remained to be seen.

Outside Government, what had begun as whispers was now developing into an increasingly loud chorus of concern that the IMF rescue has failed. There was doubt that there ever was a rescue so much as a bookkeeping exercise designed to put Indonesia's financial house in order.

A year had elapsed since Asia's financial crisis swept south from Thailand, eventually pushing Indonesia's hitherto sparkling economy flat on its face. And four successive IMF packages had come and gone with no sign that the Fund's 'medicine' was having the slightest effect on the Indonesian 'patient'.

As far as the man in the street or the rice field was concerned the burning question was not who governed Indonesia but where the next meal was coming from. The money and the meals would only start flowing normally again if something was done to stabilize the rupiah. Many were now pessimistic that it would stabilize just on the basis of the IMF's well meant reforms. In fact, in the wake of the April agreement the rupiah had promptly slumped to more than Rps 15,000 to the US dollar. Markets were described in the local media as "cheerless."

While the rupiah remained at this unrealistic level the economy would stay on hold. Few could afford to import. Exporters using imported materials were paralyzed. Offshore debt could not easily be repaid. Bad debt was piling up among domestic banks. Most major corporations remained technically bankrupt. Prices were rising beyond the pockets of the masses, threatening not only suffering but absolute want. The only measure which could turn the situation around was a spontaneous or forced appreciation of the rupiah. Commercial bank lending rates at over 70 percent were still killing Indonesian businesses large and small but the rates could be reduced so long as the rupiah remained weak.

There were firm rumblings in and out of official circles that recognition was growing that while the IMF packages were successfully patching up gaping legal, procedural, institutional and even bahavioural holes, the economy could be allowed to continue to draft downwards.

Amien Rais, Chairman of the 28 million strong Islamic Muhammadiyah had said at the end of May that he had rejected any further invitations for discussions with the IMF's Asia-Pacific Director, Hubert Neiss. He was quoted as saying in the daily 'Merdeka (Freedom) newspaper that the IMF and Washington were only playing games with Indonesia and that there would be no positive results from further meetings with the Fund's officials.

Rais's statement seemed to represent a major turn about in Indonesian public opinion about the IMF. When the Government of Indonesia requested IMF assistance in 1997, the IMF was regarded almost as a financial deity although, from the outset, there had been reservations about possible 'medicine' from the Fund. When the 'medicine' had been seen not to work, there had been definite foot dragging about further economic reforms. Deafening international condemnation of this alleged shilly shallying more or less forced the Government of Indonesia to get on with the job. Not to do so threatened to make it a pariah among nations, friendless and penniless.

But the 'medicine' really hadn't worked and something had to be done. One hope was that the IMF might now see that its 'medicine' hadn't worked and might be more amenable to permitting controlled foreign exchange. Many people, in and out of Government, feel that the situation was now so desperate that if the IMF refused to take a less ideological line concerning the currency, Indonesia might be forced to go it alone.

The voices of many IMF critics and opponents had been mute or concealed until now for fear of offending the Fund and putting at risk and progress which its 'medicine' might make possible. Asian neighbours had also been running scared of the Fund and its major backer, the USA.

On Tuesday, June 16, writing his occasional column in the daily 'Jakarta Post,' Government critic and Megawati Sukarnoputri supporter (the ousted leader of the Democratic Party of Indonesia (PDI)), economist Kwik Kian Gie had said openly that the "IMF was losing its momentum in helping Indonesia." He wrote: "The IMF has made many mistakes." A year before, Kwik could always be counted as pro-IMF. He added that the Fund was "convinced that the rupiah would strengthen if the reform programmes were accomplished. But events have proved it wrong and the rupiah (has fallen) further to Rps 15,000 (to the US dollar). Concluded Kwik: " The IMF's reform programmes are aimed at abolishing market distortions but it fails to introduce emergency programmes to push up the rupiah's value."."

Like Australia's Sheehan and Ray, Kwik Kian Gie called for an Indonesian Marshall Plan to boost foreign investment and liquidity and bail out the real sector. This, of course, was what the Indonesians hoped they were getting from the IMF in the first place. Cees de Koning, Country Manager of ABN AMRO Bank , added his voice to the argument that what Indonesia's economy needed above all was liquidity. He said: " IMF resources alone do not cover the liquidity gap (and) such funds are also not on demand and available in the size and at the time when liquidity boosts are needed."

With the IMF's back firmly turned against the use of its funds for these kinds of purposes, where could the new liquidity come from? Where might the funds needed to support a managed currency or a currency board come from? The answer, said the Australians, was friendly neighbours.

It was easy to imagine that, for example, Australia and Singapore, would have deep vested interests in keeping their huge neighbour from collapse. The Australians had both on their list of potential helpers, optimistically together with the US and Japan. To the Australian's suggestions, de Koning added that funds could perhaps be raised by placing central bank promissory notes (SBIs) in dollars with overseas investors or by selling assets to foreign buyers - a move already under way in the state sector.

The World Bank forecast that the economy would contract by 15 percent in 1998-99. Jean-Michel Severino, the Bank's Vice President for East Asia also said that to prevent economic depression crisis-hit economies should run budget deficits for the next two to four years financed by soft loans. He added darkly that the World Bank and the ADB had "more or less reached their head limits" and that the extra funds would have to come from wealthy countries, including those in the region. Clearly, budget deficits would make suffering bearable but would not reinflate punctured economies. It was again a case of treating the symptoms rather than the cause.

Senior economist Sumitro Djojohadikusumo warned during the first weekend of June that the Indonesian economy was on the "..threshold of a depression." He called for IMF funds to be used to recapitalize small and medium businesses teetering on the brink of bankruptcy. Alternatively he said that the situation was so urgent that the Government should take the money from its reserves. His comments also came on the threshold of the return to Indonesia of Hubert Neiss. The IMF director arrived back in Jakarta on Wednesday, June 10 for a three week visit. As he arrived, former finance minister Mar'ie Muhammad was quoted as saying that the Fund should speed up its disbursements to Indonesia. Being an ex minister Mar'ie could afford to speak out. He said factually that the latest US$1 billion promised by the IMF would not help much in boosting confidence and that more was needed. He was quoted as saying: " I strongly urge the IMF and other donor institutions to speed up the disbursement of their aid commitments." Mar'ie was quoted as saying that most of the reforms suggested by the IMF had either been undertaken or were in process and he inferred that there was really no good reason for further delaying the promised funds. Neiss said that his team would need three weeks to make its review but Mar'ie countered that reviewing the new macroeconomic realities should "not take long." All 103 members of the Interparliamentary Cooperation Body urged Michel Camdessus to speed up disbursements to Indonesia. A week or so later, Bank Indonesia Director Miranda Gultom warned that Indonesia's economy was headed toward stagnation.

Back in November a US$43 billion rescue package had been said to have been brought together but to date Indonesia had seen precious little of it - US$4 billion until June 12. Another US$6 billion could be released if the IMF gave the green light. It had been planned that Indonesia would receive US$3 billion in November and further quarterly tranches thereafter depending on progress with reforms. In January, not only was progress with reform deemed to be unsatisfactory but the rupiah collapsed to a record low leading to disbursements being delayed. In fact, no further disbursement was made until April and then only US$1 billion because Fund managers believed that it was more prudent to give Indonesia a billion a month rather than three billion every quarter. It was, they said, a matter of trust. It was very clear that they did not trust Indonesia. The May payment had been delayed by riots. The April payment had been held up by the impact of the March elections on the reform process. The problem was that markets were said not to have confidence in Indonesia until the IMF indicated that the country was on the right track by disbursing its aid. The more the IMF held off the more the markets held off. That was the theory.

The early June visit was Neiss's second visit to Jakarta in 10 days. The first visit had been to explore the new political situation. Satisfied that there was a good chance of stability, Neiss had duly reported to Washington with the result that he had been sent back again to make a detailed review of the economy. Much had changed. The latest visit was to review and revise Indonesia's macroeconomic targets, the state budget and the now clearly needed social safety nets. A third disbursement of IMF funds was promised in July after a post-riot review. The market ignored the promise and the rupiah stayed down at about Rps 14,500 to the US dollar. IMF First Deputy Managing Director Stanley Fisher said in Washington: " More will undoubtedly be necessary in the way of providing temporary subsidies in the next phase of the programme, which is being negotiated now, given the worsening of the exchange rate since April." These subsidies would remain in place "until incomes catch up or until the exchange rate appreciates." Fischer ruled out reductions in interest rates saying it would lead only to hyperinflation. The Fund's newfound willingness to accept subsidies represented an abrupt about turn. It was the Fund's earlier insistence on removing subsidies which had led to the devastating riots. Faced with the appalling consequences of what had been done to please it, the Fund now said that subsidies were OK. later on July 27 it would even agree to export bans.

The IMF's job in Indonesia appeared to be what the Hong Kong Chinese call 'makee learnee' - they had learnt about Indonesia as they went along. The people had paid the price.

By mid-June informed observers in Jakarta wondered more deeply than ever whether the IMF knew what it was doing. The comments of economist Kwik Kian Gie in his column in the 'Jakarta Post' on June 16 were acid: " Why does Neiss need to come to Jakarta again and again to make these studies? If he sticks to the old matrices but wants to follow hour-to-hour political developments in Indonesia, he is likely to become perpetually confused in writing reports to Washington, given the rapid social and political changes. If the IMF sustains such procedures, the effectiveness of its assistance to overcome Indonesia's economic difficulties is questionable. In almost a year it has disbursed only the first tranche of its aid. Most of the time has been used for ferrying, at great expense, its staff to and from Jakarta, where there has been "no action but talking only" (NATO). Meanwhile the economy continues to deteriorate with an annual inflation rate rising to 100 percent, a lot of factories closing down and the number of unemployed people increasing to 20 million. The danger of starvation is lurking, forcing the country to import three million tons of rice. The IMF has made many mistakes so that it has lost much of the momentum to help overcome Indonesia's economic difficulties."

Kwik's analysis was so sharp that it is well worth quoting more.: " The IMF, for example, failed to help strengthen the rupiah when it considered the currency's equilibrium value Rps 5,000 to the US$ dollar - before being revised downward to Rps 6,000. It was still convinced that the rupiah would strengthen if the reform programmes were accomplished. But events have proven it wrong and the rupiah fell further to Rps 15,000 on June 11.

"Had the IMF, as I suggested in my article on February 23, disbursed US$20 billion of its aid then, the rupiah would then have strengthened to Rps 5,000 per dollar and investors would have repatriated their dollars again into Indonesia.

"The fatal decision was the closing down of 16 banks without a full guarantee on the return of their depositor's funds in October. This drove depositors to r other private banks to cash in their savings and move them to state-owned and foreign banks. The Government's announcement on the full guarantee of savings came too late because the central bank was forced to print money - more than Rps 100 trillion (about US$8 billion) for bailing out the banks affected by the rush. Panicked by such developments, Bank Indonesia raised interest rates on its short-term promissory notes (SBIs) to up to 58 percent, thereby driving commercial banks to increase lending rates to about 60 percent or 70 percent a year. As a result, companies highly dependent on loans were forced to close down.

"The IMF's reform programmes are aimed at abolishing market distortions but it fails to introduce emergency programmes to push up the rupiah's value. This is like trying to mend a broken house but the ailing patient is left without any efficacious drugs. As soon as the house is mended the patient dies."

Kwik had now said pointedly and publicly that the IMF programmes had not worked. They had failed outstandingly to do the one thing Indonesia had always expected from the IMF - to stabilize the rupiah at a reasonable level against the US dollar. Not having stabilized the rupiah had plunged the economy into a nightmare of difficulties which the IMF seemed content to record and measure in its innumerable visits to Jakarta, each report usually more gloomy than the last and each negative report holding down domestic and international confidence - especially when coupled to the withholding of the promised aid.

On June 19, Steven Susanto and Hario Suprobo from the University of Indonesia's School of Economics wrote in the Jakarta Post:' " Without a quick resolution of the crisis, widespread hunger will cause further large-scale social turmoil and the country will be subject to further devastation, loss of property and business and threaten people's lives."

Bearing in mind the ravages caused by the devalued rupiah it was hardly surprising to see Hubert Neiss quoted as saying: " We have to accommodate more (expenditure) for subsidies and a programme to help small scale businesses so the deficit (in the state budget) will be significantly above previous assumptions of below 4 percent. The Fund would now support increased spending on food and fuel subsidies, health, education and job creation schemes. Neiss also recommended interest rate subsidies for small and medium sized enterprises.

But would any of this have been necessary if the rupiah had been stabilized in the first place? Would it have been necessary for a country proud of never having a budget deficit to now be saddled with one? Would the banking system have been close to collapse if the rupiah had been stabilized? Would corporate Indonesia be technically bankrupt? Would millions still have their jobs? Had there been no riots and no disruption of the distribution system repairs to which Neiss now said were essential? Could the political instability triggered by the riots have been avoided and with it the need for Neiss to spend so much time in the political arena, an area normally taboo for the IMF?

A whole year after the crisis first broke in Indonesia little had been done to stabilize the rupiah - the crux of the whole problem. As economic destruction intensified in Indonesia, causing economic, social and political havoc the IMF's team of measurers were performing no valuable service simply by telling the world the extent of the disaster. What Indonesia needed was help! But until mid-June there had been very little and no direct solution of the basic problem. Worse still, despite warnings from experts at home and abroad, the Habibie Government was determined not to incur the kind of international condemnation which had swamped Soeharto when he suggested a currency peg. The Habibie Government was apparently determined to hold to the IMF course, whatever the cost. Later, Steve Hanke would warn: " By the first week of February, President Soeharto knew that he would be finished if he failed to stabilize the rupiah at a reasonable level. Now President Habibie faced the very same dilemma." Toward the end of his June visit , Neiss was quoted as saying that Indonesia's economic recovery lay solely in its own hands! "The IMF and other agencies can make a useful contribution....but only Indonesia itself is in control of events." Incredible! Many Indonesians felt that the IMF was in control of a lot of important events. If Indonesia was the 'Titanic' the IMF seemed only to be recording the disaster on its radar as Indonesia Inc. sank below the waves.

Susanto and Suprobo wrote: " The economy is in worse shape because of the policy slippages advised by the IMF. As a result the Government has tripled interest rates to a mind boggling level that has brought semi-collapse to the financial and real markets. The growth-impairing measures only serve to deepen the crisis as Indonesia swallows its bitter and damaging pill from the IMF. The contractionary measures have caused job losses and economic impasse. The Government should expand the shrinking economy by applying expansionary measures. The ongoing contraction has to be offset by expansionary policies to bring the country out of its predicament. The country is presently gripped by deepening stagflation that is resulting in escalating poverty."

Warning that Indonesia's economy risked grinding to a complete halt in a matter of months the writers said that what was needed was a massive recapitalization of the economy to the tune of about US$50 billion. To get it they suggested leasing out Batam Island.

The writers said that it was "risky" to rely on the IMF's US$43 billion bailout for this purpose because of the Fund's insistence on contractionary measures and also because of the "slow and tough disbursement" of funds.

A few days later World Bank Vice President for Asia, Jean-Michel Severino was quoted as saying: " It has to be admitted that this reform process (of the IMF's) will have a limited impact on the crisis in the short-term. Structural reform will address long-term issues which will take many, many years. Restructuring the governance and supervision of the banking and corporate sector and adjusting to the globalization process is not something that can be done easily." So, as many Indonesians had feared and known, now, even the World Bank admitted that the IMF 'medicine' would have little, if any, impact on Indonesia's immediate problems. Yet the Habibie government was soldiering on with them as if they would. Of course, over two, four or five years the economy might be in better shape. But could the country wait that long?

"So, where are we today," asked Severino. " Where are we in this crisis and where are we heading to? A straightforward answer would be that we are probably at the end of a first cycle of the crisis and are entering into a deep recession, or even a depression."

Wonderful news for Indonesia! Severino said that the recession was inevitable once massive amounts of capital were withdrawn from Indonesia and other regional markets and currencies depreciated. The question in the minds of many Indonesians was whether the IMF had done anything to lessen the impact. Outside Government, the answer was near uniformly 'no.'

Severino himself provided some interesting insights. From his comments it seemed clear that the Bank and the IMF had their disagreements. The IMF had all along been applying long-term 'solutions' to Indonesia's short-term problems. Now, here was Severino saying that IMF critics had been saying. More than that, on June 26, in Melbourne Severino said that: " ...the World Bank believes that there is no alternative more expansionary micro policies right now. This is an issue that we have discussed quite intensively with our friends at the IMF and we are seeing a change in this environment." These "quite intensive' discussions seemed to mean that the Bank had had to fight hard to get the IMF to change its mind and start pumping liquidity back into the market.

Severino also had other extremely interesting things to say: " Right now, it is very clear that the way we have started to address the problems of the financial sector has been a contractionary one. We have put a lot of burden on the shoulders of the banking sectors of these (Asian) countries. They have very ambitious targets to meet in terms of capital decreasing ratios, restructuring of the balance sheets, merging and strengthening the structures, even improving the capacity of the banking sector and changing the rule of the game and governance system. One has to look at the consequences on the economy. It is clear that the credit crunch problem has partly to do with the monetary policy, but it also has a lot to do with the way the restructuring programmes are being handled. Rethinking the pace of these programmes, the nature of the measures and also the way they are funded, is something that we have to do."

Let's stop there. These few sentences carry a weight of meaning. Most importantly that even the World Bank thought the bank restructuring programmes "ambitious." If a body as August as the World Bank thought the reforms ambitious what must they have seemed to Indonesia? Should we deduce further that the "pace" of these "ambitious" programmes has been highly inimical? If so, isn't that what IMF critics were saying from the outset and what Indonesia has been made to suffer from? And if tight money resulted in a "credit crunch" whose fault, primarily was that? Severino confirmed that crisis-hit Asian countries now needed large injections of cash and he criticized even nominal contributors to IMF programmes for their slow disbursements. He said: " But most of the other participants are far from having delivered and participated concretely in the funding of the (IMF) programme. We cannot and we should not dream. Without this very practical external funding of the programme it would be impossible to move the region quickly out of the crisis." Severino was talking only about IMF programmes which critics, in any case, found of doubtful value. But now the World Bank and IMF critics seemed agreed about one thing; Asia needed money. The critics said it needed lots and not just to fund IMF or other long-term programmes.

Writing in the 'Jakarta Post' on June 23, Kwik Kian Gie accused the IMF of aiding Indonesia with small sums when what was needed was a massive injection of capital along the lines of Europe's Marshall Plan. "Without such massive aid, Indonesia's economy is likely to fall into a very serious depression marked by stagnation and high inflation." As part of a possible solution Kwik called upon Indonesian business to turn inward for the time being, to ignore export markets and instead to concentrate on the huge home market through the development of agribusiness. Kwik slammed the Soeharto government's policy of favouring the development of industries heavily dependent on foreign capital and imports. When the rupiah plunged and foreign capital dried up many factories in this sector came to a standstill.

The rupiah was not helped in mid-June when the Japanese yen nose-dived against the US dollar and there were long-feared rumblings from China about the possibility of devaluing the yuan. Even sky-high interest rates failed to halt the slide of regional currencies in the wake of the yen. By June 17, the rupiah had slumped to Rps 17,000 to the US dollar - for the third time in six months - once in January, once when it looked as if Soeharto would seek to retain power and now, once again. For the first time in six years the US spent US$2 billion propping up the yen - surely a move in theory anathema to the IMF.

Illustrating the power of the IMF, at least as an image, the 'Jakarta Post wrote in a leader on June 23: " It is important and quite encouraging to note that the IMF has been greatly impressed with the Government's performance in executing reform measures agreed to in mid-January and early April. This is greatly commendable, given the previous backtrackings on the part of the Soeharto administration in November, January and March. The IMF's flexibility in regard to subsidies reflects its understanding of the dire economic situation the nation is now facing and the good rapport it now has with the Government."

It certainly took a long time for this "understanding" to develop, not to mention all kinds of mayhem and suffering.

The "Post' went on: Needless to say, the IMF's vote of confidence is a crucial component in the efforts to lead our economy out of the economic crisis. It is catalyst and opinion leader for all other donors to the US$43 billion bailout package for Indonesia. With IMF backing, we can rest assured that new aid from the World Bank, the Asian Development Bank and other countries will soon flow into the country again. Such aid hopefully will accelerate the process of reestablishing market confidence in the economy and reinvigorate the rupiah. A stable rupiah is a prerequisite not only to economic reform but also to the overall political reform which is now underway."

Nothing could be more clear. These were the very views taken by the Government itself. If Indonesia pleased the IMF the world might be pleased with Indonesia. Unfortunately the Government and the 'Jakarta Post' were right. Such was the pedestal occupied by the IMF - whether its policies were right or wrong. To spurn the Fund would have required more courage than the Government of Indonesia apparently had, not to mention the availability of viable alternatives. Of course, IMF critics had said that there were alternatives but since they were never tried the results could never be known.

On June 23, Peter McCawley, Deputy Director General of the Australian Agency for International Development called the view that Indonesia needed total structural economic reform "very radical." He said that the demand for total reform was based on the belief that Indonesia's economic crisis had been caused by decades of corruption, collusion and nepotism. " This interpretation (than complete change is needed) is a very pessimistic view. You need 20 to 40 years to tackle the entirety of the problem."

Interesting!

On June 25, the Government of Indonesia signed a fourth Letter of Intent with the IMF. There was little in the new deal to inspire and the media described the rupiah and stocks as "cold." Investor's fears of further unrest were fuelled by news of riots in Samarinda, East Kalimantan and Gabion, North Sumatra. In an interview with Reuters, Jeffrey Winters from the US Northwestern University, commented that investors did not regard Indonesia as politically stable and that the IMF accord was not sufficient to lure them to return. He was quoted as saying: " Yesterday, a new Letter of Intent was announced in Jakarta. And yet, this morning, the Rupiah weakened rather than strengthened. In other words the markets have given their response - which is once again negative. Domestic and foreign investors have made their own assessment and they have determined that, both politically and economically, Indonesia remains unstable."

In the latest 'deal' 10 percent contraction of the economy was predicted instead of the 5 percent forecast previously; inflation was predicted to reach 80 percent instead of 40 percent and the best hope for the Rupiah - US dollar exchange rate was thought to be Rps 10,000 to the dollar by the end of 1998. The tight money policy would continue. On top of this negative news came the announcement that social spending allocations required to ameliorate some of the misery caused by the crisis might account for as much as 8.5 percent of gross domestic product - to be funded by foreign loans. In other words, IMF funds were now to be borrowed by Indonesia to provide social safety nets in the wake of the economic debacle the IMF's advice had not only failed to stem but exacerbated! - funds which under other circumstances would have been used for development. The Government said that it had already secured US$4 billion of the up to US$8 billion required to pay for the social safety nets. Even though the funds for social relief seemed large, the reaction of independent analysts to the IMF's forecasts suggested they might still be insufficient.

Making available such large funds for emergency social purposes - such as for the purchase of food - highlighted the failure of the IMF's programme for Indonesia. It must have wrenched heartstrings (or purse strings) for the Fund to agree to deficit spending, including for subsidies of basic items. The 'Indonesian Observer' quoted David Bassanese, senior economist at Bankers trust Australia as saying: " They (the IMF) have to be more lenient on social spending - its either that or walk away from the country altogether." Had it really come to that. Was it the case that at the end of June, 1998, one full year after the crisis broke, the IMF's 'help' had been so useless that observers felt that one of the Fund's options could now include "walking away!" In a sense the Fund was walking away. Wasn't that the essence of Neiss's comment that the Fund had done all it could and now recovery was in the hands of Indonesians!

The 'Indonesian Observer' of June 26, 1998 quoted Kanika Singh from Singapore's IDEA consultancy as saying: " I think we're looking at something like a 20 percent contraction this year, the rupiah target of 10,000 is optimistic and the country is basically on the brink of sovereign default." There were many who would have agreed with him.

Other provisions in the new Letter of Intent were little more than confirmation of a continuation of work in hand, for example, supporting sound banks and restructuring the capital of troubled institutions and strengthening Bank Indonesia's monetary management by allowing SBIs to be auctioned with the effect of enabling the market to set interest rates instead of the central bank. There was also reconfirmation that the finances of Pertamina, BULOG and the Forestry Fund would be audited using international accounting standards. Ensuring the supply and distribution of basic commodities particularly rice, cooking oil, sugar and soybean, launching labour intensive public work programmes and food-for-work schemes and rehabilitating and strengthening the food distribution networks seemed more like the natural responsibilities of government than assistance requiring special outside advice. While they may not have required advice, such schemes required funds and these were now forthcoming under the general description of "safety nets." Basically, there was little new. Just confirmation of the course to be clung to. Indonesia Inc., continued to wallow dangerously in the turbulent seas while the IMF advised the captain to read his manuals. Even at this late stage there was no hint of a lifeline!

One new element in the agreement was that Bank Indonesia would establish in July a pre-shipment export guarantee programme to facilitate a resumption of trade. On the positive side, if, indeed, it could be called positive, inflationary tendencies might be held in check by the new funding from the IMF because the Government had been struggling to make good deficits by increasing the money supply. This should not now be necessary. International lending institutions and bilateral donors to Indonesia might now be encouraged to release funds by the IMF's endorsement of the Habibie government. The inescapable need for subsidies had been acknowledged. BULOG was to continue in operation to maintain essential supplies. Still, all these measures treated only symptoms, not causes. And, by themselves, they were unlikely to do much to restore confidence in the economy.

Commented the "Jakarta Post' in a leader: "While the IMF's gesture may prompt foreign governments to act, foreign and domestic investors, whose funds are equally vital if the Indonesian economy is to recover, are not likely to be easily impressed, just as they were completely indifferent to the previous agreements between the Government and the IMF. Investors are primarily motivated by profits, while governments extend loans often on compassionate if not political grounds. Investors therefore, take a lot more convincing. While disbursement of the IMF money will certainly be a welcome vote of confidence for President Habibie, it is not enough. Investors will want to see real and solid, rather than make-believe, political stability before they return to Indonesia. That means a real commitment to democracy on the part of the new Government. "

The new IMF deal did indeed, prompt some action to disburse funds. On the day of the new Letter of Intent the Asian Development Bank promised US$1.5 billion to help finance Indonesia's budget deficit and strengthen its balance of payments. The loan would be released in three tranches during 1988-99; the first tranche of US$550 was available on signing. A few days later the World Bank approved a US$1.7 million oan for Indonesia to help pay for reforms to its financial and banking sectors and also to help fund key imports, including food. US$600 million was to be released immediately and the remainder throughout the balance of the year.

With Soeharto out of the way, the United States Government pledged to do everything possible to assist Indonesia in the wake of the new agreement with the IMF. US deputy Treasury Secretary, Lawrence Summers was quoted as saying in Washington: " We will be consulting

340

with the international financial institutions and other countries around the world to ensure that international support for Indonesia is sufficient for it to meet the difficult challenges it currently faces."

In Indonesia, in the wake of the new deal there were calls to do some of the things it specifically ruled out.

Reflecting the growing desperation in Indonesia, on June 30, Former Finance Minister, Mar'ie Muhammad, widely respected by overseas economists and bankers, called on the government of President Habibie to reintroduce a managed exchange rate system. He said: " The Government needs to take decisive action to prevent the situation from deteriorating further by, for example, reintroducing a managed exchange rate system."

The former Finance Minister revealed that he had been opposed to floating the Indonesian rupiah the previous August when, egged on by the IMF, other countries in the region also abandoned managed exchange rates. He said: "We had no choice because all our neighbouring countries had taken that step."

But Indonesia's rupiah had devalued far more than most other regional currencies so the time was past when it was necessary to think too much about the neighbours.

On the very same day that Mar'ie spoke out, Indonesia's most respected senior economist, Sumitro Djojohadikusumo called on the Government to revive the country's dying industry by slashing interest rates - a move that could only be taken if the rupiah appreciated against the dollar. He warned that the economy was on the brink of total collapse.

Kwik Kian Gie commented: " Because of the deteriorating economic situation and its subsequent impact on the poor, the political elite must now work hard to prepare creative and innovative concepts to bring he country out of the crisis."

Indonesia had now proved itself to be an exemplary pupil of the IMF. The Fund had shown its pleasure. The Fund's principal backer and largest vote holder was no longer concerned that IMF cash would help bailout Soeharto and his family. The king had gone: long live the Fund. But as Sumitro, Mar'ie and Kwik said and implied the problem which had caused Indonesia's crisis from the outset was still there - the devalued rupiah and the sky high interest rates applied to protect it. And there was little sign of Kwik's innovative solutions. Inflation hit 46.5 percent in the first six months of 1998.

Two months later, Indonesia would learn an unpleasant lesson from George Soros. Soros was venting his opinion about what needed to be done to save the rouble and the Russian economy. Remember! From start to finish the IMF had insisted on high interest rates to defend the rupiah, a tight money policy to ward off inflation and an austerity budget to keep pace with devaluation. Contraction had become the brand name of their product. Severino had said, as had many, many others, that what had been needed at the beginning of the crisis was liquidity and that what was needed now, in mid-1998 were measures to boost spending. Japan was being pressed to boost domestic spending, Singapore was trying to boost spending, Malaysia was trying to maintain if not boost spending, soon Taiwan would announce measures to boost spending. As always money made the world go round. No money and the wheels started to stop. Enter, George Soros.

Soros wrote to the British 'Financial Times' to air his opinion about the state of Russia's economy. In an article from Bloomberg News by Michael Lewis, the analyst wrote: " In a few short paragraphs Soros picked apart the IMF bailout package and the putative confidence of the world's political class in the Russian economy. He argued, rightly, that the IMF's goal of tight money and fiscal restraint clashed with the immediate need to bail out the Russian financial system. He demanded that Russia devalue its currency 15 to 25 percent and then peg the rouble to the US dollar. But for the peg to hold, Soros wrote, the Group of 7 (most industrialized nations) needs to put up another US$15 billion."

Well, well, well.

Many people regard George Soros as a financial genius. Wasn't this a case of the world's foremost financial genius saying that the IMF was wrong to apply contractionary measures to solve Russia's problems? Weren't these similar measures to those applied in Asia? Did this mean that the measures applied in Asia were also wrong? For example, if Indonesia had not embarked on contractionary monetary and fiscal policies, had pegged the rupiah against the US dollar as President Soeharto had wished and had been assured of adequate funds to do so, wouldn't this have saved the Indonesian economy? Wouldn't it have saved the banks? Saved the corporates? Helped overcome the debt problem? Kept the economy moving? Mightn't this have saved millions from unnecessary suffering? There were very many who thought so.

On Thursday, July 2, Bank Indonesia Governor, Sjahril Sabirin confirmed that: " If the exchange rate doesn't strengthen, it will be very difficult for Bank Indonesia to lower interest rates." The central bank governor added that if the free-floating exchange rate system proves incapable of encouraging a rupiah appreciation "We'll not be so stubborn in keeping this system without studying other alternatives." But he warned that "other alternatives" could "only work" if the IMF provided support. At this time, IMF support for any kind of currency board or peg was truly wishful thinking. Free market ideology aside, the Fund had been under heavy pressure in the US to limit its bailouts and, in any case, was running short of funds.

While ordinary people were saying that they didn't care who ran the country so long as they had money and need not go hungry Amien Rais was quoted as saying that : "It is dangerous for us to be preoccupied in discussions about basic needs. If we focus too much on our stomachs we could begin to lose our perspective of the future. Soeharto and his loyalists will use the opportunity to rise again and take power." While political reform now went on off the public stage and with little news from ABRI about the killings and disappearances some reformists feared their movement had come to almost nothing.

At the end of June, still flushed with the victory of at least witnessing the fall of Soeharto, lawless groups were popping up around the country, robbing shrimp ponds of their bounty and descending on cocoa, coffee and palm oil plantations at dead of night and making off with the crops. Trucks were held up on isolated roads or on busy roads at quiet times and their contents stolen. Joblessness, poverty and inadequacy was on the increase. Some people simply saw a chance to commit a criminal act and make money from it; others were desperate. Security forces could do little and, therefore, people still felt that security was not all that it was claimed to be. Generally speaking people were extra vigilant.

Also, at the end of June, Central Bureau of Statistics Chief, Sugito Suwito, warned that by the end of 1998, 96 million Indonesians, or almost half the population, would no longer be able to afford sufficient food. This would push the numbers of those living below the poverty line up from 11 percent in 1996, before the crisis, to a mind boggling 47 percent.

CHAPTER

PROGNOSIS

At the beginning of July Indonesia's new government, presided over by the unlikely figure of President B.J. Habibie, was in an optimistic mood. True, at 16,000, the rupiah exchange rate against the US dollar was still close to January's historic low of Rps 17,000 to the dollar but important corners seemed to have been turned.

As July progressed, most of the students and other vocal reformers had accepted the legitimacy of President Habibie's appointment - at least for the time being. In the beginning there had been considerable doubts as to whether a man as close to Soeharto as Habibie had apparently been could really lead the movement for the reforms many thought necessary. With his track record for apparently profligate spending there were many who wondered about his ability to rescue the devastated economy. Slowly, dissent had evaporated and the country generally seemed willing to give him a chance.

Critics and informed society generally had been reasonably impressed with his first steps away from the policies and practices of the Soeharto regime. Efforts to control street demonstrations and journalists met with determined opposition and months later were still in the queue of possibilities. There were lingering fears about the possibility of the return of Soeharto or of Soehartoism. A flirtation so soon with pro-

344

test and media controls seemed like an attempt to bring back hated parts of the immediate past. Aside from these stalled initiatives, there was a new sense of openness, a new sense of genuine consultation, a new sense of fair play - a new sense that at last a real process of reform was under way, albeit slowly. Cronies had been swept from the cabinet and an attack had been commenced on First Family and crony deals and wealth. Despite ominous rumblings, peaceful street demonstrations were permitted and as democracy tried its wings there seemed to be quite a few of them. The provinces, too, seemed to sense that under the new Government more advantages might soon flow there way. There were separatist demonstrations and doubtless some people thought the prospects better than ever for achieving their secessionist goals, a line of thought the Government and ABRI quashed firmly.

Some political prisoners had been released and there was naturally the hope of more. The willingness of the Armed Forces to provide answers to abuses and grievances which had culminated in the kidnappings of activists and in the riots was tested regularly and there was frustration at the slow progress made and at the realisation that it was likely that many of the ansers would not, in fact, be provided. An apology, it seemed, was deemed sufficient. On the other hand, at government level, there seemed to be a new and sincere commitment to human rights. While there was no sign that ABRI was preparing to quit politics for the barracks, there were clear indications that, in future, the Armed Forces hoped to be commanded and to function in accordance with a higher and more constructive code of ethics. ABRI would soon make the point that there was little it could do about the past, especially when it had responded to legitimate orders from the highest level. Its emphasis was on the hope that in future it would be given better orders and could therefore perform its duties more effectively and less injuriously and offensively.

President Habibie's time table for electoral reform and for holding elections had not been greeted with unanimous applause because it seemed overly long drawn out and calculated to maintain the New Order in power while wearing a few new clothes. But eventually, it was grudgingly accepted that time would be needed to work out a new electoral system, for democratic forces to take advantage of the new freedom by forming political parties and expressing their views and for this combined process to be strong enough for elections to take place. The further away from May the calendar was turned, the more people valued the new stability and the greater the Government's opportunity to introduce the reforms promised. Of course, as the clamour for reform died down there were some who feared and said openly that they hoped the Government would not water down the reforms or use the new tranquillity enhance its own chances of winning the forthcoming elections. The November meeting of the People's Consultative Assembly would be the acid test.

While political parties multiplied and obvious jockeying for power went on among the older established parties and among the political elite, the ordinary people seemed to have lost interest in the reform process - if indeed it had ever been present. Their concern was money and food. They were frequently quoted as saying that the didn't care who governed just so long as the economy and normal life could be restored. The Government had committed firmly and irrevocably to the IMF and by the time of the signing of the June Letter of Intent had carried out all the reforms agreed, some ahead of schedule. Jakarta wanted to run no risk of being again condemned by the international community for failing to implement fully the programmes of the IMF. It was a calculated risk. Even if they didn't solve the country's economic problems caused by private foreign debt and the associated loss of investor confidence, at least, after the makeover, Indonesia's micro economy would be in better, if not sound, shape. If, after introducing all the reforms the economy remained sick, surely the world would understand if Indonesia sought to change course! Meanwhile, IMF dollars were beginning to flow, appreciating the rupiah as they were injected into the economy. As luck would have it there were signs that the US dollar was beginning to weaken, further assisting the rupiah. the Frankfurt deal to restructure the offshore private debt further reduced the demand for dollars. While it was true that the IMF/CGI money was helping push up Indonesia's sovereign debt, in the short term is promised to push up the value of the rupiah against the dollar and give corporates and banks some new and very welcome room to maneuver. Indonesia's total offshore debt at this time stood at US$138 billion, US$54 billion sovereign debt and US$ 83 billion private loans. Under the end of June exchange rate climate there was little doubt that servicing the sovereign debt might soon become a problem and might even involve rescheduling, something the New Order Government had never done. Needs must, as they say.

While Indonesia waited for the political reforms to be rolled out and for economic recovery to kick in there were fears that rice supplies were running out and the Government took emergency steps to maintain the supply and to try to keep down the price. Rice shortages were reported on July 2 and five days later President Habibie made himself few friends among the people at large by urging those short of rice to fast! He said it might help keep down imports. His fasting comment was one of several which made people think he was not the stuff president's are made of, especially presidents who come to power during a time of great social upheaval and sensitivity and genuine and deep suffering. At virtually the same moment, the Central Bureau of Statistics announced that 80 million Indonesians or 40 percent of the population had fallen below the poverty line. Cooking oil exports now had to be taxed at 60 percent to discourage exports and keep down domestic prices. Earlier the IMF had insisted that there should be no ban on crude palm oil exports, leading to price hikes in the domestic markets which could again threaten social stability if left uncorrected. Great care was needed to maintain supplies of basic food and fuel items to the population, at affordable and even subsidized prices. IMF funds were used to pay for the necessary social safety nets - according to some local economists contributing to demand push inflation.

It was the economic crisis which had brought down Soeharto and little had changed since May. Would it now bring down Habibie, especially by following the IMF's advice to maintain floating exchange rates? Interest rates, jacked up in a vain effort to protect the rupiah, remained critically high. Little had happened to resolve the debt issue - lenders wanted their money back, creditors were reluctant to part with their assets, especially not at current market values. The grand hopes for substantial windfall revenue from the ill advised short-term policy of privatization of state enterprises were foundering on the twin rocks of depreciated asset values and the absence of buyers. The banking system remained massively dysfunctional, affecting investment and trade and the pace of bank mergers was very slow. Export recovery was also painfully slow. Unemployment and poverty were rising; the economy was shrinking.

Politically, at the beginning of July , the country seemed to be prepared to wait for the November meeting of the People's Consultative Assembly, but there was a feeling among observers that the public expected to see confirmation that something approaching genuine democracy was on the way as well as solutions to the crippling economic crisis - political and economic reform now being seen to be inextricably linked. Observers wondered what might happen if the Assembly failed to deliver on either or both counts! The worst scenario was that political reforms would be fudged by the Habibie Government to maintain something approaching the status quo with the result that economic recovery might not materialize.

Once again Indonesia was a nation in waiting - waiting for the announcement and agreement of political reforms on the basis of which free and fair elections had been promised in May, 1999. And waiting for the outcome of the Government's policies to rescue the economy. The problem was that these policies seemed to amount only to wait and see! Indonesians and the concerned world now wondered about Indonesia's problems and prospects more keenly than ever. Could the problems be solved in a reasonable time? Were any of the prospects truly bright? President Habibie evidently thought so. On June 30 he was quoted as saying that he had yet to decide whether or not to run again for the presidency!

Foreigners could see that Indonesia's economy had been mangled and that generational change was expected in the political structure. At the beginning of July those interested in Indonesia needed a clear road map of the economic and political problems and of the prospects immediately ahead.

Publications
from
Gateway Books

BUSINESS & POLITICAL TITLES

**Plots & Schemes
That
Brought Down
Soeharto**

**Foreign Buyers' Guide
FOR INDONESIAN EXPORTERS**
(In collaboration with the National Agency For Export
Development (NAFED),
Ministry of Industry and Trade,
Government of Indonesia)

**Resource Indonesia '98
Fair Directory and Visitors' Guide**
(In collaboration with the National Agency For Export Devel-
opment (NAFED),
Ministry of Industry and Trade,
Government of Indonesia)

**Economic Crisis In Indonesia
The full story**

**Guide to Indonesia's
Industrial Export Products
(In collaboration with theMinistry of Industry and Trade,
Government of Indonesia.)**

Guide to British Business In Indonesia 1997, 1998
(In collaboration with the Indonesian British Business
Association and the
Government of the United Kingdom.)

Indonesia Comes Of Age
50 years of Independence

Expats in Indonesia
1996. 1997

Guide To Industrial Estates
In Indonesia 1995, 1997
(In collaboration with the Indonesian Investment
Coordinating Board, (BKPM), and the
Ministry of Industry and Trade,
Government of Indonesia.)

The Culture Of Business In Indonesia
(Asia Pacific Economic Forum Conference, (APEC) 1994, 2nd
edition 1996.)

Opportunities For Australian Investment In Indonesia
(In collaboration with the Indonesian Investment
Coordinating Board, (BKPM),
Government of Indonesia.

Women's Role In Development
(In collaboration with the State Minister for the Role of
Women, Government of Indonesia and
with a special introduction by late First Lady, Ibu Tien
Soeharto.)

A Guide For British Investors
(In collaboration with the Indonesian Investment
Coordinating Board, (BKPM), Government of Indonesia and
the British Embassy, Jakarta.

United States Investment In Indonesia
(In collaboration with the Indonesian Investment
Coordinating Board, (BKPM),
Government of Indonesia.

Dutch Investment And Trade In Indonesia
Building A New Era
(In collaboration with the Indonesian Investment
Coordinating Board, (BKPM),
Government of Indonesia
and the Royal Netherlands Embassy.)

Business Travellers Guide to Indonesia
(For Garuda Indonesia)

1992-93/1995-96 /1998-99 Directory of Indonesian Exporters
(In collaboration with the National Agency For Export
Development (NAFED),
Ministry of Industry and Trade,
Government of Indonesia.)

1992-93 Guide To Batam Real Estate

Telecommunications in Indonesia:
A Guide For Private Suppliers And Operators.
(In collaboration with the Ministry of Tourism, Posts and
Telecommunications,
Government of Indonesia.)

BATAM: Step By Step Guide For Investment
(In collaboration with the Batam Industrial Development
Authority,
Government of Indonesia)

Business in Indonesia 1990, 1991-92, 1994-95, 1997, 1998-99
(In collaboration with the Indonesian Investment Coordinating Board, (BKPM), and the Ministry of Industry and
Trade
and in 1991-92 with
the National Export Development Agency (NAFED), Ministry
of Industry and Trade,
Government of Indonesia)

Doing Business in Indonesia
(For Harvest International Inc.)

Canadians in Indonesia
(Co-sponsored by the Canadian International Development
Agency, (CIDA),
Government of Canada
and in collaboration with the
Indonesian Investment Co-ordinating Board, (BKPM),
Government of Indonesia).

**International Investor Guide to
Sri Lanka**
(In collaboration with the Board of
Investment,
Government of Sri Lanka).

Business in Hong Kong
Signposts for the '90s - A positive
view

**Business Opportunities in
New Zealand**
(In collaboration with the Government
of New Zealand)
Expats in Singapore 1990 and 1991-92

Expats in Malaysia
(Co-sponsored by the Malaysian
Industrial Development Authority,
Government of Malaysia)

Canadians in Malaysia
(Co-sponsored by the Malaysian
Industrial Development Authority,
Government of Malaysia
and the
Canadian International Development
Agency, CIDA,
Government of Canada)

The Chinese in Canada

Canada Our Land

**You're Welcome:
Guide to investment opportunities
in Canada**

Relocating in Canada

How to market computer software
(Sponsored by the Department of
Regional Industrial Expansion,
Government of Canada)
and the
Ministry of Industry, Trade and
Technology,
Government of Ontario)

**The Canadian market for Australian
software**
(Sponsored by Austrade,
Government of Australia)

ENVIRONMENTAL

Battle For The Planet

**Perjuangan Untuk Lingkungan
(Indonesian language)**
(In collaboration with the State Minister for the Environment,
Government of Indonesia)

TOURISM

The Old City Of Jakarta - Today
(In collaboration with the City Government of Jakarta, (DKI))

Batam Island Souvenir Tourist Guide

. **Marine Tourism Indonesia**
(In collaboration with the Ministry of Tourism,
Posts and Telecommunications, Government of Indonesia.)

Travel Guide Indonesia
(For Singapore National Publishers Ltd)

Toronto Chinatown Guide (with
Johnny Koo)

Toronto Waterfront Guide

FICTION

Sir Thomas Stamford Raffles
- Restless Warrior
(Novel)

A Clown On The Streets Of Jakarta
(Short stories)

The Fortune Teller
(Short stories)

Murder in Batavia
(Novel)

NEWSPAPERS
Batam Times/SIJORI Times

MAGAZINES
TradeAsia magazine